XSLT and XPATH

A Guide to XML Transformations

JOHN ROBERT GARDNER
AND
ZARELLA L. RENDON

ISBN 0-13-040446-2

Prentice Hall PTR
Upper Saddle River, NJ 07458
www.phptr.com

Library of Congress Cataloging-in-Publication Data
Gardner, James Robert.
XSLT and XPath: a guide to XML transformations / James Robert Gardner and Zarella L. Rendon.
p. cm.
Includes index.
ISBN 0-13-040446-2
1. XML (Document markup language) 2. Internet programming. I. Rendon, Zarella L. II. Title. III. Series.
QA76.76.H94 R46 2001
005.7'2—dc21 2001016422

Editorial/Production Supervision: *Donna Cullen-Dolce*
Acquisitions Editor: *Mark L. Taub*
Editorial Assistant:: *Sarah Hand*
Marketing Manager: *Bryan Gambrel*
Manufacturing Buyer: *Maura Zaldivar*
Cover Design: *DesignSource*
Cover Design Direction: *Jerry Votta*
Interior Design: *Gail Cocker-Bogusz*

Prentice-Hall, Inc.
Upper Saddle River, NJ 07458

Prentice Hall books are widely used by corporations and government agencies for training, marketing, and resale.

The publisher offers discounts on this book when ordered in bulk quantities.
For more information, contact:
Corporate Sales Department,
Phone: 800-382-3419; FAX: 201-236-7141
E-mail: corpsales@prenhall.com; or write:
Prentice Hall PTR
Corp. Sales Dept.
One Lake Street
Upper Saddle River, NJ 07458

Printed in the United States of America

10 9 8 7 6 5 4 3 2 1

ISBN 0-13-040446-2

Pearson Education LTD.
Pearson Education Australia PTY, Limited
Pearson Education Singapore, Pte. Ltd
Pearson Education North Asia Ltd
Pearson Education Canada, Ltd.
Pearson Educación de Mexico, S.A. de C.V.
Pearson Education—Japan
Pearson Education Malaysia, Pte. Ltd
Pearson Education, Upper Saddle River, New Jersey

For Dale

Contents

Preface

You've heard of XML; your manager wants you to use it in your applications. Now what?

You've used HTML, and you know what a tag is; you know that it is somehow related to XML. You may even know what XML is and what it does. What you may not know is that, while XML identifies and adds structure to the content of a document, it does not tell you anything about how to *process* that content, or how to do anything useful with it beyond storage. This is good news, because this means your content can be used for many different purposes.

There are many things you can use to process content once it is marked up using XML. However, we have chosen to talk about the only *standard* application that allows you to do many different things with it. With XSLT, you can add style to XML, convert it to other XML, or simply chop it up and regenerate it in a different form.

XSLT is the power behind the throne of XML. It assures that every level of every piece of XML data is accessible and reusable across platforms and forward in time. It is not an exaggeration to say that XSLT and its companion XPath are the very glue and mortar that hold together and build the endlessly varying applications of markup data for any industry, academy, or individual. XSLT is the fastest cure for the fear of having obsolescence in a data or information architecture design.

XSLT is easy to use. In fact, XSLT *itself* is XML. XSLT "speaks the language," or the syntax, of XML with a powerful vocabulary of programming-like features that are nonetheless easy to use, learn, and understand.

XSLT attempts to be a bridge to nonprogrammers, bringing the easily understood syntax of XML together with a powerful scripting mechanism and simple pathing approach to document navigation.

It is our belief—and our approach in writing this book—that both the experienced programmer and the newly trained markup technologist can become more comfortable with the potent set of tools for preserving, augmenting, updating, and delivering XML data—whether it's on the Web or your corporation's intranet or B2B.

If you are constantly wishing you had just a little more control over your information, this book will deliver that—*and much more*. In fact, by the end of the first chapter, you will be able to perform basic conversions from XML documents to HTML that will display in any Web browser. Subsequent chapters build upon and enhance that base of knowledge, matching examples with detailed explanations and providing focus upon commonly misunderstood areas.

When you read this book, have your computer handy. Take the time to load up one of the XSLT processors and work along as you read. Learning by doing is always best, especially with XSLT and XPath. Chapter 13 will show you how to install the software included on the CD. Each example in the book is found on the CD in the `examples` directory, organized by chapter.

XSLT is rewarding and creative to use. Be prepared to enjoy this learning experience. You will be surprised by how quickly productive use of this technology increases.

Why Should You Use XSLT?

Browsers display HTML, not general XML tags. You have to do something with the XML once you have it. Can you print with XML? Can you send XML to the Web? Can you browse XML? Yes, but not alone.

XSLT lets you convert XML to HTML, other types of XML or just plain text. With a little creativity, and the proper knowledge of XSLT, you can generate practically any form of output from XML.

XSLT provides quick, easy solutions to all XML transformation issues. However, the designers of XSLT did not intend for you to use the specification without additional help.

> "This book, along with the proper tools, is what is required for XML to succeed with the average business application."
> —Sharon Adler, Co-Chair W3C XSL Working Group

The latest version of XSLT (for which this book is written) is 1.0. There are many additional features that are being considered by the W3C XSL committee, and version 2.0 promises to add some of these new features, as well as provide support for XML Schema, XML Query, and others.

Who Is This Book For?

This book is for anyone who works with electronic data and wants to enable XML transformations without a difficult programming language learning curve. If you are comfortable working with SGML, XML, or even HTML, you will benefit greatly from the common markup syntax.

Some people may find XSLT difficult because it is not a procedural programming language. Most programming languages have a very structured, concise syntax. The syntax of XSLT is XML and is designed to be human readable and easily understandable. You must have some knowledge of markup before using XSLT.

Some people may find XSLT difficult to use because it does not provide solutions to every transformation situation. For example, you cannot use XSLT to convert text to XML. There are situations when additional processing may be required. However, for most of your day-to-day XML transformations, XSLT is the tool of choice.

Organization

The book is organized to build a base of knowledge that will be added to chapter by chapter. Basic XSLT concepts and a brief overview of XML are covered in Chapter 1. The remainder of the chapters add functionality as required when creating stylesheets. The more complex the problem, the later it is covered.

Chapter 1 provides everything you need to know about XML and XSLT in a nutshell. This chapter gives a good overview with minimum syntax, and can be used by people at any level of markup experience as a review or for general information.

Chapter 2 covers stylesheet concepts that are crucial to understanding XSLT, as well as general stylesheet terminology.

Chapter 3 adds more concepts, a little more explanation and usage, and an in-depth study of templates to the basics covered in Chapters 1 and 2.

Chapter 4 defines and explains XPath expressions and patterns.

Chapter 5 covers XPath functions, which are crucial to using most of the elements in XSLT.

Chapter 6 walks through the creation of new XML elements and attributes using several different methods.

Chapter 7 discusses the use of multiple stylesheets by including and importing them, as well as a discussion on template priority.

Chapter 8 shows how to work with variables and parameters.

Chapter 9 covers anything that is in some way iterative or conditional, as well as the utilities required to copy XML from the input to the output.

Chapter 10 details the options for controlling output types, as well as stripping and preserving whitespace, and generating error messages.

Chapter 11 covers XSLT functions and their related elements, including importing external XML documents with the `document()` function, and using keys with `<xsl:key>`.

Chapter 12 discusses extensions, processors, and Java, as well as three "commercial" XSLT processors.

Chapter 13 describes three "freeware" processors: Xalan, Saxon, and XT, along with installation instructions and extension implementations.

There are three appendices that cover a variety of topics and case studies, as well as contributed material.

Conventions

XML, XSLT, and HTML elements, when discussed in the text, are always found as markup. For example `<xsl:stylesheet>` will always have the opening `<and closing>`, and will be in courier font. Any expression or function, such as `count()`, will also be in courier.

Each element has an element model definition, taken directly from the XSLT specification, when provided, as shown below. The element model is organized as an XML element with an optional category description (as a comment), followed by the start tag with any available attributes, the content (as a comment), and a closing tag (unless the element is empty). Attributes are bold if they are required, and their value is shown in italic if it has a special defined content type, or in quotes if it has a literal value. Elements in the content can be optional, designated with a ?, or optional and repeatable, designated with a *.

```
<!-- Category: instruction -->

<xsl:for-each

  select = node-set-expression>

  <!-- Content: (xsl:sort*, template) -->

</xsl:for-each>
```

Function prototypes are taken directly from the XPath and XSLT specifications, and are formatted with the key word `Function`, followed by a colon, followed by an object return type in italics, the name of the function in bold, and a parentheses containing arguments in italics, as follows.

`Function:`*`number`* **`sum`** *`(node-set)`*

Versions

This book is written according to XSL Transformations (XSLT) Version 1.0, XML Path Language (XPath) Version 1.0, and Extensible Markup Language (XML) 1.0. Additional reference material came from Namespaces in XML REC-xml-names-19990114.

The version of James Clarks' XT used for the tests in this book is 19991105. The version of Michael Kay's Saxon used is 6.2.2.

Acknowledgments

We would like to acknowledge and give proper thanks to those individuals who in no small part, due to their patience and consideration, contributed to the writing of this book. In addition, there are readers, proofers, and contributors whom we acknowledge at the end of this section.

First and foremost—apart from the irreplaceable contributions and support of those to whom this book is dedicated—we want to acknowledge each other. Working together in such a pressured way and still spending more time laughing than anything else is a feat in itself. Without figuring out each other's varied ways and memes, this book would never have gotten under way. Following that, we each have our own "cast of heroes" to thank.

John Robert thanks those loved ones, friends, and colleagues who have provided much support: Dale Leeser; the Ferntheils; Jeff Leeser; Jay Semel and the great team at the University of Iowa's Obermann Center for Advanced Studies for providing the research base where this book could begin; Michael Witzel at Harvard for providing texts and challenges which made XSLT important early on; Leslie Sims and Mary Sue Coleman; Moya and Jonathan for being so kind and cool; Dr. Mikhail Gorokhov of Atlanta for a revolutionary treatment of therapy and non-narcotic pain relief for tired and sore hands; the gang at Emory University's Center for Electronic Texts in Theology and Religion from ATLA-especially John Wagner for making us prove XSLT was necessary to a relational database world; John

Bagby, Russell and Elaine at UAQA.com; Deborah Norris; and Nichiren Nietszche Daishonin for tolerance and his own brand of support.

Practically speaking, the support of Sun Microsystems, specifically from Steven Butler and Karsten Riemer, proved make-or-break in allowing the time and focus to write properly. While finishing and proofing, the fine spirits, food, and folk at the Red Rock Bistro in Swampscott, MA, were both delightful and indispensable, and Ohio's Golden Lamb Inn.

Zarella would personally like to thank Sharon Adler, Carla Corkern, Ellen Campbell, Charles Goldfarb, G. Ken Holman, Steven Newcomb, Paul Prescod, and Jeremy Richman for all their contributions, suggestions, and support. Also a special thanks to all family and friends for their support and encouragement.

Thanks also to the team at ISOGEN for their support and contributions.

Readers and Contributors

Thanks to David Bertoni and David Marston of IBM/Lotus; Sharon Adler at IBM; Norm Walsh, David Hoffert, Donald Kerr, Marc Cannava, Caron Newman, Floyd Jones, and Scott Hudson of Sun Microsystems; Jonathan Marsh of Microsoft; Steve Muench of Oracle; Michael Kay of Software AG; Eric Lawson of ISOGEN; G. Ken Holman of Crane Softwrights, Ltd, .

Thanks to Jeni Tennison for her work on the Muenchian *key*() function; Oren Ben-Kiki for his offering on the unique use of XSLT to solve the classic N-Queens puzzle from the artificial intelligence community; and Eric Lawson, of ISOGEN, for providing a test GUI for Xalan-J.

Special thanks to the members of the W3C XSL working group for their contributions, especially Sharon Adler, Scott Boag, Michael Kay, Bob Lojek, Jonathan Marsh, Steve Muench, Norm Walsh, and of course, James Clark for making it all work.

We also extend our thanks to Deborah Norris for her work preparing the final graphics in this book.

A very special thanks goes to the patient, knowledgeable, and versatile team at Prentice Hall for their support and eagle-eyed proofing: Mark Taub, Donna Cullen-Dolce, Carol Lallier, and Camie Goffi.

XSLT and XPATH

A Guide to XML Transformations

Anatomy of an XSLT Stylesheet

- Overview of XML
- Introduction to XSLT and XPath
- Nodes
- Document Order
- Converting XML to HTML

1

XSLT, the extensible stylesheet language for transformations, is a language that provides the mechanism to transform and manipulate XML data. It is impossible to discuss XSLT without a reference to XML (extensible markup language). XML is a related W3C (World Wide Web Consortium) standard, and is the basis for standard information interchange. XML provides structure to information, and XSLT, along with another related standard, XPath (XML path language), provides the means to extract, restructure, and manipulate that information.

XSLT has the same cross-platform functionality found in XML because it is written according to the same rules. If you are an experienced markup technologist proficient in XML, you will be able to quickly maximize the uniquely powerful language of XSLT. In fact, by the end of this chapter, you will be able to write XSLT stylesheets that perform basic transformations from XML to HTML.

This chapter provides explanations and analogies for using XML, XSLT, and XPath. Any prior knowledge you have of XML markup will greatly speed up the learning process; however, a brief description is presented in the following section as a review.

1.1 What Is Markup?

Without retelling the story of how markup evolved or what it is, it is important to begin with a conceptual understanding of XML. This book is not intended to provide an explanation of the complete syntax and usage of XML, however, there are a few concepts that are worth reviewing. XML is a markup language that is a derivation—or flavor—of SGML (Standard Generalized Markup Language). You may be more familiar with HTML, a popular example of SGML that is used to mark up content for presentation on the Web.

Markup is made up of *tags*, which describe and separate the contents of an XML document instance from the presentation, style, and format of the document. The tags can be thought of as hooks, or handles, by which all material they contain—the text or data—can be accessed or identified.

The objects that the tags contain are called *elements*. Elements are the main components of an XML document, and can be identified by their element-type name, which is contained in both the start tag and the end tag, as shown below:

```
<para>This is a paragraph</para>
```

The paragraph tags, shown here as `<para>` and `</para>`, are used to separate the contents of the the paragraph from the other paragraphs and elements in the XML document. Notice that we have made up our own element-type names here (instead of using the old HTML `<p>` tags). XML allows you to create your own tag names, adding infinitely more functionality and precision of markup than HTML provides. As another feature of XML, elements can contain text, as shown above, and can also contain other elements, for example:

```
<para>This is a <index>paragraph</index></para>
```

Elements inside elements introduces the concept of nesting, and of relationships between the elements that can be addressed directly. Addressing can now be done based on the location and relationship of an element inside another, as in "all the index elements *inside* a paragraph." Nesting elements also creates a structure that can be respresented as a tree.

1.1.1 Markup Grows on Trees

When explaining markup, the image of a tree is often used to illustrate concepts, designs, processes, and other ideas, both tangible and intangible. The root, most especially, has a long signification throughout the history of human thought and philosophy as the base, or beginning. The root in XML is similar. From the root of an XML document, a tree-like structure emerges, which can be navigated and referenced with great precision. This precision is essential for working with XML. The access to and use of the entire structure of an XML document are inseparable from its representation as a tree-like structure.

Understanding the tree structure of an XML document is crucial to navigating it. The tree in markup, especially in XML, is highly abstracted and stylized to convey specific characteristics of the markup language. It hangs from the bottom, as shown in the example of a book in Figure 1–1.

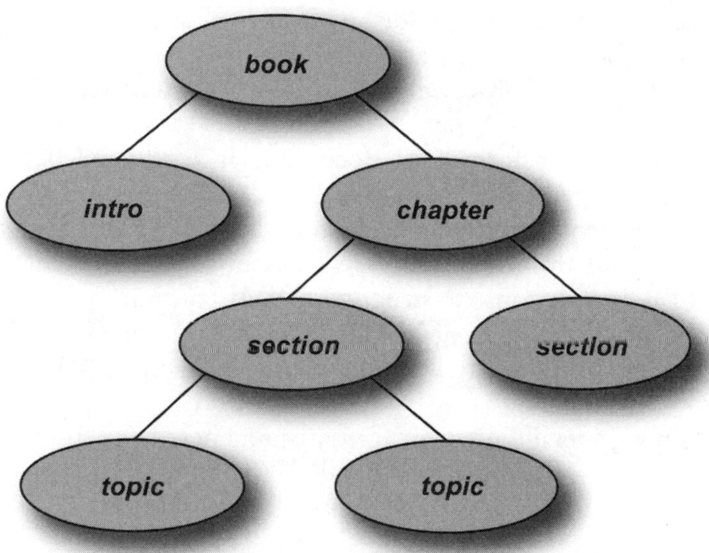

Figure 1–1 Tree representation of a basic XML document.

XML has many other aspects, enough for countless other books! Because we are dealing with XSLT as it relates to XML, we will not cover all the concepts that XML brings, only those directly related to using XSLT.

1.2 What Is XSLT?

In its most basic sense, XSLT is XML. The familiar structure of markup, using less-than and greater-than symbols ("<" and ">," as seen, for instance, in `<xsl:stylesheet>`), makes its syntax readily identifiable.

There are several benefits to thinking of XSLT as an XML document instance. Of course, aside from the familiar tagging structure, it is important to have specifications that conform to the same syntax, are platform-independent, and can be parsed by the same basic technology.

Another benefit is the notion of well-formedness, which allows the structuring of XSLT stylesheets to proceed without a particular DTD.[1] The importance of well-formedness for an XSLT stylesheet cannot be emphasized enough—both for the XSLT stylesheet to successfully parse when initially read by an XSLT processor and to be readily understood, debugged, or adjusted.

XSLT is used to transform XML documents into other XML documents. XSLT processors parse the input XML document, as well as the XSLT stylesheet, and then process the instructions found in the XSLT stylesheet, using the elements from the input XML document. During the processing of the XSLT instructions, a structured XML output is created. XSLT instructions are in the form of XML elements, and use XML attributes to access and process the content of the elements in the XML input document.

XSLT is not generally used for formatting. There is a separate specification for formatting from the W3C called XSL,[2] which is generally called XSL FO (formatting objects). XSLT *can* affect formatting if, for instance, the XSLT stylesheet is designed to output HTML tags for display in a browser, but this is only a small fragment of its capabilities.

---

1. XSLT does not conform to a specific Document Type Definition (DTD), however the basic set of elements to be supported by an XSLT processor is described in a non-normative DTD in the XSLT specification.
2. The XSL specification can be found at http://www.w3.org/TR/xsl/.

1.3 What Is XPath?

XSLT is rarely discussed without a reference to XPath.[3] XPath is a separate recommendation from the W3C that uses a simple path language to address parts of an XML document. Although XPath is used by other W3C recommendations, there is hardly a use for XSLT that does not involve XPath. Generally speaking, XSLT provides a series of operations and manipulators, while XPath provides precision of selection and addressing.

1.3.1 The XSLT Stylesheet

This structured hierarchy of elements for the book in Figure 1–1 is a useful way to begin to understand how XSLT stylesheets work. Figure 1–2 represents the same tree structure, only here it reflects some basic components of an XSLT stylesheet.

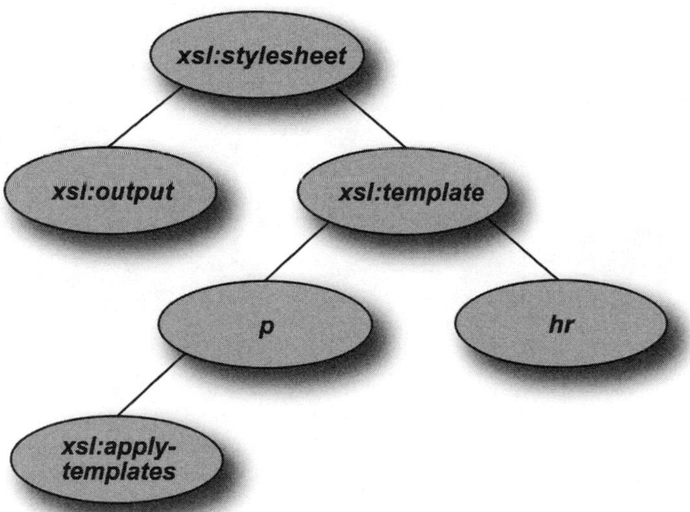

Figure 1–2 Tree representation of a basic XSLT stylesheet.

3. Both XSLT and XPath became full recommendations on the same day, November 16, 1999.

The use and explanation of these components will be provided in more detail later in this chapter, but what is important to stress here *is* that XSLT is XML, and has the same overall structure.

1.4 XSLT Stylesheet Concepts

XSLT stylesheets are best understood according to their structure and the named elements within them. It has always been a hallmark of markup languages that there be a diligent attempt at human-readability for the element-type names and, where possible, other components. With XSLT, this has been fairly well achieved, making it easier to learn and understand XSLT stylesheets.

Let's compare the XML tree structure of a book with that of an XSLT stylesheet, shown side-by-side in Figure 1–3.

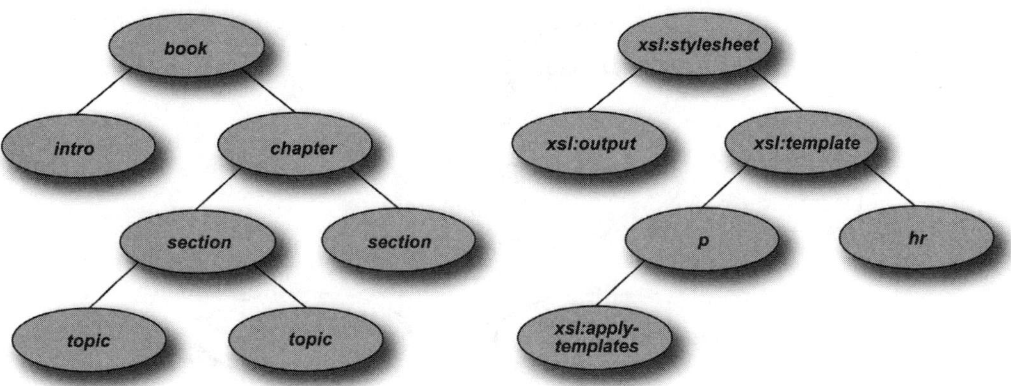

Figure 1–3 Comparing XML trees to XSLT trees.

If we rendered the XSLT side of this diagram as a stylesheet, it would look like Example 1–1.

This example shows the basic components of most XSLT stylesheets. The `<xsl:stylesheet>` element contains two other elements, an `<xsl:output>` element and an `<xsl:template>` element (sometimes called a *template rule*).

The HTML `<p>` tag simply sends the same tag to the output, as does the `<hr>` tag.

Example 1–1 : XSLT stylesheet as an XML document.

```
<?xml version="1.0"?>
<xsl:stylesheet
      xmlns:xsl="http://www.w3.org/1999/XSL/Transform"
      version="1.0">
      <xsl:output method="html" />

      <xsl:template match="topic">
           <p>
                 <xsl:apply-templates />
           </p>
           <hr/>
      </xsl:template>
</xsl:stylesheet>
```

Another component in our example is the `<xsl:apply-templates>` element, which is inside the `<p>` tags.

Using the `<book>` XML input sample would generate the output shown in Example 1–2.

Example 1–2 : Processing a topic.

INPUT:

```
<book>
      <intro></intro>
            <chapter>
                  <section>
                      <topic source="song">Xanadu</topic>
                      <topic>Topic 2</topic>
                  </section>
                  <section></section>
            </chapter>
</book>
```

OUTPUT:

```
<p>Xanadu</p>
<hr/>
<p>Topic 2</p>
<hr/>
```

Notice the structure of the XSLT stylesheet in Example 1–1 that contributed to this output. The `<xsl:template>` element found a match on a `<topic>` in the input XML document. This was replaced by the contents of that `<xsl:template>` element—in this case, the `<p></p>` and `<hr/>` elements. Then the content of the `<topic>` was sent to the output, enclosed within the `<p>` and `</p>` open and close tags. This was done by the `<xsl:apply-templates>` element, which is *contained within* the `<p>` tag in the stylesheet.

Notice also that the generated output is not well-formed XML. XSLT processors *generate* XML documents, but do not *parse* the output document.

1.4.1 Using XSLT to Convert XML to HTML

Let's use some simple XSLT to transform the elements in an XML document to HTML. As an example, we will use the common image of a year, subdivided by a loose notion of an agricultural calendar with planting, harvest, seasons, and months.[4] Example 1–3 illustrates how markup might be used to describe a year.

Suppose we need to render our year for display in a conventional Web browser. Conversion to HTML is a frequent task for XSLT stylesheets. We'll make this a simple transformation, using the HTML unordered list format (`<ul></ul>`) for displaying the `<month>`s.

Using the stylesheet in Example 1–4, we create a simple list of the months with the HTML list item tags (`<li></li>`) for the output document.

Again, consider the XML document instance structure of this XSLT stylesheet. Taking for granted the required stylesheet components that will be discussed later, the two template rules that remain are simple. The first matches the `<year>` (using the `match="year"` attribute) and replaces it with an unordered list tag (`<ul></ul>`). The `<ul>` element is a child of the `<xsl:template>` element. Then, *within* the `<ul>` is the

4. Of course, variations in planting and harvest, as well as in seasons, are widespread (with the changing global climate, your experience of the weather might be alarmingly different!), so this is a generalized presentation, based primarily on the seasons and weather of the Northern Hemisphere (though our Iowa friends might take us to task on some points!).

Example 1–3 : Marking up a year with XML.

```
<?xml version="1.0"?>
<year>
	<planting>
		<season period="spring">
			<month>March</month>
			<month>April</month>
			<month>May</month>
		</season>
		<season period="summer">
			<month>June</month>
			<month>July</month>
			<month>August</month>
		</season>
	</planting>
	<harvest>
		<season period="fall">
			<month>September</month>
			<month>October</month>
			<month>November</month>
		</season>
		<season period="winter">
			<month>December</month>
			<month>January</month>
			<month>February</month>
		</season>
	</harvest>
</year>
```

instruction—`<xsl:apply-templates>`—to process any children of `<year>`.

The `<xsl:apply-templates>` instruction element basically tells the processor to look for an `<xsl:template>` for each child of the `<year>`, recursively addressing each child of a child until all the descendants are processed. If the processor finds a rule for an element, it will follow the instructions in that template rule to process the node. If it does not, it will continue working down through the descendants until it reaches a text node. At this point, the text is sent to the output.

The second template rule matches each month in the input document. Each `<month>` tag is replaced by the contents of the template rule (which can be called simply the *template*), in this case, a list item in HTML

Example 1–4 : Basic stylesheet for unordered lists.

```
<?xml version="1.0"?>
<xsl:stylesheet
      xmlns:xsl="http://www.w3.org/1999/XSL/Transform"
      version="1.0">
<xsl:output method="html" />
<xsl:template match="year">
          <ul>
                    <xsl:apply-templates />
          </ul>
</xsl:template>
<xsl:template match="month">
          <li>
                    <xsl:apply-templates />
          </li>
</xsl:template>
</xsl:stylesheet>
```

(<li></li>). Then, the text node child of each <month> is sent to the output with <xsl:apply-templates>. To be proper HTML, the output would still need a few things, but it will actually display in most browsers as shown in Figure 1–4.

Example 1–5 shows the resulting HTML when an examination of the source for this file is made. Notice that the file does not contain the normal <html> or <body> tags that are used in most HTML files.

Without having element rules to match on the <harvest>, <planting>, and <season> elements, their tags will not be output to the result, nor will the <html> and <body> tags that are required by HTML (but most browsers would properly display this as an unordered list, anyway). It is possible to do quite a few easy XML-to-HTML transformations in this way.

During our examples we have skipped over some very basic concepts that are crucial to understanding XSLT stylesheets. With this basic example of converting XML to HTML, we will now discuss the concepts and terminology that apply to all XSLT stylesheets.

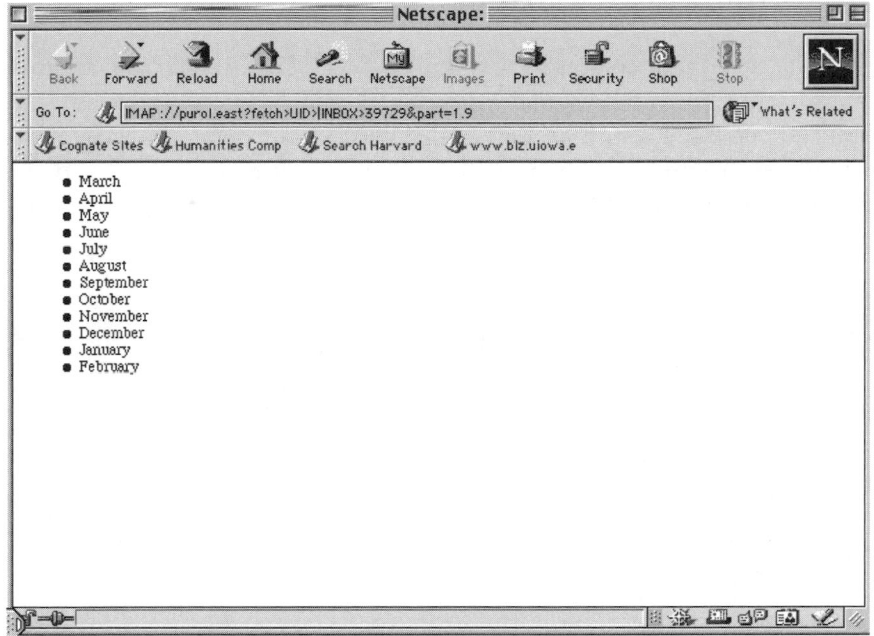

Figure 1–4 Web view of output from basic stylesheet for unordered lists.

Example 1–5 : HTML output from basic stylesheet for unordered lists.

```
<ul>
      <li>March</li>
      <li>April</li>
      <li>May</li>
      <li>June</li>
      <li>July</li>
      <li>August</li>
      <li>September</li>
      <li>October</li>
      <li>November</li>
      <li>December</li>
      <li>January</li>
      <li>February</li>
</ul>
```

1.5 Terminology for XSLT

Now that we have seen some very simple XSLT stylesheets, it is important to understand the way in which both XSLT and XPath refer to their parts. For instance, while you may be familiar with "root elements," the distinction between them and the "root" or "document root" might not be clear. Similarly, the idea of nodes and document order may be generally clear, but their precise applications deserve attention.

1.5.1 The Root of the Matter

The definition of *root,* shown below, supplies key concepts for working with XSLT stylesheets and other XML document instances.

> **root**: A unique node or vertex of a graph from which every other node can be reached.
>
> [first computer usage] Formally, a tree is a set of nodes connected by branches such that there is one and only one way of going from one node to another via branch connections, and which has a distinguished node called the root node. W. C. Gear, *Introd. Computer Sci.,* vii. 282, 1973 (*OED*, 2000, XIV: 88)

This definition introduces three key components for working with XSLT: nodes, directional navigation (though, as we'll see, when using XPath we are not limited to "one and only one way of going from one node to another"), and the uniqueness of the root node. We will address each of these in turn in the following sections, beginning—naturally—with the root.

In both XML and XSLT, the distinction between the "root" and the "root element" is often confused. The simplest way to untangle these is to look at both terms separately.

Root—that from which all else comes, on which all else is predicated, and from which every other node can be reached.

The root is not an element, it is a container for the XML document. Sometimes the root is also called the *document root* or *the root node.* The reference is to the document itself—the object that contains all the elements, attributes, comments, text, and so on. The root is not a child of any other node.

Root Element—the first element in a document, also known as the document element.

The root element is the single element of which all other elements in the XML document instance are children or descendants. The root element is itself a child of the root. The root element is also known as the *document element*, because it is the first *element* in a document, and it contains all other elements in the document.[5]

In XSLT, the root is the XSLT stylesheet. It contains the XML declaration, `<?xml version="1.0"?>`, as its first child. Following that is the document element of the XSLT stylesheet, which can be either `<xsl:stylesheet>` or `<xsl:transform>`.

The XML declaration and the document element are the only direct children of the XSLT stylesheet. All other parts of an XSLT stylesheet are contained within the XSLT document element.

Because of the general confusion between the root and the root element, we will generally refer to the root element as the document element.

When an XSLT stylesheet refers to the root of the XML document instance it is processing, the symbol "/" is used. This symbol, called a *token*, is similar in meaning to the UNIX use, which refers to the "root" on a server. In fact, the entire syntax for referencing parts of the tree descended from the root in an XML document instance is very much like the syntax used in UNIX or MS-DOS to refer to directories and subdirectories. The / symbol and other tokens are discussed in the XPath introduction in Chapter 4.

1.5.2 Branching Out: Nodes

In XML, any point you can identify in the document's tree structure is a *node*. XSLT and XPath, when used effectively, permit direct access to any node in the tree. If you refer to "this paragraph," it's a node. If you refer to "that element," "that attribute," and so on, they are all nodes.

---

5. It is the *document element* that is referenced as the document type in a Doctype Declaration. For example, in <!DOCTYPE myelement SYSTEM "mydtd.dtd">, myelement is the document element.

The terminology of nodes is used throughout both XSLT and XPath and has crucial import in understanding and accessing each object in a document.

> **node**: The point of a stem from which the leaves spring…a point or vertex of a network or graph. (*OED*, 2000, X: 459-460)

Let's reconsider the diagram of the book tree, shown again in Figure 1–5, this time with some of the nodes identified. The book, chapters, sections, and so on are all element nodes. The text contained in each topic is a text node.

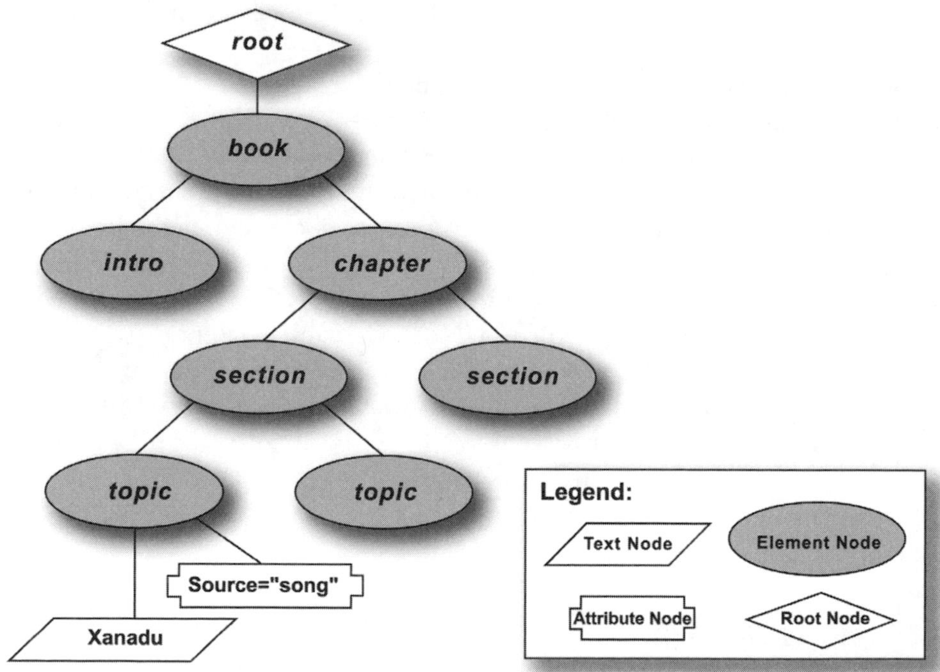

Figure 1–5 Nodes in an XML tree structure.

Suppose we used attributes to distinguish between types of topics, shown in this example as the attribute "Source" with a value of "song." This is important with the word "Xanadu," where it can mean a mythical place enshrined in the flowing words of a Coleridge poem, a pop-music song by Olivia Newton-John, or even a whimsical name used by locals for Sun

Microsystems' new campus just northwest of Boston. We could use attributes in a <topic></topic> element to mark "Xanadu" to clarify each kind of use. In this case, each attribute along with its value would comprise a node.

There are seven kinds of nodes in XSLT, but we will focus first on the *element node* as most common to both XML and XSLT stylesheets. The other six node types (that the designers of XSLT thought were significant) are discussed throughout the remainer of this book.

The nodes extending from, or "under," a chapter would be a set of nodes that is best understood as a *node branch.* A node branch is any logical structure consisting of a node and its descendants, sometimes referred to as a *subtree.* A little "pruning" of our tree terminology is implied by the notion of nodes and node branches. You will find that XML terminology does not include "leaves" or "branches." Nodes and node branches are the closest correlations to these concepts.

Consider again the diagram of a book, shown in Figure 1–6, this time with some of its parts also identified in terms of a node branch.

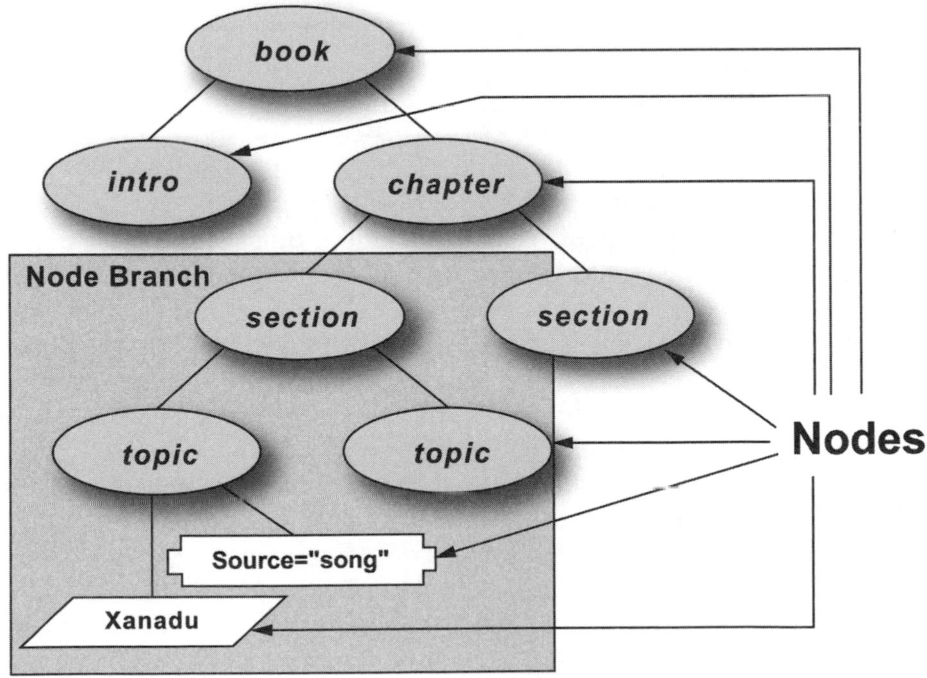

Figure 1–6 Nodes and node branches in an XML tree.

You would use XSLT and XPath to access any one of these nodes or a combination of them, as well as other types of nodes not shown here. The nodes descended from and including the "section" on the far left are a node branch.

Node-sets, on the other hand, are described in the XPath specification as "an unordered collection of nodes without duplicates." They are the set of nodes returned by an expression (discussed in Chapter 3), regardless of the location of the nodes in the tree or branch of the XML instance. For example, the set of two section elements can comprise a node-set.

1.5.3 Document Order

The concept of *document order* might seem self-evident, but it is an important concept because the process and order by which nodes are evaluated depend on it. In essence, document order is the order of nodes as they are encountered while traversing the document as it would be read left-to-right and top-to-bottom.

The elements in our `<year>` example, in document order, would be: `<year>`, `<planting>`, the `<season>` with the period attribute with a value of spring, then the `<month>` elements in the first `<season>`—March, April, May—followed by the `<season>` with the period attribute with a value of summer and its `<month>` contents, and so on. In other words, document order is what you would expect as the order according to the direction, or sequence, in which the data is read.

Sometimes, a sequence of "reverse document order" can be stipulated, which means, as you would expect, the opposite of the order in which the content would be read at the node level. The reversing of document order occurs based on a starting node. If, in the example above, an expression referred to the second `<month>` starting from July, in reverse document order, it would be referring to the `<month>` node that contained the string June. It would not, for instance, be referring to "enuJ", or the string value being read in reverse. The first element in document order is the starting element, in this case, the `<month>` containing July, so the second element in reverse document order is the `<month>` containing June.

The document order of nodes is based on the tree hierarchy of the XML instance. The first node, then, would be the root node, or document root. Element nodes are ordered prior to their children, so the first element node would be the document element (`<year>` in our example), followed by its children. Nodes are selected in document order based on their starting tag, or *opening tag*. Children nodes are processed prior to sibling nodes, and closing tags, or *end tags*, are implicitly ignored. Attribute and namespace nodes of a given element are ordered prior to the children of the element. This can be more readily seen in Figure 1–7, which shows the document order for the nodes from our `<year>` (with a few extras thrown in to demonstrate their position).

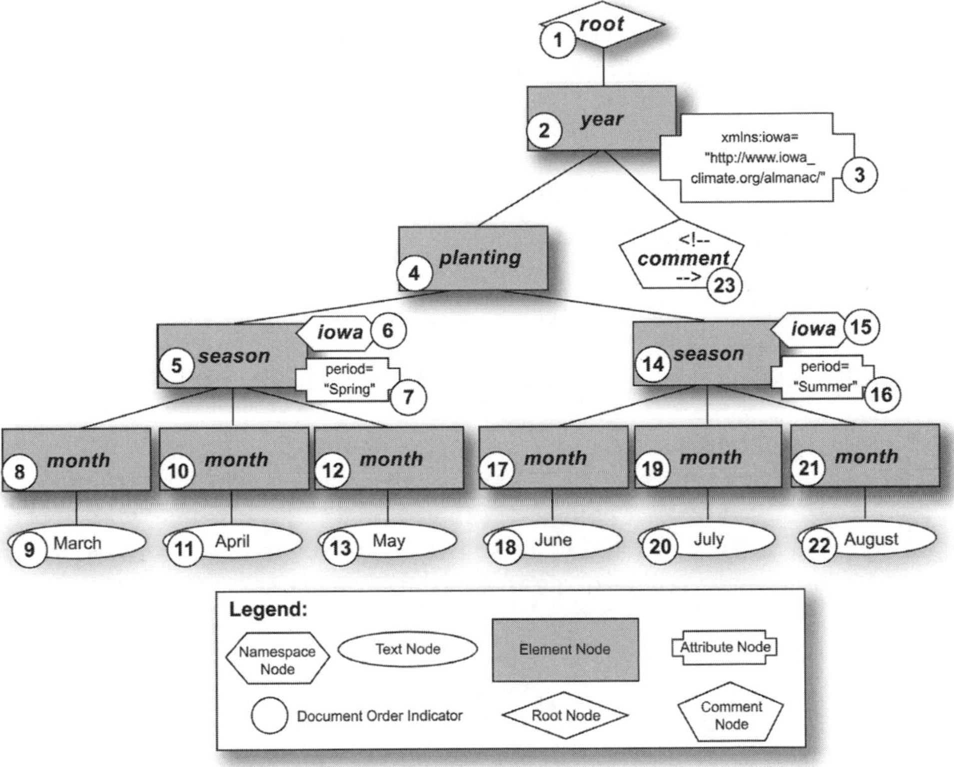

Figure 1–7 Document order using six node types.

1. The root node
2. The document element `<year>`
3. The attribute for the `iowa` namespace declaration
4. The element node `<planting>`
5. The element node `<season>`
6. The `iowa` namespace node
7. The `period` attribute with a value of `"Spring"`
8. The element node `<month>`

9. The `March` text node
10. The element node `<month>`
11. The `April` text node
12. The element node `<month>`
13. The `May` text node
14. The element node `<season>`
15. The `iowa` namespace node
16. The `period` attribute with a value of `"Summer"`
17. The element node `<month>`
18. The `June` text node
19. The element node `<month>`
20. The `July` text node
21. The element node `<month>`
22. The `August` text node
23. The comment node

Figure 1–7 displays the document order for six of the seven node types, the seventh being the processing-instruction node, which is not included in this example.

The only other possible order for the above nodes is the exact reverse, if specified in an expression as *reverse document order*. However, there is a mechanism in XSLT that will allow the sorting of nodes, which would then change the order of the nodes to something other than document order. Sorting will be addressed further in Chapter 9.

1.6 Climbing 'Round the Family Tree: Addressing in XSLT

Navigation in XSLT and XPath involves addressing the various nodes with respect to their relationship with one another. If you put "tree" and "relationships" together, a logical inference is to use a tree analogy to model how members of a family are related. So, with XPath, the terminology for how one node is positioned in an XML document instance with respect to another is done in terms of family terminology, or a family tree.

A family tree traces one's parents, grandparents, and other ancestors. XML uses the same familial terminology to describe the relationships between the nodes of a document.

Up to this point, we have used tree representations to show the structure of elements in an XML document. Now we are going to show nesting using a different form of representation, using boxes to show nesting. In Figure 1–8, consider the representation of XML and the full concept of element

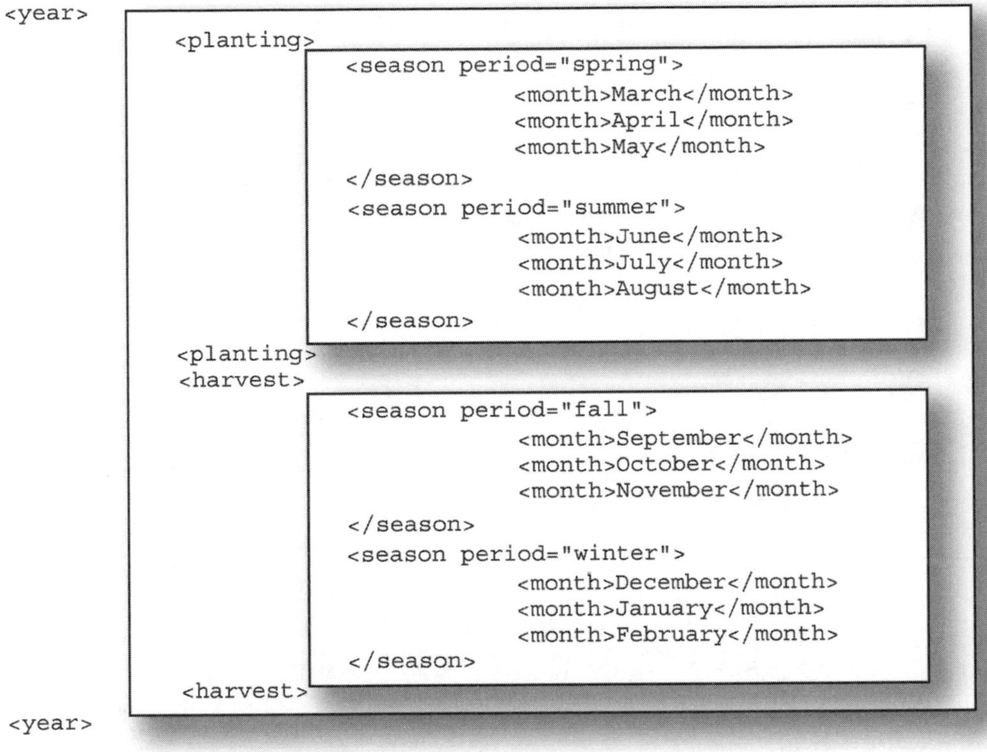

```
<year>
    <planting>
            <season period="spring">
                        <month>March</month>
                        <month>April</month>
                        <month>May</month>
            </season>
            <season period="summer">
                        <month>June</month>
                        <month>July</month>
                        <month>August</month>
            </season>
    <planting>
    <harvest>
            <season period="fall">
                        <month>September</month>
                        <month>October</month>
                        <month>November</month>
            </season>
            <season period="winter">
                        <month>December</month>
                        <month>January</month>
                        <month>February</month>
            </season>
    <harvest>
<year>
```

Figure 1–8 Nesting of XML markup using boxes.

nesting as it is presented. In this way, the logical structure of a simple XML document instance can be represented.

This example shows the document element, `<year>`, which contains (as a boxed set) the `<planting>` and `<harvest>` elements, and so on. The same logical structure can be represented in the tried and true tree paradigm, as shown in Figure 1–9.

In any family tree, the oldest traceable ancestor is always at the top. In this case, `<year>` is the *ancestor* of all the other nodes in the instance. In addition, we can say that `<year>` is the *parent* of both `<planting>`

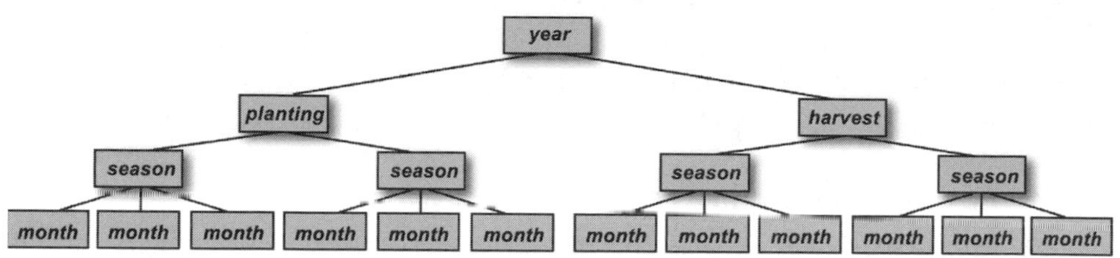

Figure 1–9 Nesting of XML markup using trees.

and `<harvest>`. Accordingly, then, `<planting>` and `<harvest>` are both *children* of `<year>`. If we asked for the parent of `<harvest>`, we would get `<year>`; for the parent of `<planting>`, we would also get `<year>`. This means that `<planting>` and `<harvest>` can also be called *siblings* to one another.

As we go further down the tree, additional features of familial relationships come into play. The various `<season>` nodes are all *descendants* of `<year>`, and `<year>` is also their shared, or common, ancestor.

In this kind of terminology that is so crucial for XPath, we do not say "grandparent" or "great-grandparent." Any predecessor in the element hierarchy of the logical structure that is more than one node level removed is an ancestor.[6]

Lines of descendancy are kept carefully intact in XML and XPath, just as they usually are in the human realm. Where `<harvest>` and `<planting>` are siblings, so also are both of them parents to their own *respective sets* of `<season>` elements. The two `<season>` elements with attribute values for period of fall and winter, are both siblings because they share the same parent, `<harvest>`. Similarly, the `<season>` elements with the period attribute values spring and summer are also siblings sharing the same parent, `<planting>`.

The summer `<season>`, then, is *not* a sibling to the winter `<season>`. They do not share the same parent. In life, we might call these cousins, but neither XPath nor XML standards as a whole use this terminology.[7] Of

6. This is correct with common practice, as a grandparent is an ancestor as well as a grandparent, and is more an ancestor than a parent with respect to the direct progenitor relationship.

7. This is partly because "cousin," among other things, can have many different familial significations in English-speaking cultures and so becomes quite problematic as an intuitive referent of a relationship.

course, every `<season>` is at the same *logical level* in this document's hierarchy, but they are not siblings.

As a definition of node relationships, each `<month>` within the fall `<season>` is:

- A sibling of the other `<month>` elements in the same `<season>`
- A child of its parent `<season period="fall">`
- A descendant of `<harvest>`
- A descendant of `<year>`
- A descendant of the document root
- The parent of the text node it contains

Another thing that might not be apparent at first glance, but is an unspoken assumption in working with the familial terminology in the tree structure, is that each of the families represented in the node branch are single-parent families. Call it a reflection of the post-modern world, but it is an important distinction of XML that no node can have more than one parent. Any node (except the root node) can have many ancestors, but only one parent.

Another point to mention is the relationship between attributes and elements. An element node such as `<season>` is called the parent of the attribute node with the attribute name `period`. However, the attribute `period` is not considered the child of `<season>`.

With this basic set of terms in mind, you can point to any part of a document based on its logical structure. This makes the value of markup and the logical structure it provides quite apparent, if, for example, the markup was in another language. In the case of our year example, providing the weather in the hemisphere from which that language arose was compatible, it would be possible to refer to the same period without knowing the specific word for that month. XPath relies heavily on this familial structure to navigate through a document when processing a particular XSLT function.

Fundamental Concepts of XSLT Stylesheets

- Boilerplate stylesheets
- `<xsl:stylesheet>` and `<xsl:transform>` document element
- Literal result element
- Literal result stylesheet
- Stylesheets embedded in an XML document
- XML declaration
- Document type declaration

2

In Chapter 1 we covered several XSLT elements and basic concepts that allowed stylesheets to be immediately useable. This chapter is devoted to fully explaining the nature—or structure—of XSLT stylesheets and the core concepts underlying them. We will discuss the `<xsl:stylesheet>` and `<xsl:transform>` document elements and their structure, along with a basic overview of their child elements, including `<xsl:template>`. We will also present boilerplate stylesheets that can be used as the base of any XSLT transformation, as well as an example of using stylesheets directly in an XML document.

2.1 Boilerplates for XSLT Stylesheets

Building upon the information presented in Chapter 1, a boilerplate XSLT stylesheet, using `<xsl:stylesheet>` as the document element, would result in the basic structure required for any stylesheet, as shown in Example 2–1.

The document element is used to contain the rest of the stylesheet, as well as providing a convenient place to declare the version and namespace for XSL. The XSLT version is shown here as `version="1.0"` and the

Example 2–1 : Basic XSLT stylesheet structure.

```
<?xml version="1.0"?>
      <xsl:stylesheet
            xmlns:xsl="http://www.w3.org/1999/XSL/Transform"
            version="1.0" >
            <!--The various top-level elements
                   go here -->
      </xsl:stylesheet>
```

XSL namespace, defined using the `xmlns` namespace declaration attribute, is shown here as:

```
xmlns:xsl="http://www.w3.org/1999/XSL/Transform"
```

The document element of an XSLT stylesheet can be either `<xsl:stylesheet>` or `<xsl:transform>`, or, as shown in Section 2.1.2, can also be a literal result element.

2.1.1 Document Element: `<xsl:stylesheet>` or `<xsl:transform>`

The document element, whether `<xsl:stylesheet>` or `<xsl:transform>`, contains the other elements in a stylesheet, and is used to declare the version of XSLT that the stylesheet conforms to. The document element is also used to tell the processor that the stylesheet *is* an XSLT stylesheet, using the `xmlns` attribute. Both elements have the same structure and content, as shown in the definitions below:

```
<xsl:stylesheet
  id = id
  extension-element-prefixes = tokens
  exclude-result-prefixes = tokens
  version = number>
  <!-- Content: (xsl:import*, top-level-elements) -->
</xsl:stylesheet>
```

Besides the required `version` attribute, both elements have an optional `id` attribute, which is used to provide an ID for the stylesheet when it is

```
<xsl:transform
  id = id
 extension-element-prefixes = tokens
 exclude-result-prefixes = tokens
 version = number>
 <!-- Content: (xsl:import*, top-level-elements) -->
</xsl:transform>
```

embedded directly in an XML document (see Section 2.2), and two attributes related to namespace prefixes (discussed in Chapter 12).

Apart from its syntactic role as the document element of an XSLT stylesheet, the `<xsl:stylesheet>` or `<xsl:transform>` element serves to establish the fact that the document is an XSTL stylesheet by declaring it as one with the `xmlns` attribute. The `xmlns` attribute, while not listed in the element model definitions from the XSLT specification, is nevertheless allowed on this element. The `xmlns` attribute on the document element is used to declare the XSL namespace (see Section 12.3.4).

The following sections provide a review of the document element's other attributes, as well as the `xml:space` attribute.

2.1.1.1 The `version` Attribute

The `version` attribute is a required attribute for the document element. It provides information to the XSLT processor to determine which version of the XSLT specification the stylesheet requires for correct processing. The following attribute model definition shows its structure:

```
ATTRIBUTE: version NMTOKEN #REQUIRED
VALUE = number
```

An example of using the `version` attribute is as follows:

```
<xsl:stylesheet xmlns:xsl="http://www.w3.org/1999/XSL/Transform"
          version="1.0" >
```

The value of the `version` attribute will be `1.0` until a new version of the XSLT specification becomes a recommendation.

2.1.1.2 The `extension-element-prefixes` Attribute

The `extension-element-prefixes` attribute is used to let the processor know if any extension elements are being used, and what their prefixes are. Prefixes for extension elements are established by adding namespaces (discussed in Chapter 12) to the document element. Any element in a template that uses a prefix other than `xsl` will be treated as a literal result element (LRE), sent to the output as is, unless the prefix is designated as an extension prefix using the `extension-element-prefixes` attribute. Once a prefix is designated as an extension prefix, elements in a template that have that prefix are treated as instruction elements and processed according to the rules of the namespace that governs that prefix. The following attribute model definition shows the proper structure of the `extension-element-prefixes` attribute:

```
ATTRIBUTE: extension-element-prefixes CDATA #IMPLIED
VALUE: = tokens
```

Declaring the XSL namespace using `xmlns` gives you access to the functions and top-level elements defined in the namespace, but it does not let you use its prefix in an element inside a template without also adding the prefix to the list of prefixes in the value of the attribute. (Note that some processors do not require this for their own extensions.)

The scope of any extension namespace is limited to the branch of the stylesheet starting with the element that contains either the `extension-element-prefixes` or `xsl:extension-element-prefixes` attribute. This does not include any stylesheets that are imported or included within the stylesheet. If the namespace is to be allowed within another stylesheet, it must be declared and designated in that stylesheet. In other words, namespaces are only available to elements that fall inside the branch of the element that declares the namespace.

> **NOTE** The attribute `extension-element-prefixes` is allowed on the document element only; however, the attribute `xsl:extension-element-prefixes` is allowed on an LRE or an extension element.

When declaring XT and Saxon namespaces in our stylesheet, we add the `extension-element-prefixes` attribute as follows:

```
<xsl:stylesheet xmlns:xsl="http://www.w3.org/1999/XSL/Transform"
      version="1.0"
      xmlns:xt="http://www.jclark.com/xt"
      xmlns:saxon="http://icl.com/saxon"
      extension-element-prefixes="xt saxon" >
```

2.1.1.3 The `exclude-result-prefixes` Attribute

The attribute `exclude-result-prefixes` allows the removal of namespace prefixes from the result tree elements. This attribute is optional, and its value is a whitespace-separated list of namespace prefixes. The namespaces listed must have been declared in the stylesheet. The attribute model definition below shows the required structure of this attribute:

```
ATTRIBUTE: exclude-result-prefixes CDATA #IMPLIED
VALUE = = tokens
```

This attribute is primarily provided to clean up any namespace prefixes from the result tree that are inconsequential for the output. It is used to exclude any namespace prefixes from the LREs included in a stylesheet.

For the following example, we might declare the namespace `"http://vedavid.org/x-nology"` with a prefix of `"veda,"` as shown below.

```
<xsl:stylesheet xmlns:xsl="http://www.w3org/1999/XSL/Transform"
      version="1.0"
      xmlns:xt="http://www.jclark.com/xt"
      xmlns:saxon="http://icl.com/saxon"
      xmlns:veda="http://vedavid.org/x-nology"
      extension-element-prefixes="xt saxon veda"
      exclude-result-prefixes="veda" >
```

To suppress the output of any prefix for the `veda` namespace used on an LRE, we add the `exclude-result-prefixes` attribute. Note that including the prefix with the `extension-element-prefixes` attribute is not a direct inverse action for excluding it with `exclude-result-prefixes`. The attributes `extension-`

element-prefixes and exclude-result-prefixes are not direct opposites, because exclude-result-prefixes only affects the output, while extension-element-prefixes affects how the processor reads the elements in the stylesheet.

2.1.1.4 The id Attribute

The id attribute is defined as a type ID, as shown in the following attribute model definition. It is used to add functionality for cross-referencing a document element.

```
ATTRIBUTE: id ID #IMPLIED
VALUE = id
```

This optional attribute is very uncommon when using the <xsl:stylesheet> or <xsl:transform> document elements. It is more common when using an LRE as the document element, when the resulting document requires IDs on elements. It is also used when embedding a stylesheet directly in an XML document later (as shown in Example 2–4).

2.1.1.5 The xml:space Attribute

The xml:space attribute comes from the XML specification and provides functionality for preserving whitespace text nodes that are found in the stylesheet. It is allowed on the document element to provide a default action for preserving or removing whitespace nodes from all the descendant elements of the document element. The value for the xml:space attribute is a choice of either default or preserve, as shown in the following attribute model definition:

```
ATTRIBUTE:  xml:space (default|preserve) #IMPLIED
VALUE = (default|preserve)
```

If other elements in the stylesheet use the xml:space attribute, they will override the value declared in the document element. This introduces the concept of inheritance. The descendant elements of the document element will inherit the value of the attribute, unless they explicitly override the value with an `xml:space` attribute of their own.

It is important to note that the `xml:space` attribute applies only to the structure of the *stylesheet,* not to the structure of the input source document. Although they perform the same function, the preserving or stripping of nodes from the source tree is controlled with a set of top-level elements, `<xsl:strip-space>` and `<xsl:preserve-space>`.

The `xml:space` attribute is not specifically shown in the content model for this element in the XSLT specification, but it is referenced later in the appendixes.

> **NOTE** If this attribute is used on an LRE, the attribute will be passed on to the resulting output as an attribute of that LRE.

2.1.2 Literal Result Element (LRE) Stylesheet

There is a unique kind of stylesheet with a document element that is itself a literal result element (LRE). A *literal result element* is any element in the stylesheet that does not have a prefix, like `xsl`, defining it to be part of a namespace. LREs are sent to the output as is, and are discussed in their capacity of generating new XML in Chapter 6. A *literal result stylesheet* is any stylesheet that has an LRE as the document element.

If an LRE is the first element, or the document element, in a stylesheet, then that LRE must use the same required attributes as either `<xsl:stylesheet>` or `<xsl:transform>`, discussed in the previous section. For instance, if the document element is `<html>`, then the `<html>` element, as the first element in the stylesheet, requires the XSL namespace declaration and the `version` attribute for XSLT, as shown in Example 2–2. However, since this is an LRE, the `version` attribute must be preceded by the `xsl` prefix. The `xmlns` attribute is already prefixed, so remains the same.

LREs that reference XSLT attributes use the prefix `xsl` in front of the attribute to let the processor know that the attribute comes from XSLT, and should be processed according to the rules for that XSLT attribute.

Stylesheets that take the form shown in Example 2–2 are handled by the processor as if the entire stylesheet was inside an `<xsl:template>` element (part of the *template*). The XSLT stylesheet in Example 2–3 is the

Example 2–2 : An LRE stylesheet showing the `version` and xsl namespace declaration.

```
<html xsl:version="1.0"
      xmlns:xsl="http://www.w3.org/1999/XSL/Transform">
      <head>
            <title>My document title.</title>
      </head>
      <body>
            <p>My document content.</p>
      </body>
</html>
```

Example 2–3 : An XSLT stylesheet that is equivalent to the LRE stylesheet in Example 2–2.

```
<xsl:stylesheet
            version="1.0"
            xmlns:xsl="http://www.w3.org/1999/XSL/Transform">
<xsl:template match="/">
      <html>
            <head>
                  <title>My document title.</title>
            </head>
            <body>
                  <p>My document content.</p>
            </body>
      </html>
</xsl:template>
</xsl:stylesheet>
```

equivalent of Example 2–2, using `<xsl:stylesheet>` as the document element.

Because a literal result stylesheet is seen by the processor as a template inside an `<xsl:template>` element—where top-level elements are not allowed—LRE stylesheets will never contain top-level XSLT elements.

The document element of an LRE stylesheet also has the option to declare other namespaces that may be used in the stylesheet (see Chapter 12).

2.1.3 Children of the Document Element

There are twelve possible element children of the XSLT stylesheet's document element. These children are called *top-level* elements because they are allowed at the top level within a document element. There is little or no requisite syntactic or logical order to the elements in an XSLT stylesheet. They may occur within any order, though you will find that writing the various template rules in a manner that reflects either the order of the source tree or the intended result tree is often the most natural procedure.

There is one *significant exception* regarding the prescribed—or otherwise *unprescribed*—order for top-level elements in an XSLT stylesheet. If the `<xsl:include>` element is to be used, it must without exception come first within the document element. All other top-level elements must follow the `<xsl:include>` element, if present.

2.1.3.1 Top-Level Elements

Top-level elements are a specific set of XSLT elements that are children of the document element of an XSLT stylesheet. Top-level elements must be direct children of either the `<xsl:stylesheet>` element or the `<xsl:transform>` element. They are not allowed inside instruction elements or any other elements that are children of the document element. They are not allowed as children of an LRE element, even if that element is used as the document element. In other words, you cannot nest top-level elements inside instructions, other top-level elements, or LREs. *Note that there are two exceptions to this rule, the* `<xsl:variable>` *and* `<xsl:param>` *elements are allowed at both the top level and at the same level as instruction elements.*

Top-level elements are not instructions per se, as they do not instruct the processor to handle nodes from the source tree in a certain way to generate an output result tree fragment. They can be considered more like assistants to or wrappers for the instruction elements and stylesheet as a whole. The `<xsl:template>` element in particular only selects a set of nodes to be handed to a template. Each top-level element has a specific function, whether passing information to and from instructions or performing administrative roles.

Each of the top-level elements is discussed in more detail in the following chapters, but it is conceptually useful to provide a short list of them here. In addition, this list gives a sampling of the scope of richness in functionality available through XSLT.

1. **<xsl:include>** enables an XSLT stylesheet to include templates and instructions from more than one stylesheet. The <xsl:include> element is the only top-level element with a specific syntactic place in the document order, and must always be the first child of the XSLT stylesheet document element.
2. **<xsl:import>** enables an XSLT stylesheet to import templates and instructions from external stylesheets.
3. **<xsl:strip-space>** removes any text nodes that contain only whitespace from the source tree prior to any further processing.
4. **<xsl:preserve-space>** does not remove text nodes that contain only whitespace from the source tree.
5. **<xsl:output>** serves to specify the kind of output from the XSLT stylesheet, other than XML. XSLT stylesheets can generate XML, as well as text or HTML.
6. **<xsl:key>** declares a set of keys for each document and works with the `key()` function for indexing elements.
7. **<xsl:decimal-format>** is used to declare a specific format for decimal numbers and works with the `format-number()` function by controlling the interpretation of a pattern.
8. **<xsl:namespace-alias>** provides functionality to declare one namespace URI as a replacement for another, which allows the use of different namespaces in the output.
9. **<xsl:attribute-set>** defines a named set of attributes that can be used as a group in an output element.
10. **<xsl:variable>** is used to define a specific value that can be used in other XSLT elements in the stylesheet.
11. **<xsl:param>** allows the definition of a variable that can be modified by the XSLT element using it.
12. **<xsl:template>** is the fundamental pattern matching construct for selecting portions of the input source that are to be treated by the instructions contained in the template.

2.2 Embedding Stylesheets in XML Documents

XSLT stylesheets are often used in a batch environment as separate files, but it is also possible to embed a stylesheet directly in an XML document, possibly to deliver the document directly to a browser for rendering. This means that the XML document must be aware of the stylesheet.

There is a separate recommendation from the W3C that identifies the process for embedding stylesheets in XML documents, called *Associating Style Sheets with XML Documents*, Version 1.0.[1] This recommendation describes a predefined XML processing instruction, or PI, that can be used at the top of any XML document to allow the XML to find the top of the XSLT stylesheet, wherever it is in the XML.

The PI uses an `href` attribute with a URI to point to the ID of the `<xsl:stylesheet>` element. This URI must be a *fragment identifier* (signalled by the # prefix) because it is a reference to a part of the document containing the PI. It is not used to reference an external stylesheet. The following PI model definition shows the two required attributes and four optional attributes for the `<?xml-stylesheet?>` PI:

```
<?xml-stylesheet
  href = string
  type = string
  title = string
  media = string
  charset = string
  alternate = "yes" | "no"
?>
```

Example 2–4, taken directly from the XSLT specification, shows an embedded stylesheet in an XML document.

Notice that this example contains a few elements from the XSL formatting objects specification. The stylesheet is called into play with the `<?xml-stylesheet?>` PI. The template rule matching on `id('foo')` in the example finds an element in the XML with an ID of "foo" and uses the instructions in the template to format it, in this case with a bold font.

1. See http://www.w3.org/TR/xml-stylesheet.

Example 2–4 : Embedding a stylesheet in an XML document.

```
<?xml-stylesheet type="text/xml" href="#style1"?>
<!DOCTYPE doc SYSTEM "doc.dtd">
<doc>
<head>
<xsl:stylesheet id="style1"
                version="1.0"
                xmlns:xsl="http://www.w3.org/1999/XSL/Transform"
               xmlns:fo="http://www.w3.org/1999/XSL/Format">
<xsl:import href="doc.xsl"/>
<xsl:template match="id('foo')">
  <fo:block font-weight="bold"><xsl:apply-templates/></fo:block>
</xsl:template>
<xsl:template match="xsl:stylesheet">
  <!-- ignore -->
</xsl:template>
</xsl:stylesheet>
</head>
<body>
<para id="foo">
...
</para>
</body>
</doc>
```

The template rule matching on "`xsl:stylesheet`" is required in all embedded stylesheets so that `<xsl:stylesheet>` elements are processed as elements.

2.3 XSLT Stylesheet Terminology

It is often possible to do a great deal of work with a given technology without ever knowing exactly what some of its terms mean. Although XSLT is basically XML, there are very specific uses for its elements and attributes. The basic concepts of stylesheet structure go beyond the basic XML tagging structure to form a logical "programming" application. It is especially important, then, that we detail the terminology of XSLT.

2.3.1 Stylesheet

The term *stylesheet* is for the most part self-explanatory, but in the context of XSLT, it requires a certain qualification. Literally, an XSLT stylesheet is an XML document instance that is processed by an XSLT engine to perform a transformation on other XML documents. A stylesheet follows XML well-formedness rules, uses XSLT-specific namespace declarations, and can contain one or more XSLT templates that select and process elements from the source XML document.

A common use for XSLT stylesheets is to transform the logical structure of an XML document instance from the semantics and syntax of one DTD or schema to another. This is more of what one might traditionally consider a transformation, as it is more an XSLT logical structure transformation than a specific "styling," but it is nonetheless an act of styling that is taking place.

2.3.2 Stylesheet Element and Transform Element

The stylesheet element (`<xsl:stylesheet>`) is a valid XML element that is the first element (i.e., document element) in a stylesheet. It is the parent or ancestor of all the other elements in a stylesheet. The transform element (`<xsl:transform>`) is allowed as a replacement for the stylesheet element. Only one of either the `<xsl:stylesheet>` or `<xsl:transform>` element is allowed in a stylesheet.

> **NOTE** `<xsl:stylesheet>` and `<xsl:transform>` are synonymous. For convenience in classifying XSLT stylesheets as opposed to XSL Formatting Object stylesheets, you may wish to use `<xsl:transform>` for all XSLT stylesheets and `<xsl:stylesheet>` for all XSL stylesheets.

2.3.3 Result Tree

The result tree is simply the output that is produced from the processing of an XSLT stylesheet. Matching the root node of the input XML document instance and generating an output based on the rules found in the stylesheet create this tree. Once the entire stylesheet has been processed, the output—the result tree—is generated. Note that the result tree does not necessarily reflect the structure of the input, or source tree. The transformation process, using the rules in the stylesheet, may restructure the information prior to generating the result tree.

The output, or result tree, from an XSLT stylesheet is always a well-formed XML document, unless another output format like HTML or text is specifically selected. (See Chapter 10 for more information on selecting different kinds of output.)

2.3.4 Source Tree

The source tree is a representation of a well-formed XML document that is created during the parsing of the XML document. The source tree is created by the XSLT processor and stored in "memory" for reference during the processing of the XSLT stylesheet.

A valid source tree will always have a root node. The source tree is the entire XML document instance, but it is a somewhat abstracted roadmap of it, as shown with the book example in Figure 2–1.

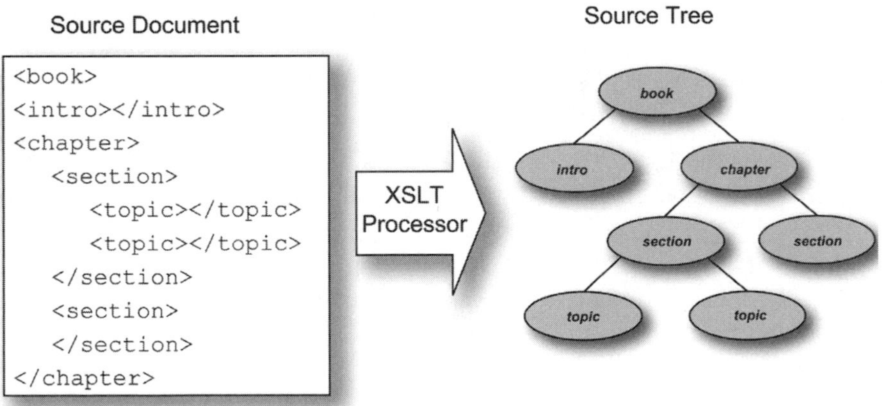

Figure 2–1 Creating a source tree.

All nodes from the input XML document, including element nodes, attribute nodes, etc., are included in the source tree, which makes the representation of the structure somewhat unintuitive, as shown in Figure 2–2. This structure was explained in detail in Chapter 1.

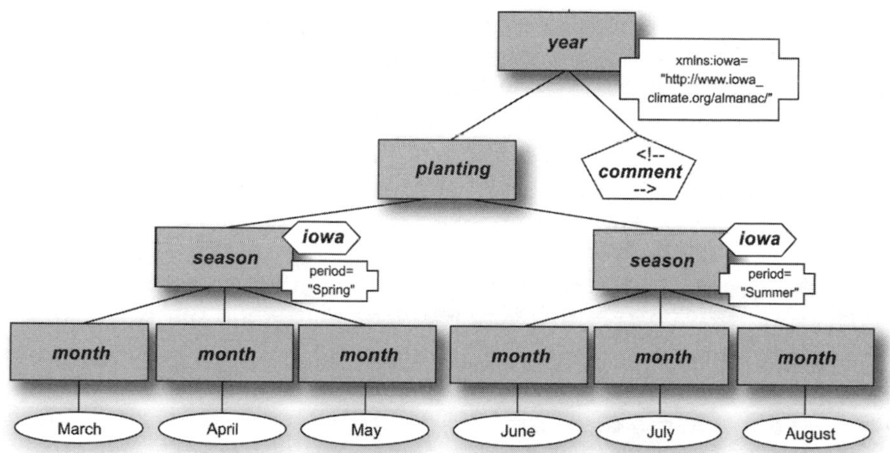

Figure 2–2 Logical structure of a source tree.

2.3.5 Whitespace

Whitespace is simply space between characters, whether tabs, line returns, or simply spaces. In most cases, whitespace does not matter to the XML processor unless we tell it to pay attention to it. Sometimes whitespace can be added to make it easier to read a complexly coded XML document.

A good way to think of whitespace is in terms of HTML. An HTML browser automatically collapses (or removes) multiple spaces between words to a single space. Hard returns in elements are also collapsed into a single space, unless the line is tagged with a line break tag (`<br>`). XML works similarly with whitespace. In HTML, you can force every bit of whitespace to be attended to and rendered by using the preformatted, or `<pre>`, tag. In XML, you can do this by adding an attribute (`xml:space='preserve'`) to an element or one of its ancestors.

In an XSLT stylesheet, whitespace is handled similarly to how it is handled in XML or HTML. For the most part, it is ignored. Within the quote marks surrounding the value for an attribute, whitespace is "compressed" or "condensed" the way it is in HTML, down to a default of one space. More spaces can be added with the ` `, or nonbreaking space, entity. Space within the output result tree can be added or preserved with an XSLT instruction element, `<xsl:text>`, discussed in detail in Chapter 6. It serves a role analogous to the HTML `<pre></pre>` tags (though it does not affect font or style in that way, only preservation of whitespace).

In XSLT stylesheets, whitespace within an attribute value is condensed to a single space. Within and between template rules, whitespace has no effect on XSLT stylesheet processing. Within the `<xsl:text>` instruction element, whitespace is preserved.

2.3.6 Well-Formedness

Well-formedness is the fundamental syntactic integrity required of every XML document. Whether there is a pre-defined markup specification using a DTD or schema or not, every XML document must be well-formed. The same is true of XSLT stylesheets. All rules apply, from proper matching of lowercase characters to the closing tag required to match every opening tag, etc. In essence, XSLT stylesheets must be well-formed because they *are* XML document instances.

The proper nesting of elements actually makes understanding each part of the XSLT stylesheet easier, as shown in Example 2–5.

Example 2–5 : Basic XSLT template showing nesting of XSLT and literal elements.

```
<xsl:template match="body">
     <xsl:for-each select="p">
          <i>
               <xsl:apply-templates />
          </i>
     </xsl:for-each>
</xsl:template>
```

Each tag that opens also closes, though in one case (`<xsl:apply-templates>`) the element is empty, so the closing of the tag is signified with the end "/" within the tag. The elements are also nested hierarchically within one another.

Even without knowing the full function of `<xsl:for-each>`, it is possible to see that something is going to be made italic using the HTML `<i>` tag. That something—assuming these are standard HTML tags—is a paragraph, selected by the `<xsl:for-each>` with the `select="p"` attribute. Not only one paragraph is selected, but each one (for-each) that may be found in the body (matched with `match="body"` on `<xsl:template>`) of the XML document instance.

Attribute values in XSLT elements must be contained in quote marks and the quote marks must match—either two single quotes (' ') or two double quotes (" "). Both of the following are *incorrect*:

```
<season period="spring'>
<season period=summer>
```

> **NOTE** It is good practice to use double quotes for attribute values, as some constructs in XSLT use expressions inside of attribute values, and therefore must use single quotes within the double quotes to avoid confusion and parsing errors.

2.4 XML Components of XSLT Stylesheets

Explanations of comments and processing-instructions in general may be unnecessary for those of you familiar with their use in XML document instances. However, these components can also be accessed by XSLT stylesheets, or even be part of XSLT stylesheets, so their application in XSLT is important to understand. There are two concepts in particular that are worth reviewing, the XML declaration and the document type declaration.

2.4.1 The XML Declaration

One of the key components of any XML document instance is the XML declaration, which is a processing-instruction, or PI, that is always the first item in the document—it even comes before the document element. The XML declaration identifies the contents of the document as XML and provides other relevant information like version and character encoding. This particular PI has a unique structure and a certain mandated content.

PIs in general are used by external applications to process the data in certain ways. PIs are empty elements that are delimited with the open tag marker <, followed by a ?, and the close tag marker >, preceded by another ?. The first word in a PI is the *target* of the instruction, or the software that is supposed to handle the instruction. The remaining content of the PI is the parameter string that the target software will need to complete the instruction. Example 2–6 shows a typical XML declaration, which is also a PI. The target of the PI in this case is `xml`, and the `version="1.0"` is a parameter that the XML processor understands.

Example 2–6 : XML document with an XML declaration.

```
<?xml version="1.0"?>
<year xmlns:iowa="http://www.iowa_climate.org/almanac/">
      <iowa:planting>
            <iowa:season period="spring">
  ...and so on...
```

It is important to note in the syntax above that there are no spaces before or after the leading and trailing `?`. This is as important to the XSLT stylesheet as it is to any XML document instance, as the XSLT processor will *not* process the XSLT stylesheet if there are errors. The XML declaration must always include the `version` attribute, and can have an `encoding` attribute to pass information about the character set of the document (for instance, something other than the XML default UTF-8, such as UTF-16).

The XML declaration can also tell you whether the document has dependencies with the `standalone` attribute. If there are other documents that go with the XML instance, the document cannot be "standalone."

2.4.2 The Document Type Declaration

XML provides a special mechanism to associate a DTD with an XML document, called a Document Type Declaration (also known as a DOCTYPE declaration). XSLT processors are not *required* to read a DTD; however, if a DTD is specified using a document type declaration, most XSLT processors will read and process the XML document according to the DTD. The DOCTYPE declaration begins with the open tag delimiter, followed by a "`!`," and the key word DOCTYPE, as shown in Example 2–7.

The DOCTYPE declaration tells in specific syntactic order what the document element is (`year`, in this case), whether the DTD is publicly declared or if it is found on the file system (SYSTEM), and where the DTD is located, using a specific address for the file (c:\dtds\calendar.dtd).[2]

2. The location of the DTD can also be just the DTDs filename in quotes if the DTD is located in the same directory as the document instance.

Example 2–7 : XML document with DOCTYPE declaration.

```
<?xml version="1.0"?>
<!DOCTYPE year SYSTEM "c:\dtds\calendar.dtd">
<year xmlns:iowa="http://www.iowa_climate.org/almanac/">
      <iowa:planting>
            <iowa:season period="spring">
  ...and so on...
```

The DOCTYPE declaration, if used, must always come before the document element.

> **NOTE** The DOCTYPE declaration can point to a DTD on a file system, or alternatively contain the DTD as part of the content of the declaration. It can also be a combination of both, allowing additions to the DTD that are specific to the document being processed.

XSLT lets you perform transformations upon and manipulate the DOCTYPE statement in addition to all the component nodes that are descendants of the document element in the logical structure of the markup. Therefore, it is important to know that the root contains the declaration, the document element does not. Otherwise, it would be very hard to access the children of the root in an XML document instance—the XML declaration, the DOCTYPE declaration (if there is one), and the document element—with an XSLT stylesheet.

Advanced Stylesheet Concepts

- Template
- Template Rule
- `<xsl:template>`
- `<xsl:apply-templates>`
- `<xsl:call-template>`
- `<xsl:value-of>`
- Built-in template rules

3

The main building block of an XSLT stylesheet is the *template*, which contains all the instructions used to process XML elements. In this chapter, we will discuss templates in general, as well as the `<xsl:template>` element and its components. Two closely related instruction elements, `<xsl:apply-templates>` and `<xsl:call-template>`, both used to select or call template rules, are included in this chapter, as well as `<xsl:value-of>`, which is used to extract a value from an expression. Additionally, we will discuss built-in template rules, the rules that kick in when a node in the input XML document is not matched.

3.1 Templates: The Building Blocks of Transformations

In the simplest sense, a template is a model. In XSLT, a template has a very specific structure, consisting of 18 instruction elements, LREs, extension elements, and text.

There are eleven elements that can contain templates: `<xsl:template>`, `<xsl:if>`, `<xsl:when>`, `<xsl:otherwise>`, `<xsl:with-param>`, `<xsl:variable>`, `<xsl:param>`, `<xsl:element>`,

> **template**: An instrument used as a gauge or guide in bringing any piece of work to the desired shape . . . a molecule or molecular pattern that determines the sequence in which other molecules are assembled . . . —unknown origin (*OED*, 2000, XVII: 753)

`<xsl:copy>`, `<xsl:message>`, and `<xsl:fallback>`. The most important and frequently used top-level element that can contain a template is the `<xsl:template>` element. This element is discussed in detail in Section 3.1.2.

Templates can also contain extension instruction elements if the extension elements are defined using namespaces. The namespace will control the function and application of the extension instruction element. If the namespace is not declared as a namespace in the stylesheet, the extension instruction element is treated like an LRE. Extension elements are discussed in Chapter 12.

Templates, template rules and the `<xsl:template>` element are all similar terms that can be a bit confusing. The `<xsl:template>` element is a top-level element that contains a set of instructions, collectively called the *template*. A *template rule* is a reference to the `<xsl:template>` element as a whole.

3.1.1 Template Processing

The XSLT stylesheet has rules that process a source tree and convert it to a result tree. The basic process associates a pattern with a template. In other words, the expression in the match statement of an `<xsl:template>` element is used to select nodes from the input tree. The nodes are then processed by the instructions in the template. The following list contains the sequence of processing from the XSLT specification (in italics), followed by a detailed explanation:

1. *A pattern is matched against elements in the source tree.*
   The expression in the `<xsl:template>` `match` attribute is evaluated against the input source document. A set of nodes (node-set) is selected and passed to the template.
2. *A template is instantiated for a particular source element to create part of the result tree.*

This is actually a two-step process. *The template is instantiated* means that each instruction element in the template is processed. The template is not processed or instantiated unless the `match` attribute of the `<xsl:template>` element is successful in actually retrieving nodes from the input. When this match occurs, the template becomes active and any instructions or LREs found in the template are processed. The statement *for a particular source element* refers to the processing of each node in the node-set selected by the match.

The second step, *to create part of the result tree,* is where the output is actually being built based on the instructions in the template.

3. *A template can contain elements that specify LRE structure.*

   LREs become part of the result tree when the template rule is instantiated.

4. *A template can also contain elements from the XSLT namespace that are instructions for creating result tree fragments (RTFs).*

   There are 18 possible XSLT instruction elements, the most common of which is the `<xsl:apply-templates>` instruction.

5. *When a template is instantiated, each instruction is executed and replaced by the RTF that it creates.*

   The instantiation process takes each instruction and, upon its execution, places the resulting structure (RTF) in the corresponding location of the result tree. This is literally the building of the output file, instruction by instruction.

6. *Instructions can select and process descendant source elements.*

   In addition to processing the node-set selected by the template rule, an expression can reach further down into the logical structure of the nodes in the node-set, including children and descendants. The input XML document instance's node hierarchy is available to the expressions in the instruction elements.

7. *Processing a descendant element creates an RTF by finding the applicable template rule and instantiating its template. Note that elements are only processed when they have been selected by the execution of an instruction.*

RTFs are created when a template rule is matched and its contents are instantiated. RTFs are "held" in memory until the actual result tree is built.

Depending on subsequent processing and selection, RTFs are written to the output file according to their position in the result tree.

8. *The result tree is constructed by finding the template rule for the root node and instantiating its template.*

   The result tree is the final version of the assemblage of all the RTFs that are instantiated by the templates. Since the root node (/) contains all the elements in the document, all other processing is complete when processing is finished for the root node. Because of the hierarchical nature of XML, processing the root node implies processing the entire document.

3.1.2 The `<xsl:template>` Top-Level Element

The most common components of XSLT stylesheets are the `<xsl:template>` elements. They form the series of template rules by which the nodes in the input XML document instance are matched and processed. The `<xsl:template>` element has several attributes, which are discussed in Section 3.1.3. The bulk of the content of an `<xsl:template>` element is called a *template,* and can consist of any combination of instruction elements, LREs, extension elements, and text. Preceding that template within an `<xsl:template>` element is one or more possible `<xsl:param>` elements, discussed in Chapter 8. The element model definition below shows the structure of the `<xsl:template>` element.

```
<!-- Category: top-level-element -->
<xsl:template
  match = pattern
  name = qname
  priority = number
  mode = qname>
  <!-- Content: (xsl:param*, template) -->
</xsl:template>
```

The `<xsl:template>` element uses an XPath pattern expression in its `match` attribute to select nodes from the input source tree, which are passed to the template for processing. The process of selecting and weeding out nodes is often the greatest effort involved in a transformation. XPath patterns expressions are discussed in Chapter 4. The attributes for `<xsl:template>` are discussed in the following section.

3.1.3 The **`<xsl:template>`** Attributes

The `<xsl:template>` has several attributes, which are all optional. The most common of these is the `match` attribute. There are also `name`, `priority`, and `mode` attributes, along with the `xml:space` attribute, which is not shown in the model. The following is a DTD representation of the attributes allowed for the `<xsl:template>` element, including the `xml:space` attribute. Each of these attributes is discussed in the following sections.

```
<!ATTLIST xsl:template
  match CDATA #IMPLIED
  name NMTOKEN #IMPLIED
  priority NMTOKEN #IMPLIED
  mode NMTOKEN #IMPLIED
  xml:space (default|preserve) #IMPLIED >
```

3.1.3.1 The `<xsl:template>` match Attribute

The `match` attribute on `<xsl:template>` contains an expression, and is used to select nodes from the input tree. The value of the expression is a *pattern*, or a path expression that addresses nodes. Note that variable references (discussed in Chapter 8) are not allowed in the match attribute. The following attribute model definition describes the characteristics of this attribute:

```
ATTRIBUTE: match CDATA #IMPLIED
VALUE = pattern
```

Once a node-set has been selected using the `match` attribute, each node in that set (also known as the *current node*) is sent to the template for processing. If no nodes are matched, the template is not used.

The match attribute is not required when the name attribute (discussed in Section 3.1.3.2) is present.

> **NOTE** Because XML cannot control the requirement of one attribute when another is absent, both the `match` and `name` attributes are optional and will not cause a parsing error if omitted.

In order to begin working with consistent XML document input for the examples in this and the following chapters, we will introduce the notion of "Markup City." Markup City is an XML representation of a set of city streets. If you can imagine a simple city with a main street with a boulevard and blocks which turn off from it, you can represent this in XML as shown in Example 3–1.

Example 3–1 : An XML representation of city streets.

```
<main>
      <boulevard>
                  <block> Panorama Street </block>
                  <block> Highland Plaza </block>
                  <block> Hutchens Avenue </block>
                  <block> Wildwood Drive </block>
                  <block> Old Chimney Road </block>
                  <block> Carrol Circle </block>
      </boulevard>
</main>
```

We can use `<xsl:template>` and `match` with LREs to see if the XML instance in Example 3–1 actually contains an element called `boulevard`, as shown in Example 3–2.

Example 3–2 : Matching a `<boulevard>` element.

```
<xsl:template match="boulevard">
            <p>Found a boulevard!</p>
</xsl:template>
```

This example shows how to determine if a match actually finds what is expected. The resulting HTML paragraph, `<p>Found a boulevard!</p>`, will only be sent to the output if a match actually occurs. The LRE shown here could then be replaced with real content. Using `<xsl:apply-templates>`, the contents of the `<boulevard>` elements would be output instead of the `<p>Found a boulevard!</p>` text. Using the same method for Example 3–3, we could find out if there are any blocks in the XML instance.

Example 3–3 : Matching a `<block>` element.

```
<xsl:template match="block">
            <p>Found a block!</p>
</xsl:template>
```

The `<p>Found a block!</p>` LRE is repeated for every block element found in the input XML document. Since there are six blocks in the input document, the output would be repeated six times. The first example would have only one `<p>Found a boulevard!</p>` result because there is only one `<boulevard>` in the input document.

In the absence of any instruction elements inside the `<xsl:template>`, the matched node-set is replaced in the output by whatever LREs are provided. This means that if both the template rules in our examples were used in the same stylesheet, the `<block>` elements in the `<boulevard>` would never be matched, because the template rule for `<boulevard>` would essentially erase the `<block>` elements. In order to understand this, consider the input, stylesheet, and output files in Example 3–4.

The processing of an XML document occurs sequentially, starting with the first element. The template rules in a stylesheet are accessed sequentially according to the hierarchy of the XML input document. The processor is effectively "walking the tree," visiting each element in the input and looking for a template rule for that element. This means that `<main>` is addressed first, followed by `<boulevard>`, and finally `<block>`. Since the content of `<boulevard>` is getting replaced by the LRE element `<p>Found a boulevard!</p>` in the output, the template rule for `"block"` is never even addressed.

Addressing of children elements is done by using `<xsl:apply-templates>`, discussed in Section 3.1.5. In effect, the stylesheet stops

Example 3–4 : One template can appear to "cancel out" the other.

INPUT:

```
<?xml version="1.0"?>
<main>
      <boulevard>
                   <block>Panorama Street</block>
                   <block>Highland Plaza</block>
                   <block>Hutchens Avenue</block>
                   <block>Wildwood Drive</block>
                   <block>Old Chimney Road</block>
                   <block>Carrol Circle</block>
      </boulevard>
</main>
```

STYLESHEET:

```
<?xml version="1.0"?>
<xsl:stylesheet xmlns:xsl="http://www.w3.org/1999/XSL/Transform"
           version="1.0">

<xsl:template match="block">
             <p>Found a block!</p>
</xsl:template>

<xsl:template match="boulevard">
             <p>Found a boulevard!</p>
</xsl:template>

</xsl:stylesheet>
```

RESULT:

```
<?xml version="1.0" encoding="utf-8"?>
      <p>Found a boulevard!</p>
```

processing after a template rule is matched unless *explicitly* told to continue with an `<xsl:apply-templates>` instruction element, as shown in Example 3–5.

Note that the order of the template rules in the stylesheet does not affect the output. Since the `<boulevard>` element comes before the

Example 3–5 : Using <xsl:apply-templates> to process <block> elements.

```
<xsl:template match="boulevard">
            <p>Found a boulevard!</p>
            <xsl:apply-templates/>
</xsl:template>
```

<block> elements in the input XML, the template rule for <boulevard> is processed first, even though it appears last in the stylesheet.

3.1.3.2 The <xsl:template> name Attribute

The name attribute is used to create a named template that can be "called" by an <xsl:call-template> rule. The <xsl:call-template> rule uses the value of the name to retrieve and process the contents of the <xsl:template>. The output resulting from the processing of the template is sent to the output result tree at the point where the <xsl:call-template> rule is invoked. The following attribute model definition describes the characteristics of this attribute:

```
ATTRIBUTE: name NMTOKEN #IMPLIED
VALUE = qname
```

The name attribute must be declared if there is no match attribute. They are not mutually exclusive, however. If the name attribute is present in the <xsl:template>, the match attribute is not required, although it is allowed.

The use of named templates will be addressed further in the section on <xsl:call-template> in Section 3.1.6.

3.1.3.3 The <xsl:template> priority Attribute

The priority attribute on a template is used to tell the processor whether this template rule should be selected over another, based on the value of the priority as compared to the value of the priority attributes of other template rules, if specified. Template rules can also have a default priority (or import precedence) based on several factors, such as position in the stylesheet or whether the template rule is imported or included. Import precedence and priority are covered in Chapter 7. The value of the `priority` attribute is a number, as shown in the following attribute model definition, and can include both positive and negative numbers:

```
ATTRIBUTE: priority NMTOKEN #IMPLIED
VALUE = number
```

The priority of an element is lower when the attribute value is negative or 0, and goes up as the number increases. Lower priority template rules are ignored in favor of higher priority template rules. For example, templates with priorities set to -2, 0, and 1 will have a selection priority order of 1, 0, and -2, -2 being the lowest priority.

This attribute is most useful when a number of possible matches for a given set of template rules is possible. The `priority` attribute, if specified, will resolve the conflict, stipulating which template rule is to be used. It is recommended to explicitly state `priority` values rather than rely on defaults, because the selection can be controlled more directly.

For instance, consider the two possible matches for a given set of template rules within the expanded Markup City shown in Example 3–6.

Example 3–6 : Markup City with additional street details.

```
<?xml version="1.0"?>
<main>
      <parkway>
            <thoroughfare>Governor Drive</thoroughfare>
            <thoroughfare name="Whitesburg Drive">
                <sidestreet>Bob Wallace Avenue</sidestreet>
                <block>1st Street</block>
                <block>2nd Street</block>
                <block>3rd Street</block>
                <sidestreet>Woodridge Street</sidestreet>
            </thoroughfare>
            <thoroughfare name="Bankhead Drive">
                <sidestreet>Tollgate Road</sidestreet>
                <block>First Street</block>
                <block>Second Street</block>
                <block>Third Street</block>
                <sidestreet>Oak Drive</sidestreet>
            </thoroughfare>
            </parkway>
            <boulevard>
                <block>Panorama Street</block>
                <block>Highland Plaza</block>
                <block>Hutchens Avenue</block>
                <block>Wildwood Drive</block>
                <block>Old Chimney Road</block>
                <block>Carrol Circle</block>
            </boulevard>
</main>
```

Building on the previous examples, we may want to have a higher priority for the <block> replacement, depending on its context. For instance, any template rules matching on <block>s that are children of <boulevard> could always have priority over any others. In that case, as shown in Example 3–7, we might want to delete the unwanted <block>s when this condition is met.

Example 3–7 : Using priority to preserve <block> children of <boulevard> elements and remove all others.

```
<?xml version="1.0"?>
<xsl:stylesheet xmlns:xsl="http://www.w3.org/1999/XSL/Transform"
            version="1.0">
<xsl:template match="//boulevard/block" priority="2">
            <p>Found a block!</p>
</xsl:template>
<xsl:template match="//block" priority="1">
            <!--These blocks have been removed as unnecessary. -->
</xsl:template>

</xsl:stylesheet>
```

The result of running this stylesheet against the Markup City XML file in Example 3–8 would be six occurrences of <p>Found a block!</p>, one for each <block> in the <boulevard>. Note that, depending on the XSLT processor you are using, the text contents of elements not addressed in the stylesheet may appear in the output. We will discuss this in Section 3.2 when discussing built-in template rules.

Example 3–8 : Input, XSLT stylesheet, and output for a template using the mode attribute.

INPUT:

```
<?xml version="1.0"?>
<main>
      <boulevard>
                  <block>Panorama Street</block>
                  <block>Highland Plaza</block>
                  <block>Hutchens Avenue</block>
                  <block>Wildwood Drive</block>
                  <block>Old Chimney Road</block>
                  <block>Carrol Circle</block>
      </boulevard>
</main>
```

STYLESHEET:

```
<xsl:stylesheet xmlns:xsl="http://www.w3.org/1999/XSL Transform"
version="1.0" >
```

Example 3–8 : Input, XSLT stylesheet, and output for a template using the mode attribute (continued).

```
    <xsl:template match="boulevard">
          <xsl:apply-templates mode="X"/>
          <xsl:apply-templates mode="Y"/>
          <xsl:apply-templates mode="Z"/>
    </xsl:template>
    <xsl:template match="block" mode="X">
          <p>Found block with mode X</p>
    </xsl:template>
    <xsl:template match="block" mode="Y">
          <p>Found block with mode Y</p>
    </xsl:template>
    <xsl:template match="block" mode="Z">
          <p>Found block with mode Z</p>
    </xsl:template>
</xsl:stylesheet>
```

RESULT: output.xml

```
<?xml version="1.0" encoding="utf-8"?>
                   <p>Found block with mode X</p>
                   <p>Found block with mode X</p>
                   <p>Found block with mode X</p>
                   <p>Found block with mode X</p>
                   <p>Found block with mode X</p>
                   <p>Found block with mode X</p>
                   <p>Found block with mode Y</p>

                   <p>Found block with mode Y</p>
                   <p>Found block with mode Y</p>
                   <p>Found block with mode Y</p>
                   <p>Found block with mode Y</p>
                   <p>Found block with mode Y</p>

                   <p>Found block with mode Z</p>
                   <p>Found block with mode Z</p>
                   <p>Found block with mode Z</p>
                   <p>Found block with mode Z</p>
                   <p>Found block with mode Z</p>
                   <p>Found block with mode Z</p>
```

3.1.3.4 The `<xsl:template>` `mode` Attribute

The `mode` attribute is used in conjunction with the `<xsl:apply-templates>` rule. Both the `<xsl:apply-templates>` and `<xsl:template>` elements must have matching `mode` attributes to work together. An `<xsl:apply-templates>` element with a mode will search for an `<xsl:template>` element with the same mode and process its template. The value of a `mode` attribute is a number, as shown in the following attribute model definition:

```
ATTRIBUTE: mode NMTOKEN #IMPLIED
VALUE = qname
```

Because multiple template rules can be defined with different modes, the content of the template rule can be processed multiple times, once for each `<xsl:apply-templates>` element that is used with that particular mode.

A `mode` attribute on a template rule is only used when there is a `match` attribute as well. The `mode` attribute only tells the parser that the template rule has a specific condition attached to it. The `match` attribute still must be implemented for the proper node-set to be selected for processing. Example 3–8 uses our simplified Markup City to demonstrate.

The processor is basically reiterating over the content of the element `<boulevard>`, repeating the call to the template rules for `<block>` for each `<xsl:apply-templates>` element in the stylesheet.

3.1.3.5 The `xml:space` Attribute[1]

The `xml:space` attribute comes from the `xml` namespace and provides functionality for handling whitespace text nodes that are found in the stylesheet. Whitespace text nodes are nodes that only contain whitespace. If they contain any other characters, they are not considered. The `xml:space` attribute is used to set a default action for either preserving or removing whitespace nodes from all the descendant elements of the `<xsl:template>` element. If other elements inside the template use

1. The `xml:space` attribute is not specifically shown in the content model for this element in the XSLT specification, but it is referenced later in the appendixes.

the xml:space attribute, they will override the value declared in this element.

The value for the xml:space attribute is a choice of either default or preserve, as shown in the following attribute model definition:

```
ATTRIBUTE:  xml:space (default|preserve) #IMPLIED
VALUE = (default|preserve)
```

It is important to note that the xml:space attribute applies only to the structure of the *stylesheet,* not to the structure of the input source document. The preserving or stripping of nodes from the source tree is controlled with a set of top-level elements, <xsl:strip-space> and <xsl:preserve-space>, discussed in Chapter 10.

> **NOTE** Be careful not to use this attribute on an LRE because it will be passed on to the resulting output.

3.1.4 Components of a Template

The bulk of the content of the <xsl:template> element is collectively called the *template.* The template consists of the 18 instruction elements, plus any LREs and extension elements that can be defined or used by the author of the stylesheet. Text is also allowed as a child of the <xsl:template> element, as noted in the following DTD representation as #PCDATA.

```
<!ELEMENT xsl:template
 (#PCDATA
  | xsl:apply-templates
  | xsl:call-template
  | xsl:apply-imports
  | xsl:for-each
  | xsl:value-of
  | xsl:copy-of
  | xsl:number
  | xsl:choose
  | xsl:if
  | xsl:text
  | xsl:copy
```

```
| xsl:variable
| xsl:message
| xsl:fallback
| xsl:processing-instruction
| xsl:comment
| xsl:element
| xsl:attribute
|%LRE-elements;
|%Extension-elements;
| xsl:param)* >
```

There is one element that is allowed as a child of the `<xsl:template>` element and is not part of the template. The `<xsl:param>` element is a top-level element that is also allowed as a child of the template element, but is not considered an instruction element.

3.1.4.1 Instruction Elements

Instruction elements are children or descendant elements of an `<xsl:template>` element and provide an "instruction" to the processor concerning the node-set selected by the template rule. The term *instruction element* is an arbitrary categorization and does not necessarily apply to all children of the `<xsl:template>`. Also, some elements that are classified as instruction elements, such as `<xsl:variable>`, are also allowed as top-level elements. Other elements that can be children of `<xsl:template>` but are not classified as instruction elements are `<xsl:param>` and LREs. The instruction elements defined by the XSLT specification are shown in Table 3–1. The XSLT specification further subdivides instruction elements into *character* instruction elements, which perform specific functions on existing structures or other templates, and *noncharacter* instruction elements, which are used to generate XML-specific structures.

Table 3–1 Instruction elements

Character Instruction Elements

1. `<xsl:apply-templates>`

2. `<xsl:call-template>`

Table 3–1 Instruction elements (continued)

Character Instruction Elements

3. `<xsl:apply-imports>`
4. `<xsl:for-each>`
5. `<xsl:value-of>`
6. `<xsl:copy-of>`
7. `<xsl:number>`
8. `<xsl:choose>`
9. `<xsl:if>`
10. `<xsl:text>`
11. `<xsl:copy>`
12. `<xsl:variable>`
13. `<xsl:message>`
14. `<xsl:fallback>`

Noncharacter Instruction Elements

15. `<xsl:processing-instruction>`
16. `<xsl:comment>`
17. `<xsl:element>`
18. `<xsl:attribute>`

User-defined instruction elements, called *extension* instruction elements, can be declared using namespaces and are also defined as instruction elements because they are found as elements in a template. Extension instruction elements are discussed in Chapter 12.

3.1.5 The <xsl:apply-templates> Instruction Element

The <xsl:apply-templates> element is used to process the content of an XML element that has been selected by a template rule. It is most commonly seen as an empty element, in the form of <xsl:apply-templates />. This instruction element has two attributes, and can contain two elements, as shown in the following element model definition:

```
<!-- Category: instruction -->
<xsl:apply-templates
  select = node-set-expression
  mode = qname>
  <!-- Content: (xsl:sort | xsl:with-param)* -->
</xsl:apply-templates>
```

The <xsl:sort> elements (discussed in Chapter 9) permitted within the <xsl:apply-templates> element enable the children of the selected node to be sorted. The <xsl:with-param> element (discussed in Chapter 8) enables the re-declaration of parameters that have been set elsewhere in the <xsl:param> top-level element.

There are two attributes for <xsl:apply-templates>, both of which are optional and not mutually dependent: the `select` and `mode` attributes. The `select` attribute can be used to "pick" nodes from the input tree for use in creating the result tree.[2] The `mode` attribute is used to select template rules that use the same mode. These attributes are discussed in detail in Sections 3.1.5.2 and 3.1.5.3, respectively.

3.1.5.1 Using the <xsl:apply-templates> Instruction Element

The <xsl:apply-templates> instruction element is the recursion component of XSLT. At the point where it is used in a template, the processing of the template stops to address the children of the element being processed before returning to continue the processing of the template. In

2. If we wanted to be sticklers about the "tree" metaphor, we could say that this element does the "grafting," but that would be going a bit far afield with the common terminology used for XML document instances.

this regard, it is similar to some programming concepts, such as subroutines or macros. However, the subprocessing is controlled by the structure of the XML, addressing each child of the selected, or current, node before ending the subprocess. If the child node's template rule also contains an `<xsl:apply-templates>` rule, the same process is followed for the children of that node.

Using `<xsl:apply-templates>` basically tells the processor to stop, get each child of the current node, find a template rule for it, and process it. This element can be thought of as the "process content" instruction.

When the `<xsl:apply-templates>` element is used without attributes, it selects the template rules for each child of the current node. In other words, if the child of the element `<boulevard>` is `<block>`, the processor will look for a template element with a `match` attribute of `"block"`. If there is no such template element, the built-in template rule (discussed in Section 3.2) kicks in and basically passes the text of the `<block>` to the output. Example 3–9 shows a template using `<xsl:apply-templates>` to process the children of `<boulevard>`.

Example 3–9 : Using `<xsl:apply-templates>`.

```
<xsl:template match="boulevard">
      <xsl:apply-templates/>
</xsl:template>
```

A sample DTD representation of the `<xsl:apply-templates>` element is as follows:

```
<!ELEMENT xsl:apply-templates
      (xsl:sort
      | xsl:with-param)*>
<!ATTLIST xsl:apply-templates
      select CDATA #IMPLIED
      mode NMTOKEN #IMPLIED >
```

3.1.5.2 The <xsl:apply-templates> select Attribute

The value of the `select` attribute, as shown in the following attribute model definition, contains an expression that identifies a specific node or node-set. The template rules for this node-set are selected instead of processing all the children of the current node:

```
ATTRIBUTE: select CDATA #IMPLIED
VALUE: node-set-expression
```

If the `select` attribute is not present in the `<xsl:apply-templates>` element, the default action is to process all the children of the current node. The "implied" `select` attribute value is the element-type name of each child node being processed.

The following two template rules are essentially the same, because, in the case of Markup City, the only children of `<boulevard>` are `<block>`s.

```
<xsl:template match="boulevard">
      <xsl:apply-templates select="block"/>
</xsl:template>
<xsl:template match="boulevard">
      <xsl:apply-templates/>
</xsl:template>
```

If there were other element-type children of `<boulevard>`, the `<xsl:apply-templates>` rule for the first `"boulevard"` would not match those children, but the second would. In both cases, the `<xsl:apply-templates>` rule would look for a template rule matching `<block>`.

Using the `select` attribute, it is possible to explicitly select a subset of children nodes, or even a group of nodes completely different than the children of the current node. The interesting concept here is that the `select` attribute is not limited to selecting from the nodes that are children of the current node. The `select` can go outside the current node and select any element within the entire structure of the input document. Example 3–10 demonstrates this using the expanded Markup City for input.

Example 3–10 : Using the select attribute to process elements other than children

INPUT:

```
<?xml version="1.0"?>
<main>
	<parkway>
		<thoroughfare>Governor Drive</thoroughfare>
		<thoroughfare name="Whitesburg Drive">
			<sidestreet>Bob Wallace Avenue</sidestreet>
			<block>1st Street</block>
			<block>2nd Street</block>
			<block>3rd Street</block>
			<sidestreet>Woodridge Street</sidestreet>
		</thoroughfare>
		<thoroughfare name="Bankhead Drive">
			<sidestreet>Tollgate Road</sidestreet>
			<block>First Street</block>
			<block>Second Street</block>
			<block>Third Street</block>
<sidestreet>Oak Drive</sidestreet>
		</thoroughfare>
	</parkway>
<boulevard>
			<block>Panorama Street</block>
			<block>Highland Plaza</block>
			<block>Hutchens Avenue</block>
<block>Wildwood Drive</block>
			<block>Old Chimney Road</block>
			<block>Carrol Circle</block>
	</boulevard>
</main>
```

TEMPLATE RULE:

```
<xsl:template match="boulevard">
		<p>
		<xsl:apply-templates select="//thoroughfare/sidestreet"/>
		</p>
</xsl:template>
```

RESULT:

```
<p>Bob Wallace Avenue
Woodridge Street
Tollgate Road
Oak Drive</p>
```

This template rule starts at the <boulevard> (the current node matched by the <xsl:template> element) and moves outside the <boulevard> using an "absolute path" to find any occurrence of any <sidestreet> in a <thoroughfare> anywhere in the document (indicated by the //). Each <sidestreet> is processed and the result replaces the contents of the children of the <boulevard> in the output result tree, surrounded by <p> tags. Note that suppressing the original content of the thoroughfare and adding the break between sidestreet names are accomplished by other template rules not shown here. The same result can be accomplished by using a more convenient "relative path" expression if the location of the <sidestreet> is known in relation to the <boulevard>, as shown in Example 3–11. Absolute and relative paths are discussed further in Chapter 4.

Example 3–11 : Use of a relative path expression in the select attribute of <xsl:apply-template>.

```
<xsl:template match="boulevard">
      <p>
             <xsl:apply-templates
select="../parkway/thoroughfare/sidestreet"/>
      </p>
</xsl:template>
```

Of course, the more common use of a select attribute is to distinguish between the children nodes of the current node and select one set over the others for processing, as shown in Example 3–12.

Example 3–12 : A simple node selection in the select attribute of <xsl:apply-templates>.

```
<xsl:template match="main">
      <p>
             <xsl:apply-templates select="boulevard"/>
      </p>
</xsl:template>
```

In this case, the // is not required because the <boulevard> is a child of the <main> element. This expression would ignore the <parkway> child and process only the <boulevard>.

As mentioned previously, when the select attribute is omitted from the <xsl:apply-templates> element, the default action is to process all the children of the current node, as shown in Example 3–13.

Example 3–13 : A basic template which processes the children of the main element.

```
<xsl:template match="main">
      <xsl:apply-templates />
</xsl:template>
```

The <xsl:apply-templates> would process both <parkway> and <boulevard> elements because that is the node-set that consists of the children of the <main> element.

> **NOTE** When this template rule is the only rule in a stylesheet, the entire document is processed because there are built-in template rules that affect the output unless they are specifically overridden with other template rules. Built-in template rules are covered in Section 3.2.

3.1.5.3 The <xsl:apply-templates> mode Attribute

The mode attribute of <xsl:apply-templates> is used to qualify the selection of the template rules that are to be used to process the children of the current node. This attribute is used in conjunction with the same mode attribute on the <xsl:template> rule. Both the <xsl:apply-templates> and the <xsl:template> elements must have matching mode attributes to work together. The value of the mode attribute is a QName, as shown in the following attribute model definition:

```
ATTRIBUTE: mode NMTOKEN #IMPLIED
VALUE: qname
```

An <xsl:apply-templates> element with a mode will search for an <xsl:template> element with the same mode and process its content template. Template rules that do not have a matching mode attribute are ignored.

The template rule that is selected must also match the select attribute on the <xsl:apply-templates> rule when the select attribute is used. When a select attribute is used in conjunction with the mode attribute, the <xsl:apply-templates> instruction will find the <xsl:template> element with the same value in the match attribute, as well as the matching mode attribute. The stylesheet in Example 3–14 contains rules for several different elements.

Example 3–14 : Using mode with select in the <xsl:apply-templates> and <xsl:template> elements.

```
<?xml version="1.0"?>
<xsl:stylesheet xmlns:xsl="http://www.w3.org/1999/XSL/Transform"
          version="1.0" >

     <xsl:template match="boulevard">
          <xsl:apply-templates select="block" mode="X"/>
     </xsl:template>

     <xsl:template match="sidestreet" mode="X">
          <p>Found sidestreet with mode X</p>
     </xsl:template>
     <xsl:template match="block" mode="X">
          <p>Found block with mode X</p>
     </xsl:template>
     <xsl:template match="block">
          <p>Found block without mode</p>
     </xsl:template>
</xsl:stylesheet>
```

In this case, the <xsl:apply-templates> in the first template rule will only select the template rule with the equivalent match and mode attributes.

```
<xsl:template match="block" mode="X">
      <p>Found block with mode X</p>
</xsl:template>
```

The result will be <p>Found block with mode X</p> for each <block> element found in the <boulevard>, and <p>Found block without mode</p> for all other <block> elements.

3.1.6 The **<xsl:call-template>** Instruction Element

The <xsl:call-template> element allows you to use other templates within the context of the template that is being processed. The template being called must have a name, declared with the name attribute on the <xsl:template> element. This functionality is similar to programming subprocesses that suspend the current process while another process is run. The current template rule stops, gets the template being called, and processes its content. Then, normal processing of the original template rule continues. The <xsl:call-template> element can contain an <xsl:with-param> element, as shown in the following element model definition:

```
<!-- Category: instruction -->
<xsl:call-template
  name = qname>
  <!-- Content: xsl:with-param* -->
</xsl:call-template>
```

The <xsl:call-template> element is very useful for storing element rules and LREs that will be used by several different elements. For example, you may want a specific HTML format to be applied to all <block> and <sidestreet> elements. If the formatting was very lengthy, it would be convenient to store it all in one place, especially for maintenance purposes. Example 3–15 shows templates used to format a table row and a table cell.

Example 3–15 : Templates to format a table row and cell.

```
<<xsl:template name="table-row">
       <tr>
              <xsl:apply-templates/>
       </tr>
</xsl:template>

<xsl:template name="table-cell">
       <td>
              <xsl:apply-templates/>
       </td>
</xsl:template>
```

Notice that these template rules do not apply directly to any element in our Markup City sample, but they can still be used. Example 3–16 shows a stylesheet that calls these two templates.

This example, while lengthy, simply applies a table format to our Markup City. Each `<block>` and `<sidestreet>` is formatted as a table cell, and each `<boulevard>` and `<thoroughfare>` is formatted as a table row. The main structure for the table is generated in the template rule for `<main>`. Instead of having repeated formatting structures in each similar element, we place them in a named template and use `<xsl:call-template>` to send the structure to the output. Notice how the structure of the named templates provides the recursion for the "calling" templates with `<xsl:apply-templates>`. Figure 3–1 shows the HTML-formatted view resulting from processing this stylesheet with the Markup City XML input.

Notice that the text content of an element (Governor Drive) gets processed even though there is no matching element rule that specifically calls for text to be sent to the output. This is being done by the built-in template rules, which will be discussed in Section 3.2. The `<thoroughfare>` that contains Governor Drive does not contain any `<block>` or `<sidestreet>` elements; therefore, the resulting HTML structure does not contain any `<td>` elements.

Example 3–16 : Stylesheet using `<xsl:call-template>`.

```
<?xml version="1.0"?>
<xsl:stylesheet xmlns:xsl="http://www.w3.org/1999/XSL/Transform"
            version="1.0">

     <xsl:template match="//block" >
            <xsl:call-template name="table-cell"/>
     </xsl:template>

     <xsl:template match="//boulevard">
            <xsl:call-template name="table-row"/>
     </xsl:template>

     <xsl:template match="//thoroughfare">
            <xsl:call-template name="table-row"/>
     </xsl:template>

     <xsl:template match="//sidestreet">
            <xsl:call-template name="table-cell"/>
     </xsl:template>

     <xsl:template match="//main">
            <table border="1">
                   <xsl:apply-templates/>
            </table>
     </xsl:template>

     <xsl:template match="/">
            <html>
            <head><title>Table Example</title>
            </head>
            <body>
                   <xsl:apply-templates/>
            </body>
            </html>
     </xsl:template>

<xsl:template name="table-row">
       <tr>
       <xsl:apply-templates/>
       </tr>
</xsl:template>
<xsl:template name="table-cell">
       <td>
       <xsl:apply-templates/>
       </td>
</xsl:template>
</xsl:stylesheet>
```

Figure 3–1 HTML file resulting from `<xsl:call-template>` stylesheet.

3.1.6.1 Current Node Processing with `<xsl:call-template>`

The match attribute on `<xsl:template>` selects a list of nodes, called the node-set, or current node list, from the nodes in the input XML document. Each of these nodes is applied individually to the template as the "current node." When a template is instantiated, the processor keeps track of the "current node" during its evaluation of further instructions. The `<xsl:call-template>` element does not change this basic processing rule. The current node that is being processed is used as the current node for the called template, regardless if there is a `match` attribute on the template being called by `<xsl:call-template>`. For example, consider the two template rules shown in Example 3–17.

The resulting output for each `<sidestreet>` is `<sidestreet>sidestreet</sidestreet>`, but the resulting output for the `<block>` element is the content of the template rule for `"block"` as well as the content of the template rule for `"sidestreet,"` as if it was inside the template rule for `block`.

```
<block><sidestreet>block</sidestreet></block>
```

Example 3–17 : Two templates using different current nodes.

```
<xsl:template name="sidestreet" match="sidestreet">
      <sidestreet>
            <xsl:value-of select="name()"/>
      </sidestreet>
</xsl:template>

<xsl:template match="block">
      <block>
            <xsl:call-template name="sidestreet"/>
      </block>
</xsl:template>
```

Notice that the first template rule for <sidestreet> is pulling the name of the element using the name() function, which is discussed further in Chapter 5. When used in the context of the <xsl:call-template> element, the <xsl:value-of select="name()"/> returns the name of the <block> element, not the name of the <sidestreet> element, because the current node in this case is "block."

3.1.7 The <xsl:value-of> Instruction Element

A very common and useful instruction element is <xsl:value-of>, which extracts the value, or "contents," of a node identified in its select attribute. It is an empty element and contains two attributes: the mandatory select attribute and the optional disable-output-escaping, as indicated in the following element model definition:

```
<!-- Category: instruction -->
<xsl:value-of
  select = string-expression
  disable-output-escaping = "yes" | "no" />
```

Because this is an empty element, the only functionality it provides is accessed through the select attribute, which supplies an expression to be evaluated. The second optional attribute, disable-output-escaping, specifically addresses the handling of certain XML character entities. These attributes are further discussed in the following sections. A DTD representation of the content model and attributes of `<xsl:value-of>` are as follows:

```
<!ELEMENT xsl:value-of EMPTY>
<!ATTLIST xsl:value-of
  select %expr; #REQUIRED
  disable-output-escaping (yes|no) "no" >
```

3.1.7.1 The `<xsl:value-of>` select Attribute

The `select` attribute of `<xsl:value-of>`, shown in the following attribute model definition, is used to define a string expression that is evaluated by the processor:

```
ATTRIBUTE: select CDATA #REQUIRED
VALUE: string-expression
```

The result of the evaluation can be any of the four possible function return types of expressions, node-set, string, Boolean, or number, which are discussed in Chapter 5, but the result is always converted to a string.

For example, when the result of the expression in the `select` attribute is a node-set, the `<xsl:value-of>` instruction element returns the text value of the content of the node. If the result of the evaluation of the expression in the `match` attribute is a Boolean, the `<xsl:value-of>` element returns a string of either "true" or "false." For example, `<xsl:value-of select="name()"/>` used in Example 3–21 evaluates the expression `"name()"` according to the current node and returns either "block" or "sidestreet." Additional examples of `<xsl:value-of>` are shown in Chapter 5 when evaluating other functions.

3.1.7.2 The `<xsl:value-of>` `disable-output-escaping` Attribute

The `disable-output-escaping` attribute is an optional attribute that requires some special attention. The first point that should be mentioned is that this is one of the most commonly misunderstood XSLT attributes. The fact is that `disable-output-escaping` applies *only* to five predefined entities—`&`, `<`, `>`, `"`, and `'`—which resolve to &, <, >, ", and ', respectively. The `disable-output-escaping` attribute does *not* apply to any other character, including hexadecimal character entities, such as ` ` for creating a space.

The second point to mention is that output escaping is affected by the output method, whether selected by default as XML, or explicitly using `<xsl:output>`, discussed in Chapter 10. The default behavior for XML is to escape these characters in the output.

Escaped entities are entities that have the preceding ampersand (&) and following semi-colon (;). When the value of `disable-output-escaping` is set to `no`, the entities remain escaped. In other words, a value of "no" keeps `&` as `&` instead of resolving it to & in the output.

When the value of `disable-output-escaping` is set to yes, the resulting output is the resolved character, regardless of output method.

The attribute model definition for `disable-output-escaping` is as follows:

```
ATTRIBUTE: disable-output-escaping (yes|no) "no"
VALUE: (yes|no)
```

The confusion of this seemingly double negative can be avoided by remembering that these character entities will always remain character entities in XML unless this attribute is set to `yes`. Because the default value is `no`, the only time you would ever use this attribute is to force the entities to be resolved. In all cases,"`disable-output-escaping`" means "resolve entities for the five specific entities."

3.2 Built-in Template Rules

Template rules use the match attribute to select nodes from the input XML document to be processed. However, XSLT provides a mechanism to handle nodes that are not explicitly addressed, using the built-in template rule. The processor implements built-in template rules automatically.

There are built-in template rules for all node types; however, not all built-in templates generate output. The built-in template for the root node and element nodes simply processes the children of each node, using `<xsl:apply-templates>` as shown in Example 3–18.

Example 3–18 : Built-in template rule for root and element nodes.

```
<xsl:template match="*|/">
  <xsl:apply-templates/>
</xsl:template>
```

The built-in template for text and attribute nodes will send the contents of the node to the output tree as a string of text, and can be represented as shown in Example 3–19. However, most processors will not send the contents of an attribute to the output unless there is an explicit rule to make it happen.

Example 3–19 : Built-in template rule for text and attribute nodes.

```
<xsl:template match="text()|@*">
  <xsl:value-of select="."/>
</xsl:template>
```

The built-in template rules for processing-instructions, comments, and namespaces do nothing, effectively ignoring the nodes. The rules for processing-instructions and comments can be represented as an empty element, shown in Example 3–20. However, there is no way to represent a namespace pattern match, so there is no example built-in template rule for namespaces.

Example 3–20 : Built-in template rule for processing-instruction and comment nodes.

```
<xsl:template match="processing-instruction()|comment()"/>
```

The built-in template rules are treated just like other template rules, however they have a lower priority and import precedence than all other template rules. Explicit template rules always override built-in template rules for the same match pattern.

When a stylesheet has templates that use the mode attribute, as discussed in Section 3.1.3.4, the built-in template rule for modes is invoked. This template rule allows the processing for each mode to continue, even if the node is not explicitly selected by a template rule with that mode. The built-in template rule for modes applies to the root node and any element nodes that are processed with a mode attribute, as shown in Example 3–21.

Example 3–21 : Built-in template rule for modes.

```
<xsl:template match="*|/" mode="modeA">
      <xsl:apply-templates mode="modeA"/>
</xsl:template>
```

It is important to remember that built-in template rules exist, because the result of processing an XML document is directly affected by these rules when nodes are not explicitly matched. For example, using a very basic stylesheet, as shown in Example 3–22, the built-in template rules apply to all nodes, even though the only explicit match is on the root node.

Example 3–22 : Using built-in template rules.

```
<?xml version="1.0"?>
<xsl:stylesheet xmlns:xsl="http://www.w3.org/1999/XSL/Transform"
          version="1.0">
<xsl:template match="/">
          <xsl:apply-templates/>
</xsl:template>
</xsl:stylesheet>
```

The content of each element is specifically processed by the `<xsl:apply-templates>` in the built-in template rule for elements, down to the text level, where the text is then passed to the output with the built-in template rule for text.

XPath Expressions

- Expressions
- Location Path
- Patterns
- Axes, node test, and predicate
- `Position()`
- Abbreviations

4

XPath enables you to access parts of an XML document instance using "family affair" navigation relationships like ancestor, descendant, parent, child, and sibling. It provides the processor-readable (and human-readable) syntax for doing this, in the form of *expressions.*

In Chapter 1, we identified the tree structure by which XML addresses nodes in a document. In this chapter, we will explain the use of expressions, in the form of patterns and location paths, as well as location steps within those paths. We begin with the basic concepts of XPath, the XPath syntax and concepts like document order, context, and proximity. Chapter 5 will build upon these concepts with XPath *functions*, rounding out the intricate mechanisms that can be part of an XPath expression.

It is no accident that both the XPath and XSLT specifications became recommendations from the W3C on the same day in November 1999. XSLT elements rely entirely on the expressions provided by XPath to select and extract nodes from the input XML document. While many common functions of XSLT could be achieved with macros and scripts, XPath adds an easy, user-friendly interface.

> **NOTE** From observation of developers' lists and user groups for extensible markup technology, it quickly becomes clear that proper knowledge of XPath is frequently more challenging than mastering the variety of XSLT functions. Typically, an XSLT template will be properly written but will fail to operate correctly—or as intended—due to improper selection of a node-set in the match expression.

XPath expressions enable you to access any node or combination of nodes of an XML document with unlimited granularity.

There is a difference between knowing the path and walking the path.
—Morpheus, *The Matrix*

XPath operates with the implicit assumption that, while you may know part of the logical structure or path for the nodes in a document, you don't need to know all of it. In other words, what you know of the document's detail and how much the XSLT processor can actually do with it can fortunately be two very different things.

4.1 XPath Syntax and Terminology

XPath provides a common syntax and semantics for addressing nodes in an XML document, and is used by both the XSLT specification and XPointer.[1] XPath was given its name to reflect its primary style of notation syntax, the path. This path reflects the same functionality as that of the URL, for instance. While the URL indicates a path to where a particular file is located, XPath indicates the particular path, based on the logical structure of an XML document, of where a given *node* is located. Paths are what the XSLT processor traverses in the course of matching, selecting, transform-

1. XPointer details an extendable syntax for addressing system-wide file and directory locations. See http://www.w3.org/TR/xptr.

ing, manipulating, and counting nodes. The paths are a form of *expressions*, which are the fundamental construct in which XPath manifests itself.

> **NOTE** XPath can be used throughout the many XML related specifications. For instance, it is used in the XSL Formatting Objects specification. It also applies to XPointer, XLink, and others. This book addresses XPath with respect to XSLT, but it should not be construed that XSLT is by any means its only venue of application!

In XSLT, XPath expressions are used as the values of attributes. Within those attributes' values, the XPath expression acts as a test for whether or not a given node matches the location path called for by the XSLT template. Before going into the details of the components of XPath, a simple example of how this syntax works will help to orient you to what follows.

Suppose you had a hard drive with a primary directory called "node", which in turn contained a folder or directory called "childnode" that had a file in it called "descendant". You would refer to the file using its location in UNIX by typing an absolute path such as:

```
/node/childnode/descendant
```

In a DOS environment, this would be the same, only the slashes would face the other direction, and you would add the drive name:

```
c:\node\childnode\descendant
```

If this looks familiar to you, then XPath syntax will be like working with an old friend. The XPath expression for this type of navigation looks like this:

```
/node/childnode/descendant
```

Usually, you will see an XPath expression as the value of an attribute like `match`, `select`, or `test` in an XSLT element, as shown in Figure 4–1.

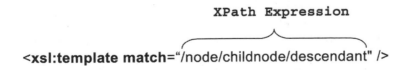

```
                    XPath Expression
<xsl:template match="/node/childnode/descendant" />
```

Figure 4–1 Using an XPath expression in XSLT.

In this figure, you can see how the syntax looks like a directory hierarchy. It is very important to note, however, that `descendant`, `node`, and `childnode` signify elements of a hypothetical XML document instance, not a file and the various directories containing it.

4.1.1 Document Order in XPath

Document order is a concept crucial to understanding and predicting how an XPath expression will behave with any given set of nodes. For Western languages, our understanding of "document order" is predicated upon the traditional narrative order in which we normally read: top to bottom and left to right. In XSLT, document order is predicated upon the hierarchical order of the elements and attributes, according to the tree structure of the XML document. Document order was covered in detail in Chapter 1.

4.1.2 The Context Node

The *context node* is the node that is selected prior to the evaluation of an expression. The context node is "handed" to the expression for evaluation, and the evaluation is performed using the context node as a starting point. The context node remains the same during the evaluation of the expression unless the expression is one of several special expression types that can change the context.

4.1.3 The Current Node

During the evaluation of an expression, each node that is being evaluated is the *current node*. The result of each evaluation is another node-set, with the current node as the new context. Sub-expressions use the new context node as their context node.

4.1.4 Context Size

The number of nodes that are being evaluated at any given point in the XPath expression is called its *context size*. Initially, this context size is equal to the number of nodes in the current node list, or the number of nodes that are children of the context node. Some expressions can change the number of nodes in the current node list, so the context size during the evaluation of an expression may be different from the original context size.

4.1.5 Proximity Position

The *proximity position* is the location of a node relative to its position in a node-set, or the numerical value of counting where a given node is (in document order) with respect to its sibling nodes in a node-set. Counting of nodes always begins with position 1 and proceeds forward, unless a reverse document order is specified.

4.1.6 Expressions

The XPath expression is a statement that the XSLT processor evaluates in order to yield a particular object as a result. The objects that are a result of an XPath expression can be one of four types:

- node-set
- Boolean (true/false)
- number
- string

Expressions are made up of tokens, as described in Section 4.1.6.1, and can contain functions (see Chapter 5) and variable references (see Chapter 8). An expression also can contain nested expressions, and so can be called either the expression or the set of expressions. Both terms are used interchangeably.

There are specific kinds of expressions called location paths that are used to extract nodes from an XML document. A subset of location path is called a pattern, which is further limited to selecting only element and attribute nodes. Location paths and patterns are discussed in Section 4.1.7.

4.1.6.1 Tokens

Each piece, or component, of an expression whether it is an element or attribute name, a symbol, an abbreviation, a forward slash, and so on is called a token. Some tokens can have several meanings, depending on their location in the expression. For example, the forward slash (/) can mean the root if it comes first in the expression, or it can indicate a step in the element hierarchy if it comes elsewhere.

The tokens are evaluated individually by the processor and then combined and/or contrasted with one another to produce a result.

Table 4–1 describes the different types of tokens and their values, some of which will be covered in further detail later in this chapter

Table 4–1 Tokens that are valid components of XPath expressions

Token	*Description*
(	Open Parenthesis
)	Close Parenthesis
{	Open Brace
}	Close Brace
[	Open Square Bracket
]	Close Square Bracket
.	Current Element
..	Parent Element
@	Attribute
*	Element
,	Comma
::	Separator
NameTest	ElementName (NCName or QName)
NodeType	Node Type (comment, text, processing instruction, or node)

Table 4–1 Tokens that are valid components of XPath expressions (continued)

<table>
<tr><th>Token</th><th>Description</th></tr>
<tr><td>Operator</td><td>OperatorName (and | or | mod | div) or MultiplyOperator (*) or (/, //, |, +, -, =, !=, <, <=, >, >=)</td></tr>
<tr><td>Function-Name</td><td>QName (used to identify a function) See Chapter 5.</td></tr>
<tr><td>AxisName</td><td>ancestor, ancestor-or-self, attribute, child, descendant, descendant-or-self, following, following-sibling, namespace, parent, preceding, preceding-sibling, self</td></tr>
<tr><td>Literal</td><td>(" [^"]* ") | (' [^']* ')
strings that are delimited by single or double quotation marks (^" means anything except ")</td></tr>
<tr><td>Number</td><td>[0-9]+('.' [0-9]+)? | '.' [0-9]+ (a floating-point number)</td></tr>
<tr><td>Variable-Reference</td><td>$QName (used to recall the value of a variable) See Chapter 8.</td></tr>
</table>

4.1.6.2 Navigating XML with XPath Expressions

The simplest possible way to think of XPath expressions is to imagine someone giving you directions for finding something in a city; for instance: Keep going north along the main road until you see the boulevard, go right, then to the third block. A rendering of Markup City, introduced in Chapter 3, is shown in Figure 4–2.

The XML version of this city was introduced in Chapter 3, and is presented again in Example 4–1.

With XPath, your expression can say: "Go to the third block in boulevard." Combining XSLT and XPath, we'd match the main road, the boulevard, and block information and test for the street we were seeking. Our XPath directions for navigating would use an expression that looks something like this:

```
/main/boulevard/block
```

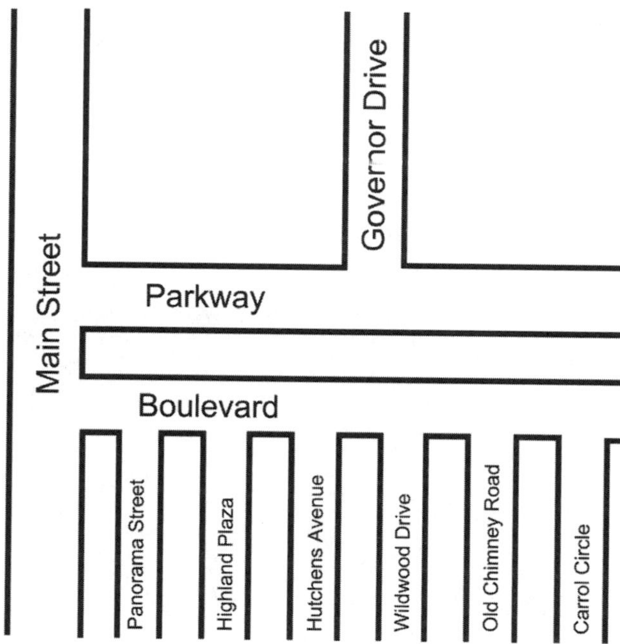

Figure 4–2 A map of Markup City.

This expression would give you all the blocks in the boulevard. You would then need to distinguish between the six blocks by picking the correct one. The best way to do this is to count them and find the third block. To do this in an XPath expression, you need a little more than just the names of the elements.

```
/main/boulevard/block[position()=3]
```

The word position here is an additional expression component that is called a *function*. Functions are the XPath version of macros. They call a process, usually passing in a parameter, and return a value. The `position()` function will be presented in more detail in Chapter 5, along with the other functions. However, it is worth introducing early on because it is extremely common and is almost indispensable for examples of how the various family heirarchy terms are used. The `position()` function does not take any parameters, and simply returns the numerical value of the position of the node within a context. In our example, we are testing to see if the value returned by the function is equal to 3.

Example 4–1 : An XML version of Markup City.

```
<?xml version="1.0"?>
<main>
      <parkway>
             <thoroughfare>Governor Drive</thoroughfare>
             <thoroughfare name="Whitesburg Drive">
                   <sidestreet>Bob Wallace Avenue</sidestreet>
                   <block>1st Street</block>
                   <block>2nd Street</block>
                   <block>3rd Street</block>
                   <sidestreet>Woodridge Street</sidestreet>
             </thoroughfare>
             <thoroughfare name="Bankhead Drive">
                   <sidestreet>Tollgate Road</sidestreet>
                   <block>First Street</block>
                   <block>Second Street</block>
                   <block>Third Street</block>
                   <sidestreet>Oak Drive</sidestreet>
             </thoroughfare>
      </parkway>
      <boulevard>
                   <block>Panorama Street</block>
                   <block>Highland Plaza</block>
                   <block>Hutchens Avenue</block>
                   <block>Wildwood Drive</block>
                   <block>Old Chimney Road</block>
                   <block>Carrol Circle</block>
      </boulevard>
</main>
```

In the XSLT stylesheet structure, using the `<xsl:template>` element, the same XPath statement appears as shown in Figure 4–3.

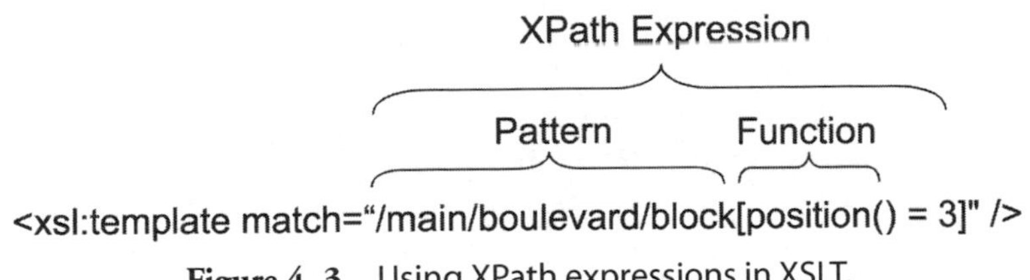

Figure 4–3 Using XPath expressions in XSLT.

In the example above, the XPath expression shows the selection of main, followed by boulevard, followed by the block found in the third position.

> **NOTE** The `position()` function works with careful reference to the concept of document order. The default sequence of nodes for XPath Is the order and/or hierarchical location they have in the XML instance unless a specific operator is used to indicate reverse document order. In our example then, you could say that XPath always assumes that people are traveling one-way through town unless explicitly directed to do otherwise.

Beginning an XPath expression with /, as shown in Figure 4–3, signifies that this is an *absolute path*, starting from the root of the input document.

In addition to absolute paths, XPath expressions can be *relative paths*, with the expression starting at the current place in the document (see Section 4.1.7.3). Figure 4–4 shows the same expression again, but this time without the initial /.

```
<xsl:template match="main/boulevard/block[position() = 3]" />
```

Figure 4–4 Relative XPath expression.

The difference is that in Figure 4–3 we are starting from the root of the document, which means that the expression matches the root, followed by main, and so on. The relative path in Figure 4–4 would match main only if the context node contained a main element.

Consider the difference in meaning with the addition of /. Like UNIX, a starting / indicates an absolute location path in XPath syntax. The absence of a starting / means a relative location path. In our example, using the initial / signalled the processor to start looking from the root. Without the initial /, the processor starts looking from whatever node is currently selected when the expression is called, or the context node. The forward slash / has many uses and significations in XPath, which will be discussed in detail below, along with a further discussion of absolute and relative location paths.

We have all had the experience, when asking more than one person for directions, of getting many different sets of directions to the same place. As noted in the preceding section, XPath enables you to select nodes based on a range of complete or incomplete information. Suppose the number of blocks was not known, but your helpful local knew that some street with the name containing the word "Highland" was somewhere along the Boulevard. He might say, "Go down Main 'til ya hit the Boulevard, and then go on a few blocks 'til ya see the word Highland and turn right."

We could simulate this navigation with a pair of XPath expressions, as shown in Example 4–2.

Example 4–2 : "Directions" to Highland Plaza, in XSLT and XPath.

```
<xsl:template match="/main/boulevard/block">
      <xsl:if test="contains(. , 'Highland')">
       <p>Turn right!</p>
      </xsl:if>
</xsl:template>
```

As shown here, with XPath it is possible to match according to the contents of a particular string of data in a given node. We'll explain the specific syntax of `contains()` in Chapter 5. For now, our purpose is to display a sample of the full range of things that an XPath expression might be able to use for selecting quite literally any node.

XPath expressions operate on the basic assumption that you either know where you are going or you have a pretty good idea of what it is you want to find, or a combination of both, inside your XML document instance. For example, the same search can be accomplished using abbreviations as follows, without knowing where the block is:

```
//block[contains(., 'Highland')]
```

Fundamentally, then, an XPath expression is a test of sorts. Notice that the names of the most frequently used attributes whose values contain XPath expressions have a meaning of evaluation: match, select, and test.

This is a key feature of XPath that must underlie all further considerations of how it works. XPath expressions are tests that are designed to yield a specific object as an outcome. The XPath expression is evaluated by the XSLT processor, and its outcome is an object, which is then "acted upon" by the attendant XSLT template functions.

4.1.6.3 Objects Yielded by Expressions

XPath expressions, regardless of their content, are designed to produce one of four object types: node-set, Boolean, number, or string.[2] While it may seem an abstract term, the "object" is simply the answer to what the XPath expression asks for, as if it were a question or query. Recall Example 4–2 from the previous section:

```
<xsl:template match="main/boulevard/block">
      <xsl:if test="contains(. , 'Highland')">
       <p>Turn left</p>
      </xsl:if>
</xsl:template>
```

In the first line of the example, `main/boulevard/block` states: Find any block that is within the boulevard that is within main. The object returned is the list of `<block>` elements that fit those requirements.

The second line of the example narrows down the selection of blocks to the one that contains the word Highland. Using the function `contains()` in the test attribute we are asking for any block that has the string 'Highland.' Node-sets and strings are two kinds of objects yielded by expressions. In addition, there are Booleans (true or false) and numbers. An example of a number object would be the result of counting how many `<block>` elements are in the `<boulevard>`.

Node-set Objects

A *node-set* is an unordered group of unique nodes that is the direct result of the evaluation of an XPath expression. Node-sets can include nodes from any of the seven different node types: element, attribute, text, namespace, processing instruction, comment, or root. Regardless of the location of the original nodes in the tree of the XML instance, each node in the node-set is considered a sibling of the other nodes in the set. If the nodes in the node-set contain children, those children are not considered part of the node-set. However, further processing of the nodes in a node-set can provide access to those children.

---

2. It is possible there could be other types. Quoting from the XPath specification, section 4.1: "An object of a type other than the four basic types is converted to a string in a way that is dependent on that type." This of course means the object could be something completely unknown!

It is important to note that node-sets are not the same as subtrees, or node branches. The resulting set of nodes from an expression does not include the children of those nodes.

In the previous example, our "directions" through the Markup City led us to the node-set consisting of a single node, the `<block>Highland</block>` element. In producing this kind of object, the XSLT processor is not required to maintain any specific document order, although most processors return the nodes in document order. Example 4–3 is our `<year>` example, repeated from Chapter 1.

Example 4–3 : XML representation of a year.

```
<year>
    <planting>
          <season period="spring">
                <month>March</month>
                <month>April</month>
                <month>May</month>
          </season>
          <season period="summer">
                <month>June</month>
                <month>July</month>
                <month>August</month>
          </season>
    </planting>
    <harvest>
          <season period="fall">
                <month>September</month>
                <month>October</month>
                <month>November</month>
          </season>
          <season period="winter">
                <month>December</month>
                <month>January</month>
                <month>February</month>
          </season>
    </harvest>
</year>
```

If we used the expression `match="/year/planting"`, then our resulting object would be a node-set containing a single node, the element node <planting>. If the expression was match="/year/planting/season", both <season> elements within the <planting> node would be selected. In other words, our object would be the node-set containing two <season> elements. The children of the nodes in the node-set, however, are not considered to be part of the node-set. They are part of the node branch. In Figure 4–5, a tree representation of an XML document instance is used to distinguish a node branch.

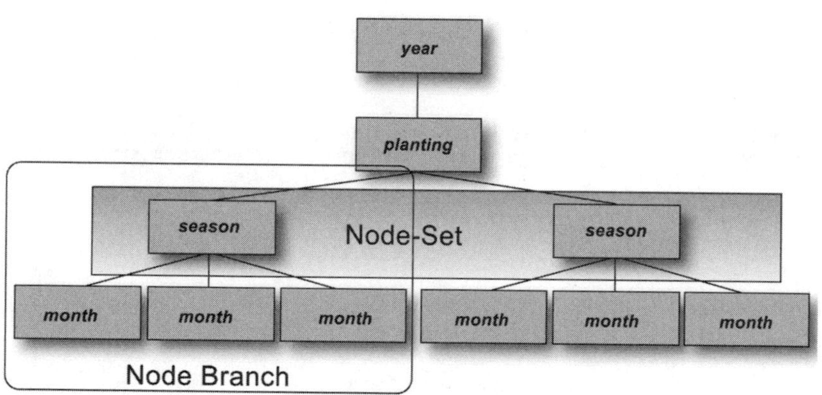

Figure 4–5 Diagram of an XML document instance showing a node-set and a node branch.

A useful way to think of the distinction between the node-set and the node branch is that a node branch always represents the original XML document's hierarchy of logical structure for that set of nodes. A node-set can contain nodes from any level and is not explicitly ordered.

Boolean Objects

An XPath expression that evaluates to either true or false returns a Boolean[3] object.

A Boolean expression is basically like a true-false question on a test. We can make a simple Boolean test for whether or not a <year> in our example happens to contain <month> descendant nodes (which it does). Using XPath specific syntax, the expression would be written as follows:

```
boolean(/year//month)
```

3. Boolean objects are named after the series of operators devised by George Boole (1815–1864).

> **Boolean:**
> [first computer usage] Boolean operation, an operation depending on the application of the rules of Boolean algebra. By extension, any operation in which the operands and results take either one of two values or states, i.e., any logical operation on single binary digits. Gloss. Autom. Data Processing (B.S.I.) 29, 1962. (*OED*, 2000, II: 398)

If the function is to be used in the XSLT `<xsl:value-of>` element, the expression would be the value of the `select` attribute:

```
<xsl:value-of select="boolean(/year//month)" />
```

> **NOTE** Throughout the XPath chapters, we will provide examples in both XPath syntax and XSLT syntax. You can use the XSLT syntax examples to test your own examples.

This expression uses the `boolean()` function to evaluate the statement `/year//month`. The evaluation produces a node-set, and the `boolean()` function converts the node-set into a true or false test. Because the result of the evaluation produces something other than a null or empty result, the final object produced is the Boolean "true" because the element `<year>` *does* contain `<month>` descendants. If the result had been null or empty, the `boolean()` function would have returned a "false" Boolean object.

Boolean objects usually result from the evaluation of an XPath expression that contains one of several kinds of tokens, called operands.

Operands are simple kinds of logical connectors and can be classified as "or" or "and" expressions, as well as various equality or relational expressions. The operands are:

- or
- and
- > (greater-than)
- < (less-than)
- = (equals)
- != (not equal)
- <= (less-than-or-equal-to)
- >= (greater-than-or-equal-to)

> **NOTE** Using the < (less-than) character will cause the XML parser to generate an error because it is not allowed in an XML document unless it is part of a tag. It must be escaped with the XML entity < when used in an expression.

The | (pipe) symbol, which is a common replacement for the `or` operator, can also be used in an expression, but results vary from the use of `or` because the processor treats the expression differently, depending on which operator is used. For example, `<xsl:value-of select="//harvest | //planting" />` returns the value of the contents of the `<planting>` node, even though `//harvest` comes first in the expression, because the expression evaluates the nodes in document order, and `<planting>` comes before `<harvest>` in our example. Because the expression uses the | symbol, the evaluation of the expression acts as if each part of the expression (each operand) stands alone. When an expression is simply a pattern, the result is a node-set, and in this case, (because of the `<xsl:value-of>`) the entire contents of the `<planting>` node are returned. In other words, the | symbol separates the two parts into individual expressions and evaluates them as such.

On the other hand, when using the `or` operator, `<xsl:value-of select="//harvest or //planting" />` results in the value `true` because, when using the `or` operator, the processor evaluates each operand and converts its value to a Boolean prior to the comparison. In other words, this expression is the same as:

```
<xsl:value-of select="boolean(//harvest)" />
```

or

```
<xsl:value-of select="boolean(//planting)" />
```

The result is true if either `//harvest` or `//planting` exist in the document. The second value (`//planting`) will not even be evaluated if the first value (`//harvest`) is found to be true.

Using our example of Markup City, the following expression "asks" whether `<main>` has a `<parkway>` and a `<boulevard>`:

```
boolean(/main/parkway and /main/boulevard)
```

or

```
<xsl:value-of select="boolean(/main/parkway and
/main/boulevard)" />
```

Notice in this example that we are using the operand `and`. In any given Boolean, the order of evaluation is from left to right. If the left-hand side of an `and` expression proves false, then the entire expression is false. The same is also the case if there are several `and` operands in a row: as soon as one comes up false, then the statement is false.

The `or` operand functions slightly differently. It is still evaluated from left to right, no matter how many `or` constructions there are. However, if you are testing for a value of true, then once any single part of the `or` expression yields true, then that entire Boolean expression is determined to be true, and no further portions of the `or` expression are evaluated (unless there are substrings, which are evaluated first).

Number Objects

XPath expressions can be constructed in such a way that when they are evaluated, their result yields a number as the object. In XPath, any object of type number is a digit or group of digits (a floating-point number).[4]

Number objects are often produced by evaluating an expression in a way that "counts" nodes. For example, we might want to know the number of months in the `<harvest>`. We can use the `count()` function (discussed in detail in Chapter 5) to count how many `<month>`s are descendants of `<harvest>` as follows:

```
count(//harvest//month)
```

Of course, we already know that the number of `<month>` nodes in the `<harvest>` portion of `<year>` is six, but what is important to realize is that the object produced by evaluating the expression is a number. The XPath expression `//harvest//month` returns a node-set of the month elements that are descendants of `<harvest>`. The `count()` function converts that node-set to a number, in this case, 6.

---

4. Number values in XPath are predicated upon the IEEE 754 specification for numerical values and equivalences. In essence, it is the basic notion of a floating-point number and can have any 64-bit format "double-precision value." For most readers, this basically means that a 6 is a 6 is a 6, unless it's three sixes in a row, which for other readers might have an entirely different signification. However, numerically, per IEEE 754, it is simply a set of number values for hexadecimal computing and mathematical manipulation following the predicated rules of algebraic logic. If terms like floating-point and double-precision are unfamiliar to you, all you really need to know about the nature of number objects in XPath is that they are—and act like—what you would normally expect of any rational number.

Numbers are often used together with Booleans for a variety of tests upon node-sets to determine whether or not to perform a given manipulation of the node-set in question. XPath number evaluation can also be used to count how many words, paragraphs, or specific element nodes an XML data instance might contain in a given chapter, section, or regional category, for example.

String Objects

What is most obvious can also be the most obscure when it comes to explaining or defining something. A "string" is simply a sequence of characters[5] whether the content of a particular element node, attribute value, attribute name, element-type name, or token in an expression. For instance, from the XML shown in Example 4–3, the word `year` is a string just as the word `August`, as the content of the `<month>` node inside the `<harvest>` portion of the `<year>`, is a string. So also are `harvest` and `month` strings, and so on.

For example, the function `name()`, discussed in Chaper 5, returns the string value of the element-type name. As shown in previous Example 3–17, `<xsl:value-of select="name()" />` returns either "block" or "sidestreet" depending on the context of the expression.

4.1.7 Location Paths

A location path is a type of expression that enables the selection of a set of nodes, based on a context. Unlike other expressions, a location path always returns a node-set. A subset of location paths in XSLT is called a pattern. Locations paths can be absolute or relative, and consist of a series of location steps separated by a /. Location paths are perhaps the most "XML-aware" expressions in XPath because they specify a location based on the XML document's tree hierarchy.

---

5. The *Oxford English Dictionary* gives the meaning for a string as "a number of things in a line; a row, chain, range" (00, XVI:922). The XPath specification states, among other things, "a sequence of zero or more characters, where a character...thus corresponds to a single Unicode abstract character with a single corresponding Unicode scalar value...this is not the same thing as a 16-bit Unicode value...." Most of the details about Unicode and scalar values have to do with the specifications for writing XSLT processing software, specifically as regards the complex issue of character coding and multilingual XML data instances.

4.1.7.1 Patterns

The most basic form of an XPath expression is a *pattern*, defined in the XSLT specification[6] as a form of location path that addresses nodes in a particular context. Patterns are a subset of location paths that only allow the use of the `child` axis, discussed in Section 4.1.8.13, and the `attribute` axis, discussed in Section 4.1.8.8.

4.1.7.2 Absolute Location Paths

An absolute location path is a path that is evaluated with the root node as the starting point. It always begins with a /, and can optionally be followed by a relative path. If the / is by itself, it references the root node of the XML data instance. In effect, an absolute location path is a relative location path, but it is one that is always relative to the root node.

An absolute location path functions similarly to an absolute location path in UNIX. Regardless which directory you are in, you can navigate to any directory on the server or network by initiating the directory or file locator path with a /. The same holds for absolute location paths in XPath.

4.1.7.3 Relative Location Paths

A relative location path is a path that is evaluated relative to the *context node*. The context node acts like the current directory—much like a relative location path in UNIX—the present working directory (pwd). You can switch to a directory that is lower in the hierarchy by naming it without a preceding /. If you were to use a preceding / in UNIX, it would take you to the root of the system, just like an absolute path (see Section 4.1.7.2).

A relative location path has a sequence of one or more *location steps* separated by /. The forward slash functions like a directory delineator in UNIX. In the XPath expression, the / serves to distinguish between one level, or step, of the markup hierarchy and another. Each step is separated by a forward slash that serves to indicate the traversing of the step. As each step is traversed, the context node changes relative to that position in the location path, and the node-set selected by each step becomes, in turn, the context node for the following step.

6. Patterns are not explicitly defined in XPath, but are a subset of expression, as defined in the XSLT specification.

4.1.7.4 Location Steps

Movement from one level in the XML hierarchy to another in a location path is called a location step. Each location step in a location path is separated by a forward slash (/).

A location step can be thought of as going up and down steps from one level to another, because you are stepping up and down the node tree, from parent to child, and so on. Using the XML in Example 4–3, a `<month>` is a step down from `<season>`, and a `<season>` is a step down from `<planting>`, giving us the following location path:

```
planting/season/month
```

A location step is made up of an *axis*, a *node test*, and optionally one or more *predicates*. In this example, only the node test for each step is shown, because the axis is defaulted, and the predicate is optional. Figure 4–6 shows a location step with its parts identified.

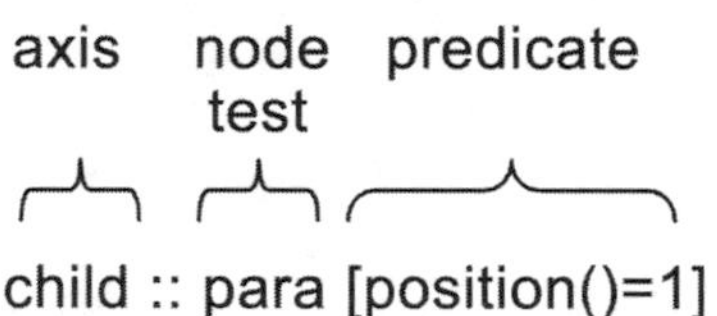

Figure 4–6 Axis, node test, and predicate in a location step.

The axis is the relationship between the location step and the context node. The node test defines which type of node to select (element, attribute, etc.) and the expanded name of the nodes to test for. If the expanded name of a node matches the node test, and the node is of the correct type, the node is selected. A predicate is an expression within a location step that qualifies or refines the selection of the node-set within the specified axis. These concepts are discussed further in the following sections.

4.1.8 The Axis

The *axis* in a location path is the relationship, with regard to the tree structure, between the location step itself and the context node. It is important to underscore that the axis is not a "place," or a node. It is a relationship.

The relationships that can be represented by the axis are: *ancestor, ancestor-or-self, attribute, child, descendant, descendant-or-self, following, following-sibling, namespace, parent, preceding, preceding-sibling, and self.*

The default axis for an XPath location expression is the `child` axis. Every node except for the root is the child of another node, so every location step begins with the `child` axis as its axis. The root, however, is not a child of anything, so its default axis is the `self` axis.

Consider again the following example:

```
planting/season/month
```

The axis for `<season>` (although it is not explicitly stated) is that of a child of `<planting>`. The axis for `<month>` is that of a child of `<season>`.

There are two ways to represent a location step, either using the abbreviated syntax as we have shown here, or using the full syntax as specified by XPath. In normal use, the abbreviated syntax is commonly used. We mentioned that the default axis for a location step is the child axis. Therefore, in all of the expression examples with location paths that we've shown you, the default axis is that of the child. However, we never explicitly wrote this out. If we had, for the example above, our location path expression would look like the following:

```
child::planting/child::season/child::month
```

As we explained, the axis for `<season>` is that of a child of `<planting>`. Since any relative path has as its default axis the child axis, it is rarely, if ever, seen in practice. This point is better understood if you remember that explicitly stating `child::` does not say anything more than what is said simply by using the element-type name alone.

We have also introduced another token in this example, the separator `::`, which serves to indicate the separation between the axis and the node test. In the location path above, `child` is the axis, and `::` indicates that what is to come next will be the node test in this case, a node test for all `<month>`s that are children of `<season>`, or all `<season>`s that are children of `<planting>`.

The separator `::` can be read as "that are." The proper way to read this is sort of like RPN (Reverse-Polish Notation). Reverse-Polish Notation, a long-standing convention of right-to-left reading of mathematical and logical expressions, is the common syntax for reading most logical expressions in XPath. To read the `::` in the location path for the expression above, we would say "all month children of season nodes that are children of planting."

4.1.8.1 Parent Axis

The parent axis contains the parent of the context node, provided such a node is available. For any given node that is a child, there is only one parent (remember, single-parent families make up the familial infrastructure of XML data instances).

From our `<year>` example, assume our context was a `<month>`. Using the location step `parent::season` would select the `<season>` node that contains the month. This literally says, "select those nodes that are called `<season>` that are parents of the context node." Of course, you would *almost never* have to specify a parent node by name, because any element has only one parent.

When considering document order, this axis is considered to be a reverse axis. A *reverse axis* specifies a reverse direction from normal document order.

4.1.8.2 Ancestor Axis

The ancestor axis contains all nodes that are one level or more above the context node. When used with a specific node name, it picks the first ancestor node with that name regardless where it appears in the hierarchy above the context node. For instance, if the context node is `<month>`, using `ancestor::planting` selects the `<planting>` node. In human terms, this example says "select any node that is called planting that is an ancestor of the context (which is `<month>`)."

The ancestor axis always includes the root node, unless the context node is the root node.

When considering document order, this axis is considered to be a reverse axis.

4.1.8.3 Descendant Axis

The descendant axis contains all nodes that are one step or more below the current context node. When used with a specific node name, it selects that node regardless where it is in the descending hierarchy from the context node, for instance, from `<year>`:

```
descendant::month
```

This selects all the <month> elements. In other words, this says "select any <month> elements that are descendants of the context node (which is <year>)."

When considering document order, this axis is considered to be a forward axis. A *forward axis* specifies a normal direction for document order.

4.1.8.4 Following-sibling Axis

The following-sibling axis contains those nodes at the same hierarchical level as the context node that follow it in document order and share the same parent:

```
following-sibling::month
```

This will select any months following the context <month>. For instance, consider an example drawn from the "winter" season.

```
<season period="winter">
        <month>December</month>
        <month>January</month>
        <month>February</month>
</season>
```

If the context <month> is the <month> containing the string January, then the only node selected by `following-sibling::month` would be the <month> containing the string February.

It is important to consider that if the context node is an attribute node or a namespace node, the `following-sibling::` axis is empty. This is because attribute and namespace nodes are not required to be in any particular order.

When considering document order, this axis is considered to be a forward axis.

4.1.8.5 Preceding-sibling Axis

The preceding-sibling axis contains those nodes that precede the context node, at the same level in the document hierarchy, sharing the same parent. Let's look at this example:

```
preceding-sibling::month
```

If our context node were the <month> containing the string February, then we would be selecting both <month>s with the respective strings

December and January. As above, if the context node were to be an attribute node or a namespace node, the `preceding-sibling::` axis would be empty.

When considering document order, this axis is considered to be a reverse axis.

4.1.8.6 Following Axis

The following axis contains those nodes that come after the context node in document order. An important consideration to this, however, is that the *descendants of the context node are not included in this axis*, but all descendants of all following siblings, and all following siblings *are* included. In other words, this axis can jump from one node branch to another.

If we were to name a node like `<harvest>`, then this node would be selected from all the nodes following the context node. Therefore, from our `<year>` example, we could select as follows, with our context node being the `<planting>` node:

```
following::harvest
```

This would select the `<harvest>` node following the `<planting>` node.

When considering document order, this axis is considered to be a forward axis.

4.1.8.7 Preceding Axis

The preceding axis contains all nodes that come before the context node. It does not select ancestors of the context node, but it does select ancestors of any other nodes that precede the context node but are not its ancestor. In other words, this axis can jump from one node branch to another.

If our context node was the `<season>` with the attribute of `fall`, we would select as follows:

```
preceding::season
```

This would *not* select anything in the `<harvest>` node, of which the "fall" `<season>` is a descendant. It would, however, select the "summer" `<season>` from the `<planting>` node branch. This would also, then, include the "spring" `<season>`, as it also precedes summer in document order, and is not in the same ancestor branch as the context node.

As with the following axis, attribute and namespace nodes are excluded.

When considering document order, this axis is considered to be a reverse axis.

4.1.8.8 Attribute Axis

The attribute axis contains all the attribute nodes of the context node. The attribute axis is represented by `attribute::`; however, this is rarely seen and we have begun working with this axis in its abbreviated form, @. The following are all correct uses for the attribute axis:

```
attribute::period
@period
attribute::*
@*
```

These examples show the use of the wildcard * to select an attribute of any name. Selecting an attribute will return the *value* of the attribute, unless that attribute is not specified, in which case it will return a null value.

When considering document order, this axis cannot be ordered either forward or reverse. It is considered a *non-ordered axis.*

4.1.8.9 Namespace Axis

The namespace axis contains the namespace node of the context node and, unless this context node is an element, it will be empty. For the following example, we might have a namespace for the seasons, and a different one for instance, `standard` for a standard calendar month which have already been declared elsewhere, such as in the root element.

```
<iowa:season period="fall">
<standard:month>September</standard:month>
<standard:month>October</standard:month>
<standard:month>November</standard:month>
</iowa:season>
```

We would select the namespace node based on the context node. If our context node was `<season>`, `namespace::iowa` would select the `iowa:` namespace.

Namespaces, like attributes, are not treated with any particular document order. This is a non-ordered axis.

4.1.8.10 Self Axis

The self axis selects exactly that: the node that *is* the context node. For example:

```
self::season
```

This would select the context node, if and only if the context node was a season. This is useful in instances where you are working through many different nodes and need to test to see if a particular node is of a certain type.

One way to think of the applicability of the self axis (and it is used frequently in more complex expressions with predicates) is with the root node, which is not contained in any child axis.

Since the resulting node-set only ever contains one node, document order is not relevant. It is, as a result, a non-ordered axis because there is nothing to order.

4.1.8.11 Descendant-or-self Axis

This axis contains the context node and all of its descendants. Specifying a name for the node test would take any node with the name that is a descendant of the context node or is the context node itself, if it has the same name.

Given `descendant-or-self::season`, if the context happened to be the root, the expression would result in a node-set of all the seasons in the document. If the context happened to be harvest, only the seasons in harvest would be returned. If the context was a season, it would return that season.

When considering document order, this axis is considered to be a forward axis.

4.1.8.12 Ancestor-or-self Axis

This is the same principle as the descendant-or-self axis, only in reverse document order. The ancestor-or-self axis selects from the context node and all of its ancestors. When considering document order, this axis is considered to be a reverse axis.

4.1.8.13 Child Axis

The child axis is designated if made explicit by `child::` and this serves to indicate that the current node is a child of whatever the context node is. Only the root does not have a child axis.

Since every node is otherwise a child of its context, the child axis is the default axis and need never be explicitly stated.

When considering document order, this axis is considered to be a forward axis.

4.1.9 The Node Test

Every location step contains a node test. The node test contains the *name* of the nodes the processor should test for. If the name of a node matches the name of the node test, and the node is of the correct type, the node is selected. If the nodes being tested for have a namespace, the expanded name of the node must be used. The node *type* being tested for is determined by the axis.

The node test depends on the axis to determine the type of node it will select. For example, if the axis is "attribute," the node test will only look at attributes. If the axis is descendant, ancestor, child, etc., which can contain elements, then the test only looks at elements.

The node test, then, uses a combination of both the axis to determine the type of node to search for, and the name of the node to only select nodes with that name.

There are two node tests in the following location path, `season` and `month`.

```
<xsl:template match="child::season/child::month" />
```

The first node test searches for any node that is a child of the context node, and also has a name "season." The second node test does the same for the month node name. The type of node the node test is looking for is an element, because the axis in this case is `child`. Only elements are considered when the `child` axis is used.

Attribute names are treated slightly differently. When looking for attributes, the axis `attribute::`, must be used, signalling that the node test is for an attribute. For instance, we could look for an attribute called period that is a child of season as follows:

```
season/attribute::period
```

Of course, <season> elements have only one kind of attribute, those called period, so this example is a little bit of overkill. One of the abbreviations for any element or attribute name is *. We could change the example to look for any attribute of season, as follows:

```
season/attribute::*
```

We can also use the // descendant abbreviation to look for any attribute called period anywhere in the document:

```
//attribute::period
```

What this path says is "start from the root and find any attribute named period." You might use this to get the elements in a document that have href for URI links, for instance.

```
//attribute::href
```

4.1.10 The Predicate

Predicates add an additional level of testing to a location step. They filter the node-set selected by the node test, within the context of the location step. Predicates are indicated by the presence of square brackets, the `[` and `]` tokens, and use additional expressions to perform additional levels of node filtering.

A common use of a predicate is to select elements based on whether they contain other elements or attributes. In our previous examples, using `season/attribute::period` returned the attribute node, not the element node. If we wanted to get the elements that *contained* attributes, but not the attributes themselves, we would use a predicate as follows:

```
season[attribute::period]
```

This returns the season element, but only if it has a period attribute. In this expression, the axis for season (not explicitly stated) is the `child::` axis. The node test is season, and the predicate is `[attribute::period]`. The predicate tests for whether or not there is a period attribute on the season.

Multiple predicates can be used, and their resulting values are passed up to the initial node test after all their filtering is completed. For example:

```
season[following-sibling::*[@period='summer']]
```

This expression asks for a <season> that has a following-sibling of any element name, *, provided it has an attribute with the name period and the value "summer". It will return the spring <season>.

Predicate expressions are evaluated for each node in the current node-set to determine if that node will be passed along to the next test or subexpression as part of a new node-set.

Some predicates can change the number of nodes in the current node list, so the context size during the evaluation of a predicate may be different from the original context size.

In `//season[following-sibling::*[@period='summer']]`, the context size for the node test of season is 4 (the number of all the seasons). The predicate asks for any elements that are following siblings, reducing the context size to 3, and the sub-predicate narrows it down to only those following siblings that have an attribute period with value of "summer", reducing the context size to 1. The result of this expression is the one node (season) that matches all the requirements.

4.1.10.1 Using `position()` with Predicates

The numerical value of the position of a node is frequently used in predicates. The `position()` function simply provides a numeric reference to the position of a given node. This is the number of the current node in the current node list. This list is counted in document order but, unlike in some programming languages, it is not zero-based. The first position, in document order, is 1.

The `position()` function can be used with mathematical operators to select specific nodes based upon their position in document order. Accordingly, in our example of the <year>, for any given season, we could select the <month> that is in first position:

```
month[position() = 1]
```

or

```
<xsl:template match="month[position() = 1]">
```

Depending on the context where this expression is used, the value returned is the first <month> in that context. If the context is the root, the first month in the document is returned:

```
<month>March</month>
```

It is also possible to test positions based on an arbitrary number or position. Suppose it was necessary to mark the middle <month> of each

<season> perhaps for an evaluation of how the respective planting or harvest progress was proceeding in accordance with the current weather based upon its position. You could use the following XSLT element and XPath expression, assuming the context node is that of <month>:

```
<xsl:if test="position() = 2" >
     <!-- do something -->
</xsl:if>
```

In this case, the test attribute yields a Boolean true or false, which when true causes whatever we had specified in between the <xsl:if> tags to be applied to the selected nodes.

Remembering that a step in a relative location path is distinguished or identified by /, we can set up a sequence of successively complex location expressions:

```
season[@period='summer']/month[position() != last()]
```

There are two steps in this expression, one with the node test of season and its predicate filter on the attribute name period with the value of summer, and the other is the node test on month, with the predicated filter specifying using !=, the "not equal" operator the position not equal to last. In this expression, we used a new function, last(), which returns the position of the last node in a node-set. last() will be discussed in more detail in Chapter 5. You should know there is a "last" function, but there is no first, second, and so on, because the numerical values of 1 and 2, and so on, are the correct format.

For this and the preceding example, the output would be:

```
<month>June</month>
<month>July</month>
```

Complexity of selection for the layers is unlimited. For example, the third <month> of the first <season> on the following:: axis would be written as:

```
following::season[position() = 1]/month[position() = 3]
```

The result of evaluating this expression when the context node is <planting> is the <month> node containing the string October. Remember that the following:: axis does not select any children of the current context.

Other mathematical operators can also be used with the position() function to specify a range, for instance, using > (greater-than), or < (less-than). However, remember that, because we are using XML, the < symbol for less-than must be replaced with the < entity:

```
following::season[position() = 1]/month[position() &lt; 3]
```

4.2 Abbreviations

Throughout the preceding sections, we have touched upon various abbreviations used for XPath axes, names, and functions. The most common is the abbreviation, by way of omission, for the `child::` axis. That abbreviation, of course, is simply an absence. The presence of a node name, such as an element-type name, indicates the child axis by default.

Another fairly "minimalist" abbreviation is that for the `self::` axis. This derives directly from UNIX directory syntax and is simply "`.`" a period by itself.

Not surprisingly, then, the common referent for the parent directory in UNIX is also seen as the abbreviation for the `parent::` axis in XPath location expressions: "`..`" two periods.

The `descendant::` axis can be abbreviated with //. The double-forward slashes represent any possible number of intervening nodes between the context node and the node being selected by the expression. Thus, the `<month>` descendants of the year can be equally referenced, as follows:

```
year/descendant::month
```

or

```
year//month
```

Another useful abbreviation, is the asterisk, *. When used alone, the * is short for "all element children of the context node." We could use the following expression to select all elements in the document.

```
/*
```

The `attribute::` axis can be abbreviated using @:

```
@period
```

Abbreviated attributes can also be used with * to indicate all attributes in the context node:

```
@*
```

Another very important abbreviation, which bears upon the frequency and importance of the numerical value of the position of any node in the XML data instance, is for the predicate `[position() = X]`, where X is a numerical value or the function `last()`. This entire predicate can be abbreviated using only the square brackets, [ ], and the number or `last()`. For example: `[2]` is the same as `[position() = 2]`. Similarly, you could have `[last()]` to select the last node of the context node.

Combining some of these abbreviations, we can select the last `<month>` in the `<season>` by using:

```
season/month[last()]
```

We can use the element name wildcard to get the last element in the season:

```
season/*[last()]
```

We can select any element that has an attribute whose value is winter:

```
//*[@* = 'winter']
```

Notice that this expression matches any attribute regardless of the name of the attribute.

Abbreviations for axes, names, and functions are the common way XPath expressions are written. The abbreviations are summarized in Table 4–2.

Table 4–2 Abbreviations for axes and functions

Abbreviation	*Function*
.	the **self::** axis, or the context node
..	the **parent::** axis
*	a "wild card" for element and attribute names
@	attribute, or the **attribute::** axis
@*	a combination of the attribute abbreviation and the "wild card" for name which selects all attributes of the context node
//	the **descendant::** axis
../	the **following-sibling::** axis
[2]	short-cut for [`position() = 2`]

XPath Functions

- XPath Function
- `boolean()`, `ceiling()`, `concat()`,`contains()`, `count()`, `false()`, `floor()`,`id()`, `lang()`, `last()`, `local-name()`, `name()`, `namespace-uri()`, `normalize-space()`, `not()`,`number()`, `position()`, `round()`, `starts-with()`, `string()`, `string-length()`, `substring()`, `substring-after()`, `substring-before()`, `sum()`, `translate()`, `true()`

5

In Chapter 4 the principles underlying XPath were introduced, but the full value of XPath is limited without functions. Functions provide a "programming" aspect to XPath. Where XPath location paths and patterns are navigational tools, functions are like little programs, they *do* something. For example, the `document()` function "goes and gets" another XML instance, similar to an import macro in a word processor.

In the XPath specification, functions are declared with a function prototype, which contains a function name, a function return type, and an argument set. Actually *using* functions is quite simple, though. Since the processing software maintains a library of functions, you only need a function call to invoke them.

This chapter will describe the functions in the XPath function library,[1] which are divided into groups based on the four object types: node-set, string, Boolean, and number. We will begin by introducing the specific principles and terminology for understanding and explaining functions.

Note that most of the examples in this chapter include the basic XPath expression, followed by an XSLT example that can be used directly in a stylesheet to get a result. XPath expressions do not of themselves return a

1. XSLT also has a set of functions described in section 12 of the W3C XSLT specification. These are introduced separately in Chapter 11.

value in a stylesheet, they must be used within the context of an XSLT attribute, such as `match` or `select`. The XSLT element `<xsl:value-of>` is a good test of the XPath expression and is used in most cases to demonstrate extracting the value of the expression.

5.1 XPath Function Library

The function library for XPath includes 27 functions, called Core Functions, which are divided into four subcategories: node-set, Boolean, string, and number. The four kinds of functions within the function library are categorized not necessarily by the object they yield, but also by the object on which they act. The object on which they act is called an *argument.*

In the following section, each function will be discussed individually within the core function group subcategory—based upon either the kind of object yielded or the kind received (i.e., "acted upon") as an argument—for that function.

Functions sometimes will yield different kinds of objects than the core function type to which they belong. It is important to realize, for instance, that just because a function such as `substring()` is included in the string core function group, it does not mean that it cannot accept number arguments within its `()` as a parameter, or argument value. The following function table (Table 5–1) can be used to determine both the kind of object acted upon and the kind of object yielded for the given function. The reference number in the last column provides a quick lookup for the section of this chapter specifically applicable to a given function.

Table 5–1 XPath functions

Function Group	*Core Function Group*	*Returns*	*Arguments*	*Argument Type*	*Ref*
`boolean()`	Boolean	Boolean	Object	required	5.4.1
`ceiling()`	Number	Number	Number	required	5.5.4

Table 5–1 XPath functions (continued)

Function Group	*Core Function Group*	*Returns*	*Arguments*	*Argument Type*	*Ref*
`concat()`	String	String	String String String	required required optional	5.3.3
`contains()`	String	Boolean	String String	required required	5.3.9
`count()`	Node-set	Number	Node-set	required	5.2.7
`false()`	Boolean	Boolean	None	none	5.4.3
`floor()`	Number	Number	Number	required	5.5.5
`id()`	Node-set	Node-set	Object	required	5.2.1
`lang()`	Boolean	Boolean	String	required	5.4.5
`last()`	Node-set	Number	None	none	5.2.5
`local-name()`	Node-set	String	Node-set	optional	5.2.2
`name()`	Node-set	String	Node-set	optional	5.2.3
`namespace-uri()`	String	String	Node-set	optional	5.2.4
`normalize-space()`	String	String	String	optional	5.3.7
`not()`	Boolean	Boolean	Boolean	required	5.4.6
`number()`	Number	Number	Object	optional	5.5.1
`position()`	Node-set	Number	None	none	5.2.6
`round()`	Number	Number	Number	required	5.5.6

Table 5–1 XPath functions (continued)

Function Group	*Core Function Group*	*Returns*	*Arguments*	*Argument Type*	*Ref*
`starts-with()`	String	Boolean	String String	required required	5.3.10
`string()`	String	String	Object	optional	5.3.1
`string-length()`	String	Number	String	optional	5.3.11
`sub-string()`	String	String	String Number Number	required required optional	5.3.4
`substring-after()`	String	String	String String	required required	5.3.5
`substring-before()`	String	String	String String	required required	5.3.6
`sum()`	Number	Number	Node-set	required	5.5.3
`trans-late()`	String	String	String String String	required required required	5.3.8
`true()`	Boolean	Boolean	None	none	5.4.4

5.1.1 XPath Function Library Terminology

There are two general categories of functions, core functions and extension functions. In this chapter, we will work with the XPath core functions, which are those functions required for implementation in any XSLT processor conforming to the XPath specification. Extension functions are those functions which have been added to the core set—specific to a given software processor implementation of XSLT and XPath. Extension functions are discussed in Chapters 12 and 13.

Before presenting the functions themselves, we will discuss the terminology for the parts that make up a function.

5.1.1.1 Function Prototype

The XPath specification presents each function in a structure called a *function prototype,* which specifies the function return type (the specification's way of saying what kind of object—node-set, string, Boolean, or number—it returns), the name of the function, and the type of the arguments (if any) that are either required or optional for the function. The function prototype is not used directly in an expression, it is only the means by which functions are declared. It is possible for functions other that those in the core function library to be declared, but they must follow the same function prototype. XPath functions are declared in the specification, using the function prototype, in the following structure:

```
Function: return type name(arguments)
```

For example:

```
Function: number sum(node-set)
```

In this example, the key word `Function:` states that a function is being declared; `number` is the function return type, `sum` is the function name, and `(node-set)` is the kind of argument that the function will accept.

5.1.1.2 Function Return Types

There are four possible function return types, corresponding to the four possible objects that an XPath expression can yield. A function return type is the category of object that a given function yields, or returns, when evaluated. Evaluation is what happens when the XSLT stylesheet containing the XPath expression is run through a conforming XSLT processor. It is concurrent with the expected mathematical meaning of "evaluate/evaluation."

The *node-set* function return type describes those functions which return node-sets; the *string* function return type describes the functions which return strings, the *boolean* function return type returns a Boolean value (either true or false), and the *number* function return type returns a number.

> **evaluate:** To work out the value of, to "reckon up," ascertain the amount of, to express in terms of something already known.
> **evaluation:** The action of appraising…statement of value…determining…estimating. (*OED,* 2000, V: 447)

Function return type values may vary from function to function and are not necessarily tied to the type of function. It is the kind of object that is *returned* which determines the function return type for any given function. The function return type does not always determine the core function group to which the function belongs.

5.1.1.3 Function Names

The function name is the name of the function as it is declared in the function prototype, and as it actually occurs in the XPath expression where the function is used. For example, in the expression predicate `[position() = 1]`, `position` is the function name. It only becomes a function—a part of an expression that *does* something—when the argument space `()` is added to it: `position()`.

5.1.1.4 Function Arguments

Function arguments[2] are the objects in the function space that are evaluated by the processor to return a value. Whether implicitly or explicitly stated, the argument—the object being evaluated—is simply what will be acted upon by the function.

> **argument:** A quantity from which another required quantity may be deduced, on which [the] calculation depends. (*OED*, 2000, I: 625)

2. You may not immediately realize that in this usage, argument does not have a connotation of contention. It derives from the Latin connotation of *argumentum,* which refers to a particular quanta that influences a consideration, rather than to an act of arguing. However, this nuance is still synonymous, as the computer meaning of argument is to provide content to influence a particular process. Of course, when a given function employing one or more arguments is not yielding the desired result, you might easily feel a contentious sense of argument with the given function!

Explicit function arguments are not necessarily required for all functions. For instance, `position()` maintains the argument space—the `()`—for an argument, but never is there anything placed within the parentheses. All functions will have this syntactic argument space represented by the parentheses, regardless of whether the function uses the arguments. When an argument is not explicitly stated, the object that will be evaluated by the processor is always the current node.

The argument is not limited to a numerical value; it can be any of the possible object types. For example, with the node-set function `count()`, which has a function return type of *number*, the argument is that of a node-set. In other words, the argument for `count()` simply specifies that the type of object it is expecting is a node-set. The value of that node-set will be expressed as a number—the number of nodes. In this way, a function can effectively "convert" an object of one type to another.

A function can have optional arguments, denoted by a `?` in the function's prototype, or optional and repeatable arguments, denoted by a `*`. When neither a `?` or a `*` denotation follows the declared object type for an argument, then that argument is *required.*

Failure to provide required arguments causes the function to fail. Further evaluation of the given XPath expression containing the function, and the XSLT template within which the expression occurs, will also fail or return a null—empty—result. Syntactically, when more than one argument is furnished, each must be separated by a comma and a space. If strings of text are used as arguments, they must be enclosed in quote marks with the required comma separator outside those marks, as in the following example:

```
[function name]("some text", */my_element,@my_attribute)
```

In addition to the four basic argument types, some function prototypes specify a value of *object* for the argument type. This allows for more than one of the four kinds of XPath object types to be used as an argument. With arguments of type object, the argument provided can be of any type.

> **NOTE** The argument of type object is used only in the four basic conversion functions, `string()`, `boolean()`, `id()`, and `number()`, which are used mainly to convert objects from one type to another.

The types and values of arguments can be *prescribed,* or expected in a certain order. For example, the function `substring()` takes arguments in the form of `(string, number, number?)`. The third number argument is optional, as denoted by the `?`; thus it can be omitted. These three arguments specify not only the order, but also the argument types that are permitted.

5.1.1.5 Function Calls

Functions are declared using the function prototype, but they are *used* with a function call. The function call is the name of the function, followed by the argument space, indicated by the `()`. For example, in the expression `[position() = 1]`, `position()` is the function call. The processor evaluates the function call by looking up the function name in the function library and evaluating each of the arguments in the argument space. Each argument is converted to the proper type (indicated by the function return type) and passed back to the calling function. XPath functions can be used wherever XPath expressions are appropriate in XSLT templates.

5.1.1.6 Core Function Groups

A core function group corresponds to one of the four groupings of XPath functions, node-set, Boolean, string, or number. There are seven functions in the node-set group, ten in the string group, and five each in the Boolean and number groups.

1. **Node-set Functions** – contain those functions that perform conversions involving node-set objects, always converting from or to a node-set.
   a. *from* a node-set, which is converted to another object type, such as a number, as with the `count()` function
   b. *to* a node-set from a string or other type, as with some arguments allowed in the `id()` function

2. **String Functions** – contain those functions that perform conversions involving strings, always converting from or to a string.
    a. *from* a set of strings, which are then converted to something else, such as a Boolean, as with the `starts-with()` function
    b. *to* a string from a number, node-set, Boolean, or other object, as with the `string()` function
3. **Boolean Functions** – those functions that perform conversions involving Booleans, always converting from or to a Boolean.
    a. *from* a Boolean to a Boolean, as with the `not()` function.

> **NOTE** The function return type for all five functions in the Boolean core function group is always a Boolean. In other words, Boolean functions *only* return Booleans, i.e., only return true or false.

    b. *to* a Boolean from a node-set, string, number, or other object, as with the `boolean()` function itself
4. **Number Functions** – those functions that perform conversions involving numbers, always converting from or to a number.
    a. *from* a number to a number, as with the `floor()`, `ceiling()`, and `round()` functions
    b. *to* a number from a node-set, string, Boolean, or other object, as with the `number()` function itself

> **NOTE** Like the Boolean core function group, the function return type for all five functions in the number core function group is always a number. In other words, number functions *only* return numbers.

Boolean and number functions are restricted in their function return types; they only return Boolean or number values respectively. By contrast, the node-set and string core function groups contain functions whose function return type can be something other than the respective object type designated by the core group. Some string functions can return objects other than strings; some node-set functions can return objects other than node-sets.

Another characteristic of each of the core function groups is that each one contains a function which, in effect, converts any given object to the respective type of the function group. For instance, the `string()` function converts objects to a string, `number()` converts objects to a number, and `boolean()` converts objects to a Boolean. The node-set core function group, unlike the other three function groups, does not contain a function of the same name as its primary core function type. In other words, there is no "node-set()" function. The only function that returns a node-set is `id()`.

5.2 The Node-set Core Function Group

There are seven node-set functions. Each of these operates upon the current node-set at the given stage in the evaluation of the expression in which the function is called. Our `<year>` example is duplicated for convenience in Example 5–1.

Consider the expression `count(//harvest//month)`. In this expression, `harvest` is the ancestor node from which descendant `month` elements are to be counted. Notice how we have used a pattern expression comprising the argument to `count()` function. This is because `count()` is a node-set function, expecting a node-set as an argument, and pattern expressions return node-sets. The node-set acted upon in this example is the set of `<month>` elements descended from `<harvest>`. Because it *acts* upon a set of nodes, `count()` is considered a node-set function. What is returned, however, will be a number. The resulting

Example 5–1 : Example of our <year>.

```
<?xml version="1.0"?>
<year>
      <planting>
            <season period="spring">
                  <month>March</month>
                  <month>April</month>
                  <month>May</month>
            </season>
            <season period="summer">
                  <month>June</month>
                  <month>July</month>
                  <month>August</month>
            </season>
      </planting>
      <harvest>
            <season period="fall">
                  <month>September</month>
                  <month>October</month>
                  <month>November</month>
            </season>
            <season period="winter">
                  <month>December</month>
                  <month>January</month>
                  <month>February</month>
            </season>
      </harvest>
</year>
```

number in this case will be the number of those `<month>` nodes that are descended from `<harvest>`, which will yield the number 6.

The node-set core function group, unlike the other three function groups, does not contain a function of the same name as its primary core function type. In other words, there is no "node-set()" function. If considered for a moment, this makes sense. A node-set has an implicit structure, each component of which can be of seven possible types, each with a specific syntax and hierarchy. It is not within the scope of a standard such as XSLT or XPath to have a single function that can render a node-set from, for instance, a string or a number. There are far too many subjective options in such a process that preclude making such a function possible—or even viable.

There is, however, one function whose function return type—object returned—is a node-set. The `id()` function can accept most kinds of objects as an argument and returns a node-set. In spite of the length of its explanation, which concerns how the ID itself is identified, this is a relatively simple function. It has a few limits for use with XSLT processors, however, because it requires the processor to reference the ID attribute declaration in the DTD.

Presented next are three functions that return strings, all of which have optional node-set arguments, `local-name()`, `name()`, and `namespace-uri()`. These three functions work together to access the various parts of namespaced nodes, including the name that comes after the colon (the local name), the name that comes before the colon (the qualified, or QName), and the actual identifier, or Uniform Resource Identifier (URI), respectively. In each case, then, the name or URI returned is of the return type *string*.

Following those are three functions that return numbers; two with no arguments and a third, which requires a node-set (`last()`, `position()`, and `count()`). These functions are not unlike "inventory" functions for determining quantitatively the numerical values represented in each function name. Thus, the `last()` function gives the count value of the final node in the node-set, which is, accordingly, the total number of nodes in the node-set being evaluated by the expression. Slightly different is the `count()` function, which totals *all* nodes in the node-set referenced by the argument. The `position()` function simply gives the numerical count of where the node is with respect to its location within the node-set, in document order, based on the expression's evaluation context. No functions in the node-set core function group return or operate on Booleans.

5.2.1 The `id()` Function

The `id()` function will select an element based on the unique ID of the element. The `id()` function operates mainly on node-sets, but will also accept any other object, which it converts to a string prior to processing. The `id()` function is the only node-set core function that returns a node-set. Therefore, its function return type is that of *node-set,* and it has a required argument of object, as shown in the following function prototype.

Function: *node-set* **id**(*object*)

Function Name	*Core Function Group*	*Returns*	*Arguments*	*Argument Type*
`id()`	Node-set	Node-set	Object	required

The `id()` function specifically looks for an element with an attribute of type ID in the given node-set. IDs are a particular type of attribute in XML, which must be declared as such in the DTD. Thus the `id()` function can only be used with valid XML documents—those conforming to a DTD.

While many XSLT processors have been designed to read attribute definitions and therefore recognize ID attribute content model types, they are not required to do so. If you use `id()` with a processor that does not read attibute definitions, the `id()` function will *always* return an empty result, or no object whatsoever. Note that the specification for XSLT does *not* require parsing of a document in relation to a DTD, so it should not be considered a fault or bug of the processing software.

> **NOTE** You are encouraged to review the XSLT `key()` function, presented in Chapter 11, as in many cases it can be more advantageous for processing efficiency and wider applicability than the XPath `id()` function.

To use the `id()` function, it is necessarily assumed that when calling this function, you know the ID structure in the XML data instance source. In other words, consider the following example:

```
id('n13-9-63')
```

This function call will return the single element node with an attribute of type ID that is precisely equal to `n13-9-63`. It does not matter, in this case, what the element is; the only thing that will be selected for matching is an attribute with a value of `n13-9-63`. The result will be the node-set of the one node that corresponds to the element with that attribute having that value.

Notice in the example that the object type of the argument for the `id()` function in this case is a string, denoted by the quotes. If the object type of the argument is anything other than a string, the object is converted to a string prior to processing the `id()` function. The process essentially takes an object of a given kind—node-set or non-node-set—and turns it into a string order for the processor to find the ID, as follows.

1. If the `id()` function's argument is *not* a node-set, the argument is converted to a string according to the `string()` function rules (see Section 5.3.1).
2. If the `id()` function's argument type is a node-set, the same rules as above apply for producing a string; however, each node in the node-set is processed. Each node in the node-set is converted to a string according to the `string()` rules, based on the type of the node.

The resulting string is treated as a whitespace-separated string of tokens. Each of these strings is then evaluated until a matching ID value is found.

If an ID is not found, it is not an error, but the function will produce an empty node-set after being evaluated. For instance, in the example above with `id('n13-9-63')`, if there is no such ID, then the result node-set is empty.

In order to use the `id()` function properly, the following items must be provided:

1. An XML source instance with an attribute whose content model type is specified as, and conforms to, type ID
2. A DTD that defines the attributes as the declared attribute content model type ID
3. An XSLT processor that is, at the very least, equipped to recognize attribute declarations
4. A knowledge of the possible IDs and their syntax in the source document such that you have a chance of targeting a match in the `id()` function call.

5.2.2 The `local-name()` Function

The `local-name()` function returns the local part of the expanded name of the first node in the node-set. The function has a string as its function return type, that is, its result object is a string. It has one optional argument, which is a node-set, as shown in the following function prototype. If no argument is supplied, then the current node will be used. This function only operates on node-sets.

`Function:` *`string`* **`local-name`**`(`*`node-set?`*`)`

Function Name	*Core Function Group*	*Returns*	*Arguments*	*Argument Type*
`local-name()`	Node-set	String	Node-set	optional

In practice, this means that when you have a node—for example, an attribute or element—with an expanded namespace, the `local-name()` function returns the portion of the expanded namespace that follows the colon (`:`). For example, if `iowa:harvest` is the expanded namespace, the word `harvest` is the result of evaluating the function.

This function is particularly useful if you have a source node-set that has a lot of namespaced nodes (nodes with qualified names, or QNames) and the intended output will only have element-type names from a single namespace. In some cases, it might be preferred that the output data be simplified by removing the namespace prefix (in this case, the `iowa:`). This function can be used to extract only the local name (in this case, the `harvest`), in effect removing the namespace prefix, or the portion preceding and including the colon.

The default processing model will return only the first conforming, or matching, node's name for this expression. In other words, you could say the following, and still get the same return:

```
local-name(../*[@period="winter"] | ../*[@period="spring")]
```

Here, you are using a predicate with `[]`, and asking by identifying the attribute (@) `period` whose value is `winter` to identify the parent (..)

of any element (*) with that attribute and value. Even though this actually matches `<season period="winter">`, the parent of which would be `<iowa:harvest>` and (using the | operator) `<season period="spring">`, the parent of which would be `<iowa:planting>`, the first match in document order is `<iowa:harvest>`. The return would, then, still be `harvest`, as that is the `local-name()` of the first match for the expression, in document order. You could not get more than one without using some of the other XSLT elements.

If there is no colon in the matched node's name string, then the entire name is taken to be the local name, and the entire node's name is returned. For example, there might be a source document with a default namespace declared for a `<figure>` element, and an additional namespace—such as from the MathML DTD—which is `<math:figure>`. If you want to have your XPath expression act upon any element of the element-type name `figure`, regardless of its namespace, you would use the `local-name()` as part of an equivalence evaluation. For instance:

```
//*[local-name()='figure']
```

or

```
<xsl:value-of select="//*[local-name()='figure']" />
```

In this expression, which has a node test of any element (represented by the * abbreviation) at any level in the node-tree (represented by the //), using the function for the local name of figure returns figure elements of any type, whether or not the element has a namespace declared.

A few additional considerations are worth noting. While commonly used to select the local-name of an element or attribute node, elements and attributes are not the only possible nodes that can be supplied as the node-set argument to `local-name()`. In addition to attribute and element nodes, there are comment, namespace, processing-instructions (PIs), root (or document root) nodes, and text nodes. Each, in turn, is treated differently when supplied as the argument to `local-name()`.

If the argument to the `local-name()` function is the root, there can be no distinction allowing for a local-name. The root is simply the document root; it does not have a name or namespace, so the result is an empty string. Text and comment nodes also return an empty string.

If the node-set referenced by the argument is the namespace itself, then the prefix is returned. If the namespace is the default namespace for the input XML document or data, nothing is returned. If you think about it, this makes more sense than perhaps does the technical description. If the node in the argument is the namespace itself, then the name that is local to that namespace is the namespace prefix itself—in other words, that which comes before the colon.

If the argument is a processing-instruction, the attribute value for the "target" of the processing-instruction, which says what kind of software is supposed to be called by the PI, is returned (see Section 6.7.2 for more information on PIs). For example, in `<?Pub Caret?>`, the `Pub` is a signal to a specific publishing software (Arbortext), and `Caret` is the instruction (`Caret` is the location last edited by an author in Arbortext). Using `local-name()` on this PI would return `Pub`.

Table 5–2 indicates the various objects returned from the `local-name()` function, in the form of a string, when applied to different types of nodes.

Table 5–2 Summary of object types returned by the `local-name()`

Node Type	*Object Returned by* ***`local-name()`***
Attribute	QName - Name of the attribute
Comment	Empty
Element	QName - Name of the element
Namespace	Namespace prefix - if defined
Processing-instruction	Target
Root	Empty
Text	Empty

The `local-name()` function provides the user of XPath with the ability to access the part of a node name after the colon when there is an expanded namespace. This function is part of a trio of functions that includes the `name()` function and the `namespace-uri()`.

The three functions can be used to access all the various parts of an expanded namespace. There are some qualifications to this general statement; however, it is useful to have this conceptual understanding of `local-name()` as a frame of reference before proceeding with the `name()` function.

5.2.3 The **`name()`** Function

The `name()` function returns the QName, or the entire expanded name of any namespaced node. QNames are composed of a namespace prefix, a separator (the `:`), and a local name, and the `name()` function returns the entire string.

This function returns a string, so string is also its function return type. The only argument it accepts, which is optional, is a node-set, as shown in the following function prototype. If no argument is supplied, the default node-set is the current node at that point in the XPath expression. The `name()` function operates only on node-sets.

Function: *string* **name**(*node-set?*)

Function Name	*Core Function Group*	*Returns*	*Arguments*	*Argument Type*
`name()`	Node-set	String	Node-set	optional

In the previous section we discussed getting `figure` elements, but in this case we are using the expanded namespace version, applying the `name()` function. The following expression will return the contents of the first node in the node-set of all elements (`*`) in any context (`//`), whose expanded name, or the QName, is `math:figure`.

```
//*[name()='math:figure']
```

or

```
<xsl:template match="/">
```

```
        <xsl:value-of select="//*[name()='math:figure']" />
    </xsl:template>
```

The same thing would be the case with an attribute that has a namespace, the entire QName is returned. If the attribute was `html:href` to identify the HTML hypertext reference attribute, then `name()` applied to that attribute node would return `html:href`. The `name()` function is useful, then, as a means of analyzing what the various names of different nodes in a document might be, or for performing transformations that preserve the entire QName of a node.

Like the `local-name()` function, each of the seven kinds of nodes is treated differently when used as an argument to `name()` (see Table 5–3). For example, text, root, and comment nodes, when furnished as an argument to `name()`, return an empty string. Namespace nodes return the namespace prefix—the text that comes before the colon. Since the namespace URI is null on all processing-instructions, the return value is the PI's "target," or the identity of the application being called by the PI when furnished as the argument to `name()`.

Table 5–3 Summary of object types returned by the `name()` function

Node Type	***Name()*** *result*
Attribute	QName - name of the attribute
Comment	Empty
Element	QName - name of the element
Namespace	Namespace prefix - if defined
Processing-instruction	Target
Root	Empty
Text	Empty

5.2.4 The `namespace-uri()` Function

The `namespace-uri()` function, together with `local-name()` and `name()`, completes the trio of namespace functions that selectively accesses the various components of namespaced nodes. Where `local-name()` retrieved the portion of the name following the colon, and `name()` retrieved the entire name, `namespace-uri()` accesses the URI itself.

The `namespace-uri()` function return type is a string, as shown in the following function prototype. The string returned is the URI that was declared as the identifier for the namespace—if any—in the namespace declaration. This function accepts an optional node-set argument, and only operates on node-sets.

`Function: `*`string`* **`namespace-uri`**`(`*`node-set?`*`)`

Function Name	*Core Function Group*	*Returns*	*Arguments*	*Argument Type*
`namespace-uri`	String	String	Node-set	optional

It is very important to understand that the `namespace-uri()` function *does not* return the prefix of the expanded namespace, which is found prior to the `:` in an expanded namespace, or QName. The result of this function is the value *defined* for the namespace. More specifically, the function returns a string equivalent to the attribute value for the namespace declaration of the first node, in document order, of the node-set supplied in the argument.

> **NOTE** There is no specific function to access the prefix portion of an expanded namespace, but using creative combinations of these and other functions could provide the value.

If no argument is supplied, then the current node at that point in the evaluation of the XPath expression is the node whose namespace-uri is returned. If there is no declared URI, or if it is the default namespace, an empty string is returned.

The `namespace-uri()` function will only return a string for an element or attribute node. This makes sense because a text, comment, or PI node does not have a URI, and a namespace prefix does not, itself, have a URI. This may sound contradictory, but the prefix *represents* a URI; it does not have its own URI per se. It if did, this would in fact be redundant and would amount to a namespace for a namespace! Example 5–2 shows our `<year>` specific to Iowa.

Example 5–2 : The `<year>` specific to Iowa.

```
<?xml version="1.0"?>
<year xmlns:iowa="http://www.iowa_climate.org/almanac/">
      <iowa:planting>
            <iowa:season period="spring">
                  <month>March</month>
                  <month>April</month>
                  <month>May</month>
            </iowa:season>
            <iowa:season period="summer">
                  <month>June</month>
                  <month>July</month>
                  <month>August</month>
            </iowa:season>
      </iowa:planting>
      <iowa:harvest>
            <iowa:season period="fall">
                  <month>September</month>
                  <month>October</month>
                  <month>November</month>
            </iowa:season>
            <iowa:season period="winter">
                  <month>December</month>
                  <month>January</month>
                  <month>February</month>
            </iowa:season>
      </iowa:harvest>
</year>
```

Since our example has declared the iowa namespace for the element <harvest>, the returned value using namespace-uri() would be the attribute value for the xmlns:iowa attribute, or http://www.iowa_climate.org/almanac/. However, you can't reference a namespaced node directly in an XSLT stylesheet, so you have to do a little manipulating to get the value. For example, to match on a <harvest> element, use the following XSLT template rule:

```
<xsl:template match="//*[local-name() = 'harvest']">
     <xsl:value-of select="namespace-uri()"/>
</xsl:template>
```

> **NOTE** Be aware that even though we have used the *http://* URL format for the URI, it is not necessary that it actually point to a specific place on the Web. The URI is intended primarily to *provide a method* for following up on the source of a particular set of element-type names or attribute names.

If we have more than one namespace, the node-set argument enables us to be more specific, as in Example 5–3.

The result is http://www.us_geological.service.gov/, or, the value for the xmlns:usgeo attribute defined for the usgeo namespace on the <year> element, selected from the <usgeo:planting> element's namespace.

If we change this example slightly, we can take advantage of the default document order processing, using wildcards to get the first child node of <year>, which is <usgeo:planting>:

```
namespace-uri(//year//*)
```

In this case, http://www.us_geological.service.gov/ will still be the URI returned. The pattern expression //year//* includes all descendants of <year>, but of these, the first in document order is usgeo:planting, so its URI is the one returned. Notice that pattern expressions can be arguments to functions, provided the function accepts a node-set as its argument.

Example 5–3 : Declaration of multiple namespaces.

INPUT:

```
<?xml version="1.0"?>
<year xmlns:iowa="http://www.iowa_climate.org/almanac/"
      xmlns:usgeo="http://www.us_geological.service.gov/">
      <usgeo:planting>
            <iowa:season period="spring">
                  <month>March</month>
                  <month>April</month>
                  <month>May</month>
            </iowa:season>
            <iowa:season period="summer">
                  <month>June</month>
                  <month>July</month>
                  <month>August</month>
            </iowa:season>
      </usgeo:planting>
      <usgeo:harvest>
            <iowa:season period="fall">
                  <month>September</month>
                  <month>October</month>
                  <month>November</month>
            </iowa:season>
            <iowa:season period="winter">
                  <month>December</month>
                  <month>January</month>
                  <month>February</month>
            </iowa:season>
      </usgeo:harvest>
</year>
```

TEMPLATE RULE:

```
<xsl:template match="//*[local-name() = 'planting']">
      <xsl:value-of select="namespace-uri()"/>
</xsl:template>
```

5.2.5 The `last()` Function

The `last()` function returns the total number of nodes in the context node-set. This number is also equivalent to the context size of the node-set, because the numerical value of the last node for the context node-set is equal to the total number of nodes in the node-set (not including descendants). The `last()` function is one of three node-counting functions in the node-set core function group, which return numbers. It does not accept an argument and operates only on node-sets, as shown in the following function prototype.

Function: *number* **last()**

Function Name	*Core Function Group*	*Returns*	*Arguments*	*Argument Type*
`last()`	Node-set	Number	None	—

The `last()` function returns a number, however, since it doesn't accept arguments, the resulting number can only be used in another context. The function can never really return the number by itself. To actually *see* the value of the number, use the `number()` function described in Section 5.5.1.

We can, however, use this function to access the contents of the last node in a node-set:

```
//harvest//month[last()]
```

or

```
<xsl:template match="/">
      <xsl:value-of select="//harvest//month[last()]" />
</xsl:template>
```

The `last()` function will give us the total number of months in the first season of the harvest period, which is 3, but the entire XSLT expression with `<xsl:value-of>` will actually return *November*, which is the contents of the last `<month>` in the first `<season>` element in the `<harvest>` element.

Recall from Chapter 4 that the context node is the node from which the current portion of an expression is being evaluated. Because the `<harvest>` element contains two `<season>` elements, each one is used as the context node for the evaluation of the `month[last()]` portion of the expression.

The `last()` function can also be used as a sort of "on/off" testing switch if you are performing a transformation on a number of nodes, but do not want to perform that transformation on the last node.

```
//harvest//month[position()!=last()]
```

or

```
<xsl:template match="/">
      <xsl:value-of select="//harvest//month[position()!=last()]"
      />
</xsl:template>
```

When used with another function in the node-set core function group, `position()` and the operator `!=` (not equal to), the function will return the contents of any `<month>` that was not the last in the set specified by the current context (assuming you are processing each `<month>` with some sort of looping or iterative mechanism, like the `<xsl:for-each>` function described in Chapter 9).

> **NOTE** Predicates can change the size of the node-set by selecting or eliminating nodes, so the number that is returned by the `last()` function is the number of the last node of the current node-set for the given stage in the processing of the XPath expression where the function is called. In other words, as the current context node can change in the course of a predicate's evaluation, so then can the count of the current context of nodes change.

5.2.6 The `position()` Function

Like the `last()` function, the `position()` function returns a number, but since it doesn't accept arguments, the function is only really useful when used in combination with other functions. For example, this function can be used in an equivalence expression like `position() = 1`, or in XSLT elements like `<xsl:value-of>` that can pull out the value of the `position()`.

This function has a return type of number and is part of a trio with `last()` and `count()`, which together enable a range of inventory and numerical sequence-based operations on node-sets. The `position()` function does not accept an argument, as shown in the following function prototype. The implicit argument is the current node, which is why this function is classified as a node-set function. It only operates on node-sets.

Function: *number* **position()**

Function Name	*Core Function Group*	*Returns*	*Arguments*	*Argument Type*
position()	Node-set	Number	None	—

Using the Markup City model, slightly revised in Example 5–4, we can navigate without knowing the street names. Note that it may be necessary to remove any extra space and tabs from this example because some processors consider whitespace objects as "children" and they are counted as text nodes.

If our local expert, at whose mercy we are when asking directions, doesn't know the street names (and we've all had that frustrating occurrence) but does know that the store we're seeking is in the fifth block, it's still possible to find it. So with XPath, choosing the fifth block as we "drive"—or traverse, in proper XPath terminology—the <boulevard> is quite simple:

```
//boulevard/block[position() = 5]
```

or

```
<xsl:template match="/">
      <xsl:value-of select="//boulevard/block[position() = 5]" />
</xsl:template>
```

This expression, using <xsl:value-of>, returns the text value of the fifth <block> element in the <boulevard>, or Old Chimney Road.

As demonstrated previously, position() is often used together with last(), either with the "not" operator (!=) to exclude the last node, or with equal (=) when the last node is to be used.

```
//boulevard/block[position() = last()]
```

or

Example 5–4 : Revised Markup City model.

```
<?xml version="1.0"?>
<main>
     <parkway>
          <thoroughfare>Governor Drive</thoroughfare>
          <thoroughfare name="Whitesburg Drive">
               <sidestreet>Bob Wallace Avenue</sidestreet>
               <sidestreet>Woodridge Street</sidestreet>
          </thoroughfare>
          <thoroughfare name="Bankhead">
               <sidestreet>Tollgate Road</sidestreet>
               <sidestreet>Oak Drive</sidestreet>
          </thoroughfare>
     </parkway>
     <boulevard>
          <block>Panorama Street</block>
          <block>Highland Plaza</block>
          <block>Hutchens Avenue</block>
          <block>Wildwood Drive</block>
          <block>Old Chimney Road</block>
          <block>Carrol Circle</block>
     </boulevard>
</main>
```

```
<xsl:template match="/">
     <xsl:value-of select="//boulevard/block[position() =
        last()]" />
</xsl:template>
```

The result of this expression would be the content of the last `<block>` element in the `<boulevard>`, or `Carrol Circle`.

5.2.6.1 The `position()` Function with Regard to Context

Because nodes are counted in context, the numbering for `position()` resets at the context element. Context is not determined by the `position()` function itself, but by the XSLT element in which the `position()` function is used. Most XSLT elements get their context from the `<xsl:template>` element (see Chapter 3, Section 3.1.2 for more on the `<xsl:template>` element).

When matching beginning from the root, the context is the root, and `position()` starts at the first element with 1, and sequentially counts elements to the end, as shown in Example 5–5.

Example 5–5 : Using `position()` in an iteration.

```
<xsl:template match="/">
     <xsl:for-each select="//*">
          <xsl:value-of select="position()"/>
     </xsl:for-each>
</xsl:template>
```

The result of this template using our Markup City from Example 5–4 is a count of all elements starting at 1 and ending at 16: `1 2 3 4 5 6 7 8 9 10 11 12 13 14 15 16.`

Matching from the root, the context for the following template is the root, so the position of the sidestreets is counted sequentially without regard to direct parentage:

```
<xsl:template match="/">
     <xsl:for-each select="//sidestreet">
          <xsl:value-of select="position()"/>
     </xsl:for-each>
</xsl:template>
```

The result of this template is a sequential count of the sidestreets starting at 1, regardless of their parent: `1 2 3 4.`

Changing the template to match on any sidestreet, the context is changed to the parent element of sidestreet (recall that even though the // is used to denote any sidestreet, the context of the sidestreet is still its parent node):

```
<xsl:template match="//sidestreet">
     <xsl:value-of select="position()"/>
</xsl:template>
```

The result of this template is the count of each sidestreet in context of its parent, or `1 2 1 2`. The processor takes each element as the context element, starting from the root (//), and looks for sidestreets within that element, first resetting the `position()` count to 1. Note that if you have any whitespace in your input file, it may be counted as a child of `<thoroughfare>` and cause your resulting numbers to be off.

5.2.7 The count() Function

The count() function simply counts the nodes—not including their descendants—in the node-set specified in the argument. This function is the third component of the node sequencing and numerical inventory trio of functions. Of the three—count(), last(), and position()—only count() has an argument, which is required, and must be a node-set. The count() function operates on node-sets and returns a number, as shown in the following function prototype.

```
Function: number count(node-set)
```

Function Name	*Core Function Group*	*Returns*	*Arguments*	*Argument Type*
count()	Node-set	Number	Node-set	required

If we wanted to know how many blocks were in the entire Markup City, we would use count() as shown in Example 5–6.

Example 5–6 : Using count() to count blocks.

```
count(//block)
```

or

```
<xsl:template match="/">
      <xsl:value-of select="count(//block)" />
</xsl:template>
```

This would give us the total number of blocks, in this case 6, regardless their parents. Of course, in our current city, we have only <block>s along the <boulevard>. We could use the union operator | with the count() function to find the total number of either <block>s or <sidestreet>s.

```
count(//block | //sidestreet)
```

or

```
<xsl:template match="/">
      <xsl:value-of select="count(//block | //sidestreet)" />
</xsl:template>
```

This expression would result in 10, the total of 6 <block>s and 4 <sidestreet>s. Working with more complex expressions within the argument, we could add a predicate that limits which <sidestreet>s we count.

```
count(//block | //*[@name='Bankhead']/sidestreet)
```

or

```
<xsl:template match="/">
      <xsl:value-of select="count(//block |
      //*[@name='Bankhead']/sidestreet)" />
</xsl:template>
```

This counts all <block>s, regardless from which node they are descended (//), which is equal to 6, and it also counts all <sidestreet>s whose parent (the / preceding sidestreet steps up to the parent of <sidestreet>) is any element (*) with the attribute (@) name with the value Bankhead, which results in 2, for an expression total of 8. If there was a kind of street other than <thoroughfare> with a name attribute with the value Bankhead, its <sidestreet> children would be counted too. To be more specific, but with the same result in this case, we could do the following:

```
count(//block | //thoroughfare[@name='Bankhead']/sidestreet)
```

or

```
<xsl:template match="/">
      <xsl:value-of select="count(//block |
      //thoroughfare[@name='Bankhead']/sidestreet)" />
</xsl:template>
```

5.3 String Core Function Group

There are ten functions in the string core function group, seven of which return strings. The string() function serves to convert the range of objects supplied as an argument into a string according to the string conversion rules for that object type (covered in Section 5.3.2). The concat() function concatenates the group of strings supplied in the argument. The `substring()`, `substring-after()`, and `substring-before()` functions operate on subsets of strings. The next two functions manipulate the characters of the strings themselves. The first, `normalize-space()`, equalizes the whitespace in the strings supplied in the argument. The other, `translate()`, interprets two sets of arguments and replaces one set with the other.

Two functions in the string core function group return Booleans. The `starts-with()` function returns a true/false value when a given string starts with members of another string. The `contains()` function simply checks if the components of one string in the supplied arguments contains the components of the second string.

The `string-length()` function has a number return type, and returns the total count of the characters in the supplied string.

5.3.1 The **`string()`** Function

The `string()` function is the basic conversion function that takes a given object of the four types specified in XPath and converts it to a string.[3] This object argument is optional, as shown in the following function prototype. The `string()` function operates on any type of input, designated by the argument type of *object.*

Function: *string* **string**(*object?*)

Function Name	*Core Function Group*	*Returns*	*Arguments*	*Argument Type*
`string()`	String	String	Object	optional

3. A glance in the *Oxford English Dictionary* indicates that the meaning of string is surely not singular, even without considering its programming connotations. We could call this a moment's pondering on "string theory," but that too is still another connotation (the latest and greatest rage in the never-ending "theory of everything quest" among physicists...in terms of being a viable goal in markup terms, consider it as sort of like finding a set of semantics suitable for all possible data).

To understand the `string()` function, it's best to think of it as a process of segmenting the input arguments into a form that is simply a sequence of characters with no syntactic meaning, other than the separating whitespace. In other words, when XML-processing or XSLT-processing software sees, for instance, `<block>`, it reads the less-than < and greater-than > in such a way that makes `block` an element-type name and `<block>` an element. Similarly, when an XSLT processor sees true or false in a Boolean context, then that literally means an answer to a query of sorts as to whether or not a given condition exists. Taken together, then, the characters that comprise `<block>` and those that comprise the word true have a *meaning* that goes beyond the simple combination of characters. The syntax, or arrangement of those characters, and the context in which they occur add meaning to what they signify.

> **string:** A thread or file with a number of objects strung upon it. (circa 1488)
> **string:** computers: A linear sequence of records or data. (1956) (*OED*, 2000, XVI: 922)

In each of the cases just described, the so-called "combination of characters," or "sequence of characters," can also be a string. In fact, they literally *are* strings in the everyday sense of the word string: A number of things in a line; a row, chain, range (*OED*, 2000, XVI: 922). However, when considered as a whole, the string of `t`, `r`, `u`, and `e` means an answer in a given context—that of a Boolean—which affirms the presence of a particular condition about which an inquiry has been made. All of these significations accompany the word true in a Boolean context. Converting it to a string means, among other things, removing the "sense" of being a Boolean, which that syntax and context conveys as an additional meaning to just the word constructed of those letters.

When the word true becomes a string with the conversion afforded by the `string()` function, it is still visible to human-reading as "true." The attendant significations are gone, however, as far as the computer software is concerned.

In a related way, when a node-set is converted to a string, the significations of the tags as well as the hierarchy of elements within the given node-set, are all removed. The result is simply the text within the node, without all the XML markup.

There are particular reasons for doing this. As seen with `id()`, when the various object types become strings, then it is a simple matter to match character-for-character. In addition, as will be seen with the other functions in the string core function group that take strings as arguments, if in a given operation you wish to affect an element or number in a certain way—such as to translate an element-type name from uppercase to lowercase—the only way to do that is to have the element-type name be a string as an argument to the `translate()` function.

So, much like the ubiquity of `position()`, the `string()` function is both very powerful and very essential for transforming all manner of structures in the XML data source instance. There is a great irony here, however, as the `string()` function is rarely, if ever, explicitly called. As in the case of the `id()` function—as also with node-sets when given as arguments to the `number()` function—the `string()` function is *implicitly* invoked in the course of performing other operations, still adhering to the string conversion rules. Lots of string conversions take place in the course evaluating other XPath functions, but `string()` itself is not often explicitly invoked.

5.3.2 String Conversion Rules

To convert objects to a string, certain rules of order must be observed so there is a predictable structure in the resulting string. When you construct an XPath expression using the `string()` function—explicitly or implicitly—it is helpful to know exactly what is going to happen to the input data in order to successfully work with the resulting output.

1. Numbers are converted to strings as follows (refer to Section 5.5.2 on number conversions for a more detailed explanation of NaN, positives, negatives, etc.):
   a. A non-numerical number value (e.g., sequenced letters), denoted as NaN, is converted to the string `NaN`.
   b. Any zero number, positive or negative, is converted to the string `0`.

> **NOTE** An integer is returned, regardless of whether the number happens to be positive, as in 0.3, or negative, as in -0.3. In each case, the number will return the nearest integer (moving towards positive infinity). In the case of 0.5, the nearest positive integer 1 is returned. Any negative number between -0.5 and 0 will return a negative 0. (-0.000000001 is still a negative 0).

c. Infinity, positive or negative, is converted to the string `Infinity` or `-Infinity`.

d. Numbers that are integers are represented in decimal form as numbers (according to IEEE 754) with no decimal point and no leading zeros, with a preceding minus sign if negative.

e. Other numbers are presented as numbers (IEEE 754), including a decimal point and at least one digit after the decimal point, with leading minus sign if negative. No leading zeros other than optionally the one preceding the decimal, and only as many digits beyond the decimal as are needed to distinguish the number from any other such numbers in the XML data instance source.

2. Boolean true or false values are converted to the strings `true` and `false` respectively.
3. Node-sets are converted to strings using specific rules for each node type. Each type of node has a specific string conversion rule, resulting in a *string-value*. In some cases, a node's string-value will be part of the node. In other cases, the string-value of the node comes from the string-value of the text nodes of the node's descendants.

4. If a string is passed to the `string()` function, it remains a string.
5. Objects other than the four basic types are converted to strings according to the type of object.

Table 5–4 shows the resulting string-values for each converted node type:

Table 5–4 String values for converted node types

Node Type	**`String-Value`**
Attribute	value of the attribute, if specified
Comment	text of the comment
Element	value of the element's descendant's text nodes, concatenated together in document order
Namespace	the text of the URI
Processing-instruction	text of the processing-instruction
Root	value of the element's descendant's text nodes, concatenated together in document order
Text	text of the node

The resulting string is treated as a whitespace-separated string of tokens[4] (basically, words or groups of characters separated by spaces).

The `string()` function is often used to prepare a particular object for being operated upon by some other function. By itself, it has limits. This is

4. Tokens are equivalent to the series of characters. If there is more than one string, it is demarcated by whitespace (spaces separating each set of characters). In effect, whether the sequence is a token or a word to the human eye, it is still nothing more than just a line-up of digital "stuff" to the computer, once it has become a string.

consistent with its basic function because the output has no other inherent meaning than the sequence of characters it produces.

5.3.3 The `concat()` Function

The `concat()` function operates on strings, and returns a string that is a result of joining (or concatenating) two or more strings, which are furnished as arguments. At least two strings are required as arguments, though an unlimited number may be optionally furnished. Optional additional strings are specified in the function prototype below, using an asterisk * following the argument declaration, which technically means zero or more. A comma separates each argument. If a non-string object is specified as an argument, it will be converted to a string according to the string conversion rules (see Section 5.3.2) prior to processing.

Function: *string* **concat**(*string, string, string**)

Function Name	*Core Function Group*	*Returns*	*Arguments*	*Argument Type*
`concat()`	String	String	String	required
			String	required
			String*	optional

It is useful to think of `concat()` as a sort of daisy-chaining function.[5] It ties the strings provided as arguments together end-upon-end (it does not loop them, however). You can supply a number of items in the arguments, which can be used to generate output text.

5. If you're familiar with UNIX, `concat()` performs the same function as the UNIX "cat" function. Another example is the *cons* and *concatenate* functions in Lisp, except in Reverse-Polish Notation (RPN) order, wherein the input string in `concat()` is the first argument, not the last, as with *cons* in Lisp. Unlike Lisp *concatenate,* `concat()` does not require specification of an object type because, of course, its input arguments are predefined by the W3C specification to be of type string.

With `concat()` you can construct content with a mixture of text strings, pattern expressions, and functions. For instance, we could get the contents of the first and last `<block>` in Markup City, as shown in Example 5–7.

Example 5–7 : XML input from Markup City for `concat()` example.

```
<?xml version="1.0"?>
<main>
      <parkway>
          <thoroughfare>Governor Drive</thoroughfare>
          <thoroughfare name="Whitesburg Drive">
               <sidestreet>Bob Wallace Avenue</sidestreet>
               <sidestreet>Woodridge Street</sidestreet>
          </thoroughfare>
          <thoroughfare name="Bankhead">
               <sidestreet>Tollgate Road</sidestreet>
               <sidestreet>Oak Drive</sidestreet>
          </thoroughfare>
      </parkway>
      <boulevard>
          <block>Panorama Street</block>
          <block>Highland Plaza</block>
          <block>Hutchens Avenue</block>
          <block>Wildwood Drive</block>
          <block>Old Chimney Road</block>
          <block>Carrol Circle</block>
      </boulevard>
</main>
```

In the following example, the first argument (`//block`) is a simple pattern expression to get the name of the first `<block>`, the second (`' and '`) is a string to put in the word and after it, and the third (`//block[last()]`) is a pattern expression with a predicate:

```
concat(//block, ' and ', //block[last()])
```

or

```
<xsl:template match="/">
    <xsl:value-of select="concat(//block, ' and ',
    //block[last()]) " />
```

```
</xsl:template>
```

As a result, we're able to get the following narrative output:

```
Panorama Street and Carrol Circle
```

Recall from the `string()` function that any node-set that is converted to a string returns the value of the *first* node, which is why the first argument (in this case, `//block`) returns the text contents of the first `<block>` element.

The two `<block>` names are separated by the word `and` (in the English language, not operand, sense) by using a literal string as the second argument. The third argument returns the value of the last `<block>`, testing whether it is the last `<block>` by using the `last()` function.

Another possible use might be to determine all names of `<thoroughfare>`s along the `<parkway>` in Markup City. You will remember from the example above that some names of `<thoroughfare>`s were given as element content, and others as values to the `name` attribute.

We could put together a list in human-sensible syntax by using several arguments with `concat()` and the `local-name()` function.

Assume you knew there were three `<thoroughfare>`s and which ones had the attribute `name` instead of a name in the content.

```
concat('There are several ', local-name(//parkway/
*), 's, the first is called ', //parkway/*, ', the
second is called ', //parkway/*[position()=2]/
@name, ', and the third is called ', //parkway/
*[position()=3]/@name, '.')
```

Notice that it is necessary to include any additional text inside quote marks, including the spaces. Element and attribute names as parts of pattern expressions do not require quote marks, as is also the case with other functions, such as the use of `local-name()`. The output of this XPath function expression, using `concat()` on the input file from Markup City, is:

```
There are several thoroughfares, the first is
called Governor Drive, the second is called
Whitesburg Drive, and the third is called
Bankhead.
```

The parts of that sentence generated from function or pattern expressions as components are underlined. Notice, for instance, how the commas and the "s" after "thoroughfare" are attached by `concat()`.

If you didn't know that there were three `<thoroughfare>`s, or which ones had the attribute `name` instead of a name in the content, you would need to use more advanced functions, such as the XSLT function `<xsl:for-each>`. See Chapter 9 for more information on the `<xsl:for-each>` instruction element.

5.3.4 The **substring()** Function

The `substring()` function is one of a trio of functions, including `substring-after()` and `substring-before()`, in the string core function group, which work, in some way or another, with subcomponents of strings. The substring trio functions begin with a string and then provide additional processing granularity for accessing and manipulating smaller portions of the initial string. The `substring()` function accepts three arguments, as shown in the following function prototype.

```
Function: string substring(string, number,
number?)
```

Function Name	*Core Function Group*	*Returns*	*Arguments*	*Argument Type*
`substring()`	String	String	String	required
			Number	required
			Number	optional

The first two arguments (a string and a number) are required, and the third (a number) is optional. Although the function only operates on strings, the input string can be any object that is implicitly converted to a string with the string conversion rules (see Section 5.3.2).

The `substring()` function is a positional function, based on the parameters delineated by the supplied arguments. In other words, this function operates on the initial string using the position of the characters within that string to extract a substring. The first argument is always the starting, or input string. The second argument specifies which character with which to begin the substring, numerically counted from the first character in the string, using a base of 1 (not 0, as in some programming languages). The new substring created is the subset of the initial string that starts from the positional character in the second argument and continues to the end of the initial string. The substring will include all the characters to the end of the initial string unless there is a third argument to the function to specify where to stop.

If provided, the third argument specifies how many sequential characters in the input string, beginning with the character specified in the second argument, are to be included in the resulting substring. For example, given the string `my string`, count the characters in the string as follows (numbers below `my string` indicate which character, in numerical sequence, each is when counted):

```
my string
123456789
```

Using the function `substring('my string', 4, 3)`, the resulting substring is `str`, which comes from the fourth, fifth, and sixth characters. This function essentially states: Start from the fourth character in the string `my string` and count three characters.

Think of the second argument as saying "all sequential pieces of the input/starting string that are greater than or equal to me." Think of the third argument, if given, as saying "all sequential pieces of the input/starting string that are less than or equal to me."

5.3.4.1 Using `substring()` on Node-sets.

If the first argument of the `substring()` function happens to be a node-set, the result of the conversion of the node-set to a string would be the value of the first node in the node-set, as is shown in Example 5–8 of our Markup City.

The result of this function call would be the three characters `ora` from the fourth, fifth, and sixth characters in the string value of the first `<block>` element, or `Panorama Street`.

The `substring()` function should be considered "destructive," in that all portions of the base or starting string not selected by the second and third arguments (if used) are discarded by the XSLT processor in the subsequent evaluation of the XPath expression containing this function.

Example 5–8 : XML for `substring()` function example.

INPUT:

```
<?xml version="1.0"?>
<boulevard>
            <block>Panorama Street</block>
            <block>Highland Plaza</block>
            <block>Hutchens Avenue</block>
            <block>Wildwood Drive</block>
            <block>Old Chimney Road</block>
            <block>Carrol Circle</block>
</boulevard>
```

FUNCTION:

```
substring(//block, 4, 3)
```

or

```
<xsl:template match="/">
      <xsl:value-of select="substring(//block, 4, 3)" />
</xsl:template>
```

5.3.4.2 Using `substring()` on Numbers.

The `substring()` function becomes a bit complex when the arguments supplied are numbers. Number objects have specific properties, which affect XPath expressions that are using them in differing ways. All of these properties have a universal set of rules to which they conform, as defined in the IEEE 754 set of rules for numerical values. We will deal with these in more detail in the number core function group, but must introduce them here as different types of properties affecting numbers will, in turn, affect how the sequences supplied as arguments to the `substring()` function are counted.

It is likely that some of the following discussion will not be essential to extracting substrings. For example, if—as in the example above—your use of `substring()` always has sort of "everyday, bread-and-butter whole numbers," then you can rest assured that IEEE 754 rules simply ensure that 3 will always mean a 3.

However, when the second and third arguments are decimals, negative values, or zeroes, for instance, IEEE 754 rules and the principles of rounding numbers come into play (see Section 5.5.6 for more information on the principles of the `round()` function). This rounding results in the following kinds of results for a simple input string of `abcde`, as used in the W3C XPath specification.

1. `substring('abcde', 1.5, 2.6)` returns `bcd`, because 1.5 and 2.6 will round to 2 and 3 respectively. So, `b` is greater than or equal to the position value represented by 1.5—which rounds to 2—as is `c` and `d`. The sum of rounded 1.5 and 2.6, or 2 + 3, is 5. The position of `d` is 4, which is less than 5.
2. `substring('abcde', 0, 3)` returns `ab`, the 0 remains 0, so there is no corresponding point in the input string to be included. Zero represents a point prior to the beginning of the string (because XPath is not zero-based as are other programming languages), and that point plus two more beyond it would only comprise `a` and `b` because the position occupied by `a` is greater than or equal to 0.
3. `substring('abcde', 0 div 0, 3)` returns `""`, or an empty set. The `div` is the number function for "divided by." Because 0 divided by 0 is not a number (returns NaN), the result of any such division will be an empty string.
4. `substring('abcde', 1, 0 div 0)` also returns `""`, for the same reason as 3 above.
5. `substring('abcde', -42, 1 div 0)` returns `abcde` because the string function will always start at the first character when the number supplied for the first character is less than the starting value of 1, and `1 div 0` is Infinity, so all the characters are selected.
6. `substring('abcde', -1 div 0, 1 div 0)` returns `""` because -1 divided by 0 is -Infinity, and even though 1 divided by 0 is Infinity and it would make sense to return all the characters, the function cannot find the starting point.

5.3.5 The `substring-after()` Function

The second in the trio of functions that work with subcomponents of strings is the `substring-after()` function, which also returns a string. It takes two required arguments, which are themselves strings, as shown in the following function prototype:

Function: *string* **substring-after**(*string*, *string*)

Function Name	*Core Function Group*	*Returns*	*Arguments*	*Argument Type*
`substring-after()`	String	String	String String	required required

The `substring-after()` function operates on strings, or objects that are converted to strings prior to processing. The first argument to `substring-after()` is an input or initial string, and the second specifies the character or group of characters in the input string *after* which the remainder of the input string is returned.

For example, given the expression `substring-after("1963/02/13", "/")`, the function returns everything after the first match on the second argument (in document order), in this case the forward slash (/), and so yields `02/13`.

If there is no match for the second argument, then there will be nothing returned or, more specifically, the empty string is returned. If the entire string of the second argument matches, character for character, the equivalent string in the input string provided in the first argument such that the match continues right up to the very last character of the input string, there is nothing left to return. This is because the string in the second argument specifies the point *after which* the resulting substring to be returned begins. Thus using the function `substring-after("1963/02/13", "02/13")` will return the empty string because nothing comes after `02/13`.

In Example 5–9 of Markup City, it may be necessary to know what kind of <block>s—avenues, streets, plazas, and so on—are along the <boulevard>.

Example 5–9 : XML for the following substring-before() and substring-after() functions.

```
<?xml version="1.0"?>
<boulevard>
            <block>Panorama Street</block>
            <block>Highland Plaza</block>
            <block>Hutchens Avenue</block>
            <block>Wildwood Drive</block>
            <block>Old Chimney Road</block>
            <block>Carrol Circle</block>
</boulevard>
```

Using the substring-after() function with a pattern to extract the names of the <block> will return the string after the space in each name:

```
    substring-after(//boulevard/block, ' ')
```

or

```
    <xsl:template match="/">
          <xsl:value-of select="substring-after(//boulevard/block, '
          ')" />
    </xsl:template>
```

The result of testing this function, because the context of the <xsl:value-of> element is the root, returns the string Street because it only returns the first <block>. You can add a position() function to test each block individually, but this may be a time consuming process:

```
          substring-after(//boulevard/block[position()=2], ' ')
          substring-after(//boulevard/block[position()=3], ' ')
    ... etc.
```

The best solution is to change the context of the previous test by changing the match attribute of <xsl:template>:

```
          <xsl:template match="//boulevard/block">
              <xsl:value-of select="substring-after(., ' ')" />
```

```
</xsl:template>
```

Recall from Chapter 4 that the "self" token passes the value of the current node to the expression, in this case the text of each `<block>`.

The resulting strings from each `<block>` would be:

```
Street
Plaza
Avenue
Drive
Chimney Road
Circle
```

Note that the fifth `<block>` will not return `Road` for the expression above, but instead `Chimney Road`, as the space after `Old` is the first of two. We could then add an additional `substring-after()` function, nesting the first `substring-after()` function within it, to correct this occurrence.

```
substring-after(substring-after(//boulevard block[position()=5],
' '), ' ')
```

or

```
<xsl:template match="/">
      <xsl:value-of select="substring-after(substring
      after(//boulevard/block[position()=5], ' '), ' ')"
      />
</xsl:template>
```

This results in the substring `Road`.

5.3.6 The `substring-before()` Function

The `substring-before()` function completes the substring trio of functions and performs, as might be expected, the reverse of the `sub-string-after()` function. It also returns a string and takes two required arguments, which are themselves strings, as shown in the following function prototype. The `substring-before()` function operates on strings or on objects that are converted to strings prior to processing.

Function: *string* **substring-before**(*string*, *string*)

Function Name	*Core Function Group*	*Returns*	*Arguments*	*Argument Type*
`substring-before()`	String	String	String String	required required

The first argument in `substring-before()` furnishes the initial or input string. The second argument will return any portion of the input string that *precedes* the portion represented in the second argument, but not including the second argument portion. Thus, with the previous example of dates, `substring-before("1963/02/13", "/")` returns whatever comes before the first match—in document order—to the second argument. In this case, using / for the second argument will return `1963` because this precedes the first forward slash match in the initial string.

In the case where the characters in the second argument exactly match the first characters in the first argument, the result returned is an empty string, because nothing comes before the first character of the string in the first argument. If no part of the first argument is matched by the second argument, the result is also an empty string:

```
substring-before("1963/02/13", "1963")
```

The function will return the empty string because nothing comes before `1963`.

Suppose we wanted the name of any `<block>`s in Markup City, as shown in Example 5–10, that were also "circle" type of roads.

Example 5–10 : Using the `substring-before()` function.

```
<xsl:template match="//boulevard/block">
     <xsl:value-of select="substring-before(., ' ')" />
</xsl:template>
```

We could simply reverse our example from the `substring-after()` function to get all the names of the streets.

If used with `<xsl:for-each>`, this results in the names of all the `<block>`s (except of course, "Old Chimney," which is truncated to `Old`), but that would not tell us which one was a circle resulting in:

```
Panorama
Highland
Hutchens
Wildwood
Old
Carrol
```

The easiest way to get the name of the `<block>` that is a circle is to use the word `Circle` in the test string:

```
substring-before(., 'Circle')
```

or

```
<xsl:template match="//boulevard/block">
      <xsl:value-of select="substring-before(., 'Circle')" />
</xsl:template>
```

This would result in the string '`Carrol  `' (which also includes the space between `Carrol` and `Circle`). Adding a space to the second argument would, in effect, erase the space in the result:

```
substring-before(//boulevard/block, ' Circle')
```

5.3.7 The **normalize-space()** Function

The `normalize-space()` function returns a string with the extra spaces within it removed. It takes a single optional argument, which is also a string, as shown in the following function prototype. If the argument is not supplied, the string corresponding to the current node at that point in the evaluation of the XPath expression is used.

Function: *string* **normalize-space**(*string?*)

Function Name	*Core Function Group*	*Returns*	*Arguments*	*Argument Type*
`normalize-space()`	String	String	String	optional

The `normalize-space()` function is used to prepare data for subsequent actions. The "normal" in `normalize-space()` refers to the default use of a single space between strings in a markup document. The `normalize-space()` function reduces any extra spaces down to the normal single space, unless the space is expressly preserved by using either the ` ` (nonbreaking space entity) or the `xml:space` attribute with the value set to `preserve`. See Chapter 2 for more information on the `xml:space` attribute.

> **NOTE** The result of preserving space using the `xml:space` attribute is similar to using the "pre" tag for preformatted text in HTML, except the font is not affected. The `normalize-space()` function could be used to override this setting in the input XML data instance if needed, for instance, to make a single space a point for substring manipulations.

If the source string has multiple spaces between words, these will be reduced to one space separating each word. Leading and trailing spaces before and after strings will also be stripped by `normalize-space()`.

As an example, if we tried to use the example from `substring-after()`, where we were searching for a space and returning the string after the space, and if the input from the Markup City were a bit more sloppy, the results would be very unpredictable, as Example 5–11 shows.

Example 5–11 : XML with disorderly white space to demonstrate the `normalize-space()` function.

```
<boulevard>
     <block> Panorama    Street</block>
     <block>Highland  Plaza </block>
     <block>   Hutchens          Avenue</block>
     <block>Wildwood    Drive   </block>
     <block> Old    Chimney  Road</block>
     <block>Carrol    Circle  </block>
</boulevard>
```

Using `normalize-space()` on this data will clean it up to assure the substring functions mentioned previously work properly.

```
normalize-space(//boulevard/block)
```

or

```
<xsl:template match="//boulevard/block">
     <xsl:value-of select="normalize-space(.)" />
</xsl:template>
```

Once the data has been normalized, the expressions can be used as shown before, and the result will still come out right.

```
substring-after(normalize-space(//boulevard/block), ' ')
```

or

```
<xsl:template match="//boulevard/block">
     <xsl:value-of select="substring-after(normalize-space(.), '
     ')" />
</xsl:template>
```

5.3.8 The **translate()** Function

The `translate()` function is used to convert one set of strings to another.[6] It returns a string as its function return type, as shown in the following function prototype. This function requires three arguments, the first of which provides an initial or input string. The second argument specifies which characters of the first string are to be replaced. The third argument provides the characters that will be used as the replacement characters. This function operates on strings or on objects that will be converted to strings prior to processing.

Function: *string* **translate**(*string, string, string*)

Function Name	*Core Function Group*	*Returns*	*Arguments*	*Argument Type*
`translate()`	String	String	String	required
			String	required
			String	required

6. Programmers may recognize `translate()` as a function somewhat like *intersection* in the Lisp programming language, which takes arguments, the results of which reflect the commonality between the arguments.

Before proceeding, the example from the XPath W3C specification serves to make this abstract notion of substitution and intersection more concrete. If you have a string such as `bar` and you want to capitalize only those letters that match a specific set, such as `abc`, then you would supply `bar` as the first argument as a starting or input string, `abc` as second argument, and `ABC` as the third string, indicating what is to be translated to.

So, for `translate('bar', 'abc', 'ABC')`, the processor will first check for which characters in the second argument match characters in the first argument—in this case, `a` and `b`. Then the processor will look up the appropriate conversion for the `a` and `b` matches in the corresponding positions from the characters in the third argument—in this case, `A`, and `B`. The result would then be `BAr`, because only `b` and `a` of the first argument were matched by the options in the second argument, and the appropriate replacements for them from the third argument were the uppercase `B` and the uppercase `A`.

Think of the first argument as you would a starting or input string. The second argument is the list of what is to be replaced from the first string. The third string is simply a lookup table of appropriate substitutions, where each position of each character corresponds to the position of the character specified in the second argument. If the first argument has characters unmatched by any from the second argument, they are output unaffected.

Working with the `translate()` function is always predicated on supplying a complete set for what the input string is to be translated to. There is nothing "intuitive" about the `translate()` function. It is better thought of as a sophisticated search and replace function, and also as a tool for changing the case from upper to lower or vice versa for many, but not all, character sets of various languages.

Because of the rules governing the syntax of the three arguments to the `translate()` function, it is also possible to remove characters from the first argument by matching them in the second argument and supplying no replacement for them in the third argument. This necessarily means the second argument will be longer—contain more characters—than the third argument.

In the example above, we could change the second argument as follows: `translate('bar', 'abcr', 'ABC')`. This would allow the second argument to match all characters of the first argument. However, the third argument has no fourth character with which to match the `r`, which comes fourth in the second argument. The return would therefore be

BA. This means also that the third argument can simply be empty, meaning that the characters listed for replacement in the second argument are, in effect, deleted or removed.

For example, if our Markup City <block> names were in lowercase, you might want to use the `translate()` function to capitalize them. We will use a couple of other functions in combination with `translate()` to accomplish this in Example 5–12.

Example 5–12 : XML for the `translate()` function examples.

```
<boulevard>
               <block>panorama street</block>
               <block>highland plaza</block>
               <block>hutchens avenue</block>
               <block>wildwood drive</block>
               <block>old chimney road</block>
               <block>carrol circle</block>
</boulevard>
```

The XPath function expression could be written as follows.

```
translate(substring(//block, 1, 1), 'abcdefghijklmnopqrstuvwxyz',
'ABCDEFGHIJKLMNOPQRSTUVWXYZ')
```

or

```
<xsl:template match="/">
    <xsl:value-of select="translate(substring(//block, 1, 1),
    'abcdefghijklmnopqrstuvwxyz',
    'ABCDEFGHIJKLMNOPQRSTUVWXYZ')" />
</xsl:template>
```

This function will return the first letter of the first node, converted to uppercase. In this specific example, it returns a `P` because `panorama street` is the content of the first node. Combine this with the `concat()` function (Section 5.1.3.2) to get the rest of the string as follows:

```
concat(translate(substring(//block, 1, 1),
'abcdefghijklmnopqrstuvwxyz','ABCDEFGHIJKLMNOPQRSTUVWXYZ'),
substring(//block, 2))
```

or

```
<xsl:template match="/">
     <xsl:value-of select="concat(translate(substring(//block,
     1, 1), 'abcdefghijklmnopqrstuvwxyz',
     'ABCDEFGHIJKLMNOPQRSTUVWXYZ'), substring(//block, 2))" />
</xsl:template>
```

The result of this expression will be `Panorama street`. This of course doesn't address the lower case "s" in street, so we would use yet more functions, `substring-after()` and `substring-before()`, as shown in Example 5–13.

Example 5–13 : Extended example of nested functions.

```
concat
(translate
(substring(//block, 1, 1),
'abcdefghijklmnopqrstuvwxyz','ABCDEFGHIJKLMNOPQRSTUVWXYZ'),
substring(substring-before
(//block, ' '), 2), ' ', translate
(substring(substring-after
(//block, ' '), 1, 1), 'abcdefghijklmnopqrstuvwxyz',
  'ABCDEFGHIJKLMNOPQRSTUVWXYZ'), substring(substring-after
(//block, ' '), 2))
```

or

```
<xsl:template match="/">
      <xsl:value-of select="concat(translate(substring(//block,
      1, 1), 'abcdefghijklmnopqrstuvwxyz',
      'ABCDEFGHIJKLMNOPQRSTUVWXYZ'), substring(substring
      before(//block, ' '), 2), ' ',
      translate(substring(substring-after(//block, ' '), 1, 1),
      'abcdefghijklmnopqrstuvwxyz',
      'ABCDEFGHIJKLMNOPQRSTUVWXYZ'), substring(substring
      after(//block, ' '), 2))" />
</xsl:template>
```

After all this trouble of using several functions, in many cases nested inside other functions, we finally get our result, `Panorama Street`. While this may seem a daunting task to get such a simple result, consider running this on a database of millions of names. A few lines of nested expressions actually seem worth the time spent to get the correct results. Change the XSLT example slightly to get a list of all the blocks, with the case changed in each:

```
<xsl:template match="//block">
     <xsl:value-of select="concat(translate(substring(., 1, 1),
     'abcdefghijklmnopqrstuvwxyz',
     'ABCDEFGHIJKLMNOPQRSTUVWXYZ'), substring(substring-
     before(., ' '), 2), ' ', translate(substring(substring-
     after(., ' '), 1, 1), 'abcdefghijklmnopqrstuvwxyz',
     'ABCDEFGHIJKLMNOPQRSTUVWXYZ'), substring(substring-after(.,
     ' '), 2))" />
</xsl:template>
```

There are many possible uses for the `translate()` function, the most common for uppercase/lowercase conversions. It is important to consider this function also as a way of weeding out specific characters by not supplying appropriate replacements in the third argument for those selected for action by the second argument. Other functions can be used to supply the value for the second argument, so that a single `translate()` function could be contingent upon a number of factors in the input XML data instance.

5.3.9 The `contains()` Function

The `contains()` function tests for the existence of a substring within an initial string. Even though the `contains()` function is in the string core function group, it has the return type of *boolean*, because it will only return a Boolean true or false answer. It requires two string arguments, as shown in the following function prototype, an input or initial string, and a second argument, which is the string being matched or tested for in the input string. This function operates on strings or objects that will be converted to strings prior to processing, using the string conversion rules as described in Section 5.3.2.

Function: *boolean* **contains**(*string*, *string*)

Function Name	*Core Function Group*	*Returns*	*Arguments*	*Argument Type*
`contains()`	String	Boolean	String	required
			String	required

The `contains()` function is an existential function because, while it is used to match on strings, it returns a Boolean true or false value, not the string. It is actually testing for the *existence* of the substring within the initial string. For example:

```
contains('xml', 'x')
```

This expression will result in a true value because the string `xml` actually does contain the substring `x`. On the other hand, the following expression using our Markup City will result in a `false` value:

```
contains(//block, 'x')
```

This is because the expression is testing to see if there is an "`x`" in the string that is the result of the node-set conversion for each `<block>`, none of which contain an `x`.

The function can also be used in combination with other functions—as predicates, for instance—so that the node test that contains the predicate allows for the containing node itself to be returned. For example,

```
//block[contains(., 'Circle')]
```

or

```
<xsl:template match="/">
      <xsl:value-of select="//block[contains(., 'Circle')]" />
</xsl:template>
```

In this use of the function, any `<block>` element with the word `Circle` in it is returned. The result would be

```
Carrol Circle
```

As noted previously, in this example for the `<block>` element, the first argument to the `contains()` function is often the `self:: axis`, or a `"."` in abbreviated form. In the case of the expression with `<block>`, this means that where the expression is part of an `<xsl:value-of>` element, which is necessarily looking at the contents of `<block>`, those contents are the `self::` axis to which `Circle` is being matched or tested for. Thus, the expanded representation of the `"."` would be the full contents of a given block, such as `Highland Plaza` (no match there), `Hutchens Avenue` (no match there), or `Carrol Circle` (match found, answer returned is true). The `"."` stands, in turn, for the contents of each `<block>` as determined by the `<xsl:value-of>` context. If there is no match, then the return is, of course, false and no `<block>` name would be output because the `contains()` function test in its predicate had failed.

A few little details about contains() require further explanation, as they are not, perhaps, self-evident. If there is an empty string furnished for the second argument, the return will always be true. If the first string is empty, the answer is false unless the second is also empty, in which case the return is truc. You might wonder how this could be the case. For clarity in our examples, we have supplied functions in expressions as arguments to other functions; however, it is possible that a subexpression as an argument to contains() might produce an empty string, so there must be an accounting for this contingency.

In Markup City, it might be a dark and stormy night and quite late, and all we know is that there is some turn we must take (our cellphone blipped out of range while getting directions) from one of the roads in town that has "Street" in its name. We don't know anything more than this. The local expert says he doesn't know that part of town, but thinks there may be something called Street off one of the <thoroughfare>s along the <parkway>. This disquieting absence of information is not a problem for our XPath navigator, however, because as Example 5–14 shows, we need only find <thoroughfare>s with turns going off of them that have Street in their name.

Example 5–14 : XML for the contains() function example.

```
<?xml version="1.0"?>
<parkway>
      <thoroughfare>Governor Drive</thoroughfare>
      <thoroughfare name="Whitesburg Drive">
           <sidestreet>Bob Wallace Avenue</sidestreet>
           <sidestreet>Woodridge Street</sidestreet>
      </thoroughfare>
      <thoroughfare name="Bankhead">
           <sidestreet>Tollgate Road</sidestreet>
           <sidestreet>Oak Drive</sidestreet>
      </thoroughfare>
</parkway>
```

The XPath expression using the contains() function will have a node test for a <thoroughfare> that contains a predicate testing for true if the children of that <thoroughfare> have the desired Street component in their names.

```
//thoroughfare//*[contains(., 'Street')]
```

or

```
<xsl:template match="/">
    <xsl:value-of select="//thoroughfare//*[contains(.,
    'Street')]" />
</xsl:template>
```

The result would be the string value of the node that contains Street, or Woodridge Street. We are simply looking for any descendent of <thoroughfare> whose own contents—designated by the "." abbreviation given as the first argument to contains()—contain Street. We could also get the name of that <thoroughfare> by selecting on its attribute value.

```
//thoroughfare/@name[//*[contains(., 'Street')]]
```

or

```
<xsl:template match="/">
      <xsl:value-of select="//thoroughfare/@name[//*[contains(.,
      'Street')]]" />
</xsl:template>
```

This gives the value of any attribute (@) called name, which is part of a <thoroughfare> whose descendent contains the word Street somewhere in it. The return would be Whitesburg Drive. Thus, with the contains() function, you can include or exclude various nodes and strings from the output result based on the presence or absence of a particular set of characters.

5.3.10 The `starts-with()` Function

The starts-with() function provides a way to test a string for a starting value. Although this function is in the string core function group, it has the return type of *boolean*. It will only return a Boolean true or false answer. It requires two string arguments, as shown in the following function prototype, an input or initial string, and a second argument, which is the string being matched or tested for in the input string. The starts-with() function operates on strings or objects that will be converted to strings prior to processing.

Function: *boolean* **starts-with**(*string, string*)

Function Name	*Core Function Group*	*Returns*	*Arguments*	*Argument Type*
`starts-with()`	String	Boolean	String	required
			String	required

The `starts-with()` function is an existential function because, while it is used to match on strings, it returns a Boolean true or false value, not the string. It is actually testing for the *existence* of a substring within the string. It acts somewhat like a position-specific `contains()` function, checking to see if the string contains a substring, but specifically at the beginning of the string. For example, `starts-with('xml', 'x')` will result in a true value, because `xml` starts with an `x`.

On the other hand, the following expression from Markup City will result in a false value:

```
starts-with(//block, 'x')
```

This function call returns a false because the expression is testing to see if the string that is the result of the node-set conversion, which yields `Panorama Street`, starts with an `x`, which is false.

The arguments to `starts-with()` are the same as for `contains()`. The first is a input string and the second is the required match test. The distinction, of course, is that `starts-with()` can only return true if the test string in the second argument is matched in exact order by the corresponding first characters of the string in the first argument. As above, if the second argument is an empty string, the result is true, but if the first argument is empty, the result is true only if the second argument is also empty.

As long as there is a match in the first argument, beginning with its first character, then the processor will continue testing character-by-character until all the characters of the second set have been matched in order, and the return is true. It stands to reason, then, if the second argument is longer than the first, there can only be a return of false, because all its characters cannot be matched.

5.3.11 The `string-length()` Function

The `string-length()` function counts the number of characters in the initial string. It will take the string supplied in the argument—or the current node if no argument is supplied, converted to a string—and return the number of characters the string contains. The `string-length()` function is the only string function that returns a number. It takes one optional string argument, as shown in the following function prototype. Like most string functions, it operates on strings or any object that will be converted to a string prior to processing.

`Function: number string-length(string?)`

Function Name	*Core Function Group*	*Returns*	*Arguments*	*Argument Type*
`string-length()`	String	Number	String	optional

The `string-length()` function, because it returns a number, can be used in equivalence tests, using the various number operators such as less-than, equals, greater-than, and so on. It can also be manipulated by other functions that act on numbers.

We can use the `string-length()` function, as shown in Example 5–15, if we want to take the names of our `<block>`s and automatically center them on a printed page (assuming that we don't have automatic centering on our printer). We would start with the length of the longest block name, in this case `Old Chimney Road`, which is the fifth `<block>`.

The result of this expression is 16. Normally, a page is 80 characters wide, so we would subtract 16 from 80, which would be 64, then divide by 2, which is 32. So we would need to start our centered title on the thirty-second character of the page. If we wanted to list all of them, we could work with `<xsl:for-each>` and use a similar expression with `string-length()`.

Example 5–15 : Using the `string-length()` function.

INPUT:

```
<?xml version="1.0"?>
<boulevard>
            <block>Panorama Street</block>
            <block>Highland Plaza</block>
            <block>Hutchens Avenue</block>
            <block>Wildwood Drive</block>
            <block>Old Chimney Road</block>
            <block>Carrol Circle</block>
</boulevard>
```

FUNCTION:

```
string-length(//boulevard//block[5])
```

TEMPLATE RULE:

```
<xsl:template match="/">
   <xsl:value-of select="string-length(//boulevard//block[5])" />
</xsl:template>
```

> **NOTE** Character entity references, such as ` ` or `<`, for the non-breaking space and for the less-than symbol, respectively, will be counted as one character because the entities that represent those characters are resolved prior to processing; the entities themselves are not strings according to the `string-length()` function's argument evaluation protocol.

5.4 Boolean Core Function Group

The Boolean core function group deals with all four kinds of XPath objects, however, the results are always converted to a Boolean. The Boolean functions build upon principles that lay at the core of all programming languages, prepositional logic and artificial intelligence. Boolean functions serve as binary operators—true or false—that act as switches in the course of an XPath function expression. They determine whether a given context's content meets a specific criteria and, depending upon the outcome and syntax, whether the evaluation of the expression will continue.

All five Boolean functions have a function return type of Boolean. Accordingly, they are discussed in order, with respect to the type of arguments they accept, beginning with the `boolean()` function itself, which requires an argument of general type object, that is converted to a Boolean by the evaluation of the function. Next are treated two functions that take no arguments, the `false()` and `true()` functions. There is a unique `lang()` function, which simply tests if the given language of the context—furnished as a required string argument—matches the `xml:lang` attribute on the context node. The `xml:lang` is not treated specially by XSLT since there is an XSLT specific attribute (`lang`) that covers the same functionality. The XSLT `lang` attribute is discussed in Chapter 9. Finally, there is a Boolean-to-Boolean function, the `not()` function, which requires a Boolean argument.

5.4.1 The `boolean()` Function

The `boolean()` function is the fundamental conversion function for rendering a binary—true or false—value from any type of object furnished as its required argument. Very much like the `string()` function, the `boolean()` function is implicitly used in any function that returns a Boolean. It operates "under the hood" of many functions, such as `contains()` and `starts-with()`. It will rarely be used other than to deliberately convert an object to a Boolean in some context other than one in which a given function already does so by the nature of its specified function return type.

`Function: `*`boolean`*` `**`boolean`**`(`*`object`*`)`

Function Name	*Core Function Group*	*Returns*	*Arguments*	*Argument Type*
`boolean()`	Boolean	Boolean	Object	required

Since this function is rarely called explicitly, concocting a representative example is difficult and prompts a certain punchiness on the part of the authors. Listeners—with either love or hate—to Rush Limbaugh will notice a frequent, and arguably funky, guitar riff when he returns to the microphone from a station or sponsor break. This song's primary refrain is "I went back to Ohio, and my city was gone."

If we went back to the original Markup City (Example 5–4) on the aforementioned dark and stormy night, we might have visibility problems and simply want to know if the city was there at all. We could expeditiously test for the document element of `<main>` using `boolean()`, as shown in Example 5–16.

Example 5–16 : Boolean test for existance.

```
boolean(main)
```

or

```
<xsl:template match="/">
      <xsl:value-of select="boolean(main)" />
</xsl:template>
```

This simply asks, is the main element there? Since the city is indeed there, we get the result of `true`. Then we could ask if it has a given kind of road, as follows.

```
boolean(//block | //lane | //sidestreet)
```

or

```
<xsl:template match="/">
      <xsl:value-of select="boolean(//block | //lane |
      //sidestreet)" />
</xsl:template>
```

This will return true because there are blocks. Using an `or` operand (here abbreviated with `|`), as soon as a true case is found, evaluation is discontinued. We could easily make this false as follows.

```
boolean(//block and //lane and //sidestreet)
```

or

```
<xsl:template match="/">
      <xsl:value-of select="boolean(//block and //lane and
```

```
            //sidestreet)" />
    </xsl:template>
```

When evaluating `and` operands, as soon as one turns up false, the rest of the expression is not evaluated and the answer returned is false.

5.4.2 Boolean Conversion Rules

The basic criteria for evaluating a `boolean()` function according to object type is as follows:

1. **Node-sets** – As long as there is a node in the node-set, or it is non-empty, this argument will permit the `boolean()` function to return true.
2. **Strings** – As long as the string is of a length other than zero, this argument will permit the `boolean()` function to return true.
3. **Numbers** – In this case, we see some degree of interpretation of the rather esoteric positive and negative zeros: as long as the number is neither type of zero, and is not NaN, is not "not a number," or is anything other than a number, this argument will permit the `boolean()` function to return true.
4. **Other** – Any other object is converted to a Boolean according to rules dependant upon its respective type. If this is unsettling, rest assured that the lion's share of objects in XPath will always be of the four basic types with hard-to-imagine exception.

5.4.3 The `false()` Function

The `false()` function returns a Boolean only of the type false. It accepts no arguments, as shown in the following function prototype.

Function: *boolean* **false()**

Function Name	*Core Function Group*	*Returns*	*Arguments*	*Argument Type*
`false()`	Boolean	Boolean	None	none

Although it is not very useful alone, this function can be used in combination with other functions and in equivalence tests. For example, the function `string()` expects an object as an argument, but passing in the word `false` results in a null string. Passing in `false()` results in the string value of `false`.

5.4.4 The `true()` Function

The `true()` function returns a Boolean only of the type true. It accepts no arguments, but applies to the current node.

`Function: boolean true()`

Function Name	*Core Function Group*	*Returns*	*Arguments*	*Argument Type*
`true()`	Boolean	Boolean	None	—

Although it is not very useful alone, this function can be used in combination with other functions and in equivalence tests. For example, the function `string()` expects an object as an argument, but passing in the word `true` results in a null string. Passing in `true()` results in the string value of `true`.

5.4.5 The `lang()` Function

The Boolean `lang()` function is used to verify the current language as specified in the context node, or an ancestor of the context node, with the `xml:lang` attribute. The `lang()` function operates on a string, provided as its required argument, and returns either a true or a false Boolean when evaluated. The following function prototype describes the structure of the `lang()` function.

Function: *boolean* **lang**(*string*)

Function Name	*Core Function Group*	*Returns*	*Arguments*	*Argument Type*
`lang()`	Boolean	Boolean	String	required

When a node has a language declared with the `xml:lang` attribute, this information is available to the node and all its descendants, and can be tested for using the `lang()` function. The language codes tested for are either two-letter codes specified in the ISO 639 table of language abbreviations, or a code with a subcode for country specific languages, specified in ISO 3166.[7] If there is no language specified, the `lang()` function returns false.

Regrettably, there is nothing intuitive about this function. It does not check the actual strings of the node to see if they are, indeed, French, for instance. So, it is worth noting that just because someone declares a chapter to be in Greek (with `<chapter xml:lang="gr">`), the entire following text could be English, and using the function call `lang("gr")` will still return true. In effect, regardless what kind of string content is contained in the `<chapter xml:lang="gr">` node, the XSLT processor will rightly say, "It's all Greek to me," (or, of course, more literally and less euphemistically, true).

The `lang()` function is case insensitive and ignores suffixes when testing the value of the language. For example, from the XSLT specification, the following will always be true for `lang("en")`.

```
<para xml:lang="en"/>
<div xml:lang="en"><para/></div>
<para xml:lang="EN"/>
<para xml:lang="en-us"/>
```

5.4.6 The `not()` Function

The `not()` function returns true when its argument is false, and false if its argument is true. The single required argument is a Boolean, as shown in the following function prototype. The `not()` function operates on Boolean objects, or any object that can be converted to a Boolean value prior to processing.

7. See http://www.w3.org/TR/1998/REC-xml-19980210#ISO3166.

Function: *boolean* **not**(*Boolean*)

Function Name	*Core Function Group*	*Returns*	*Arguments*	*Argument Type*
not()	Boolean	Boolean	Boolean	required

With the Boolean not() function, a great deal of contradictory layering can be strung together, producing amusing—or infuriating, depending on your relative patience with extended contradictions—expressions. For example, not(true()) returns a false value, while not(false()) returns a true value. We will use the XML in Example 5–17 for the following examples.

Example 5–17 : XML for the not() function.

```
<?xml version="1.0"?>
<parkway>
      <thoroughfare>Governor Drive</thoroughfare>
      <thoroughfare name="Whitesburg Drive">
            <sidestreet>Bob Wallace Avenue</sidestreet>
            <block>1st Street</block>
            <block>2nd Street</block>
            <block>3rd Street</block>
            <sidestreet>Woodridge Street</sidestreet>
      </thoroughfare>
      <thoroughfare name="Bankhead">
            <sidestreet>Tollgate Road</sidestreet>
            <block>First Street</block>
            <block>Second Street</block>
            <block>Third Street</block>
            <sidestreet>Oak Drive</sidestreet>
      </thoroughfare>
</parkway>
```

Using the expression //thoroughfare[block] we could search for only thoroughfares that contained block elements. If we add a not()

to the predicate, we could then search for only thoroughfares that did not contain blocks.

```
<xsl:template match="/">
     <xsl:value-of select="//thoroughfare[not(block)]"/>
</xsl:template>
```

This would select the first thoroughfare that did not contain a <block>, or Governor Drive.

In another case, we might want to make sure we only use the <block>s that have a numerical value, for example 3rd Street, but not Third Street. The following XPath expression looks for <block> descendents, using `substring()` and `number()` functions, as well as the `not()` function, as follows.

```
number(substring(//block, 1, 1)) = not(NaN)
```

or

```
<xsl:template match="/">
    <xsl:value-of select="number(substring(., 1, 1)) =
    not(NaN)" />
</xsl:template>
```

This expression will return the value true for every <block> element that contains a digit as the first character. The logic behind this expression can be unpacked (inside-out) as shown in Table 5–5.

Table 5–5 Possible function returns using number operators on Markup City from Example 5–15

Function Name	*Object Returned*	*Markup City Equivalent*
`//block`	Returns the string of the node	1st Street
`substring(., 1, 1)`	Returns the 1st character of the text node	"1"
`number(substring(., 1, 1))`	Converts the string "1" to a number	1

Table 5–5 Possible function returns using number operators on Markup City from Example 5–15(continued)

Function Name	*Object Returned*	*Markup City Equivalent*
`number(substring(., 1, 1)) = not(NaN)`	Tests to see if the number resulting from the `substring()` and `number()` functions is not equal to NaN (not a number) using the `not()` function	true

The reversal of NaN using the `not()` function returns true for any number, which is the value we want if the first character actually is a number. Testing `not(NaN)` asks, in fact, if the argument's value is not something that is not a number. In other words, is it a number? The only other way to ask if something *is* a number would be to ask if the starting position, for instance, contained (using `contains()`) 1, 2, 3, 4, 5, 6, 7, 8, 9, or 0. This is a long and clearly inefficient way to make such determinations and is open to many possible errors. It is simplest to remember that to ask if something *is* a number, ask if it is *not* "not a number," or `not(NaN)`.

5.5 Number Core Function Group

The number functions all return a number as their function return type. It contains five functions, one of which, `number()`, serves as the fundamental conversion of any object to a number.

The five functions in the number core function group are covered below, beginning with the `number()` conversion function, which takes an optional object argument to be converted to a number. This function is similar to `string()` and `boolean()` in that it works ubiquitously under the hood while not frequently being explicitly called itself. Following this is the `sum()` function, which serves to convert a required node-set object's string value to a number. The remaining three functions include a top-end test of a given numerical sequence, the `ceiling()` function, a bottom-end test, the `floor()` function, and the `round()` function, to which we referred earlier.

5.5.1 The `number()` Function

The `number()` function is the primary conversion function used to convert an object to a number. It has one optional argument of type object, as shown in the following function prototype. If no argument is supplied, the default is the current node.

Function: *number* **number**(*object?*)

Function Name	*Core Function Group*	*Returns*	*Arguments*	*Argument Type*
`number()`	Number	Number	Object	optional

The `number()` function is implicitly used in any other function that returns a number, such as the `count()` function in the node-set core function group or the `string-length()` function in the string core function group. Accordingly, `number()` is not often called on its own.

Because the argument to the `number()` function is of type object, any of the four object types, node-set, string, Boolean, or number can be used. Converting each of these object types to a number has a specific set of rules, which are covered in the next section.

5.5.2 Number Conversion Rules

The four object types, node-set, string, Boolean, or number can be converted to a number following the conversion rules specified by the W3C XPath recommendation (section 4.4) as follows.

1. *A string that consists of optional whitespace followed by an optional minus sign followed by a Number followed by*

whitespace is converted to the IEEE 754 number that is nearest (according to the IEEE 754 round-to-nearest rule) to the mathematical value represented by the string; any other string is converted to NaN.

This basically says that if the string looks like a number, it is converted to that number. Whitespace is stripped, and the value is given for that number according to IEEE 754 and rounding; otherwise it is not a number, and the string is NaN in its numerical value.For example, using our Markup City, *`number(//block)`* will return the value NaN because the resolved value of *`//block`* returns a string that is not numbers, the text value of the node. If the resolved value of an expression is a string that looks like a number, it can be converted to a number for use by other functions that are expecting a number. For example, *`number('1235')`* returns the number 1235, which can then be interpreted by another function.

A more useful example includes using `number(substring('1st Street', 1, 1))` to extract the street number from the element `<block>1st Street</block>`, using the `substring()` and `number()` functions.

This would return the number 1. If you did not use the `number()` function, the returned value would be the string "1."

2. *Boolean true is converted to 1; boolean false is converted to 0.*

   This rule follows basic "bit" rules where 0 is off and 1 is on; a 1 (the existence of something) will always be true, a 0 (the absence of something) will always be false.[8] Recall from our `contains()` example that we had an expression that returned a true value. If we wrap that same function in the `number()` function, `number(contains('xml', 'x'))`, the result will be to convert the string `true` to a number 1.

8. What that "something" is can be potentially fuel conversations on existentialism. What does it mean to be something that signifies nothing? One has to wonder, do bits and bytes ask "why am I here?"

3. *A node-set is first converted to a string as if by a call to the* `string()` *function and then converted in the same way as a string argument.*

   Node-sets are converted to a string according to the string conversion rules in Section 5.3.2, in which the node-set's first node is converted to a string and its string-value is then converted to a number according to the string-to-number conversion rules (see 1 above). Again, if the resulting string is not a number, the value will be NaN.

4. *An object of a type other than the four basic types is converted to a number in a way that is dependent on that type.*

   The fact that there can be other types of objects leaves the interpretation of the conversion of those objects up to the creator of those objects. If a new object type is created and managed, for example, by an extension element, the namespace for that extension should supply the conversion rules for that object.

5.5.3 The **sum()** Function

The `sum()` function adds the value of each node in a node-set, after it has been converted to a number. This of course means that the nodes in the node-set being converted must contain numbers or digits; otherwise the result of this function will be NaN. The `sum()` function returns a number as a function return type. It requires a single argument of a type node-set, as shown in the following function prototype. The node-set supplied will be converted to a number according to the conversion rules for node-sets, mentioned in the previous section on `number()`.

`Function: number sum(node-set)`

Function Name	*Core Function Group*	*Returns*	*Arguments*	*Argument Type*
`sum()`	Number	number	Node-set	required

If our Markup City had yet another set of streets, perhaps in the French Quarter, called `<rue>`s, we could then use the `sum()` function to add up the contents of the `<rue>` elements,[9] as shown in Example 5–18.

Example 5–18 : XML for the `sum()` function example.

```
<parkway>
     <thoroughfare>Governor Drive</thoroughfare>
     <thoroughfare name="Whitesburg Drive">
          <sidestreet>Bob Wallace Avenue</sidestreet>
          <block>1st Street</block>
          <block>2nd Street</block>
          <block>3rd Street</block>
          <sidestreet>Woodridge Street</sidestreet>
     </thoroughfare>
     <thoroughfare name="Concord">
          <rue>47</rue>
          <rue>48</rue>
          <rue>49</rue>
     </thoroughfare>
</parkway>
```

FUNCTION:

```
sum(//rue)
```

TEMPLATE RULE:

```
<xsl:template match="/">
<xsl:value-of select="sum(//rue)"/>
</xsl:template>
```

Using the `sum()` function would return the value of the sum of 47, 48, and 49, which is equal to 144.

9. This summing up of a node-set could get quite complicated if there were elements of the same name nested inside each other, for example if our Markup City was in Bangkok, where a side street is called a soi and a soi can get big enough to have its own branching sois.

5.5.4 The **`ceiling()`** Function

The `ceiling()` function finds the nearest integer—that is, not a decimal number—larger than the number supplied as its argument. In effect, it works like a rounding function that always rounds up. It has one required argument, which is of type number, as shown in the following function prototype.

The `ceiling()` function is one of a pair with a complimentary function, the `floor()` function, discussed immediately below. The `ceiling()` function operates on numbers or objects that are converted to numbers prior to processing.

Function: *number* **ceiling**(*number*)

Function Name	*Core Function Group*	*Returns*	*Arguments*	*Argument Type*
`ceiling()`	Number	number	Number	required

In effect, the `ceiling()` function is like the `round()` function, except the `ceiling()` function will find the nearest possible integer that is *greater* than the input argument. For example, the function call `ceiling(2.8)`, would return 3; the `ceiling()` for 2.1 is also 3. Negative numbers work the same as rounding, finding the nearest negative integer greater than the argument; `ceiling(-36.3)` would be –36, and so on.

The `ceiling()` function is similar to `round()`, except that `ceiling()` always rounds up, whereas the `round()` function rounds up or down, depending on the number.

5.5.5 The **`floor()`** Function

The `floor()` function provides a sort of backward rounding functionality. It finds the nearest integer—that is, not a decimal number—smaller than the number supplied as its argument. Where normal rounding goes upward or downward, depending on the number, `floor()` always rounds down, finding the smallest integer nearest to the input argument. The `floor()` function has one required argument, which is a number, as shown in the following function prototype. It is one of a pair with a complimentary function, the `ceiling()` function, and performs the reverse of `ceiling()`.

```
Function: number floor(number)
```

Function Name	*Core Function Group*	*Returns*	*Arguments*	*Argument Type*
`floor()`	Number	Number	Number	required

For example, the function call `floor(2.8)` returns a value of 2, and `floor(2.1)` is also 2. Using `floor()` with negative numbers, the rounding goes to the nearest integer in the opposite direction. For example, `floor(-36.3)` gives –37, which is the nearest integer still smaller than –36.3.

The `floor()` function is similar to `round()`, except that `floor()` always rounds down, whereas the `round()` function rounds up or down, depending on the number.

5.5.6 The `round()` Function

The `round()` function returns a number that is the result of rounding according to the rules specified in IEEE 754. It requires a single number input argument and operates on numbers or objects that are converted to numbers prior to processing. The following function prototype shows the structure of the `round()` function.

```
Function: number round(number)
```

Function Name	*Core Function Group*	*Returns*	*Arguments*	*Argument Type*
`round()`	Number	Number	Number	required

In XPath, rounding functions work the way you would normally expect rounding to work. The decimal counting idea of "5 or more rounds upward" is observed consistently. Accordingly, when using the function call `substring(1.5)`, the result would be rounded up to 2, since 1.5 is not an integer, but 2 is. The rounding is always done to the nearest integer. Obviously, then, 1.8 would also round to 2, and 1.4 would round down to 1.

Things get more complicated with negative integers, however. An input argument of –0.5 up to 0 rounds to negative zero. Positive zero is always positive zero after rounding, and the same is true of negative zero. The same also holds for positive and negative infinity, which remain positive and negative infinity, respectively, when rounded. If the input argument is not a number, or NaN, then it remains NaN.

Building New XML Documents with XSLT

- Creating new XML elements
- `<xsl:element>`
- `<xsl:attribute>`
- Literal result elements (LREs)
- Attribute value templates (AVTs)
- `<xsl:processing-instruction>`
- `<xsl:comment>`
- `<xsl:namespace-alias>`

6

One of the most convenient features of XSLT stylesheets is the ability to generate new content in the process of transformation. This generated content can be derived through a series of XPath expressions in combination with LREs, text that you add, or with other elements in XSLT yet to be introduced.

There are many ways to work with the existing structure and content of an XML document. However, there are only a few specific XSLT elements that deal directly with the creation of new elements and content. In this chapter, we will look at how content can be created using LREs, as well as the following XSLT elements: `<xsl:element>`, which is used to generate new XML elements; `<xsl:attribute>`, which is used to generate new XML attributes; `<xsl:attribute-set>`, which is used to create a group of attributes; and `<xsl:text>`, which is used to generate text. We will also discuss attribute value templates (AVTs), which provide the capability to use expressions in attributes. At the end of this chapter, we will also discuss two elements that are used to generate processing-instructions and comments. Finally, the last section will discuss the use of the `<xsl:namespace-alias>` element, which is useful when generating namespaced elements using LREs.

There are two specific ways to add new elements: either using LREs or using the `<xsl:element>` element. While both methods generate new elements, there are some specific nuances that may make one method preferable over the other, depending on the circumstances. Specifically, dealing with namespaces and attributes may be easier using `<xsl:element>` rather than LREs. Both methods are presented in the following sections.

6.1 Creating Elements with LREs

Elements that are not part of the input source document can be created using a literal result element, also known as an LRE. LREs are XML elements that are not part of the XSL specification or extension set of elements. They are "literal" elements that are passed through to the output, with the same element-type name and any attributes that are added by the stylesheet. LREs are added by the author of the stylesheet and placed according to the desired output. They are considered templates and can contain instruction elements, but cannot contain top-level elements. An LRE can also be used as the document element of the stylesheet, if the attribute defining it as a stylesheet is used.

An LRE generates an element of the same name in the output tree whenever the template rule that contains it is invoked. A common use of this is to transform XML to HTML, where the LRE is the HTML element specified for output.

For example, if your source XML refers to paragraphs with a `<para>` element, you might want to change them to the HTML `<p>` element by typing the `<p>` directly in the template, as in Example 6–1.

Example 6–1 : Simple transformation of element-type names using LREs.

```
<xsl:template match="para">
     <p>
          <xsl:apply-templates />
     </p>
</xsl:template>
```

In this template, `<p>` is an LRE. The template matches any element called `<para>` and outputs a `<p>` element in its place. The `<xsl:apply-templates>` instruction can be considered as an instruction to send any children of <para> on through to the next template rule, or output if there are no more template rules.

6.2 The <xsl:element> Instruction Element

The <xsl:element> instruction element provides a more structured approach to adding new XML elements directly to the output result tree. The following element model definition shows the correct structure of the <xsl:element> instruction element:

```
<!-- Category: instruction -->
<xsl:element
  name = { qname }
  namespace = { uri-reference }
  use-attribute-sets = qnames>
  <!-- Content: template -->
</xsl:element>
```

The <xsl:element> instruction element has three attributes, one of which is mandatory: the name attribute. The name attribute contains the element-type name of the new element in the result tree. This attribute is required because an element without an element-type name is not valid XML, and using the <xsl:element> implies that the output will be either XML or HTML.

> **NOTE** Using <xsl:element> when the output type is text will cause the new element's tags to be ignored (not even sent to the output). LREs will also be ignored. The output type is specified with the <xsl:output> element's method attribute, discussed in Chapter 10.

The optional `namespace` attribute permits the declaration of a URI, if the new element requires a namespace to be shown in the result. In addition, `<xsl:element>` contains the optional `use-attribute-sets` attribute, which allows the new element to reference a pre-determined set of attributes (see Section 6.4).

In our Markup City in Example 6–2, the `<xsl:element>` element could enable the city planners to begin drawing neighborhood grids.

The template rule shown adds houses to each block using the `<xsl:element>` with an element-type name (specified in the `name` attribute) of `house`. This may seem a little over-complicated, since the same effect can easily be accomplished using LREs as follows:

```
<xsl:template match="block">
     <block>
          <house>1</house>
          <house>2</house>
          <house>3</house>
          <house>4</house>
          <house>5</house>
     </block>
</xsl:template>
```

However, the advantage of using `<xsl:element>` instead of an LRE is that the name of the new element can be calculated using expressions, which are not allowed in the start or end tags of an LRE. The name attribute of `<xsl:element>` is interpreted by the XSLT processor as an AVT (see Section 6.6.1 for more information about AVTs). Using AVTs allows the content of the name attribute to be an XPath expression, as long as the value is surrounded by curly braces `{ }`. For example, instead of naming our houses just `house`, we could compute the value of the element-type name using an expression:

```
<xsl:element name="{concat(translate(ancestor::thoroughfare/@name, ' ',
'-'), '-', 'house')}">
```

The result of this expression would return a different element-type name depending on which `<thoroughfare>` the `<block>` is in. The value of the `name` attribute of each `<thoroughfare>` is put through a `translate()` to convert the spaces to dashes. Then, the value is concatenated with a dash and the word "`house`." The two new element-type names are `<Whitesburg-Drive-house>` and `<Bankhead-house>`.

Example 6–2 : Using `<xsl:element>` to add houses to each block.

INPUT:

```
<?xml version="1.0"?>
<parkway>
            <thoroughfare>Governor Drive</thoroughfare>
            <thoroughfare name="Whitesburg Drive">
                  <sidestreet name="Bob Wallace Avenue">
                         <block>1st Street</block>
                         <block>2nd Street</block>
                         <block>3rd Street</block>
                  </sidestreet>
                  <sidestreet>Woodridge Street</sidestreet>
            </thoroughfare>
            <thoroughfare name="Bankhead">
                  <sidestreet name="Tollgate Road">
                         <block>First Street</block>
                         <block>Second Street</block>
                         <block>Third Street</block>
                  </sidestreet>
                  <sidestreet>Oak Drive</sidestreet>
            </thoroughfare>
</parkway>
```

TEMPLATE RULE:

```
<xsl:template match="block">
      <block>
            <xsl:element name="house">1</xsl:element>
            <xsl:element name="house">2</xsl:element>
            <xsl:element name="house">3</xsl:element>
            xsl:element name="house">4</xsl:element>
            <xsl:element name="house">5</xsl:element>
      </block>
      </xsl:template>
```

OUTPUT:

```
<block>
<house>1</house>
<house>2</house>
<house>3</house>
<house>4</house>
<house>5</house>
</block>
      <!-- other blocks removed for brevity -->
```

Expressions are not allowed in an LRE name because the special characters in an expression are not valid XML and are not allowed in an element-type name. For example, if we wanted to just repeat the element `<block>` without typing "`<block>`," it would seem to make sense to use `<name()>` to extract the name of the element, but this would cause an error. This format is not a valid LRE because parentheses `()` are not allowed in element-type names, and the XSLT processor would attempt to interpret `<name()>` as a literal XML element. You could, however, use the name() function as follows:

```
<xsl:element name="{name()}">
```

Once new elements are created, using either `<xsl:element>` or LREs, you can add attributes as necessary using the `<xsl:attribute>` element. Note that `<xsl:attribute>` can also be used to add attributes to elements generated or copied from the input with other XSLT elements; its use is not restricted to just new elements.

6.3 Creating Attributes with the <xsl:attribute> Instruction Element

One of the most useful instruction elements is the `<xsl:attribute>` element, which, as its name indicates, creates attributes. It has two attributes, as shown in the following element model definition: the `name` attribute, which establishes the new attribute's name, and the `namespace` attribute, which can give a namespace URI for the attribute, if necessary.

```
<!-- Category: instruction -->
<xsl:attribute
  name = { qname }
  namespace = { uri-reference }>
  <!-- Content: template -->
</xsl:attribute>
```

Using `<xsl:attribute>` is a good example of how XSLT stylesheets, as well-formed XML data instances themselves, benefit from and can be interpreted by means of XML syntax rules for the logical syntax of their structure. Based on the placement of the `<xsl:attribute>` element, the attributes created will be inserted into the element whether an LRE or otherwise in which the `<xsl:attribute>` instruction element is nested, as Example 6–3 illustrates. Assume that we want to add an address attribute to the houses in our previous example.

Example 6–3 : Adding attributes with `<xsl:attribute>`.

TEMPLATE RULE:

```
<xsl:template match="block">
    <block>
    <xsl:element name="house">
          <xsl:attribute name="address">1</xsl:attribute>
    </xsl:element>
    <xsl:element name="house">
          <xsl:attribute name="address">2</xsl:attribute>
    </xsl:element>
    <xsl:element name="house">
          <xsl:attribute name="address">3</xsl:attribute>
    </xsl:element>
    <xsl:element name="house">
          <xsl:attribute name="address">4</xsl:attribute>
    </xsl:element>
    <xsl:element name="house">
          <xsl:attribute name="address">5</xsl:attribute>
    </xsl:element>
    </block>
</xsl:template>
```

OUTPUT:

```
<block>
    <house address="1"/>
    <house address="2"/>
    <house address="3"/>
    <house address="4"/>
    <house address="5"/>
</block>
```

The result of this stylesheet adds the address attribute to each new house. Note that the XSLT processor automatically converts empty elements to the proper format.

Again, this example can be accomplished using a few LREs, but the usage demonstrated in the previous section with AVTs also applies to `<xsl:attribute>`. The `name` attribute value can be an expression when used as an AVT by adding curly braces { }. As an added bonus, the content of the attribute value to be generated can now be calculated using any of the XSLT elements that are valid within a template. This is because the content of the `<xsl:attribute>` element is defined as a *template*.

A more complex usage, as shown in Example 6–4, might involve generating an address using the `position()` function to find out which `<block>` the houses are on. See Section 5.2.6.1 for an explanation of how context affects the value of the `position()`.

Example 6–4 : Creating house numbers with `<xsl:attribute>` using `concat()`, and `position()`.

TEMPLATE:

```
<xsl:template match="block">
<block>
<xsl:element name="house">
<xsl:attribute name="address"><xsl:value-of
select="concat(position(),
'01')"/></xsl:attribute>
</xsl:element>
<xsl:element name="house">
<xsl:attribute name="address"><xsl:value-of
select="concat(position(), '02')"/></xsl:attribute>
</xsl:element>
<xsl:element name="house">
<xsl:attribute name="address"><xsl:value-of
select="concat(position(), '03')"/></xsl:attribute>
</xsl:element>
<xsl:element name="house">
<xsl:attribute name="address"><xsl:value-of
select="concat(position(), '04')"/></xsl:attribute>
</xsl:element>
<xsl:element name="house">
<xsl:attribute name="address"><xsl:value-of
select="concat(position(), '05')"/></xsl:attribute>
</xsl:element>
</block>
</xsl:template>
```

Example 6–4 : Creating house numbers with `<xsl:attribute>` using `concat()`, and `position()` (continued).

OUTPUT:

```
<?xml version="1.0" encoding="utf-8"?>
<block>
<house address="101"/>
<house address="102"/>
<house address="103"/>
<house address="104"/>
<house address="105"/>
</block>
<block>
<house address="201"/>
<house address="202"/>
<house address="203"/>
<house address="204"/>
<house address="205"/>
</block>
<block>
<house address="301"/>
<house address="302"/>
<house address="303"/>
<house address="304"/>
<house address="305"/>
</block>
<block>
<house address="401"/>
<house address="402"/>
<house address="403"/>
<house address="404"/>
<house address="405"/>
</block>
<block>
<house address="501"/>
<house address="502"/>
<house address="503"/>
<house address="504"/>
<house address="505"/>
</block>
<block>
<house address="601"/>
<house address="602"/>
<house address="603"/>
<house address="604"/>
<house address="605"/>
</block>
```

The resulting XML file contains the new `<house>`s with their appropriate number, based on the number of the `<block>` they are on. The `position()` function gets the number of the current `<block>`, and the `concat()` function combines it with the number of the house for each `<house>`.

Some of the city planners have approved the addition of several homes and addresses to Woodridge Street, and we want to make `Woodridge Street` the value of a `name` attribute for `<sidestreet>`, so that `<sidestreet>` can also contain several `<house>` elements, as shown in Example 6–5.

Example 6–5 : Creating attributes with `<xsl:attribute>`.

TEMPLATE RULE:

```
<xsl:template match="//sidestreet[contains(., 'Woodridge')]">
<sidestreet>
<xsl:attribute name="name"><xsl:value-of
select="text()"/></xsl:attribute>
      <house><xsl:attribute name="address">1100</
xsl:attribute>
      </house>
      <house><xsl:attribute name="address">1101</
xsl:attribute>
      </house>
      <house><xsl:attribute name="address">1102</
xsl:attribute>
      </house>
</sidestreet>
</xsl:template>
```

OUTPUT:

```
<sidestreet name="Woodridge Street">
<house address="1100"/>
<house address="1101"/>
<house address="1102"/>
</sidestreet>
```

Here we are using LREs to create the houses, and adding the attribute directly to each LRE with the `<xsl:attribute>` element. We could then add other contents to the `<house>` elements as needed. Notice that we did *not* use `<xsl:apply-templates>`, and so the original text data or PCDATA that listed `Woodridge Street` as the only content of `<sidestreet>` was *not* output again as content of the new `<sidestreet>`.

The nesting of `<xsl:attribute>` in the `<house>` LREs serves to situate the resulting `address` attribute inside, or as part of, the `<house>` in the output result tree. Remember from Chapter 1 that the parent of an attribute is the element that contains it, but at the same time, the attribute is not and cannot be considered a child of the element itself. Accordingly, then, nesting the `<xsl:attribute>` element within the element makes the attribute part of the new element.

> **NOTE** The `<xsl:attribute>` element must always appear first inside an LRE or `<xsl:element>`, prior to any additional LREs or instruction elements; otherwise, the attribute being defined is ignored in the output.

6.3.1 Using `<xsl:attribute>` with Namespaces

The `<xsl:attribute>` instruction provides a way to declare a namespace for the attribute being created, using the optional `namespace` attribute to declare it. The value of the `namespace` attribute can be an expression, in the form of an AVT, but it should resolve to a URI.

There is no special provision (no attribute) for declaring a prefix for the namespace that is being declared, but it can be added in the `name` attribute, using the form `name="prefix:element-name"` as the declaration. However, the XSLT processor decides whether to use a prefix defined in this manner. If the prefix defined for an attribute happens to be `xmlns`, the XSLT processor will not generate the namespace in the result tree. The `xmlns` is a reserved prefix and should not be used in an `<xsl:attribute>` name attribute. In Example 6–6, we add a namespace when declaring an attribute by simply adding the namespace attribute to the `<xsl:attribute>` element; but in this case, we do not add a prefix.

The resulting `<font>` element has the XSLT processor specific prefix (generated by James Clark's XT) automatically inserted as shown in bold. The namespace URI, `"http://www.our_company.com,"` is clear,

Example 6–6 : Creating a series of HTML font attributes with `<xsl:attribute>` inside LREs.

TEMPLATE RULE:

```
<xsl:template match="/">
<font>
      <xsl:attribute name="fontface">courier</xsl:attribute>
      <xsl:attribute name="size">4</xsl:attribute>
      <xsl:attribute name="our_company_color"
      namespace="http://www.our_company.com">quadraseptic-
chartreuse-
      taupe</xsl:attribute>
</font>
</xsl:template>
```

OUTPUT:

```
<font fontface="courier" size="4"
ns0:our_company_color="quadraseptic-chartreuse-taupe"
xmlns:ns0="http://www.our_company.com"/>
```

as is the defined attribute name, "our_company_color," but the prefix is still up in the air. In fact, the temptation to make the attribute declaration stipulate the prefix`'namespace="xmlns:WRONG='http://www.our_company.com'"'` may seem logical, but is *not* correct. Example 6–7 shows the proper way to declare a prefix for a namespaced attribute.

Example 6–7 : Adding a prefix to a namespace with `<xsl:attribute>`.

```
<font>
<xsl:attribute name="fontface">courier</xsl:attribute>
<xsl:attribute name="size">4</xsl:attribute>
<xsl:attribute name="myprefix:our_company_color"
namespace="http://www.our_company.com">quadraseptic-chartreuse-
taupe</xsl:attribute>
</font>
```

So, the author of the XSLT stylesheet creating a namespaced attribute with `<xsl:attribute>` is at the mercy of the chosen processor as to what prefix will result, even if it is defined correctly. Happily, XT does pick up on the prefix value defined in the name attribute, resulting in:

```
<font fontface="courier" size="4"
myprefix:our_company_color="quadraseptic-chartreuse-taupe"
xmlns:myprefix="http://www.our_company.com"/>
```

Regardless of the range of uses for `<xsl:attribute>`, the variety of possible namespace prefixes, or the values or names for the created attributes being specified, this element provides indispensable functionality for a range of contexts. Most applicably, for industrial-strength applications of XSLT stylesheets, the `<xsl:attribute-set>` element offers additional versatility.

6.4 The `<xsl:attribute-set>` Top-Level Element

The `<xsl:attribute-set>` top-level element provides the ability to set up a group of `<xsl:attribute>` elements that generate attributes that can be inserted collectively into an element in the result tree.

The `<xsl:attribute-set>` element has two attributes: the `name` attribute, which is used to name and call the attribute set created, and the `use-attribute-set` attribute. The allowed content of the `<xsl:attribute-set>` element is zero or more `<xsl:attribute>` elements, as shown in the following element model definition:

```
<!-- Category: top-level-element -->

<xsl:attribute-set

  name = qname

  use-attribute-sets = qnames>

  <!-- Content: xsl:attribute* -->

</xsl:attribute-set>
```

Having a content of zero or more elements means that the `<xsl:attribute-set>` element can be an empty element, but it has the ability to call other `<xsl:attribute-set>` elements and include their content as its own. Note that an empty `<xsl:attribute-set>` element with no `use-attribute-sets` attribute is perfectly valid, but not very useful. A sample DTD element and attribute declaration detailing the structure of `<xsl:attribute-set>` is shown below.

```
<!ELEMENT xsl:attribute-set (xsl:attribute)*>
<!ATTLIST xsl:attribute-set
    name %qname; #REQUIRED
    use-attribute-sets %qnames; #IMPLIED >
```

6.4.1 The `name` Attribute

The value of the name attribute for `<xsl:attribute-set>` is a QName that is used to name the group of attributes. The value of the `name` attribute is the same as the value used for `use-attribute-sets` when the attribute set is being called.

```
ATTRIBUTE:  name NMTOKEN #REQUIRED
VALUE = QName
```

6.4.2 The `use-attribute-sets` Attribute

The attribute `use-attribute-sets` is used to access the content of an `<xsl:attribute-set>` and send the resulting attributes and their values to the result tree. This attribute is also found on two other XSLT elements, `<xsl:element>` and `<xsl:copy>`, and can be used by LRE elements if prefixed with the `xsl` namespace prefix (`xsl:use-attribute-sets`):

```
ATTRIBUTE:  use-attribute-sets NMTOKENS #IMPLIED
VALUE = QNames
```

When used on an `<xsl:attribute-set>` element, the `use-attribute-sets` attribute serves to sort of nest attribute sets. Any attribute set called by another <xsl:attribute-set> is placed before the ones that the calling set defines, if any. For example, if an <xsl:attribute-set> named "calling-set"called an <xsl:attribute-set> named "boilerplate-set," the attributes in the "boilerplate-set" would appear before the attributes in "calling-set," as shown below.

```
<xsl:attribute-set name="calling-set" use-attribute-sets="boilerplate-
set" >
      <xsl:attribute name="att1">Attribute1</xsl:attribute>
</xsl:attribute-set>
<xsl:attribute-set name="boilerplate-set">
      <xsl:attribute name="att2">Attribute2</xsl:attribute>
</xsl:attribute-set>
```

The result of combining these two attribute sets (to the processor) is a single <xsl:attribute-set>, with the <xsl:attribute> elements placed in the calling set as if they were in the same set, but the called attributes appear first, as shown below.

```
<xsl:attribute-set name="calling-set">
      <xsl:attribute name="att2">Attribute2
       </xsl:attribute>
<xsl:attribute name="att1">Attribute1
</xsl:attribute>
</xsl:attribute-set>
```

Of course, you would not see the above combined set because it is an example of how the XSLT processor *sees* the two sets during processing.

6.4.3 Using Attribute Sets with <xsl:attribute-set>

Often in the course of writing an XSLT stylesheet, it is necessary to create additional elements and attributes in the output result tree. There are many times when the same attributes are needed over and over again, although usually with different values. It is therefore convenient to declare such groups of attributes that are likely to be repeatedly utilized in a group, so that they can be inserted all at once by a single named reference, not unlike a macro or subroutine.

A common use for <xsl:attribute-set> would be to have a set of attributes defined for different types of table styles, one with borders and one without in typical HTML style. With our table formatting example for

Markup City, it is now possible to call the defined set of attributes by name, as shown in Example 6–8.

Example 6–8 : Two attribute sets for bordered and unbordered HTML tables, called by the `use-attribute-sets` attribute.

```
<?xml version="1.0"?>
<xsl:stylesheet xmlns:xsl="http://www.w3.org/1999/XSL/
Transform"
            version="1.0">
<!-- attribute set definitions -->
<xsl:attribute-set name="plain_table">
      <xsl:attribute name="border">0</xsl:attribute>
      <xsl:attribute name="cellpadding">3</xsl:attribute>
      <xsl:attribute name="cellspacing">4</xsl:attribute>
</xsl:attribute-set>
<xsl:attribute-set name="bordered_table">
      <xsl:attribute name="border">1</xsl:attribute>
      <xsl:attribute name="cellpadding">2</xsl:attribute>
      <xsl:attribute name="cellspacing">3</xsl:attribute>
</xsl:attribute-set>

<!-- template rules -->
      <xsl:template match="block" >
             <xsl:call-template name="table-cell"/>
</xsl:template>
<xsl:template match="boulevard">
      <xsl:call-template name="table-row"/>
</xsl:template>

<xsl:template match="thoroughfare">
      <xsl:call-template name="table-row"/>
</xsl:template>

<xsl:template match="sidestreet">
      <xsl:call-template name="table-cell"/>
</xsl:template>
<xsl:template match="main">
<xsl:element name="table" use-attribute-
sets="bordered_table">
                <xsl:apply-templates/>
      </xsl:element>
      </xsl:template>
```

Example 6–8 : Two attribute sets for bordered and unbordered HTML tables, called by the `use-attribute-sets` attribute (continued).

```
      <xsl:template match="/">
            <html>
            <head><title>Table Example</title>
            <head>
            <body>
                  <xsl:apply-templates/>
            </body>
            </html>
      </xsl:template>

<xsl:template name="table-row">
      <tr>
      <xsl:apply-templates/>
      </tr>
</xsl:template>
<xsl:template name="table-cell">
      <td>
      <xsl:apply-templates/>
      </td>
</xsl:template>
            </xsl:stylesheet>
```

The `<table>` element that is created contains the new attributes for border, cellpadding and cellspacing, as selected with the `use-attribute-sets`. The table can easily be converted from a table with borders to a table with no borders by changing the attribute value of `use-attribute-sets` from `bordered_table` to `plain_table`.

Example 6–9 shows the use of attribute sets which applies to LREs: you can apply attribute sets, using the `use-attribute-set` attribute in the LRE itself, by adding the `xsl` prefix.

If a series or set of attributes is to be repeatedly used throughout an XSLT stylesheet, you can declare it once and invoke it by a convenient name. This decreases the likelihood of error in cutting and pasting or, worse, retyping. Further, the values and the attribute names themselves can be generated based on the input XML data instance, adding flexibility to the output.

Example 6–9 : Using the attribute `xsl:use-attribute-set` in an LRE

```
<xsl:template match="main">
   <table xsl:use-attribute-sets="plain_table">
        <xsl:apply-templates/>
   </table>
</xsl:template>
```

6.5 The <xsl:text> Instruction Element

Another way to supplement the output result tree is to add text directly using the <xsl:text> element. While this can also be accomplished by typing text directly in the template, the <xsl:text> element serves to distinguish the actual text from other parts of the stylesheet. Sequences of <xsl:text> elements are sent to the output without any line breaks, making it possible to concatenate several strings. The <xsl:text> element, which has one optional attribute, disable-output-escaping, as shown in the following element model definition, can be used to output literal whitespace as well.

```
<!-- Category: instruction -->

<xsl:text

disable-output-escaping = "yes" | "no">

<!-- Content: #PCDATA -->

</xsl:text>
```

In effect, <xsl:text> instructs the XSLT processor to output the exact sequence of keystrokes that are found between the <xsl:text> and </xsl:text> tags. This includes line breaks and tabs. However, there are two special characters, < and &, that are not allowed in the content of <xsl:text> unless they are included as the special character entities, < and &. This is because these two characters are special XML characters and are processed as such when the document is parsed. It is the XML parser, not the XSLT processor, that will generate an error if these characters are used. The processing of these characters can be affected using the `disable-output-escaping` attribute.

6.5.1 The `disable-output-escaping` Attribute

When the output method of the document is `xml` or `html`, whether declared as such in the `<xsl:output>` element (see Chapter 10), or defaulted by the lack of an `<xsl:output>` element, certain special character entities are escaped. In other words, they will appear in the output as the same character entity reference that appeared in the input document. Note that this behavior is only valid for a few character entities, based on the XSLT processor used. The XSLT specification states that:

> *Normally, the xml output method escapes & and <* ***(and possibly other characters)*** *when outputting text nodes. This ensures that the output is well-formed XML.* (XSLT specification, section 16.4)

This means that only & and < are guaranteed to appear in the output as `&` and `<`, but that the processor is free to add other characters to this list. In order to by-pass this functionality, you can use the `disable-output-escaping` to output the characters they represent, which are the text strings the entities resolve to. This is achieved by setting the attribute `disable-output-escaping` to a value of `yes`.

```
ATTRIBUTE:  disable-output-escaping (yes|no) "no"
VALUE = (yes|no) "no"
```

The default value of the `disable-output-escaping` attribute is `no`, as shown in the following sample DTD element declaration for `<xsl:text>`.

```
<!ELEMENT xsl:text (#PCDATA)>
<!ATTLIST xsl:text
  disable-output-escaping (yes|no) "no" >
```

When the value of the `method` attribute of the `<xsl:output>` element is set to `text`, the processor ignores any use of the `disable-output-escaping` attribute altogether, and defaults to generating the actual character in the output. Table 6–1 shows the possible combinations of the disable-output-escaping attribute and the xsl:output method (either "text" or "xml/html") and the results using James Clark's XT.

Table 6–1 Output method and disable-output-escaping

disable-output-escaping *value*	*text*		*xml/html*	
	yes	*no*	*yes*	*no*
&	&	&	&	&
<	<	<	<	<
>	>	>	>	>
>	>	>	>	>
"	"	"	"	"
"	"	"	"	"
'	'	'	'	'

6.5.2 Using **<xsl:text>** to Generate Text

New text that is added to the output can be placed inside the <xsl:text> element to distinguish it from other text. Several <xsl:text> elements can be used to output sequential text elements without any additional whitespace because generating text with <xsl:text>, or any other XSLT element, does not generate any additional line-breaks outside the tag in the output. For example, the following lines generate the single line "line1line2line3line4" in the output:

```
<xsl:text>line1</xsl:text>
<xsl:text>line2</xsl:text>
<xsl:text>line3</xsl:text>
```

```
<xsl:text>line4</xsl:text>
```

Line breaks inside the `<xsl:text>` element, however, do appear in the output:

```
<xsl:text>line1

</xsl:text>
<xsl:text>line2</xsl:text>
<xsl:text>line3</xsl:text>
<xsl:text>line4</xsl:text>
```

Adding the two line breaks inside the `<xsl:text>` element for line 1 generates the literal line breaks in the output:

```
line1

line2line3line4
```

The `<xsl:text>` element is very useful for placing extra whitespace like linebreaks and tabs between text generated by other elements. For example, most of the output examples in this book have line breaks added to make them readable, but in reality, the output is bunched up, as shown in Example 6–10.

Example 6–10 : Generated elements without line breaks.

STYLESHEET:

```
<?xml version="1.0"?>
<xsl:stylesheet
          xmlns:xsl="http://www.w3.org/1999/XSL/Transform"
     version="1.0">

<xsl:template match="/">
<block>
     <xsl:element name="house">1</xsl:element>
     <xsl:element name="house">2</xsl:element>
     <xsl:element name="house">3</xsl:element>
     <xsl:element name="house">4</xsl:element>
<xsl:element name="house">5</xsl:element>
</block>
</xsl:template>
</xsl:stylesheet>
```

RESULT:

```
<?xml version="1.0" encoding="utf-8"?>
<block><house>1</house><house>2</house><house>3/house><house>4</
house>
<house>5</house></block>
```

In order to have readable output, with line breaks between the <house> elements, we can add <xsl:text> elements with line breaks inside them, as shown in Example 6–11.

Example 6–11 : Generating line breaks with <xsl:text>

STYLESHEET:

```
<?xml version="1.0"?>
<xsl:stylesheet
          xmlns:xsl="http://www.w3.org/1999/XSL/Transform"
     version="1.0">

<xsl:template match="/">
<block>
<xsl:text>
</xsl:text>
     <xsl:element name="house">1</xsl:element>
<xsl:text>
</xsl:text>
     <xsl:element name="house">2</xsl:element>
<xsl:text>
</xsl:text>
     <xsl:element name="house">3</xsl:element>
<xsl:text>
</xsl:text>
     <xsl:element name="house">4</xsl:element>
<xsl:text>
</xsl:text>
     <xsl:element name="house">5</xsl:element>
<xsl:text>
</xsl:text>
</block>
</xsl:template>
</xsl:stylesheet>
```

RESULT:

```
<?xml version="1.0" encoding="utf-8"?>
<block>
<house>1</house>
<house>2</house>
<house>3</house>
<house>4</house>
<house>5</house>
</block>
```

Note that simply putting line breaks between elements in the stylesheet will not generate line breaks in the output, as shown in Example 6–12.

Example 6–12 : No line breaks generated without `<xsl:text>`.

STYLESHEET:

```
<?xml version="1.0"?>
<xsl:stylesheet
            xmlns:xsl="http://www.w3.org/1999/XSL/Transform"
      version="1.0">

<xsl:template match="/">
<block>

      <xsl:element name="house">1</xsl:element>

      <xsl:element name="house">2</xsl:element>

      <xsl:element name="house">3</xsl:element>

      <xsl:element name="house">4</xsl:element>

      <xsl:element name="house">5</xsl:element>

</block>
</xsl:template>

</xsl:stylesheet>
```

RESULT:

```
<?xml version="1.0" encoding="utf-8"?>

<block><house>1</house><house>2</house><house>3</house><house>4</house>
<house>5</house></block>
```

6.5.3 Generating Text without `<xsl:text>`

It is possible to generate text in the output result tree without using `<xsl:text>` by simply typing the text in the stylesheet. The issues with using text in this way are subtle in the fact that they deal mostly with whitespace. When the processor sees a text string, it normalizes the string before sending it to the output. This means that any extra whitespace is removed according to the XSLT rules for normalizing whitespace. In most cases this means that, if the text between elements is simply line breaks, the line breaks will not appear in the output. If, on the other hand, the text includes line breaks between other text, the line breaks will be preserved. This is demonstrated in Example 6–13.

Example 6–13 : Using text in a stylesheet with line breaks.

STYLESHEET:

```
<?xml version="1.0"?>
<xsl:stylesheet
            xmlns:xsl="http://www.w3.org/1999/XSL/Transform"
      version="1.0">
<xsl:template match="/">
<block>
text line1

text line2
<xsl:element name="house">1</xsl:element>
<xsl:element name="house">2</xsl:element>
<xsl:element name="house">3</xsl:element>
<xsl:element name="house">4</xsl:element>
<xsl:element name="house">5</xsl:element>
</block>
</xsl:template>
</xsl:stylesheet>
```

RESULT:

```
<?xml version="1.0" encoding="utf-8"?>
<block>
text line1

text line2
<house>1</house><house>2</house><house>3</house><house>4</house><house>
5</house></block>
```

6.6 Adding Attributes to LREs

Attributes can be added to LREs in three ways: by directly typing the attribute and its value in the LRE, by using the `<xsl:attribute>` element, or by using the `<xsl:attribute-set>` element in conjunction with either the `use-attribute-sets` on an element or `xsl:use-attribute-sets` attribute on an LRE. Because LREs are passed through to the output result tree, using attributes directly in LRE elements can be difficult if the value of the attribute is to be generated or extracted from some node-set in the input document. For example, if we wanted to output a new element called `<newblock>` instead of our `<block>`s in Markup City, and then add an attribute with the text content of the `<block>`, the template in Example 6–14 would not accomplish our goal.

Example 6–14 : An ineffective way to add attributes to LREs.

```
<xsl:template match="block">
     <newblock name="text()"/>
</xsl:template>
```

The result of this template rule would replace each `<block>` element in the input with a literal element `<newblock name="text()"/>` in the output. The content of the new attribute would be the literal string `text()`. It is not possible to use a function directly in an LRE attribute. For this reason, the value of an attribute of a literal result element can be an Attribute Value Template, or AVT.

6.6.1 Attribute Value Templates

Normally, LRE attributes are passed through verbatim to the output result tree. However, if the attribute of an LRE contains curly braces ({ }), the content of the curly braces is considered an Attribute Value Template, or AVT. AVTs can contain expressions and patterns, allowing the value of the resulting attribute to be extracted or generated from the input source document, or from some other result of an expression.

If we add curly braces to the attribute value of the LRE in the previous example, the result will actually be the correct value of each `text()` node

> **NOTE** The word template in Attribute Value Template should not be misconstrued to mean that it can contain children or anything of the sort, and should not be mistaken with the template contained in the `<xsl:template>` element.

of each `<block>` element, as shown in Example 6–15. Note that in this example we are removing any extra text or stylesheet elements that do not apply to the result.

Example 6–15 : Using an AVT to create a new attribute in an LRE.

INPUT:

```
<?xml version="1.0"?>
<main>
      <parkway>
             <thoroughfare>Governor Drive</thoroughfare>
             <thoroughfare name="Whitesburg Drive">
                   <sidestreet>Bob Wallace Avenue</sidestreet>
                   <block>1st Street</block>
                   <block>2nd Street</block>
                   <block>3rd Street</block>
                   <sidestreet>Woodridge Street</sidestreet>
             </thoroughfare>
             <thoroughfare name="Bankhead">
                   <sidestreet>Tollgate Road</sidestreet>
                   <block>First Street</block>
                   <block>Second Street</block>
                   <block>Third Street</block>
                   <sidestreet>Oak Drive</sidestreet>
             </thoroughfare>
      </parkway>
      <boulevard>
                   <block>Panorama Street</block>
                   <block>Highland Plaza</block>
                   <block>Hutchens Avenue</block>
                   <block>Wildwood Drive</block>
                   <block>Old Chimney Road</block>
                   <block>Carrol Circle</block>
      </boulevard>
                   </main>
```

Example 6–15 : Using an AVT to create a new attribute in an LRE (continued).

TEMPLATE RULE:

```
<xsl:template match="block">
      <newblock name="{text()}"/>
</xsl:template>
```

OUTPUT:

```
<newblock name="1st Street"/>
<newblock name="2nd Street"/>
<newblock name="3rd Street"/>
<newblock name="First Street"/>
<newblock name="Second Street"/>
<newblock name="Third Street"/>
<newblock name="Panorama Street"/>
<newblock name="Highland Plaza"/>
<newblock name="Hutchens Avenue"/>
<newblock name="Wildwood Drive"/>
<newblock name="Old Chimney Road"/>
<newblock name="Carrol Circle"/>
```

6.6.2 Using `<xsl:attribute>` with LREs

Adding attributes to LREs can also be accomplished by using the `<xsl:attribute>` element directly following the open tag for the LRE, as shown in Example 6–16.

Of course, the value of the resulting attribute, which is determined by the content of the `<xsl:attribute>` element, will be once again hard-coded, or literally output, for each `<newblock>` as `MyAtt`, which is not really useful. But because we've moved the resolution of the value of the attribute to an instruction element instead of an AVT, we can now add instruction elements, such as `<xsl:value-of>`, as the content of the `<xsl:attribute>` element, as shown in Example 6–17.

The template will result in the same output as was shown in Example 6–15, but this stucture allows additional elements to be included to expand the functionality of the `<xsl:attribute>` element. In addition, `<xsl:attributes>` can be nested in `<xsl:attribute-set>` elements and used on LRE elements as discussed in the next section.

Example 6–16 : Adding attributes to LREs using `<xsl:attribute>`.

```
<xsl:template match="block">
      <newblock>
            <xsl:attribute name="name">MyAtt<xsl:attribute>
      </newblock>
</xsl:template>
```

Example 6–17 : Using `<xsl:value-of>` to add attributes to LREs.

```
<xsl:template match="block">
      <newblock>
            <xsl:attribute name="name">
                  <xsl:value-of select="."/>
            </xsl:attribute>
      </newblock>
</xsl:template>
```

6.6.3 Using `<xsl:attribute-set>` and the `xsl:use-attribute-sets` Attribute with LREs

LREs can take advantage of attributes defined in attribute sets by calling them directly in the LRE, using the `xsl` prefix on the `use-attribute-sets` attribute. For example, the element `<newblock>` created in Example 6–17 can use the `xsl:use-attribute-sets` to call a predefined set of attributes. The attributes in the set are added to the `<newblock>` element in the output result tree, as shown in Example 6–18.

The two attributes, name and context, are added to each `<newblock>` element, with their value calculated from each node as it is processed.

6.7 Comments and Processing-Instructions

There are two XSLT instruction elements that create what is considered content internal to the output XML document. Normally, internal content is not intended for end users. This internal content can be in the form of XML processing instructions, or XML comments. Processing instructions, or PIs, and comments are embedded in the output XML document as part

Example 6–18 : Demonstration of <xsl:attribute-set> with LREs.

STYLESHEET:

```
<xsl:template match="block">
      <newblock xsl:use-attribute-sets="block-atts"/>
</xsl:template>

<xsl:attribute-set name="block-atts">
      <xsl:attribute name="name">
<xsl:value-of select="."/>
</xsl:attribute>
      <xsl:attribute name="context">
<xsl:value-of select="name(..)"/>
</xsl:attribute>
</xsl:attribute-set>
```

OUTPUT:

```
<newblock name="1st Street" context="thoroughfare"/>
<newblock name="2nd Street" context="thoroughfare"/>
<newblock name="3rd Street" context="thoroughfare"/>
<newblock name="First Street" context="thoroughfare"/>
<newblock name="Second Street" context="thoroughfare"/>
<newblock name="Third Street" context="thoroughfare"/>
<newblock name="Panorama Street" context="boulevard"/>
<newblock name="Highland Plaza" context="boulevard"/>
<newblock name="Hutchens Avenue" context="boulevard"/>
<newblock name="Wildwood Drive" context="boulevard"/>
<newblock name="Old Chimney Road" context="boulevard"/>
<newblock name="Carrol Circle" context="boulevard"/>
```

of the document *structure*, but are not considered part of the document *content,* and cannot be seen by most rendering engines.

Processing instructions generated with `<xsl:processing-instruction>` are used by an external process, identified by the target of the PI, to handle the XML file in a specific way, based on the parameters of the PI. Comments generated with `<xsl:comment>` are used for special handling of the XML by a human.

The loose categorization of internal output holds for processing instructions and comments in that this output is only accessed that is, is only humanly readable *inside* the XML document containing it. They can, however, be extracted as PI and comment nodes by an XSLT stylesheet.

6.7.1 The <xsl:comment> Instruction Element

The <xsl:comment> element creates an XML comment, identified by the comment delimiters <!-- and -->, in the output result tree. This element has no attributes and its content is a template, as shown in the following element model definition.

```
<!-- Category: instruction -->
<xsl:comment>
  <!-- Content: template -->
</xsl:comment>
```

The result of instantiating the template contained in this element can only be text. Any other kind of node will create an error, because comments are by nature empty elements.

Comments are internal to the XML document, and can be found anywhere in the XML document except within markup. There is no processor specific handling of XML comments, and XML or HTML browsers will not display them. Most XML parsers ignore any characters in the comment, except for the use of the delimiter characters --. Note that using a string of two sequential dashes (--) inside an <xsl:comment> element will cause some XSLT processors to place a space between them. Two sequential dashes are the reserved string that signals the end of a comment and are not allowed inside a comment.

As Example 6–19 shows, the instructions included in the template of the <xsl:commment> element can be used to generate the content of the comment in the output.

Example 6–19 : Using <xsl:comment> to make context-specific comments.

```
<xsl:template match="/">
      <xsl:comment>
            <xsl:text>This city has </xsl:text>
            <xsl:value-of select="count(//block)" />
            <xsl:text> blocks in it. </xsl:text>
      </xsl:comment>
</xsl:template>
```

The result of instantiating this template against a Markup City with 12 <block> elements is the XML comment:

```
<!--This city has 12 blocks in it. -->
```

The template in the <xsl:comment> element contains <xsl:text> elements used to generate text output, as well as an <xsl:value-of> element using the count() function in its match attribute to get the number of blocks.

6.7.2 The <xsl:processing-instruction> Instruction Element

The <xsl:processing-instruction> instruction element is used to generate XML processing instructions in the output document instance. The content of this element, as shown in the following element model definition, is a template. It has one required name attribute that sets the name of the PI.

```
<!-- Category: instruction -->
<xsl:processing-instruction
  name = { ncname }>
  <!-- Content: template -->
</xsl:processing-instruction>
```

The name of the PI, generated from the name attribute, becomes the target of the PI, which is the name of the application that will be used to process the PI. The template inside the <xsl:processing-instruction> element is instantiated to create the text content of the PI following the name. This text becomes the parameters of the PI that will be passed to the application when the PI is parsed.

Example 6–20 shows a typical use for the <xsl:processing-instruction> element to include a PI to reference to an external cascading stylesheet (CSS).

This would generate the following processing instruction in the XML document instance.

```
<?xml-stylesheet href="mystyles.css" type="text/css"?>
```

Example 6–20 : Creating a processing instruction with `<xsl:processing-instruction>`.

```
<xsl:processing-instruction name="xml
stylesheet">href="mystyles.css"
type="text/css"</xsl:processing-instruction>
```

Notice that the content of the `<xsl:processing-instruction>` element is used as the text of the PI, following the name (`xml-stylesheet`) that is generated with the `name` attribute. The question marks at the beginning and end of the generated PI are automatically placed in the output by the `<xsl:processing-instruction>` element.

6.8 Namespace Aliases

When creating new elements it may be necessary to create an element that has a namespace. However, it is often not feasible to use the namespace directly as the name of an LRE, so the XSLT specification provides a mechanism to supply an alias for the prefix of a namespace. The `<xsl:namespace-alias>` element is used to define an alias for a namespace prefix. As shown in the following element model definition, the `<xsl:namespace-alias>` element is an empty top-level element with two attributes.

```
<!-- Category: top-level-element -->
<xsl:namespace-alias
  stylesheet-prefix = prefix | "#default"
  result-prefix = prefix | "#default" />
```

The `stylesheet-prefix` attribute is used to specify the namespace prefix that will be used in the stylesheet. The `result-prefix` attribute specifies the namespace prefix that will appear in the result tree. Either value can use the default namespace if specified by using `#default`.

For example, if the stylesheet is being used to generate another stylesheet, or an XML document with an embedded stylesheet, you cannot use the `xsl` prefix for the new elements, because they will be interpreted by the processor to be real XSLT stylesheet elements. In this case a prefix alias can be defined, and the processor will convert the alias to the real prefix in the output. Example 6–21 shows the use of `<xsl:namespace-alias>` to define a prefix alias.

Example 6–21 : Using `<xsl:namespace-alias>` to define a prefix alias.

```
<?xml version="1.0"?>
<xsl:stylesheet
  version="1.0"
    xmlns:xsl="http://www.w3.org/1999/XSL/Transform"
    xmlns:myxsl="http://MyxslPrefixAlias">

<xsl:namespace-alias stylesheet-prefix="myxsl" result-
prefix="xsl"/>

<xsl:template match="text()"/>

<xsl:template match="/">
<myxsl:stylesheet>
<xsl:attribute name="version">1.0</xsl:attribute>
<xsl:apply-templates/>
</myxsl:stylesheet>
</xsl:template>

<xsl:template match="//*">
<myxsl:template match="{name()}">
     <myxsl:apply-templates/>
  </myxsl:template>
<xsl:apply-templates/>
</xsl:template>
</xsl:stylesheet>
```

Using this stylesheet on any XML document will generate a stylesheet for each element from the input. The `myxsl` prefix is converted to the `xsl` prefix in the output, using the `<xsl:namespace-alias>` element. Notice that the namespace for the alias is defined in the `<xsl:stylesheet>` element.

The first template rule matching on `text()` is used to suppress the output of any text nodes from the XML.

The template rule matching on the root (/) is generating the final `<xsl:stylesheet>` element. The `<xsl:attribute>` element is adding the version information to the output. Note that the processor automatically adds the xmlns attribute to the <xsl:stylesheet> element in the output (there is no way to define a prefix alias for the xmlns attribute).

The template rule matching the rest of the elements in the document (//*) supplies the new template rules for each element by pulling the name of the element with the name() function. Notice that the name() function in this case is in an attribute value template, signalled by the {} curly braces. Even though the alias prefix is being used, the <myxsl:template> element is considered an LRE, so the attribute values must be pulled using an attribute value template.

We then use <xsl:apply-templates> in each template rule to process the children of each matched node.

Note that there will be duplicate template rules because the template rule used to generate <xsl:template> elements is matching on every element in the document.

Note that XT does not support the <xsl:namespace-alias> element.

Using Multiple Stylesheets

* `<xsl:include>`
* `<xsl:import>`
* `<xsl:apply-imports>`
* Conflict resolution for template rules

7

Up to this point in our discussion of XSLT stylesheets, we have talked about the stylesheet as the only file that contains all the templates that are being processed. XSLT also allows you to work with more than one stylesheet at a time.

The possibility of using multiple stylesheets and accessing their content selectively provides a means of grouping related template rules, packaging them together according to their function. For example, you may want to have a separate stylesheet that only handles tables, or one that handles list formatting. These separate stylesheets do not need to be physically incorporated into the main stylesheet. They can be called into use with one of two top-level elements, `<xsl:include>` or `<xsl:import>`.

In this chapter, we will address the two top-level elements, `<xsl:include>` and `<xsl:import>`, along with the related instruction element, `<xsl:apply-imports>`. We will also discuss the multiple ways in which conflicts between template rules can be resolved.

7.1 Working with External Stylesheets

Several elements in XSLT are used specifically to access stylesheets and template rules that are external to the current (or calling) stylesheet. These elements are `<xsl:include>` and `<xsl:import>`, which are the top-level elements used to bring in the external stylesheets, and `<xsl:apply-imports>`, which is an instruction element used specifically to choose an imported template rule over those in the current stylesheet.

7.1.1 The <xsl:include> Top-Level Element

The `<xsl:include>` element is used to access and incorporate the contents of another stylesheet into the current, or calling, stylesheet. It can be used anywhere in an XSLT stylesheet as long as it is a direct child of the `<xsl:stylesheet>` or `<xsl:transform>` document element. The `<xsl:include>` top-level element is an empty element, as shown in the following element model definition. It has one required attribute, `href`, whose value is a URI reference to an external stylesheet that will be included at the point of that the `<xsl:include>` element is used.

```
<!-- Category: top-level-element -->
<xsl:include
  href = uri-reference />
```

When the XSLT processor finds the XSLT stylesheet referenced by the `href` attribute's value, the top-level elements of that referenced XSLT stylesheet are inserted into the current stylesheet, literally in place of the `<xsl:include>` element. It inserts the entire included stylesheet—minus its PI and `<xsl:stylesheet>` or `<xsl:transform>` document element—as though it was originally part of the stylesheet in which the `<xsl:include>` element was invoked.

As an XML or SGML reference, the `<xsl:include>` element acts very much like an entity reference. When the parser sees the entity reference, it goes and resolves the entity and replaces the reference with the content of the entity.

7.1.1.1 Conditions Affecting Included Top-Level Elements

There are a variety of contingencies that can affect the behavior of included top-level elements when `<xsl:include>` is invoked, such as references to relative URIs in the included elements and namespace declarations from the XSLT stylesheet being included.

The simplest way to think of the included elements when `<xsl:include>` is invoked is to remember that they retain all the characteristics of their "home" stylesheet. The included top-level elements function like top-level elements of the including stylesheet to begin with, but they retain the relative paths in their URIs. For example, if the included elements reference a file in the home directory in which the stylesheet being included is found, it keeps the reference to that file's location. They also retain namespace declarations and any version, extension-element-prefixes, and exclude-result-prefixes of the home stylesheet.

The only exception is in the case of an `<xsl:import>` top-level element that is part of the included elements. What happens if one of the top-level elements being included is an `<xsl:import>` element? Following the rules for `<xsl:import>`, discussed in Section 7.1.2, the imported elements among the included elements of the XSLT stylesheet referenced with `<xsl:include>` are treated as though they were imported in the original stylesheet.

For example, if stylesheet `main.xsl` has an `<xsl:include>` element that points to `included.xsl`, and `included.xsl` has an `<xsl:import>` element that points to `imported.xsl`, then any top-level elements from `xsl.imported` will be treated as though they were referenced by an `<xsl:import>` element in `main.xsl`. The imported elements referenced by `included.xsl` "leap-frog" the stylesheet, importing them to behave as though they were in the original `main.xsl` stylesheet in which the `<xsl:include>` element that triggered this triple-chain was invoked in the first place. We will discuss this in more detail in the comparisons between `<xsl:include>` and `<xsl:import>` in Section 7.1.3.

7.1.1.2 Using the <xsl:include> Top-Level Element

The use of <xsl:include> enables an enterprise to boilerplate certain features of its stylesheets. Grouping stylesheets based on their functionality allows them to be shared and reused. For instance, in the ongoing series of examples with Markup City, we may need to have several different versions of an XSLT stylesheet, perhaps to prepare reports for several different agencies. This might be the case again with the area of town accessed via the <parkway>. Instead of several different stylesheets, which may be very large and difficult to maintain, we could have several modular stylesheets, each with its own title format. In Example 7–1 we show one such module stylesheet being included into a "main" stylesheet.

Example 7–1 : Using <xsl:include> to add a separate stylesheet.

NPUT:

```
<?xml version="1.0"?>
<parkway>
      <thoroughfare name="Governor Drive" />
      <thoroughfare name="Whitesburg Drive">
           <sidestreet name="Bob Wallace Avenue">
           <block name="1st Street"></block>
                  <block name="2nd Street"></block>
                  <block name="3rd Street"></block>
           </sidestreet>
           <sidestreet name="Woodridge Street">
           </sidestreet>
      </thoroughfare>
      <thoroughfare name="Bankhead Drive">
           <sidestreet name="Tollgate Road">
                  <block name="First Street"></block>
                  <block name="Second Street"></block>
                  <block name="Third Street"></block>
           </sidestreet>
           <sidestreet> Oak Drive </sidestreet>
      </thoroughfare>

</parkway>
```

Example 7–1 : Using `<xsl:include>` to add a separate stylesheet (continued).

MAIN STYLESHEET:

```
<?xml version="1.0"?>
<!-- FILE NAME main.xsl -->
<xsl:stylesheet xmlns:xsl="http://www.w3.org/1999/XSL/Transform"
          version="1.0">
<xsl:include href="audit.xsl" />
<xsl:template match="parkway">
      <html>
      <body>
            <xsl:call-template name="doc-title" />
      <dl>
            <xsl:apply-templates/>
      </dl>
      </body>
      </html>
</xsl:template>
<xsl:template match="sidestreet">
            <dt>

                  <xsl:value-of select="@name | text()"/>
            </dt>
            <dd><ul>
                  <xsl:apply-templates select="block" />
            </ul></dd>
</xsl:template>
<xsl:template match="block">
      <li>
            <xsl:value-of select="@name | text()"/>
      </li>
</xsl:template>
      </xsl:stylesheet>
```

INCLUDED STYLESHEET:

```
<?xml version="1.0"?>
<!-- FILE NAME audit.xsl -->
<xsl:stylesheet xmlns:xsl="http://www.w3.org/1999/XSL/Transform"
              version="1.0"
                    >
```

Example 7–1 : Using <xsl:include> to add a separate stylesheet (continued).

```
<xsl:template name="doc-title">
     <center>
          <h1>Prepared for the Auditor's Office</h1>
          <h2>Borough of Monte Sano Boulevard</h2>
     </center>
</xsl:template>
</xsl:stylesheet>
```

The person running the scripts only needs to change one line, the `<xsl:include>` element in the main XSLT stylesheet, to include the correct stylesheet for the title for each report. Additional title stylesheets, as shown in Example 7–2, can be easily swapped out using the correct value for `<xsl:include>`.

For all intents and purposes, the main stylesheet and the included stylesheet are combined into one by the XSLT processor. After the first pass through the XSLT processor, which checks the basic logical structure of the XSLT elements for being a well-formed XML data instance, the `<xsl:include>` element URIs are resolved, or "looked up." The children of the document element of the included stylesheet—in other words, its top-level element(s)—are then inserted *in place of* the actual `<xsl:include>` element. This does not mean that the original XSLT stylesheet that used `<xsl:include>` has itself been transformed. Instead, to the processor's perception—or, more accurately, parsing—of the resulting XSLT stylesheet, there is a new template rule, extracted from the external stylesheet, in place of where `<xsl:include>` was to begin with.

7.1.2 The `<xsl:import>` Top-Level Element

The `<xsl:import>` top-level element is used to bring in elements from another stylesheet, similar to `<xsl:include>` discussed in the previous section. There are some basic differences between the two, however. The `<xsl:import>` top-level element *must* always come first among the children of the `<xsl:stylesheet>` or `<xsl:transform>` document element when it is used. Also, the templates found in an imported

Example 7–2 : Additional modular stylesheets for report titles.

OPTIONAL STYLESHEET 1:

```
<?xml version="1.0"?>
<!-- FILE NAME mayor.xsl -->

<xsl:stylesheet xmlns:xsl="http://www.w3.org/1999/XSL/Transform"
                version="1.0" >

<xsl:template name="doc-title">
      <center>
             <h1>Prepared for the Mayor's Office</h1>
             <h2>Borough of Monte Sano Boulevard</h2>
      </center>
</xsl:template>
</xsl:stylesheet>
```

OPTIONAL STYLESHEET 2:

```
<?xml version="1.0"?>
<!-- FILE NAME utilities.xsl -->
<xsl:stylesheet xmlns:xsl="http://www.w3.org/1999/XSL/Transform"
                version="1.0" >

<xsl:template name="doc-title">
      <center>
             <h1>Prepared for the Water Utilities Office</h1>
             <h2>Borough of Monte Sano Boulevard</h2>
      </center>
</xsl:template>
</xsl:stylesheet>
```

stylesheet have a lower precedence than templates found in an included stylesheet.

The `<xsl:import>` top-level element is an empty element, which is optional and repeatable. It has one required attribute, `href`, as shown in the following element model definition:

```
<!-- Category: top-level-element -->
<xsl:import
  href = uri-reference />
```

The `<xsl:import>` element uses its single required `href` attribute to retrieve the contents of an external XSLT stylesheet. The `href` attribute value is a URI pointing to another XSLT stylesheet.

Before addressing any elements in a stylesheet, the XSLT processor builds a tree of the stylesheet. All `<xsl:import>` elements are retrieved from the location specified in the `href` attribute and placed in the tree at the point where the `<xsl:import>` element was found in the original stylesheet. Once this stylesheet tree is built, the processor continues.

7.1.2.1 The Import Process

The use of `<xsl:import>` is essentially the same as given above for `<xsl:include>`, except that the imported elements come first in the importing XSLT stylesheet. This does not mean that they come first in priority or precedence in the event of competing or conflicting template rules, as discussed in Section 7.2.2. In fact, *imported* top-level elements are automatically considered last in priority to any top-level elements of the calling stylesheet. Imported top-level elements are also prioritized below any top-level elements included with `<xsl:include>`.

The top-level elements referenced by `<xsl:import>` are placed first in the calling XSLT stylesheet. When an XSLT processor operates on an XSLT stylesheet, the order of procedure is as follows.

1. The XSLT stylesheet is parsed and checked for whether it is a well-formed XML data instance.
2. Any external stylesheets referenced by `<xsl:import>` are accessed and their corresponding top-level elements are imported, provided the imported XSLT stylesheet itself is a well-formed XML data instance.
3. Any top-level elements of external stylesheets referenced by `<xsl:include>` are included.
4. This complete set of top-level elements is checked for conflicts and resolved according to the conflict resolution model presented in Section 7.2.2.

The imported top-level elements retain their base URI, namespace declarations, version, and extension-element-prefix and exclude-result-prefix attribute characteristics declared in the `<xsl:stylesheet>` or `<xsl:transform>` document element of their home XSLT stylesheet.

Again, if any elements of the imported set of top-level elements are themselves imported elements, they are treated as though referenced by an <xsl:import> element in the original importing XSLT stylesheet.

7.1.3 Comparing the <xsl:import> and <xsl:include> Top-Level Elements

The comparison between <xsl:import> and <xsl:include> is primarily based on the matter of conflict resolution. The simplest summary of their difference is that top-level elements brought into an XSLT stylesheet using the <xsl:import> element have lower precedence than the importing stylesheet's top-level elements or any top-level elements included with the use of <xsl:include>.

Remember that <xsl:include> effectively inserts additional top-level elements into the stylesheet in which it is invoked. The href attribute of <xsl:include> directs the XSLT processor to go to the URI given as its value, and from the stylesheet at that URI, the top-level elements are taken and put in place of—in other words, at the same point in the including XSLT stylesheet—the <xsl:include> element. The <xsl:import> element does this also, but with two distinctions. First, the <xsl:import> element comes first in document order in the XSLT stylesheet in which it is invoked. Therefore, the top-level elements from the XSLT stylesheet being imported come first. Second, the <xsl:import> top-level elements are *not* ranked above any top-level elements of the importing stylesheet.

The top-level elements brought into an XSLT stylesheet using <xsl:import> and <xsl:include> are the same in that they both retain the base URI, relative URIs, namespace declarations, and so forth of the included or imported top-level elements. In other words, the top-level elements combined into any XSLT stylesheet always retain all of their home stylesheet's—the stylesheet from which they were either included or imported—characteristics. As noted, the top-level elements referenced by way of <xsl:import>, when <xsl:import> is part of the elements included with <xsl:include>, are treated differently.

The basic thing to remember is that all <xsl:import> elements are resolved and placed at the front of the importing stylesheet before any further processing of additional elements is done.

The best way to explain this set of contingencies for conflict resolution and general import, and include procedures, is with a simplified example.

Consider that we have a primary XSLT stylesheet, called `primary.xsl`, and three referenced stylesheets, as shown in Example 7–3. The additional stylesheets are located in the same directory as `primary.xsl` to simplify their reference.

Example 7–3 : Using imported and included stylesheets.

PRIMARY STYLESHEET:

```
<?xml version="1.0"?>
<!-- Primary Stylesheet primary.xsl -->
<xsl:stylesheet
      xmlns:xsl="http://www.w3.org/1999/XSL/Transform"
      version="1.0">
<xsl:import href="imported.xsl" />
<xsl:template match="/" priority="1">
      <p>I'm the content of the original
      template in primary.xsl.</p>
</xsl:template>
<xsl:include href="included.xsl" />
</xsl:stylesheet>
```

IMPORTED STYLESHEET:

```
<?xml version="1.0"?>
<!-- Imported Stylesheet imported.xsl -->
<xsl:stylesheet
      xmlns:xsl="http://www.w3.org/1999/XSL/Transform"
      version="1.0">
<xsl:template match="/">
      <p>I'm the content of imported.xsl. </p>
</xsl:template>
</xsl:stylesheet>
```

NCLUDED STYLESHEET:

```
<?xml version="1.0"?>
<!-- Included Stylesheet included.xsl -->
<xsl:stylesheet
xmlns:xsl="http://www.w3.org/1999/XSL/Transform"
version="1.0">
```

Example 7–3 : Using imported and included stylesheets (continued).

```
<xsl:import href="import2.xsl" />
<xsl:template match="/">
      <p>I'm the content of included.xsl.</p>
</xsl:template>
</xsl:stylesheet>
```

2nd IMPORTED STYLESHEET:

```
<?xml version="1.0"?>
<!-- 2nd Imported Stylesheet import2.xsl -->
<xsl:stylesheet
      xmlns:xsl="http://www.w3.org/1999/XSL/Transform"
      version="1.0">
<xsl:template match="/" priority="2">
      <p>I'm the content of import2.xsl.</p>
</xsl:template>
</xsl:stylesheet>
```

In the primary stylesheet above, we declared a priority value of 1 for the template. Each of the additional three XSLT stylesheets is referenced directly or indirectly by the `primary.xsl` stylesheet. The `imported.xsl` and `included.xsl` stylesheets are referenced directly in the `primary.xsl` stylesheet, but their templates do not have a priority set. The second imported stylesheet, `import2.xsl`, is referenced in `included.xsl`, and contains a template with a priority of 2.

Now, we will look at what happens to `primary.xsl` when all the imports and includes are resolved. Example 7–4 gives all the resulting contents, the imported and included top-level elements of `primary.xsl` to which the conflict resolution model must be applied. It is important to remember that the following is not meant to indicate that `primary.xsl` *itself* has changed in any way, but that once resolved, the `<xsl:import>` and `<xsl:include>` top-level elements have been "replaced" by the top-level elements of the stylesheets to which their `href` attributes referred. Therefore, we have put those referenced top-level elements that are being included and imported *in place of* the `<xsl:import>` and `<xsl:include>` elements that referenced them. We've also added comments that would not normally result from this process, but that help orient you to the origin of the material. Note that Example 7–4 is for demonstration purposes only—to demonstrate how `primary.xsl` "looks" to the XSLT processor after imports and includes are done.

Example 7–4 : The parsed `primary.xsl` stylesheet.

```
<?xml version="1.0"?>
<xsl:stylesheet xmlns:xsl="http://www.w3.org/1999/XSL/Transform"
                version="1.0">
<!-- The top-level elements from the imported.xsl XSLT
stylesheet come first because the <xsl:import> element comes
first itself. Therefore, from the perspective of the XSLT
processor, this template rule, the only top-level element
imported.xsl, has effectively "replaced" the <xsl:import>
element which references it.-->
<xsl:template match="/"><p>I'm the content of imported.xsl. </p>
</xsl:template>

<!-- This is the import2.xsl file, which was referenced in
the included.xsl file. It comes at the beginning in document
order because imported top-level elements from included files
are treated as if they were referenced by an <xsl:import>
element in the original including stylesheet. In other words,
in this case, the contents of import2.xsl, referenced by
included.xsl, are presented as though primary.xsl itself
contained the <xsl:import> element used in included.xsl. The
other top-level elements of included.xsl come below in the
same document order of primary.xsl, in which the
<xsl:include> was declared.  -->
      <xsl:template match="/" priority="2">
            <p>I'm the content of import2.xsl.</p>
      </xsl:template>
<!-- This is the original template rule of primary.xsl -->
<xsl:template match="/" priority="1">
      <p>I'm the content of the only
template in primary.xsl.</p>
</xsl:template>
<!-- This is the top-level element from included.xsl, which was
included by means of the <xsl:include> element in primary.xsl,
last in document order. One of its top-level elements, this
template rule, is included here in place of the <xsl:include>
element that referenced it. The other top-level element, which
referenced the import2.xsl stylesheet that was also part of
included.xsl, was moved up in document order as though it was
an <xsl:import> that was part of primary.xsl. -->
<xsl:template match="/">
      <p>I'm the content of included.xsl. </p>
</xsl:template>
</xsl:stylesheet>
```

Most of the criteria for determining which template rules are placed where in the resulting pseudo-stylesheet above were explained in the intervening comment sections.

Regarding the matter of conflict resolution, notice that in each case, the `<xsl:template>` element's `match` attribute is the same, matching the root or document root with / as an abbreviation. There are therefore four conflicting template rules. This can be simply resolved by the criteria mentioned in Section 7.2.2. In the case of both the `imported.xsl` template rule *and* the `import2.xsl` template rule, they are automatically removed from contention for top priority by virtue of being imported top-level elements. If there are no `priority` attributes defined, the last template rule in the stylesheet (after all includes and imports have been resolved) is selected. This "order rule" of template selection can be overridden using the `<xsl:apply-imports>` instruction element, discussed in Section 7.1.4, by effectively reinserting the imported template at that location.

Any imported top-level element that conflicts with another non-imported top-level element will always lose out. This is true even when the template has a priority value higher than any other template in the stylesheet, as in our example, where `import2.xsl` has a template with a declared priority of 2. Again, the fact that the template rule from `import2.xsl` is imported (by virtue of being an import into the `included.xsl` file) obviates any stated priority with the `priority` attribute. Also, using `<xsl:apply-imports>`, discussed in the next section, does not change this implicit priority. An imported template with a higher `priority` attribute value cannot override any conflicting non-imported template rule. Internal templates will always have priority over external templates—imported or included—regardless of the priority given to the imported or included templates.

This leaves the original template rules from `primary.xsl` and `included.xsl` as "contenders" for priority among the four templates. In the case of the declaration of priority, even if the number is 1—or, for that matter, 1000—a declared priority will take precedence over a template with no `priority` attribute. Therefore—the envelope, please...—the one template of all four that will be invoked is the content of the `primary.xsl`, which stipulates a `priority` attribute.

> **NOTE** Some parsers may not support more than two nested levels of included or imported files. For example, in the previous example, XT returns a different value when `included.xsl` contains an imported (`import2.xsl`) stylesheet.

7.1.4 The `<xsl:apply-imports>` Instruction Element

The `<xsl:apply-imports>` instruction element is used to effectively "requery" imported templates to find one that matches the current template rule's match. It allows a nesting of another template inside the calling template.

The `<xsl:apply-imports>` element has no attributes and is an empty element, as shown in the following element model definition. It can only be used inside a template, and is categorized as an instruction element.

```
<!-- Category: instruction -->
<xsl:apply-imports />
```

The `<xsl:apply-imports>` element searches for an imported template rule with the same match criteria as the `<xsl:template>` element that calls it. For example, if a template rule is matching on `"thoroughfare,"` `<xsl:apply-imports>` in that template rule will search for an imported template with a match value of `"thoroughfare,"` as shown in Example 7–5.

The main stylesheet is doing the basic formatting for the lists, and the imported templates add titles for each thoroughfare and boulevard. We add an `<xsl:import>` element to the main stylesheet to import `title.xsl` and an `<xsl:apply-imports>` in the thoroughfare and boulevard template rules to use the contents of the imported templates.

The `<xsl:apply-imports>` effectively takes the content of the template rule in the imported stylesheet and uses it at the point it is called. The imported template does not affect the contents of the original template rule. They are both processed in order.

If there are several imported template rules that match the same criteria, the processor uses the same priority selection rules as a normal stylesheet, except that only the imported templates are checked.

Example 7–5 : The using `<xsl:apply-imports>` to call an imported template.

MAIN STYLESHEET:

```
<?xml version="1.0"?>
<xsl:stylesheet
      xmlns:xsl="http://www.w3.org/1999/XSL/Transform"
      version="1.0">
<xsl:import href="title.xsl" />

<xsl:template match="/">
      <html>
      <body>
             <xsl:apply-templates/>
      </body>
      </html>
</xsl:template>

<xsl:template match="thoroughfare">

             <xsl:apply-imports/>
      <ul>
             <xsl:apply-templates/>
      </ul>
</xsl:template>

<xsl:template match="boulevard">

             <xsl:apply-imports/>
      <ul>
             <xsl:apply-templates/>
      </ul>
</xsl:template>


<xsl:template match="sidestreet | block">
      <li>
             <xsl:apply-templates/>
      </li>
</xsl:template>

</xsl:stylesheet>
```

IMPORTED STYLESHEET:

Example 7–5 : The using `<xsl:apply-imports>` to call an imported template (continued).

```
<?xml version="1.0"?>
<!-- imported stylesheet title.xsl -->
<xsl:stylesheet
xmlns:xsl="http://www.w3.org/1999/XSL/Transform"
version="1.0">
<xsl:template match="thoroughfare">
      <center>
            <h1>Listing for <xsl:value-of select="@name |
text()"/></h1>
      </center>
</xsl:template>
<xsl:template match="boulevard">
      <center>
            <h1>Listing for the Boulevard</h1>
      </center>
</xsl:template>
</xsl:stylesheet>
```

OUTPUT:

```
<html>
<body>
<center>
<h1>Listing for Governor Drive</h1>
</center>
<ul>Governor Drive</ul>
<center>
<h1>Listing for Whitesburg Drive</h1>
</center>
<ul>
<li>Bob Wallace Avenue</li>
<li>Woodridge Street</li>
</ul>
<center>
<h1>Listing for Bankhead</h1>
</center>
<ul>
<li>Tollgate Road</li>
<li>Oak Drive</li>
</ul>
<center>
<h1>Listing for the Boulevard</h1>
```

Example 7–5 : The using <xsl:apply-imports> to call an imported template (continued).

```
</center>
<ul>
<li>Panorama Street</li>
<li>Highland Plaza</li>
<li>Hutchens Avenue</li>
<li>Wildwood Drive</li>
<li>Old Chimney Road</li>
<li>Carrol Circle</li>
</ul>
</body>
</html>
```

The `<xsl:apply-imports>` element is not a recursive rule like `<xsl:apply-templates>`, which looks for the children of the current element. However, if the included template contains an `<xsl:apply-templates>` element, the children will be processed at that point.

7.2 Template Rule Processing and Priorities

In this section, we will review the concepts of processing template rules and the procedures for resolving conflicts.

Almost every one of the priorities for resolving conflicts discussed in the following sections fall along the general lines that imported elements always have the lowest priority. Any processing or template priority resolution, however, is contingent upon the concept of the current template rule.

7.2.1 The Current Template Rule

The current template rule is always that rule which is being instantiated at any given point in the processing of an XSLT stylesheet. A given template rule becomes the current template rule once its `match` pattern has been successfully matched in the input XML data instance. The template rule is not the current template rule while the matching evaluation is occurring, but becomes so immediately upon a successful match and subsequent instantiation of the template it contains.

7.2.2 Conflict Resolution for Template Rules

The use of `<xsl:import>` and `<xsl:include>` elements raises additional considerations for the overall processing model of XSLT stylesheets. Specifically, it is quite possible that there can be competing or conflicting template rules. In other words, two or more `<xsl:template>` elements might match on the same node-set, for example. While it is possible for duplicate template rules to be defined in one stylesheet, it is much more likely that there will be duplicates when stylesheets are included or imported. The XSLT processor selects the appropriate template rule to use at any given time during the instantiation of the stylesheet, based on specific precedence and priority rules. The default selection criteria is based on the order rule of precedence.

7.2.2.1 The Order Rule of Precedence

There is a general procedure, or default processing model, for resolving conflicts or competing components in XML, which applies to precedence. For example, when defining entities in a DTD or document instance, if you define the same entity more than once, the last—in document order as processed—is given precedence. The same applies for template rules when no other factors affecting precedence are present.

When this happens, the same standard principle of "order" for resolving such conflicts (which is somewhat like the Biblical notion that the last shall be first) is used. In other words, the default processing model will always assign highest precedence to the last of any given set of equivalent or competing template rules. Order is used as the default precedence—or conflict resolution—when no other specific factors are identified to establish priority.

This basic "last shall be first" resolution rule is subject to several mediating provisions. As noted in Section 3.1.3.3, `<xsl:template>` elements can use the `priority` attribute to explicitly stipulate a precedence for resolution. If a priority is not specified, or priority is declared with an empty value, the precedence of template rules is selected using the "order rule" for precedence, according to the order they appear in the stylesheet.

When a `match` attribute on a template rule contains a union indicator (|) to effectively select more than one node-set, the template rule is treated as two separate rules, one for each choice in the order they occur. Once the two separate rules have been "split" in the processor's view, the same template selection rules apply.

7.2.2.2 Import Precedence of Template Rules

When imported templates are involved, the XSLT specification refers to this as the import precedence of a template. Templates are selected based on the order in which they were imported into the calling stylesheet. If the conflicting template comes before a template in the stylesheet, it has a lower import precedence, because imported templates are always first in the stylesheet. It may be helpful to remember that the last template rule in the document has the highest precedence. Using the example from the XSLT specification, Section 2.6.2:

- stylesheet *A* imports stylesheets *B* and *C* in that order;
- stylesheet *B* imports stylesheet *D*;
- stylesheet *C* imports stylesheet *E*.

Then the order of import precedence (lowest first) is *D*, *B*, *E*, *C*, *A*. It is easier to imagine the order of import precedence with a diagram showing the implicit nested priority given to each as in Figure 7–1.

In this case, using `<xsl:apply-templates select="block">` would automatically match the `<xsl:template>` rule 5 in stylesheet A, because it is the last template rule in the stylesheet.

Import precedence is lowest when the number is low and highest when the number is high, so in this example, 1 is lowest, which is the template rule in stylesheet D, and 5 is highest, which is the template rule from stylesheet A.

7.2.2.3 Priority of Template Rules

The priority attribute of the `<xsl:template>` element provides a means for an explicit order of selection to be used on template rules. Again, the higher numbers take higher priority.

Negative numbers are treated just like normal real negative numbers on a number scale; the higher the number, the lower the priority. In other words,

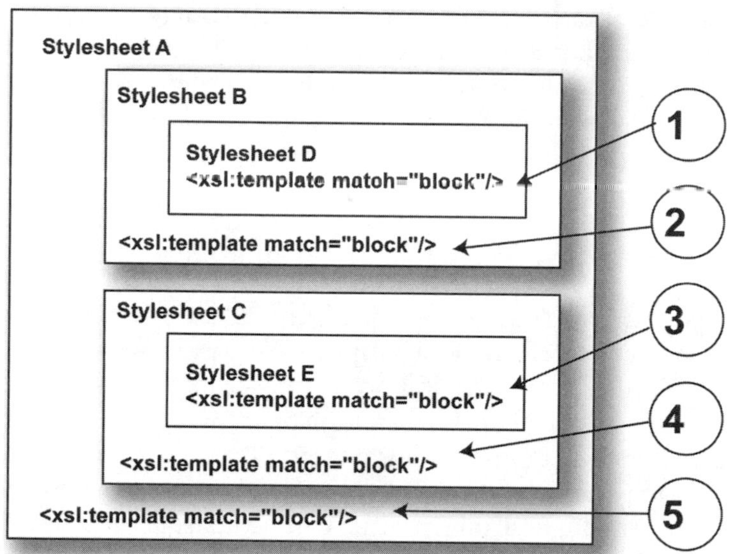

Figure 7–1 Model of import precedence among five stylesheets.

-5 is lower than -2, so in a conflict, the template rule with a priority of -2 would get selected over the same template rule with a priority of -5.

Any `<xsl:include>` elements are resolved before the conflict resolution starts, much like resolving entities before parsing. The resulting template rule is treated as if it was originally written in the stylesheet, and not "included." Once `<xsl:include>` elements have been resolved, the conflict resolution process begins with these rules:

1. If any conflicting rules result from an `<xsl:import>`, they are removed from consideration because they appear first in the fully resolved stylesheet.
2. If a numerical priority has been stipulated with the `priority` attribute, the template rules are selected based on their priority value.
3. If no priority has been stipulated, there is a default priority that is determined based on the nature of the pattern, which is the value of the `<xsl:template>` element's `match` attribute. Basically, the more specific the pattern, the higher the priority.

   If there are range of alternatives separated by |, then these are treated like individual rules. For example, `<xsl:template`

match="block | sidestreet"> is treated as two separate template rules:

```
<xsl:template match="block">
<xsl:template match="sidestreet">
```

Priority is assigned to template rules that do not have explicit priority values assigned as follows:

a. If the pattern is either namespaced or is a processing-instruction, and has an axis of either child or attribute, it is considered to have priority value of 0.

b. If it is non-namespaced, or an NCName, and has an axis of either child or attribute, it has a slightly lower priority value of -0.25.

c. If it just a node test, preceded by a child or attribute axis, then it is still lower with a value of -0.5.

d. In any other case, the default priority is 0.5.

Many of these concepts are rarely necessary to consciously consider when writing a stylesheet, though they are worth referring to in debugging the unexpected results from one. The default priorities are already at work in any template rule, and so you need not memorize or be actively aware of them in order to construct and work with XSLT stylesheets. However, it is sometimes necessary to override the precedence and priorities of a template.

7.2.3 Overriding Import Template Rule Precedence and Priorities

When writing an XSLT stylesheet, you have two options of providing for anticipated or possible conflicts when you know in advance how you want them to be resolved. The first is by using the priority attribute on the <xsl:template> element. The second is by forcing a template to be selected at a certain location in a stylesheet, which entails the use of one of two XSLT instruction elements, either <xsl:apply-imports> or

<xsl:call-template>. These elements are used within the context of an <xsl:template> to call and use the content of another <xsl:template> element. These two methods are discussed in the following sections.

7.2.3.1 Establishing Priority with the priority Attribute in <xsl:template>

In Chapter 3, we introduced the priority attribute of the <xsl:template> top-level element. In short, it is an optional attribute whose value can be a number, or an expression that resolves to a number, establishing the relative priority among two or more otherwise conflicting <xsl:template> elements.

Using priority is a simple matter of knowing how many possible conflicts one has and numbering them according to the preferred resolution for order of precedence, as shown in Example 7–6.

Example 7–6 : Resolving conflicts with the priority attribute in a template.

```
<xsl:template match="/" priority="1">
     <!-- do some stuff -->
</xsl:template>
<xsl:template match="/" priority="2">
     <!-- do different stuff -->
</xsl:template>
```

In this example, the priority attribute—or even the need for two different template rules—seems sort of pointless. As it is written, the template rule with a priority of 2 always wins out, simply because it comes last in the document. However, the processor is not using the "order rule" in this case because the <xsl:template> elements have a priority attribute, so if the order of the template rules was reversed, the priority 2 template would still be used instead of the one with a priority of 1.

In all cases with template rules that are not imported, if the priority attribute is declared, it will determine which of the conflicting template rules is invoked. The priority attribute value for an imported top-level element, however, cannot under any circumstances elevate the relative priority of an imported element over a non-imported element. However, top-level elements brought into a stylesheet with <xsl:include> are *not* considered to be imported, so their relative priority attribute values, if given, *do* apply.

7.2.3.2 Overriding Import Priority with <xsl:apply-imports>

The <xsl:apply-imports> instruction element, discussed in Section 7.1.4, works within the context of the current template rule in which it is called. In effect, it references <xsl:template> elements imported with a declaration of <xsl:import> and applies the content of the imported template to the current template rule at the point where it is referenced. Where imported elements are otherwise lowest on the possible priority list for conflicting elements, they are "redeemed" when <xsl:apply-imports> is used. The selection of the template that is used still follows the rules for priority, but the selection is limited to only those templates that were imported. This does not affect the original priority that was used to select the current template rule. Because <xsl:apply-imports> can only be used inside a template rule, the original template rule must be matched and instantiated, using the original priority rules, prior to processing the imported rule.

Using the <xsl:apply-imports> element does not "remove" the other template rules. It is used to allow nested processing of template rules that would otherwise never be matched because they were imported.

7.2.3.3 Overriding Import Priority with <xsl:call-template>

The <xsl:call-template> element, covered in Chapter 3, is used to call template elements that have been specifically named. The <xsl:call template> element is only used within the context of an <xsl:template> element and is used to force the use of a named template at the point where it is called. When using the <xsl:call-template> element, it is necessary to have declared a template by name and use that name for calling it.

One of the most interesting things about <xsl:call-template> is that it can be used to invoke imported templates by name—provided they have been given a name with the name attribute—such that their otherwise lowly position in the hierarchy is obviated. Again, this is largely the same effect as the <xsl:apply-imports>, but the selection of the template rule is specifically targeted by using a name, whether the named template is declared in the home stylesheet or in an external stylesheet. While the <xsl:apply-imports> element only selects the imported template with the highest priority, <xsl:call template> selects a specific template, ignoring all priority and import rules.

For example, working with the files from Example 7–5, we could add a name to the imported template, title.xsl, as shown in Example 7–7.

Example 7–7 : Modified title.xsl with a named template.

```
<?xml version="1.0"?>
<!-- imported stylesheet title.xsl -->
<xsl:stylesheet
xmlns:xsl="http://www.w3.org/1999/XSL/Transform"
version="1.0">
<xsl:template match="thoroughfare" name="called-template">
      <center>
            <h1>Listing for <xsl:value-of select="@name |
text()"/></h1>
      </center>
</xsl:template>
<xsl:template match="boulevard">
      <center>
            <h1>Listing for the Boulevard</h1>
      </center>
</xsl:template>

</xsl:stylesheet>
```

We could then use <xsl:call-template> in the main stylesheet to elevate that part of title.xsl so that the precedence of the imported elements is ignored. The named template is called using the name attribute of the <xsl:call-template> element, as shown below.

```
<xsl:template match="thoroughfare">
            <xsl:call-template name="called-template"/>
      <ul>
            <xsl:apply-templates/>
      </ul>
</xsl:template>
```

Once again, all the included and imported stylesheets will be resolved, and since the named template `called-template` is part of the imported elements from `title.xsl`, it can be invoked by name. The `match` attribute on the called template is ignored, and the content of the template is used within the context of the template calling the `called-template`. The same rules of precedence apply to the calling template when using the `<xsl:call-template>` element, and the called template's content is used, regardless of its original precedence or priority. The other template rules from the imported elements are not addressed directly, so they keep their order in the priority rules.

Working with Variables

- `<xsl:variable>`
- `<xsl:param>`
- `<xsl:with-param>`

8

XSLT provides the functionality to create special values that can be declared and used by expressions in other elements in the stylesheet. These values are attached, or bound, to named objects called *variables.* A variable in XSLT can be either global (available throughout the stylesheet) or local (available only to the element where it is declared), and it *must* be declared before it can be used.

In this chapter, we will discuss the two ways to declare variables in XSLT, using either `<xsl:variable>` or `<xsl:param>`, and the process of calling, or referencing, variable values. We will also discuss `<xsl:with-param>`, which allows a template to override the value of a variable that was previously declared using an `<xsl:param>` element.

8.1 Declaring and Binding Variables

Variables are declared in an XSLT stylesheet with either the `<xsl:variable>` element or the `<xsl:param>` element. Binding a value to a variable is the process of *assigning* the variable to a value. Therefore, when a value is assigned to a variable, it is said to be *bound* to that variable. Declaring a variable and binding a value to a variable happen simultaneously. It is not possible to declare a variable without also assigning a value to it. It may help to remember that, when a variable is *declared*, it refers to the physical location of the `<xsl:variable>` or `<xsl:param>` in the stylesheet, and when a variable is *bound*, it refers to the processor's instantiation of the value of that variable.

Variable values are bound at the point in the stylesheet where they are declared, not where they are called. This means that any evaluation of an expression in a variable uses the context of the variable declaration as its context. In other words, *where* the variable is declared is very important because the value of the variable is tied to the current context.

Global variables declared with `<xsl:variable>` are not *variable* in the true sense of the word. They are bound to a value using the root node as the context, and they keep their assigned value throughout the processing of the stylesheet. Once a global variable that is declared with `<xsl:variable>` is bound to a value, that variable will remain the same. However, it is possible to declare a local variable of the same name to temporarily override that global variable value.

Global variables that are declared using the `<xsl:param>` element *are* variable because they have an initial default value that can be overridden with the `<xsl:with-param>` element during the processing of a template.

Local variables (declared with either `<xsl:variable>` or `<xsl:param>`) are also variable because they are reinstantiated; that is, their values are reassigned according to the current context during the processing of a template.

8.1.1 The `<xsl:variable>` Top-Level Element

The `<xsl:variable>` element is used to declare a variable with a fixed value, and can function both as a top-level element and as an instruction element. When declared as a top-level element, the variable is considered to be global. When declared as an instruction element, it is considered to be local. The `<xsl:variable>` element accepts two attributes: the `name` attribute, which is required, and the `select` attribute, which is optional. The following element model definition shows the content of the `<xsl:variable>` element as a template, but the content is not allowed if the `select` attribute contains an expression:

```
<!-- Category: top-level-element -->

<!-- Category: instruction -->

<xsl:variable

  name = qname

  select = expression>

  <!-- Content: template -->

</xsl:variable>
```

The required `name` attribute of the `<xsl:variable>` element is used to identify the variable and takes the form of a QName. A variable reference uses the same name to retrieve the value of the variable (see Section 8.3 for more information on variable references).

The optional `select` attribute contains an expression and is used to bind the value of the variable to the object that is the result of evaluating the expression. If the `select` attribute is used, the content of the `<xsl:variable>` element must be empty.

If there is no `select` attribute, the content of the `<xsl:variable>` element is a template, and the value bound to the variable is the result of instantiating that template. Note that the result of instantiating a template in an `<xsl:variable>` element is a result tree fragment, or RTF (see Section 8.2 for more information on result tree fragments).

The value bound to a variable is available to the expressions in other elements based on where it is declared. When declared within an `<xsl:template>` element at the instruction element level, it is a variable local to that context only, and it is only available to the functions and elements that follow it, within that template. In other words, the value of that variable is only valid inside the realm of the template where it is declared, and is only available to elements that occur after its declaration. On the other hand, if a variable is declared with an `<xsl:variable>` as a top-level element, the value of the variable is available globally to the remaining elements in the stylesheet following its declaration.

8.1.2 The <xsl:param> Top-Level Element

The <xsl:param> element is used to declare a variable with a default value. It accepts two attributes: the name attribute, which is required, and the select attribute, which is optional. The content of the <xsl:param> element is a template, but the content is not allowed if the select attribute contains an expression.

The value of the variable declared using the <xsl:param> element is only a default value, which is used unless another explicit value is supplied before the variable is referenced, or called. This default value can be modified prior to use by the <xsl:with-param> element, which is discussed in the following section.

Although not explicitly categorized as an instruction element in the element model definition shown below, the <xsl:param> element is allowed at the same level as instruction elements.[1] However, when used inside a template, it *must* occur before any other elements in the template. When declared as a top-level element, the variable is considered to be global; when declared at the instruction level, the variable is considered to be local.

```
<!-- Category: top-level-element -->

<xsl:param

  name = qname

  select = expression>

  <!-- Content: template -->

</xsl:param>
```

The required name attribute of the <xsl:param> element is used to identify the variable and takes the form of a QName. A variable reference uses the same name to retrieve the value of the variable (see Section 8.3).

1. Technically, <xsl:param> is not a true "instruction element" even though it is allowed at the same level as instruction elements. Instruction elements are executed and replaced by the RTFs that they create, while an <xsl:param> element only defines a default value.

The optional select attribute contains an expression and is used to bind the value of the variable to the object that is the result of evaluating the expression. If the select attribute is used, the content of the <xsl:param> element must be empty.

If there is no select attribute, the content of the <xsl:param> element is a template, and the value bound to the variable is the result of instantiating that template. Note that the result of instantiating the template in an <xsl:param> element is an RTF (see Section 8.2).

The value bound to the variable is available to the expressions in other elements based on where it is declared. When declared within an <xsl:param> element at the instruction element level, it is a variable local to that context only, and only available to the functions and elements that follow it. In other words, the value of that variable is only valid inside the realm of the template where it is declared, and is only available to elements that occur after its declaration. On the other hand, if the variable is declared with an <xsl:param> as a top-level element, the value of the variable is available globally to the remaining elements in the stylesheet following its declaration.

8.1.3 The <xsl:with-param> Element

The <xsl:with-param> element is used to override the value of a variable declared with <xsl:param>. It has the same basic model, shown in the element model definition below, as <xsl:variable> and <xsl:param>. However, a variable must be declared using <xsl:param> prior to using <xsl:with-param> to override it.

```
<xsl:with-param

  name = qname

  select = expression>

  <!-- Content: template -->

</xsl:with-param>
```

The required name attribute of the <xsl:with-param> element is used to identify the variable and takes the form of a QName. A variable reference uses the same name to retrieve the value of the variable (see Section 8.3). Note that a variable with the same name must have been declared using `<xsl:param>` prior to using this element.

The optional `select` attribute contains an expression and is used to bind the value of the variable to the object that is the result of evaluating the expression. If the `select` attribute is used, the content of the `<xsl:with-param>` element must be empty.

If there is no `select` attribute, the content of the `<xsl:with-param>` element is a template, and the value bound to the variable is the result of instantiating that template. Note that the result of instantiating the template in an `<xsl:with-param>` element is an RTF (see Section 8.2).

Using `<xsl:with-param>` makes the value of a parameter more flexible. After you have declared a variable with a default value using `<xsl:param>`, you can use the `<xsl:with-param>` element to reset that value within the current template's context. In other words, `<xsl:with-param>` gives a context-specific value for the variable, which affects only the template being called.

The `<xsl:with-param>` element is neither a top-level element nor an instruction element. It can only be used within the `<xsl:call-template>` element or the `<xsl:apply-templates>` elements. The template called or applied using either `<xsl:call-template>` or `<xsl:apply-templates>` is therefore the only context that uses the new value of the variable declared with `<xsl:with-param>`. The original value for the variable declared with `<xsl:param>` is overridden for the context of the template being called. It is important to note that `<xsl:with-param>` can only be used to affect the values of variables already declared using `<xsl:param>`. If there is no declaration of the original variable in place for a template, it is ignored.

8.2 Result Tree Fragments

When a variable declaration element contains a template, the content of the template is instantiated and the resulting object is an RTF. This creates a new kind of object, different from the four standard object types (node-set, string, Boolean, and number). An RTF is a node-set that contains one node, whose children are the nodes that are produced by the instruction elements in the template.

Although an RTF is technically a node-set, there are restrictions on how this new type of node-set can be accessed or used. The way in which the variable is referenced in subsequent template rules determines how that RTF will be written to the actual output result tree. If the RTF is output using `<xsl:copy-of>`, the nodes in the RTF are sent to the output, including the tags and text content. Otherwise, the output will be the text content of the RTF, without any markup.

When a variable is bound to an RTF, a portion of the actual output result tree is being bound. Additional processing on RTFs resulting from variables is allowed, but not all functions are available. Only functions that can be applied to strings are allowed on RTFs. For example, using `count()` on an RTF will return an error. Operations that involve patterns and predicates are not allowed. Also, an RTF cannot be further processed using any `/`, `//`, or `[]` tokens in it—in other words, no absolute location path tokens, no descendant axis abbreviations, and no predicates. Otherwise, operations performed of the type permitted on strings, when performed on RTFs, behave just as they would on any other equivalent node-set.

Example 8–1 shows a variable that contains a template with three LREs, each containing an instruction element.

Example 8–1 : Variable declaration with template content.

```
<xsl:variable name="numvar">
     <num><xsl:value-of select="1"/></num>
     <num><xsl:value-of select="2"/></num>
     <num><xsl:value-of select="3"/></num>
</xsl:variable>
```

The result of instantiating the variable is a node-set containing the three `<num>` nodes. Using `<xsl:copy-of select="$numvar">` returns the nodes and their content:

```
<num>1</num>
<num>2</num>
<num>3</num>
```

The value of the node-set, when extracted using `<xsl:value-of select="$numvar">`, is the string value of a concatenation of its children; in this case, the string is "`123`." However, using a node-set function like `<xsl:value-of select="count($numvar)">` is an error because node-set operations on RTFs are not allowed.

In an example using Markup City, it is possible to store nodes from the input in a variable as follows:

```
<xsl:variable name="blocks">
<xsl:copy-of select="//block"/>
</xsl:variable>
```

This example stores all the `<block>` elements and their text children in the variable as a single node-set. The value of the new node-set can then be extracted using `<xsl:value-of select="$blocks">`, which returns the concatenation of the text in each block.

Using `<xsl:copy-of select="$blocks">` retrieves the entire set of `<block>` nodes, including their children text nodes, as shown in Example 8–2.

Example 8–2 : Extracting a node-set in a variable using `<xsl:copy-of>`.

INPUT:

```
<?xml version="1.0"?>
<main>
      <parkway>
            <thoroughfare>Governor Drive</thoroughfare>
            <thoroughfare name="Whitesburg Drive">
                  <sidestreet>Bob Wallace Avenue</sidestreet>
                  <block>1st Street</block>
                  <block>2nd Street</block>
<block>3rd Street</block>
                  <sidestreet>Woodridge Street</sidestreet>
            </thoroughfare>
            <thoroughfare name="Bankhead">
                  <sidestreet>Tollgate Road</sidestreet>
                  <block>First Street</block>
                  <block>Second Street</block>
                  <block>Third Street</block>
                  <sidestreet>Oak Drive</sidestreet>
            </thoroughfare>
      </parkway>
      <boulevard>
                  <block>Panorama Street</block>
                  <block>Highland Plaza</block>
```

Example 8–2 : Extracting a node-set in a variable using `<xsl:copy-of>` (continued).

```
      <block>Hutchens Avenue</block>
                  <block>Wildwood Drive</block>
                  <block>Old Chimney Road</block>
                  <block>Carrol Circle</block>
      </boulevard>
</main>
```

STYLESHEET:

```
<?xml version="1.0"?>
<xsl:stylesheet xmlns:xsl="http://www.w3.org/1999/XSL/Transform"
           version="1.0">
<xsl:variable name="blocks">
<xsl:copy-of select="//block"/>
</xsl:variable>
<xsl:template match="/">
<xsl:copy-of select="$blocks"/>
</xsl:template>
</xsl:stylesheet>
```

RESULT:

```
<?xml version="1.0" encoding="utf-8"?>
<block>1st Street</block>
<block>2nd Street</block>
<block>3rd Street</block>
<block>First Street</block>
<block>Second Street</block>
<block>Third Street</block>
<block>Panorama Street</block>
<block>Highland Plaza</block>
<block>Hutchens Avenue</block>
<block>Wildwood Drive</block>
<block>Old Chimney Road</block>
<block>Carrol Circle</block>
```

The template inside the `<xsl:variable>` element shown in this example is retrieved when the variable is referenced, or *called,* using the variable reference, `$blocks`.

8.3 Using Variable References

Regardless of how a variable is declared, either with `<xsl:variable>` or `<xsl:param>`, or if it is overridden with `<xsl:with-param>`, the value bound to the variable is accessed using a *variable reference.*[2] A variable reference is the mechanism used to retrieve the value of a variable. Variable reference takes the form `$variable-name`, where "variable-name" is the name of the variable declared using the `name` attribute on the declaring element. Note that this means the variable name is also by definition a QName.

The template rule in Example 8–3 declares a variable named `myparent` and gets its value using the `name()` function. The value of the variable is output with the `$myparent` variable reference in the `<xsl:value-of>` element.

Example 8–3 : Declaration of a variable with `<xsl:variable>`.

```
<xsl:template match="block">
<xsl:variable name="myparent" select="name(..)" />
<xsl:value-of select="$myparent"/>
</xsl:template>
```

The result of this template is to output the name of the parent for each `<block>` element. Variable references can only be used in the context of expressions. However, you cannot use a variable reference directly in a `match` or `use` attribute. Some processors do allow variable references inside the *predicate* of an expression within the `match` or `use` attribute. For example, in XT, it is not valid to use `$num` in a match for the template rule `<xsl:template match="$num"/>`, but it is valid in the predicate of match for the template rule `<xsl:template match="//*[$num]"/>`. If the value of `$num` is 3, the template rule will match every element that has a position of 3. While this functionality is available with some processors, it is not guaranteed to work with all or future versions of processors.

2. Although variables are defined in XSLT, variable references are the realm of XPath because they are used in expressions.

8.3.1 Local vs. Global Variables

The value of a variable is bound to the variable within the context of the declaration. In other words, the value is determined based on *where* the variable is declared. The value is available to the elements that occur after the declaration has been made, but only within the same context as the declaration. However, if the variable is declared using a top-level element, it is considered a *global* variable and its value is bound based on the root node as a context. Global variables are available to all elements and their children, regardless of where reference to the variable occurs in the stylesheet.

If a variable is declared within the context of a template rule, that variable is a *local* variable and is only available to the contents of that template rule. Local variables do not pass on their value to any templates called by the template rule with `<xsl:apply-templates>`, `<xsl:call-template>`, or `<xsl:apply-imports>`. However, variable values can be passed to templates using the `<xsl:with-param>` element in either `<xsl:apply-templates>` or `<xsl:call-template>`.

Example 8–4 shows a template matching on `<parkway>` that contains a local variable. An additional template matching on `<block>` tries to use the same variable, but cannot, because the value of the local variable is not defined in the context of `<block>`.

Example 8–4 : Using local variables incorrectly.

```
<?xml version="1.0"?>
<xsl:stylesheet
      xmlns:xsl="http://www.w3.org/1999/XSL/Transform"
      version="1.0">
<xsl:template match="parkway">
<xsl:variable name="num" select="3" />
<xsl:value-of select="$num"/>
<xsl:apply-templates/>
</xsl:template>
<xsl:template match="block">
<xsl:value-of select="$num"/>
<xsl:apply-templates/>
</xsl:template>
</xsl:stylesheet>
```

Using this example would produce an error because the variable num is declared as a local variable in the context of <parkway>. The template matching on block cannot "see" the value of the variable. Declaring the variable at the top level as a global variable would resolve this problem, as shown in Example 8–5.

Example 8–5 : Using global variables.

```
<?xml version="1.0"?>
<xsl:stylesheet
      xmlns:xsl="http://www.w3.org/1999/XSL/Transform"
      version="1.0">

<xsl:variable name="num" select="3" />

<xsl:template match="parkway">
<xsl:value-of select="$num"/>
<xsl:apply-templates/>
</xsl:template>

<xsl:template match="block">
<xsl:value-of select="$num"/>
<xsl:apply-templates/>
</xsl:template>

</xsl:stylesheet>
```

8.3.2 Duplicate Declarations (Shadowing)

When a value is bound to a variable, the value of the variable becomes static, or fixed, within the context of its binding. The value of a variable can only be changed after it has been bound by rebinding the value with a new declaration or, if it was originally declared using the <xsl:param> element, by using the <xsl:with-param> element to pass a new variable value in its place. Declaring a variable that is a duplicate of a previously declared variable is called *shadowing*.

According to the XSLT specification, shadowing at the *same level* by declaring two variables with the same name is not allowed. If this occurs, the results vary depending on the processor used. Some processors may return an error, while others may use the last variable declared. Declaring variables with the same name in different contexts, however, is allowed.

Declaring a local variable with the same name as one that was previously declared at the top level is valid. A local variable with the same name as a global variable temporarily overrides the value of the global variable within the context of the local declaration of the variable. Example 8–6 demonstrates the order of precedence for variables with duplicate names.

Example 8–6 : Order of precedence for variables with duplicate names.

```
<?xml version="1.0"?>
<xsl:stylesheet
      xmlns:xsl="http://www.w3.org/1999/XSL/Transform"
      version="1.0">

<xsl:variable name="num" select="1" />
<xsl:param name="num" select="2" />

<xsl:template match="parkway">
<xsl:param name="num" select="3" />
<xsl:value-of select="$num"/>
<xsl:apply-templates/>
</xsl:template>

<xsl:template match="block">
<xsl:value-of select="$num"/>
<xsl:apply-templates/>
</xsl:template>

</xsl:stylesheet>
```

In this stylesheet, the variable named num is defined three times, two at the top, or the global, level and once locally within the context of the <parkway> element. The resulting value of the variable is 2 in the global sense, but 3 when it is redeclared as a local attribute inside the template rule for <parkway>.

> **NOTE** Some processors will simply ignore the first <xsl:variable> declaration (the one with a value of 1). Other processors will generate an error when any shadowing in the same context occurs.

Variable values declared locally in a template are not inherited by the template rules for the children of the element. So, the template rule for <block> would use the global value of 2, not the local value of 3.

Using our Markup City, Example 8–7 shows a variable declaration that returns a different value based on which element is the parent of the current block.

Example 8–7 : Context based <xsl:variable> declaration.

STYLESHEET:

```
<xsl:stylesheet
      xmlns:xsl="http://www.w3.org/1999/XSL/Transform"
      version="1.0">
<xsl:template match="text()"/>
<xsl:template match="block">
<xsl:variable name="myparent" select="name(..)" />
<xsl:value-of select="$myparent"/><xsl:text>: </xsl:text>
<xsl:value-of select="text()"/>
<xsl:text>
</xsl:text>
</xsl:template>
</xsl:stylesheet>
```

RESULT:

```
thoroughfare: 1st Street
thoroughfare: 2nd Street
thoroughfare: 3rd Street
thoroughfare: First Street
thoroughfare: Second Street
thoroughfare: Third Street
boulevard: Panorama Street
boulevard: Highland Plaza
boulevard: Hutchens Avenue
boulevard: Wildwood Drive
boulevard: Old Chimney Road
boulevard: Carrol Circle
```

Based on the context, the value of the variable myparent is different depending on which <block> is being processed. Using the name() function with two dots .. (the abbreviation for the parent) in the variable declaration <xsl:variable name="myparent" select="name(..)" /> binds the name of the parent of the context node to the variable. The variable is referenced using <xsl:value-of select="$myparent"/>. A little creative use of <xsl:text> puts in line breaks and the colon, and <xsl:value-of select="text()"/> pulls out the text nodes in the blocks (notice that the first template rule, <xsl:template match="text()"/>, is used to suppress all the text nodes initially). If the context node is a <block> in the <thoroughfare>, the value of the variable is thoroughfare. If the context node is a <block> in the <boulevard>, the value of the variable is boulevard. The local variable myparent is being reinstantiated for each <block> element that it encounters.

8.3.3 Using the **<xsl:with-param>** Instruction Element

The <xsl:with-param> element can be used to change the value of a variable used in a template rule by passing a new value for that variable from another template rule. The variable that is being passed in must have been previously declared in the context of the template being called, or the new variable will just be ignored. This allows parent templates to pass values into templates for children elements. Recall that variables are limited to the scope of the context where they are declared, so simply declaring the variable in the parent template of an element does not make that variable available to the child element's template.

For example, suppose we wanted to divide up our city by precinct based on the kind of street, either a thoroughfare or a boulevard. We could change the value of the "precinct" variable defined in the <block> template using an <xsl:with-param> element inside an <xsl:apply-templates> element, as shown below.

```
<xsl:template match="thoroughfare">
      <xsl:apply-templates select="block">
            <xsl:with-param name="precinct" select="5"/>
      </xsl:apply-templates>
</xsl:template>
<xsl:template match="block">
      <xsl:param name="precinct" select="4"/>
      <xsl:value-of select="$precinct"/>
</xsl:template>
```

In this case, the <block>s that are in <thoroughfare>s would use the "precinct" value 5, but the <block>s in any other context would use the default value declared in the <block> template rule, 4. Normally, templates would not be able to pass the value of a variable to other templates, but <xsl:with-param> allows this to happen. Example 8–8 shows a complete stylesheet.

8.4 Comparing <xsl:variable> and <xsl:param>

Syntactically, there is no difference between <xsl:variable> and <xsl:param>. The content model of both elements is the same. The way these elements declare variables is the same. However, the value of the variable declared using <xsl:param> is only a default that can be changed with the <xsl:with-param> element, while the <xsl:variable> value cannot be changed. The only other difference is that there is a restriction on *where* the <xsl:param> element can be used. It must always come before any other elements if used within a template rule.

Because <xsl:variable> and <xsl:param> declare variables in the same way, if they are both present in the same context and they both have the same name, they are considered duplicates and result in an error. Duplicate declarations, or shadowing, are discussed in Section 8.3.2.

Using <xsl:param> together with <xsl:variable> raises certain contextual restrictions on syntax. When a variable and parameter are both declared in a template, the <xsl:param> must come first.

8.5 Comparing <xsl:with-param> to <xsl:param> and <xsl:variable>

The <xsl:with-param> element has the same content model and declares a variable in the same manner as <xsl:variable> and <xsl:param>. However, <xsl:with-param> must be used inside either <xsl:apply-templates> or <xsl:call-template>, and using it replaces the value of the variable that was declared using the

Example 8–8 : Extended example using `<xsl:param>` and `<xsl:with-param>`.

STYLESHEET:

```
<xsl:stylesheet
      xmlns:xsl="http://www.w3.org/1999/XSL/Transform"
      version="1.0">
<xsl:template match="text()"/>
<xsl:template match="thoroughfare">
<xsl:apply-templates select="block">
<xsl:with-param name="precinct" select="5"/>
</xsl:apply-templates>
</xsl:template>
<xsl:template match="block">
<xsl:param name="precinct" select="4"/>
Precinct: <xsl:value-of select="$precinct"/>
Block name: <xsl:value-of select="text()"/>
</xsl:template>
</xsl:stylesheet>
```

OUTPUT:

```
Precinct: 5
Block name: 1st Street
Precinct: 5
Block name: 2nd Street
Precinct: 5
Block name: 3rd Street
Precinct: 5
Block name: First Street
Precinct: 5
Block name: Second Street
Precinct: 5
Block name: Third Street
Precinct: 4
Block name: Panorama Street
Precinct: 4
Block name: Highland Plaza
Precinct: 4
Block name: Hutchens Avenue
Precinct: 4
Block name: Wildwood Drive
Precinct: 4
Block name: Old Chimney Road
Precinct: 4
Block name: Carrol Circle
```

original `<xsl:param>`. If there is no `<xsl:param>` declaration in the template being called, the variable is ignored. The `<xsl:with-param>` element cannot be used to change the value of a variable declared with `<xsl:variable>`.

Duplication, Iteration, and Conditional XSLT Elements

- <xsl:copy-of>
- <xsl:copy>
- <xsl:if>
- <xsl:for-each>
- <xsl:choose>
- <xsl:when>
- <xsl:otherwise>
- <xsl:sort>
- <xsl:number>
- <xsl:fallback>

9

There are three very important concepts in XSLT, as in any programming language, that encompass the ability to duplicate objects, conditionally process objects, and iterate through a list of objects sequentially. This chapter will discuss these three concepts and their applicable XSLT elements.

The duplication elements in XSLT that provide the ability to copy an entire XML structure, or just a tag name, are `<xsl:copy-of>` and `<xsl:copy>`. Conditional elements, those that involve a condition or test to select objects, are `<xsl:if>`, `<xsl:choose>`, and `<xsl:fallback>`. The elements that are in some way iterative are `<xsl:for-each>`, `<xsl:sort>`, and `<xsl:number>`. The `<xsl:sort>` element, while not necessarily iterative, works on node-sets to reorder them prior to an iteration. The two children of `<xsl:choose>`, `<xsl:when>` and `<xsl:otherwise>`, are also covered in this chapter.

The `<xsl:fallback>` instruction element, while not technically a conditional element, is used to provide an alternative process when an XSLT instruction fails. It is covered in the last section of this chapter.

9.1 The <xsl:copy-of> Instruction Element

The <xsl:copy-of> instruction element is used to create a copy of a node branch, or subtree, from the input tree. It is an empty element that has one required attribute, `select`, which contains an expression, as shown in the following element model definition:

```
<!-- Category: instruction -->

<xsl:copy-of

  select = expression />
```

When the expression in the `select` attribute is evaluated, the resulting object is copied to the output result tree. However, *what* is copied depends on the type of object produced by the expression.

If the expression produces either a node-set or an RTF, <xsl:copy-of> will copy each node in the node-set or RTF, including markup, children elements, and descendents of the node, and place the results in the output result tree. Attributes, namespaces, text, PIs, and comments in the node-set are also copied. The <xsl:copy-of> instruction element effectively "transplants" a node branch to the output result tree. If the `select` attribute matches a root, or document root node (/), then that root and its children and descendants are copied to the output result tree.

If the expression in the select attribute returns any object other than a node-set or RTF, then that object is converted to a string and copied to the output.

It is important to know that <xsl:copy-of> does *not* allow you to perform operations on the object returned by the expression before sending it to the output. It is, effectively, a "cut-and-paste" of the matched node. For example, it is not possible to selectively exclude some of the nodes, or to include new elements with LREs. For this reason the <xsl:copy-of> element is empty.

The stylesheet shown in Example 9–1 shows the use of <xsl:copy-of> with a pattern to select the <thoroughfare> elements and copy them into a new element-type name. Because the pattern returns a node-set, the entire <thoroughfare> node is copied for each match.

Example 9–1 : Using `<xsl:copy-of>` to copy a node branch.

INPUT:

```
<?xml version="1.0"?>
<main>
      <parkway>
            <thoroughfare>Governor Drive</thoroughfare>
            <thoroughfare name="Whitesburg Drive">
                  <sidestreet>Bob Wallace Avenue</sidestreet>
                  <block>1st Street</block>
                  <block>2nd Street</block>
                  <block>3rd Street</block>
                  <sidestreet>Woodridge Street</sidestreet>
            </thoroughfare>
            <thoroughfare name="Bankhead">
                  <sidestreet>Tollgate Road</sidestreet>
                  <block>First Street</block>
                  <block>Second Street</block>
                  <block>Third Street</block>
                  <sidestreet>Oak Drive</sidestreet>
            </thoroughfare>
      </parkway>
      <boulevard>
            <block>Panorama Street</block>
            <block>Highland Plaza</block>
            <block>Hutchens Avenue</block>
            <block>Wildwood Drive</block>
            <block>Old Chimney Road</block>
            <block>Carrol Circle</block>
      </boulevard>
</main>
```

STYLESHEET:

```
<?xml version="1.0"?>
<xsl:stylesheet xmlns:xsl="http://www.w3.org/1999/XSL/Transform"
               version="1.0">
<xsl:template match="boulevard"/>
<xsl:template match="parkway">
      <new-parkway>
<xsl:copy-of select="thoroughfare"/>
      </new-parkway>
</xsl:template>
</xsl:stylesheet>
```

Example 9–1 : Using <xsl:copy-of> to copy a node branch (continued).

RESULT:

```
<?xml version="1.0" encoding="utf-8"?>
<new-parkway>
<thoroughfare>Governor Drive</thoroughfare>
<thoroughfare name="Whitesburg Drive">
<sidestreet>Bob Wallace Avenue</sidestreet>
<block>1st Street</block>
<block>2nd Street</block>
<block>3rd Street</block>
<sidestreet>Woodridge Street</sidestreet>
</thoroughfare>
<thoroughfare name="Bankhead">
<sidestreet>Tollgate Road</sidestreet>
<block>First Street</block>
<block>Second Street</block>
<block>Third Street</block>
<sidestreet>Oak Drive</sidestreet>
</thoroughfare>
</new-parkway>
```

This example shows two template rules: `<xsl:template match="boulevard"/>` to match the `<boulevard>` element and suppress its contents, and `<xsl:template match="parkway">` to match the `<parkway>` element and replace it with the `<new-parkway>` element. The template rule that matches on `<parkway>` contains an LRE for the `<new-parkway>` and uses the `<xsl:copy-of select="thoroughfare"/>` to send each `<thoroughfare>` element to the output result tree.

9.2 The <xsl:copy> Instruction Element

The `<xsl:copy>` element creates a copy of the current node's markup. If the current node is an element, the element's tags, including the element-type name and its associated namespace, are copied. However, `<xsl:copy>` does not copy the attribute or children nodes of the element. The optional attribute, `use-attribute-sets`, can be used to include a set of attributes that was defined using the `<xsl:attribute-`

set> element (see Section 6.6.1 for more information on the <xsl:attribute-set> element).The <xsl:copy> element is an instruction element that contains a template, as shown in the following element model definition:

```
<!-- Category: instruction -->

<xsl:copy

  use-attribute-sets = qnames>

  <!-- Content: template -->

</xsl:copy>
```

Working with <xsl:copy> is distinctively different from working with <xsl:copy-of> in two primary ways. On the one hand, the <xsl:copy> instruction element can contain children instruction elements, where the <xsl:copy-of> element cannot. Far more significantly, <xsl:copy-of> copies an entire node branch or RTF, where <xsl:copy> only copies the current node's markup. The children of the matched node are ignored, as are any attribute nodes. The <xsl:copy> effectively erases all the matched element's attributes in the output.

Using <xsl:copy> without any content in the template simply copies the element's tags from the input to the output. Because the <xsl:copy> element ignores children of the current node, this output will be an empty element, as shown in Example 9–2.

Example 9–2 : Simple demonstration of <xsl:copy>.

```
<xsl:template match="block">
      <xsl:copy></xsl:copy>
</xsl:template>
```

This produces <block/>, an empty block element, for each block matched in the input. However, because <xsl:copy> contains a template, it is possible to use additional instruction elements and LREs to process and/or modify the content of the current node when it is copied. As shown in Example 9–3, adding content to the template causes the instantiation of the template to be applied to the current node within the context of the copied tag.

Example 9–3 : Using <xsl:copy> to add content to the current node.

```
<xsl:template match="block">
      <xsl:copy>
            <name>
            <xsl:apply-templates/>
            </name>
      </xsl:copy>
</xsl:template>
```

In this example, the <xsl:copy> element sends the <block> and </block> tags to the output result tree for each <block> element. The <name> LRE appears in the output exactly as-is, and the children of the original input <block> element are sent through using the <xsl:apply-templates> element. The resulting XML structure, using the first <block>, is as follows:

```
<block><name>1st Street</name></block>
```

When <xsl:copy> is used to copy a namespaced node, the local name of the element is copied to the output as well as the prefix for that namespace.

If the element that was used to declare the namespace is not copied to the output with a template rule, the first element that uses the prefix for the namespace will be used to declare the namespace in the output result tree. The processor automatically handles the namespace declaration if it is not copied with a template rule.

Using <xsl:copy> and <xsl:copy-of> together, it is possible to create combinations of otherwise fairly unaltered node-sets from the XML data instance. As Example 9–4 shows, our obsessive city planners in the municipal division of Markup City are rearranging the streets, this time to have all <block>s in just one area, that of the <boulevard>.

Example 9–4 : Using `<xsl:copy>` together with `<xsl:copy-of>`.

STYLESHEET:

```
<?xml version="1.0">
<xsl:stylesheet
      xmlns:xsl="http://www.w3.org/1999/XSL/Transform"
      version="1.0">
<xsl:template match="boulevard">
      <xsl:copy>
            <xsl:copy-of select="//block" />
      </xsl:copy>
</xsl:template>
<xsl:template match="parkway"/>
</xsl:stylesheet>
```

RESULT:

```
<boulevard>
<block>1st Street</block>
<block>2nd Street</block>
<block>3rd Street</block>
<block>First Street</block>
<block>Second Street</block>
<block>Third Street</block>
<block>Panorama Street</block>
<block>Highland Plaza</block>
<block>Hutchens Avenue</block>
<block>Wildwood Drive</block>
<block>Old Chimney Road</block>
<block>Carrol Circle</block>
</boulevard>
```

The template rule matching on the `<boulevard>` element contains an `<xsl:copy>` element used to copy the `<boulevard>` tags into the output result tree. We then take each `<block>` element from the input source document, regardless of its original location, and copy it with the `<xsl:copy-of select="//block"/>` instruction element. Finally, to remove the contents of the old `<parkway>`, we add an empty template rule, `<xsl:template match="parkway"/>`.

While it may not seem very useful to copy just the element's tags to the output, `<xsl:copy>` becomes very useful when the name of the current node is not known. As shown in Example 9–5, using `<xsl:copy>` inside a template that employs the wildcard * to match all the elements, each element's tags, will be copied into the output.

Example 9–5 : Using `<xsl:copy>` to copy all elements.

```
<xsl:template match="*">
      <xsl:copy>
            <xsl:apply-templates />
      </xsl:copy>
</xsl:template>
```

This template will effectively copy the structure of the document, removing all the attributes. New attributes can then be added using `<xsl:attribute>` or the `use-attribute-sets` attribute. You can also copy the original attributes from an element using a combination of `<xsl:for-each>` (discussed in Section 9.3) and `<xsl:copy>`, as shown in Example 9–6.

Example 9–6 : Using `<xsl:copy>` and `<xsl:for-each>` to copy attributes.

```
<xsl:template match="*">
      <xsl:copy>
            <xsl:for-each select="@*">
                  <xsl:copy/>
            </xsl:for-each>
            <xsl:apply-templates />
      </xsl:copy>
</xsl:template>
```

The `<xsl:for-each>` element selects all attributes, using the `"@*"` abbreviation, and the `<xsl:copy>` element inside the `<xsl:for-each>` copies the attribute name and its original value into the output result tree. The content of each element is processed with `<xsl:apply-templates>`. Note that the text nodes are still sent to the output because of built-in template rules, discussed in Chapter 3. To suppress text output, it would be necessary to add an empty template rule, `<xsl:template match="text()"/>`.

9.3 The <xsl:for-each> Instruction Element

The <xsl:for-each> element provides the ability to recursively process a list of nodes. It is an instruction element that can contain zero or more <xsl:sort> elements (see Section 9.4), followed by a template, as shown in the following element model definition.

```
<!-- Category: instruction -->

<xsl:for-each

  select = node-set-expression>

  <!-- Content: (xsl:sort*, template) -->

</xsl:for-each>
```

The value for the required select attribute is a special kind of expression, a *node-set-expression*, which must always result in a node-set. It is an error to use an expression that returns any other kind of object. The instructions contained in the template will be applied to each node matched by the select attribute. The matched nodes are processed in document order, unless a revised order has been selected using <xsl:sort>.

Using Markup City, the stylesheet shown in Example 9–7 allows us to use <xsl:for-each> to process each <block> and use the name of its parent as an attribute named branch on each new <block> element in the output result tree.

Notice that the instruction elements in <xsl:for-each> apply to the current node as selected by the <xsl:for-each> element's select attribute, not the current node matched by the <xsl:template> element. The <xsl:for-each> element is one of the few instruction elements that can change the context of the current node list. It effectively suspends the processing of the node-set matched with <xsl:template>'s match attribute while it processes the new node-set.

If any <xsl:sort> elements are used in an <xsl:for-each>, they must come before any other elements or LREs in the template. The

Example 9–7 : Using <xsl:for-each> to add attributes.

STYLESHEET:

```
<xsl:stylesheet
      xmlns:xsl="http://www.w3.org/1999/XSL/Transform"
      version="1.0">

<xsl:template match="text()"/>
<xsl:output indent="yes"/>

<xsl:template match="boulevard">
<xsl:copy>
      <xsl:for-each select="//block">
            <xsl:copy>
            <xsl:attribute name="branch">
                  <xsl:value-of select="name(..)" />
            </xsl:attribute>
            <xsl:value-of select="text()"/>
            </xsl:copy>
      </xsl:for-each>
</xsl:copy>
</xsl:template>

</xsl:stylesheet>
```

RESULT:

```
<boulevard>
<block branch="thoroughfare">1st Street</block>
<block branch="thoroughfare">2nd Street</block>
<block branch="thoroughfare">3rd Street</block>
<block branch="thoroughfare">First Street</block>
<block branch="thoroughfare">Second Street</block>
<block branch="thoroughfare">Third Street</block>
<block branch="boulevard">Panorama Street</block>
<block branch="boulevard">Highland Plaza</block>
<block branch="boulevard">Hutchens Avenue</block>
<block branch="boulevard">Wildwood Drive</block>
<block branch="boulevard">Old Chimney Road</block>
<block branch="boulevard">Carrol Circle</block>
</boulevard>
```

`<xsl:sort>` element sorts the nodes matched by the select attribute on `<xsl:for-each>` prior to instantiating the template for each node. This means that the nodes in the node-set are processed in the new sorted order, which may affect the output.

9.4 The `<xsl:sort>` Element

The `<xsl:sort>` element is used to reorder each node in the current node-set prior to processing the node list further with instruction elements. The current node-set for `<xsl:sort>` is the list of nodes returned from the select attribute of either `<xsl:apply-templates>` or `<xsl:for-each>`. Technically, `<xsl:sort>` is not classified as an instruction element because it is only allowed within two specific elements: `<xsl:apply-templates>` and `<xsl:for-each>`. The `<xsl:sort>` element is empty and has five optional attributes, as shown in the following element model definition. The main attribute is `select`, which contains an expression used as the key for sorting the node list.

```
<xsl:sort

  select = string-expression

  lang = { nmtoken }

  data-type = { "text" | "number" | qname-but-not-
ncname }

  order = { "ascending" | "descending" }

  case-order = { "upper-first" | "lower-first" } />
```

If there is a value for the `select` attribute, each node in the current node-set is evaluated based on the expression in the `select` attribute and the result is converted to a string. This string is then used as the sort key. A sort key is the value used by the processor to perform the sort. The default value for the select attribute is `.`, which means that when the `select` attribute is not used, the sorting key is the content of the current node.

Example 9–8 : Using <xsl:sort> to reorder elements.

STYLESHEET:

```
<xsl:stylesheet xmlns:xsl="http://www.w3.org/1999/XSL/Transform"
            version="1.0">
<xsl:template match="text()" />
<xsl:template match="boulevard">
<xsl:copy>
      <xsl:for-each select="//block">
      <xsl:sort/>
            <xsl:copy>
            <xsl:attribute name="branch">
                  <xsl:value-of select="name(..)" />
            </xsl:attribute>
                  <xsl:value-of select="text()"/>
            </xsl:copy>
      </xsl:for-each>
</xsl:copy>
</xsl:template>
</xsl:stylesheet>
```

RESULT:

```
<?xml version="1.0" encoding="utf-8"?>
<boulevard>
<block branch="thoroughfare">1st Street</block>
<block branch="thoroughfare">2nd Street</block>
<block branch="thoroughfare">3rd Street</block>
<block branch="boulevard">Carrol Circle</block>
<block branch="thoroughfare">First Street</block>
<block branch="boulevard">Highland Plaza</block>
<block branch="boulevard">Hutchens Avenue</block>
<block branch="boulevard">Old Chimney Road</block>
<block branch="boulevard">Panorama Street</block>
<block branch="thoroughfare">Second Street</block>
<block branch="thoroughfare">Third Street</block>
<block branch="boulevard">Wildwood Drive</block>
</boulevard>
```

In Example 9–8, we use our previous stylesheet for creating a new boulevard to reorder all the <block>s in Markup City, using the default values of the five <xsl:sort> attributes.

The sort works on the nodes that are selected by the <xsl:for-each> element, without changing the result of the instantiation of the rest of the instructions that follow it. The result is basically the same as in Example 9–7, except that now the <block>s are in alphabetical order based on the text they contain. Numbered streets come first, in ascending order, followed by the alphabetized streets.

When used within the <xsl:for-each> element, <xsl:sort> must come before any other instruction element, and the instructions are then applied to the nodes in *sorted* order. When used within <xsl:apply-templates>, <xsl:sort> can come before or after any <xsl:with-param> elements, which are the only other valid children of <xsl:apply-templates>.

Multiple <xsl:sort> elements are allowed in both <xsl:for-each> and <xsl:apply-templates>, and each <xsl:sort> element is used as an additional sort key; the first <xsl:sort> is used to specify the primary sort key, the second <xsl:sort> is used to specify the secondary sort key, and so on.

The four other attributes on <xsl:sort> are: lang, data-type, order, and case-order. Each of the attributes for <xsl:sort>, including select, are discussed in the following sections.

9.4.1 The select Attribute of <xsl:sort>

The select attribute contains an expression that returns a string. Each node in the current node-set is evaluated based on the expression in the select attribute, and the value is converted into a string, which is then used as the sort key for the sort.

Sort keys are often used to decide which child of the current node to sort on. If the node-set selected by the <xsl:apply-templates> or <xsl:for-each> elements returns a set of nodes that contains children, those children or descendants can be specified as sort keys. If there is no select attribute specified, the text of the current node is used as the default sort key. Note that using a select attribute to select children on a node-set that contains no children nodes may cause unpredictable results, if any. The select attribute can also be used to identify other objects to be used as a sort key, such as a parent or ancestor node, or an attribute value from the input element.

Using the same example from the previous section, we could modify our <xsl:sort> element to add a select attribute as follows:

```
<xsl:sort select="name(..)"/>
```

Using the `name(..)` value for the `select` attribute sorts the `<block>` elements in order based on the *parent* of the `<block>`, as shown in Example 9–9.

Example 9–9 : Result of using the `<xsl:sort>` select attribute.

```
<?xml version="1.0" encoding="utf-8"?>
<boulevard>
<block branch="boulevard">Panorama Street</block>
<block branch="boulevard">Highland Plaza</block>
<block branch="boulevard">Hutchens Avenue</block>
<block branch="boulevard">Wildwood Drive</block>
<block branch="boulevard">Old Chimney Road</block>
<block branch="boulevard">Carrol Circle</block>
<block branch="thoroughfare">1st Street</block>
<block branch="thoroughfare">2nd Street</block>
<block branch="thoroughfare">3rd Street</block>
<block branch="thoroughfare">First Street</block>
<block branch="thoroughfare">Second Street</block>
<block branch="thoroughfare">Third Street</block>
</boulevard>
```

Notice in this example that although the `<block>`s are now sorted according to either boulevard or thoroughfare, they are still in document order within that sorting. In other words, each `<block>` is in the original order it was in from the input document, within the context of its parent element. We can do an additional sort using another `<xsl:sort>` element to specify the secondary sort key for the text of the `<block>`s, as shown in Example 9–10.

The additional `<xsl:sort>` in this example is using the default values to select the content of each `<block>` as the secondary sort key. The result is to sort the `<block>` elements by their text node within the original sort based on the parent of each `<block>`. In this case, the same effect can be accomplished using `<xsl:sort/>`, `<xsl:sort select="."/>`, or `<xsl:sort select="text()"/>`. The first two values of `select` apply to the *content* of the currently selected element, and in our example, each selected element is a `<block>` that only contains text, allowing the third value of `select` to also apply.

Example 9–10 : Using multiple `<xsl:sort>` elements.

MODIFIED TEMPLATE RULE:

```
<xsl:template match="boulevard">
<xsl:copy>
      <xsl:for-each select="//block">
      <xsl:sort select="name(..)"/>
      <xsl:sort/>
            <xsl:copy>
            <xsl:attribute name="branch">
                  <xsl:value-of select="name(..)" />
            </xsl:attribute>
                  <xsl:value-of select="text()"/>
            </xsl:copy>
      </xsl:for-each>
</xsl:copy>
</xsl:template>
```

RESULT:

```
<?xml version="1.0" encoding="utf-8"?>
<boulevard>
<block branch="boulevard">Carrol Circle</block>
<block branch="boulevard">Highland Plaza</block>
<block branch="boulevard">Hutchens Avenue</block>
<block branch="boulevard">Old Chimney Road</block>
<block branch="boulevard">Panorama Street</block>
<block branch="boulevard">Wildwood Drive</block>
<block branch="thoroughfare">1st Street</block>
<block branch="thoroughfare">2nd Street</block>
<block branch="thoroughfare">3rd Street</block>
<block branch="thoroughfare">First Street</block>
<block branch="thoroughfare">Second Street</block>
<block branch="thoroughfare">Third Street</block>
</boulevard>
```

9.4.2 The `data-type` Attribute of `<xsl:sort>`

The `data-type` attribute determines what kind of data the sort process uses: text, numeric, or some other unspecified type. The options for the value of `data-type` are: `text`, `number`, or a namespace-prefixed

QName. A `text` value is the default that is assumed if no `data-type` is explicitly declared.

Text sorting converts the value of the node being sorted to a string prior to sorting, and uses sorting algorithms to sort lexicographically according to the language being used, defined in the `lang` attribute (see Section 9.4.5).

Numerical sorting converts the value of the node being sorted to a number prior to sorting, and then sorts the nodes numerically according to the value returned by that conversion. The `lang` attribute is ignored when the `data-type` is `number`.

A QName as the value of the `data-type` attribute may be used by some extension functions to define some other type of sorting criteria. In the case of a prefixed QName, the W3C specification for XSLT, section 10, states, "...the behavior in this case is not specified by this document." The namespace for this value will determine the functionality of the sorting.

Example 9–11 shows the different results of sorting the numbers 1, 01, 001, 2, 02, and 002 using either `text` or `number` as the value of the data-type attribute.

Notice that the sorting order using `number` recognizes each value of 1 as a 1, ignoring the preceding zeros. As far as the processor is concerned, the values, 1, 01, and 001 all have the same value, so it does not sort them further than placing them together. Their original sequence in the input is maintained. The sorting order using text, however, recognizes the leading zeros as part of the string and sorts them accordingly. In `text` sorting, leading zeros are sorted before other numbers, so 002 comes *before* 01.

The values of `text` or `number` for the most part behave as you would expect. However, there is an element of "conversion" that occurs that can at first be surprising when there is mixed content of numbers and text in the sort key.

9.4.2.1 Sorting Numbers as Text

Using `<xsl:sort>` to sort numbers with a `data-type` of `text` converts the value of the number being sorted to a string prior to sorting. For example, sorting numbers using the `text data-type`, the number 13 will come before the number 6. This is because, as a text string, the value 1 as the first digit of 13 comes before 6. By contrast, if the same pair of values was sorted with a specified `data-type` of `number`, the 6 would precede the 13, as you would normally expect with numerical sequences.

Example 9–11 : Results of sorting using number vs. using text.

INPUT:

```
<?xml version="1.0"?>
<list>
      <num>002</num>
      <num>01</num>
      <num>1</num>
      <num>2</num>
      <num>001</num>
      <num>02</num>
</list>
```

STYLESHEET:

```
<xsl:stylesheet
      xmlns:xsl="http://www.w3.org/1999/XSL/Transform"
      version="1.0">
<xsl:template match="/">
<xsl:for-each select="//num">
      <xsl:sort data-type="number"/>
      <xsl:value-of select="."/>
<xsl:text>
</xsl:text>
</xsl:for-each>
</xsl:template>
</xsl:stylesheet>
```

TEXT SORT RESULT:

```
      001
      002
      01
      02
      1
      2
```

NUMBER SORT RESULT:

```
      01
      1
      001
      002
      2
      02
```

9.4.2.2 Sorting Text as Numbers

When number is set for the data-type and the nodes being sorted contain a mixture of text and numbers, or just text, sorting is essentially ignored. This is because the use of number as the value for the data-type attribute causes the processor to attempt to convert the data to a number. If the data contains text, the result of the conversion will be the value "NaN" and the data will be sorted accordingly. This means that, if we tried to sort our <block> elements using number as the value of data-type, the result would be the same order as the inputs, because in all cases, the resulting value of the sort key for each <block> would be NaN.

9.4.3 The order Attribute of <xsl:sort>

The order attribute is used to specify whether the sort (alphabetic or numerical) is ascending or descending. These are the only two values allowed for the order attribute. The default order is ascending, so the order attribute only needs to be specified if descending order is needed. This would then reverse the order of the results. For example, using Markup City as input, the <block>s in our new <boulevard> would end up in reverse order, as shown in Example 9–12.

9.4.4 The case-order Attribute of <xsl:sort>

The case-order attribute provides the means to specify a case-specific sort, sorting either uppercase at the top, using the upper-first value, or lowercase at the top, using the lower-first value.

In Example 9–13, we have created duplicate <block>s, except for changing the case of every duplicated block name (panorama and Panorama, highland and Highland, etc.).

The default value of case-order is language-dependent, so that for English, for example, it would be upper-first. Language is specified using the lang attribute, discussed in the next section.

Example 9–12 : Using the `order` attribute with the descending value.

STYLESHEET:

```
<?xml version="1.0"?>
<xsl:stylesheet xmlns:xsl="http://www.w3.org/1999/XSL/Transform"
           version="1.0">
<xsl:output indent="yes"/>
<xsl:template match="text()" />

<xsl:template match="boulevard">
      <xsl:copy>
            <xsl:for-each select="//block">
                  <xsl:sort order="descending"/>
                  <xsl:copy>
                        <xsl:value-of select="text()"/>
                  </xsl:copy>
            </xsl:for-each>
      </xsl:copy>
</xsl:template>
</xsl:stylesheet>
```

RESULT:

```
<?xml version="1.0" encoding="utf-8"?>
<boulevard>
<block>Wildwood Drive</block>
<block>Third Street</block>
<block>Second Street</block>
<block>Panorama Street</block>
<block>Old Chimney Road</block>
<block>Hutchens Avenue</block>
<block>Highland Plaza</block>
<block>First Street</block>
<block>Carrol Circle</block>
<block>3rd Street</block>
<block>2nd Street</block>
<block>1st Street</block>
</boulevard>
```

Example 9–13 : Using <xsl:sort> with the case-order attribute.

INPUT:

```
<boulevard>
      <block>panorama Street</block>
      <block>Panorama Street</block>
      <block>highland Plaza</block>
      <block>Highland Plaza</block>
      <block>hutchens Avenue</block>
      <block>Hutchens Avenue</block>
      <block>wildwood Drive</block>
      <block>Wildwood Drive</block>
      <block>old Chimney Road</block>
      <block>Old Chimney Road</block>
      <block>carrol Circle</block>
      <block>Carrol Circle</block>
</boulevard>
```

STYLESHEET:

```
<?xml version="1.0"?>
<xsl:stylesheet xmlns:xsl="http://www.w3.org/1999/XSL/Transform"
           version="1.0">
<xsl:output indent="yes"/>
<xsl:template match="text()" />
<xsl:template match="boulevard">
      <xsl:copy>
            <xsl:for-each select="//block">
                  <xsl:sort case-order="upper-first"/>
                  <xsl:copy>
                        <xsl:value-of select="text()"/>
                  </xsl:copy>
            </xsl:for-each>
      </xsl:copy>
</xsl:template>
</xsl:stylesheet>
```

RESULT:

```
<?xml version="1.0" encoding="utf-8"?>
<boulevard>
<block>Carrol Circle</block>
```

Example 9–13 : Using `<xsl:sort>` with the `case-order` attribute (continued).

```
<block>carrol Circle</block>
<block>Highland Plaza</block>
<block>highland Plaza</block>
<block>Hutchens Avenue</block>
<block>hutchens Avenue</block>
<block>Old Chimney Road</block>
<block>old Chimney Road</block>
<block>Panorama Street</block>
<block>panorama Street</block>
<block>Wildwood Drive</block>
<block>wildwood Drive</block>
</boulevard>
```

When `case-order` is declared as `lower-first`, the reverse would apply, as follows:

```
<?xml version="1.0" encoding="utf-8"?>
<boulevard>
<block>carrol Circle</block>
<block>Carrol Circle</block>
<block>highland Plaza</block>
<block>Highland Plaza</block>
<block>hutchens Avenue</block>
<block>Hutchens Avenue</block>
<block>old Chimney Road</block>
<block>Old Chimney Road</block>
<block>panorama Street</block>
<block>Panorama Street</block>
<block>wildwood Drive</block>
<block>Wildwood Drive</block>
</boulevard>
```

9.4.5 The `lang` Attribute of `<xsl:sort>`

The `lang` attribute is used to specify the language that is being used for sorting. It accepts a two-character language value, such as "en" for English, from the ISO 639 specification, or a subcode, such as "en-US," for specific countries defined by the ISO 3166 specification. The XML recommendation[1] suggests using lowercase prefixes, followed by uppercase suffixes, even though the value of the `lang` attribute is not case-sensitive.

Using the `lang` attribute enables specific nuances of alphabetic order with languages other than English to be explicitly accommodated in `<xsl:sort>`. If there is no language specified, the default value for the `lang` attribute is based on the language that is specified by the system environment or regional settings.

9.5 The `<xsl:if>` Instruction Element

The `<xsl:if>` element performs a simple Boolean test, evaluating an expression in the required `test` attribute and returning either true or false. The content of `<xsl:if>`, which is a template, is instantiated if the result of evaluating the expression returns true; otherwise, it is ignored. The special kind of expression (*`boolean-expression`*) designated as the value of the `test` attribute can only produce a Boolean result. In other words, the expression will be evaluated and converted to a Boolean by the XSLT processor. The `<xsl:if>` element is an instruction element, as shown in the following element model definition:

```
<!-- Category: instruction -->

<xsl:if

  test = boolean-expression>

  <!-- Content: template -->

</xsl:if>
```

The most simple use of `<xsl:if>` is a test for existence. Using a pattern in the expression will test to see if the element returned by the pattern actually exists, and return true if it does. The content of the template in `<xsl:if>` will then be instantiated. In Example 9–14, the `<xsl:if>` element's test attribute is checking to see if the `<boulevard>` exists somewhere in the document.

1. The XML recommendation can be found at http://www.w3.org/TR/REC-xml.

Example 9–14 : Simple test for existence with `<xsl:if>`.

```
<xsl:template match="/">
     <xsl:if test="//boulevard">
          <xsl:text>Found a Boulevard!</xsl:text>
     </xsl:if>
</xsl:template>
```

Since the `<boulevard>` does exist, the result of the test is true and the template is instantiated. Additionally, pattern expressions can be used to check for the existence of children elements, text, or attribute nodes.

```
<xsl:if test="//boulevard/block">
```

In this example, the `<xsl:if>` element is checking to see if there are any `<block>` elements in the `<boulevard>`. The result of this expression using Markup City is true.

```
<xsl:if test="//boulevard/text()">
```

In this example, the `<xsl:if>` element's test attribute is checking to see if the `<boulevard>` contains `text()` elements. Note that this may be true or false depending on if the `<boulevard>` contains whitespace. If it contains any whitespace that is not stripped, the result will be true, because whitespace is considered text.

```
<xsl:if test="//boulevard/@*">
```

In this example, the `<xsl:if>` element's test attribute is checking to see if the `<boulevard>` contains any attribute nodes. The result of this expression using Markup City is false because `<boulevard>` does not have any attributes.

For programmers who use `if` constructs in other programming languages, it may be helpful to know that there are no elements (or instructions) in XSLT corresponding to `then`, `else`, or `else-if` statements in conjunction with `<xsl:if>`. The `<xsl:choose>` element (see Section 9.6) provides functionality similar to an if-then-else programming construct.

However, the `<xsl:if>` element can contain other `<xsl:if>` elements to provide the necessary functionality for `then`, `else`, or `else-if` structures. The power of nesting elements in XML can be leveraged in this case to use many layers of `<xsl:if>` elements. For example, if we wanted to change the tags of a `<thoroughfare>` in our full Markup City based on whether the element has an attribute, the value of the attribute, and the content of the element, we could use nested <xsl:if> elements, as shown in Example 9–15.

Example 9–15 : Using nested <xsl:if> elements.

STYLESHEET:

```
<xsl:stylesheet xmlns:xsl="http://www.w3.org/1999/XSL/Transform"
           version="1.0">
<xsl:template match="text()"/>
<xsl:template match="thoroughfare">
      <!-- check to see if there's a name attribute -->
      <xsl:if test="@name">
            <xsl:copy>
            <name>
            <xsl:value-of select="@name"/>
            </name>
            <!-- check to see if the attribute has a specific value -->
            <xsl:if test="@name[contains(., 'Drive')]">
                  <drive>
            <!-- check to see if it has a block child -->
            <xsl:if test="block">
                  <xsl:copy-of select="block"/>
            </xsl:if>
            </drive>
         </xsl:if>
         </xsl:copy>
      </xsl:if>
</xsl:template>
</xsl:stylesheet>
```

RESULT:

```
<?xml version="1.0" encoding="utf-8"?>
<thoroughfare>
<name>Whitesburg Drive</name>
<drive>
<block>1st Street</block>
<block>2nd Street</block>
<block>3rd Street</block>
</drive>
</thoroughfare>
<thoroughfare>
<name>Bankhead</name>
</thoroughfare>
```

Walking through the process, the first `<thoroughfare>` does not have an attribute called `name`, so the `<xsl:if>` template is skipped for that element and no content is sent to the output.

The second `<thoroughfare>` *does* have a `name` attribute, so the processor instantiates the template. It uses the second `<xsl:if>` rule in the template to check the content of the name attribute for the text `Drive`. Since the value of the name attribute contains `Drive`, a new tag called `<drive>` is created. The third `<xsl:if>` element checks to see if one of the children of the `<thoroughfare>` is a `<block>`, and if so, all the `<block>` elements are copied to the output using the `<xsl:copy>` element.

The third `<thoroughfare>` has a `name` attribute, so it is copied to the output with the new `<name>` element. Since the `name` attribute does not have the text `Drive` in it, the rest of the instructions are skipped.

9.6 The `<xsl:choose>` Instruction Element

The `<xsl:choose>` instruction element allows several conditions to be tested for the selective processing of nodes. Using two child elements, `<xsl:when>` and `<xsl:otherwise>`, it provides alternatives to be used for testing and one default if no condition is met. Each test provides a new template for instantiation when the condition for that test is met. The `<xsl:choose>` element must contain one or more `<xsl:when>` elements, followed by one optional `<xsl:otherwise>` element. The `<xsl:choose>` element does not have any attributes, as shown in the following element model definition:

```
<!-- Category: instruction -->

<xsl:choose>

  <!-- Content: (xsl:when+, xsl:otherwise?) -->

</xsl:choose>
```

The `<xsl:choose>` instruction element offers a significant advantage over `<xsl:if>`, because `<xsl:if>` only provides a singular instance of a test resulting in either true or false. On the other hand, `<xsl:choose>` allows for multiple mutually exclusive conditions, using `<xsl:when>`, plus a default template, using `<xsl:otherwise>`, to be instantiated when none of the `<xsl:when>` elements are chosen. If no `<xsl:otherwise>` is supplied and no `<xsl:when>` elements return a value of true, then the template rule is not instantiated.

> **NOTE** As a simple reference to programming language structures, `<xsl:choose>` can be compared with a "case" statement, which provides a test, several possible results, and a default process.

Each `<xsl:when>` in an `<xsl:choose>` element is checked until a match is found, or until the default `<xsl:otherwise>` is reached. Once an `<xsl:when>` element's `test` returns true, then no further `<xsl:when>` elements will be evaluated.

9.6.1 The <xsl:when> Conditional Element

The `<xsl:when>` element is used within an `<xsl:choose>` element to stipulate a condition that, when evaluated to a value of true, instantiates the instructions contained in the template. The `<xsl:when>` element has one required attribute, which is a `test` attribute, as shown in the following element model definition:

```
<xsl:when
  test = boolean-expression>
  <!-- Content: template -->
</xsl:when>
```

The `test` attribute returns a Boolean true or false, which then determines if the template contained within `<xsl:when>` will be instantiated. This element must come as the first child to `<xsl:choose>` (it is *only* allowed as a child of `<xsl:choose>`), and there must be at least one

<xsl:when> in an <xsl:choose> instruction element or else the stylesheet will be invalid.

9.6.2 The <xsl:otherwise> Contingency Condition

The <xsl:otherwise> provides a default, or contingency, process in the case that any <xsl:when> elements within an <xsl:choose> element fail to return a value of true. The <xsl:otherwise> element accepts no attributes, and its content is a template, as shown in the following element model definition:

```
<xsl:otherwise>

  <!-- Content: template -->

</xsl:otherwise>
```

The <xsl:otherwise> element can only appear as a child of <xsl:choose>, and it must be the *last* child in the <xsl:choose>, preceded by at least one <xsl:when> element. The <xsl:otherwise> provides as its name indicates a set of instructions for what to do "otherwise," when all the <xsl:when> elements have been tested and a true value is not found. It contains a set of instructions that are instantiated if all the <xsl:when> elements preceding it in the <xsl:choose> return Boolean false.

9.6.3 Using <xsl:when> and <xsl:otherwise> with <xsl:choose>

The strength of <xsl:choose> is the ability to add as many <xsl:when> elements as are required to do a proper test. Where <xsl:if> only evaluates one condition to return true or false, <xsl:choose> gives the process additional tests if the first one doesn't match, recursively through the rest of the possible matches. If the same functionality was to be accomplished with <xsl:if>, it would require multiple nested <xsl:if>s for each choice, and additional nested

<xsl:if>s with the opposite test to process the options when the <xsl:if>s didn't match. For example, in our first use of <xsl:if>, we had the following rule:

```
<xsl:if test="block">
```

To catch any elements that did not match that test, we would need to add another opposite <xsl:if> element, using the not() function as follows:

```
<xsl:if test="not(block)">
```

The same functionality in these two instructions can be accomplished with one <xsl:choose>, as shown in Example 9–16.

Example 9–16 : Demonstration of the efficiency of <xsl:choose>.

```
<xsl:choose>
      <xsl:when test="block">
            <xsl:text>Found a block.</xsl:text>
      </xsl:when>
      <xsl:otherwise>
            <xsl:text>Something other than a block was found.
            </xsl:text>
      </xsl:otherwise>
</xsl:choose>
```

The best part is that you can keep adding tests that are not necessarily opposites, as in Example 9–17.

In this example we've added <xsl:when> elements to "catch" occurrences of sidestreet and boulevard elements, and our <xsl:otherwise> lets us know when we've found something else, this time using the name() function to pull the value of the name of the element. Now we can add instruction elements or LREs as required to create meaningful output for each choice.

Example 9–17 : Adding additional `<xsl:when>` tests to `<xsl:choose>`.

```
<xsl:stylesheet xmlns:xsl="http://www.w3.org/1999/XSL/Transform"
           version="1.0">

<xsl:template match="text()"/>
<xsl:output indent="yes"/>

<xsl:template match="*">
<xsl:choose>
      <xsl:when test="name() = 'block'">
            <xsl:text>Found a block.
            </xsl:text>
      </xsl:when>
      <xsl:when test="name() = 'sidestreet'">
            <xsl:text>Found a sidestreet.
            </xsl:text>
      </xsl:when>
      <xsl:when test="name() = 'boulevard'">
            <xsl:text>Found a boulevard.
            </xsl:text>
      </xsl:when>
      <xsl:otherwise>
            <xsl:text>Found a </xsl:text>
            <xsl:value-of select="name()"/>
            <xsl:text>.
            </xsl:text>
      </xsl:otherwise>
</xsl:choose>
<xsl:apply-templates/>
</xsl:template>
</xsl:stylesheet>
```

9.7 The `<xsl:number>` Instruction Element

The `<xsl:number>` element performs the traditional numbering role, which you might be accustomed to in the HTML ordered list (`<ol>`) or in word processor Bullets and Numbering tools. Its nine attributes are all optional, as shown in the following element model definition, and serve to nuance the format, starting number, and so on for the numbering:

```
<!-- Category: instruction -->
<xsl:number
level = "single" | "multiple" | "any"
count = pattern
from = pattern
value = number-expression
format = { string }
lang = { nmtoken }
letter-value = { "alphabetic" | "traditional" }
grouping-separator = { char }
grouping-size = { number } />
```

The <xsl:number> element can be used anywhere in a template and is always an empty element. Its output is a text node, which represents the appropriate level and respective number for the given context of the current node being numbered.

The simplest use of <xsl:number> is without attributes, using the default values which return the current node number, equal to the position of the node in its current context. Example 9–18 shows the use of an empty <xsl:number> to generate numbers for each <block> element.

The result of this template rule lists each <block> element preceded by the number of the node, generated with <xsl:number>. The numbering is essentially reset at the parent element of <block>, regardless of the type of parent. The additional formatting using <xsl:text> adds a dash and the break between lines.

More complex combinations of numbering can be accomplished using the attributes specified for <xsl:number>. Most of the attributes are directly affected by the use of the `count` attribute, which is used to select the nodes to be counted. Without the `count` attribute, the default behavior is to number only the elements with the same name as the currently selected node, matched from the template rule containing the <xsl:number> element.

9.7.1 The `count` Attribute of <xsl:number>

The `count` attribute determines which nodes will be counted in the numbering. Its value is a pattern expression, which can reference any node in the input document. This includes the root node, element nodes, text nodes, attribute nodes (although numbering is not valid for attribute nodes

Example 9–18 : Using an empty <xsl:number> to generate basic numbers.

TEMPLATE:

```
<xsl:template match="block">
<xsl:number/>
<xsl:text> - </xsl:text>
<xsl:value-of select="."/>
<xsl:text>
</xsl:text>
</xsl:template>
```

RESULT:

```
1 - 1st Street
2 - 2nd Street
3 - 3rd Street
1 - First Street
2 - Second Street
3 - Third Street
1 - Panorama Street
2 - Highland Plaza
3 - Hutchens Avenue
4 - Wildwood Drive
5 - Old Chimney Road
6 - Carrol Circle
```

because they do not have a specified order in a node list), etc. The `count` attribute can be used to select one or more element-type names, or to select a specific subset of nodes to number, using predicates. Nodes identified in the `count` attribute can also be ancestors or descendants of the current node. For example:

```
<xsl:number count="block|thoroughfare"/>
<xsl:number count="thoroughfare[@*]"/>
<xsl:number count="block|thoroughfare[@*]"/>
```

These elements show different combinations of the count attribute, the first counting both `<block>` and `<thoroughfare>` elements, the second counting only `<thoroughfare>` elements that have an attribute, and the third a combination of the first two.

Note that although a node can be identified in the `count` attribute, it is not necessarily sent to the output result tree, but it is counted in the numbering. Any elements that are sent to the output result tree will reflect the numbering, including the elements not shown. In Example 9–19, we are changing our stylesheet to count both `<block>` and `<sidestreet>` elements. This will increment the numbering by including the `<sidestreet>` elements in the count. However, if we don't actually *use* the `<sidestreet>` in our output, the numbering will appear to skip wherever the `<sidestreet>` originally appeared.

Example 9–19 : Output counting two element types when one is not displayed.

TEMPLATE:

```
<xsl:template match="block">
<xsl:number count="block|sidestreet"/>
<xsl:text> - </xsl:text>
<xsl:value-of select="."/>
<xsl:text>
</xsl:text>
<xsl:apply-templates/>
</xsl:template>
```

RESULT:

```
2 - 1st Street
3 - 2nd Street
4 - 3rd Street
2 - First Street
3 - Second Street
4 - Third Street
1 - Panorama Street
2 - Highland Plaza
3 - Hutchens Avenue
4 - Wildwood Drive
5 - Old Chimney Road
6 - Carrol Circle
```

The three `<sidestreet>` elements from the input are counted as 1 and 5 in the first `<thoroughfare>`, and 1 in the second. However, since the `<sidestreet>`s are not being sent to the output, these numbers do not show up, but are still used in the overall count.

9.7.2 The `level` Attribute of `<xsl:number>`

The `level` attribute of `<xsl:number>` is used to stipulate which levels of numbering will be output for each object. It has three predefined values—`single`, `multiple`, and `any`. A value of `single` only outputs the number of the count for that object; for example, 1, 2, and 3. A value of `multiple` outputs all the numbers according to which level the object is at in the hierarchy; for example, 1, 2.1, and 2.1.1. Numbering is still reset at the parent of the current node for each level. The `any` value basically ignores hierarchical levels to generate a single sequence of numbers that do not reset.

9.7.2.1 The `single` Value for the `level` Attribute

The `single` value for the `level` attribute numbers each node in the matched node-set sequentially within the context of each parent node. The XSLT processor will reset the count to begin numbering with a value of 1 for each level in the hierarchy. The `single` value is the default setting for `<xsl:number>'s level` attribute, so it need not be declared. Simply invoking <xsl:number> without attributes will generate the single-level count of the current node type, as shown in Example 9–20.

9.7.2.2 The `multiple` Value for the `level` Attribute

Using `level` with a value of `multiple` numbers each node in the node-set according to the hierarchy, including the number of the parent and ancestor elements. The parent or ancestor elements to be used must be included in the count attribute for their value to be included. Nested elements of the same element-type name will also be treated as multiple values for numbering. Using the same input from Example 9–20, `<xsl:number level="multiple"/>` would result in a hierarchical count of `<block>`s, with the numbers of each level displayed, as shown in Example 9–21.

Example 9–20 : Using an <xsl:number> with single-level numbering.

INPUT:

```
<?xml version="1.0"?>
<block>Block 1
      <block>Child 1 of Block 1
            <block>Child 1 of Child 1 of Block 1</block>
            <block>Child 2 of Child 1 of Block 1</block>
            <block>Child 3 of Child 1 of Block 1</block>
      </block>
      <block>Child 2 of Block 1</block>
      <block>Child 3 of Block 1
            <block>Child 1 of Child 3 of Block 1</block>
            <block>Child 2 of Child 3 of Block 1</block>
            <block>Child 3 of Child 3 of Block 1</block>
      </block>
</block>
```

TEMPLATE:

```
<xsl:template match="block">
<xsl:number level="single"/>
<xsl:text> - </xsl:text>
<xsl:apply-templates/>
</xsl:template>
```

RESULT:

```
<?xml version="1.0" encoding="utf-8"?>
1 - Block 1
      1 - Child 1 of Block 1
            1 - Child 1 of Child 1 of Block 1
            2 - Child 2 of Child 1 of Block 1
            3 - Child 3 of Child 1 of Block 1

      2 - Child 2 of Block 1
      3 - Child 3 of Block 1
            1 - Child 1 of Child 3 of Block 1
            2 - Child 2 of Child 3 of Block 1
            3 - Child 3 of Child 3 of Block 1
```

Example 9–21 : Using an <xsl:number> with multiple-level <block>s.

TEMPLATE:

```
<xsl:template match="block">
<xsl:number level="multiple"/>
<xsl:text> - </xsl:text>
<xsl:apply-templates/>
</xsl:template>
```

RESULT:

```
<?xml version="1.0" encoding="utf-8"?>
1 - Block 1
      1.1 - Child 1 of Block 1
            1.1.1 - Child 1 of Child 1 of Block 1
            1.1.2 - Child 2 of Child 1 of Block 1
            1.1.3 - Child 3 of Child 1 of Block 1

      1.2 - Child 2 of Block 1
      1.3 - Child 3 of Block 1
            1.3.1 - Child 1 of Child 3 of Block 1
            1.3.2 - Child 2 of Child 3 of Block 1
            1.3.3 - Child 3 of Child 3 of Block 1
```

The more common use of the `level` attribute is when elements of different element-type names are used to number hierarchically. Example 9–22 shows multiple elements numbered using the `count` and `level` attributes.

We are using `<block>`s and `<thoroughfare>`s that contain `<block>`s as levels of counting. We don't want to count `<thoroughfare>` elements that don't have `<block>`s, so we use the predicate `[block]` on thoroughfare. Notice the use of `<xsl:template match="text()"/>` to suppress the output of unwanted text nodes.

9.7.2.3 The any Value for the `level` Attribute

Using `level` with a value of `any` numbers the nodes globally, without considering the context of the current node. With this value, it is possible to sequentially number nodes that occur at any level of the document's hierarchy. For example, using `<xsl:number level="any"/>`

Example 9–22 : Using multiple `level` elements with `count`.

INPUT:

```
<?xml version="1.0"?>
<main>
      <parkway>
            <thoroughfare>Governor Drive</thoroughfare>
            <thoroughfare name="Whitesburg Drive">
                  <sidestreet>Bob Wallace Avenue</sidestreet>
                  <block>1st Street</block>
                  <block>2nd Street</block>
                  <block>3rd Street</block>
                  <sidestreet>Woodridge Street</sidestreet>
            </thoroughfare>
            <thoroughfare name="Bankhead">
                  <sidestreet>Tollgate Road</sidestreet>
                  <block>First Street</block>
                  <block>Second Street</block>
                  <block>Third Street</block>
                  <sidestreet>Oak Drive</sidestreet>
            </thoroughfare>
      </parkway>
      <boulevard>
            <block>Panorama Street</block>
            <block>Highland Plaza</block>
            <block>Hutchens Avenue</block>
            <block>Wildwood Drive</block>
            <block>Old Chimney Road</block>
            <block>Carrol Circle</block>
      </boulevard>
</main>
```

STYLESHEET:

```
<xsl:stylesheet
      xmlns:xsl="http://www.w3.org/1999/XSL/Transform"
      version="1.0">
<xsl:template match="text()"/>
<xsl:template match="thoroughfare/block">
<xsl:number level="multiple"count="block|thoroughfare[block]"/>
<xsl:text> - </xsl:text>
```

Example 9–22 : Using multiple `level` elements with `count` (continued).

```
<xsl:value-of select="text()"/>
<xsl:text>
</xsl:text>
</xsl:template>
</xsl:stylesheet>
```

RESULT:

```
1.1 - 1st Street
1.2 - 2nd Street
1.3 - 3rd Street
2.1 - First Street
2.2 - Second Street
2.3 - Third Street
<xsl:text> - </xsl:text>
```

would result in a sequential count of `<block>`s, without resetting the number at the parent of `<block>`, as shown in Example 9–23.

A typical use for the `any` value of the `level` attribute is to number global elements, such as tables or figures that need to be numbered independently of the relative hierarchical position each occupies in the input XML document instance.

9.7.3 The `from` Attribute of `<xsl:number>`

The `from` attribute of `<xsl:number>` is used to identify an element (or elements) from the input document to use as the starting point for the numbering. Its value is a pattern expression that identifies specific nodes, essentially restarting the numbering at that point, instead of using the normal contextual resetting. This allows the stylesheet to reset the numbering using a different ancestor than the immediate parent. For example, the numbering for `<block>` resets at the parent element, which is either `<thoroughfare>` or `<boulevard>`. Using the `from` attribute, in combination with the `level` attribute set to `any`, we can change the starting point of the numbering to `<parkway>` and `<boulevard>`, as shown in Example 9–24.

Example 9–23 : Result of using the `level` attribute with a value of `any`.

TEMPLATE:

```
<xsl:template match="block">
<xsl:number level="any"/>
<xsl:text> - </xsl:text>
<xsl:value-of select="text()"/>
<xsl:text>
</xsl:text>
</xsl:template>
```

RESULT:

```
1 - 1st Street
2 - 2nd Street
3 - 3rd Street
4 - First Street
5 - Second Street
6 - Third Street
7 - Panorama Street
8 - Highland Plaza
9 - Hutchens Avenue
10 - Wildwood Drive
11 - Old Chimney Road
12 - Carrol Circle
```

The numbering for all the `<block>`s inside `<thoroughfare>` elements are now numbering sequentially, starting at 1, without regard to which `<thoroughfare>` they're in, while the `<block>`s inside the `<boulevard>` are also numbered sequentially starting at 1.

9.7.4 The `value` Attribute

The `value` attribute allows the use of a specified number, generated by an expression, for the numbering sequence. The expression contained in the `value` attribute is evaluated and converted to a number, rounded, and then converted to a string prior to being used. The default, if there is no `value` specified, is to number each node according to its position in con-

Example 9–24 : Using the `from` attribute to reset numbering.

TEMPLATE:

```
<xsl:template match="block">
<xsl:number level="any" from="parkway|boulevard"/>
<xsl:text> - </xsl:text>
<xsl:value-of select="text()"/>
<xsl:text>
</xsl:text>
</xsl:template>
```

RESULT:

```
1 - 1st Street
2 - 2nd Street
3 - 3rd Street
4 - First Street
5 - Second Street
6 - Third Street
1 - Panorama Street
2 - Highland Plaza
3 - Hutchens Avenue
4 - Wildwood Drive
5 - Old Chimney Road
6 - Carrol Circle
```

text. For example, using `<xsl:number value="position()"/>` performs the same function as an empty `<xsl:number>` element, assuming no whitespace nodes between elements in the input document structure.

Using expressions in the `value` attribute, it is possible to extract a different value for the numbering, for example, if your numbering scheme starts with 0 instead of the default starting value of 1. Example 9–25 shows the renumbering of the `<block>`s in the `<boulevard>` to start from 0.

The numbering is now effectively changed to start at 0 instead of 1. Notice that we are using the `<xsl:strip-space>` element, discussed in Chapter 10, to remove any extra whitespace from our input so that the empty nodes are not counted.

Example 9–25 : Using the `value` attribute to change the starting value of the numbering.

STYLESHEET:

```
<?xml version="1.0"?>
<xsl:stylesheet
      xmlns:xsl="http://www.w3.org/1999/XSL/Transform"
      version="1.0">
<xsl:template match="text()"/>
<xsl:output omit-xml-declaration="yes"/>
<xsl:strip-space elements="*"/>

<xsl:template match="boulevard/block">
<xsl:number value="position() - 1"/>
<xsl:text> - </xsl:text>
<xsl:value-of select="."/>
<xsl:text>
</xsl:text>
<xsl:apply-templates/>
</xsl:template>
</xsl:stylesheet>
```

RESULT:

```
0 - Panorama Street
1 - Highland Plaza
2 - Hutchens Avenue
3 - Wildwood Drive
4 - Old Chimney Road
5 - Carrol Circle
```

9.7.5 The `format` Attribute

The `format` attribute is used to specify the model that will be used to represent numbering sequences in the output. The value of the `format` attribute is parsed and separated according to two classes of characters, either alphanumeric or non-alphanumeric. Alphanumeric characters are used as character models for the sequencing, and non-alphanumeric characters are used as punctuation or *separators*. Punctuation and separator characters are added to each sequence in the output in the same position they occupy in the `format` attribute, using the same character specified.

The `format` attribute can model five types of sequences: numeric, represented by `1` or `0`; alphabetic lowercase, represented by `a`; alphabetic uppercase, represented by `A`; Roman numeral lowercase, represented by `i`; and Roman numeral uppercase, represented by `I`.

When using a numeric format, any combination of concurrent numbers is interpreted to be a complete number for the start of the sequence, such as 0001, which will increment as 0002, 0003, etc. Note that other digits besides 0 and 1 are allowed, but do not change the numbering sequence. So, using 9999 or 1111 will default the numbering to either 1 or 0001, depending on the processor used. The functionality of zero-padding, or zero-fill, for the `format` attribute is discussed in Section 9.7.5.2.

Alphabetic sequencing does not allow multiple combinations of characters, and any extra characters are ignored by the processor. Depending on the processor used, the combination "aaa" will be interpreted as the single character `a`, or default to `1`. Any alphabetic character other than `a` or `A` may be interpreted by the processor as a separator, or default to `1`, depending on the processor used.

Other sequences may be defined and supported based on processor-specific implementations, possibly to support language-specific character sequences.

9.7.5.1 Attribute Value Templates in the `format` Attribute

The value of the `format` attribute can be interpreted as an AVT (discussed in Section 6.6.1) when used with { }, allowing the sequencing format to be derived from an expression. The expression is processed based on the context of the current node and the result is converted to a string to determine the model for the sequencing. For example, the value for the format could be stored in a variable and retrieved with a variable reference, as shown in Example 9–26.

9.7.5.2 Zero-padding with the `format` Attribute

Especially handy is the option to pad a number with right-justified zeros, sometimes known as RJZF, or *right-justified, zero-fill.*[2] This enables a user to

2. RJZF is used in specifications such as the Machine Readable Record format, or MARC record digital cataloguing system, used by most online library catalogs such as the Library of Congress.

Example 9–26 : Using AVTs to retrieve a variable for `format`.

STYLESHEET:

```
<?xml version="1.0"?>
<xsl:stylesheet xmlns:xsl="http://www.w3.org/1999/XSL/Transform"
          version="1.0">
<xsl:output indent="yes"/>
<xsl:output omit-xml-declaration="yes"/>
<xsl:template match="text()"/>
<xsl:variable name="list-form" select="'1.a - '"/>
<xsl:template match="thoroughfare/block">
      <xsl:number count="block|thoroughfare[block]" level="multiple"
format="{$list-form}"/>
      <xsl:value-of select="."/>
      <xsl:text>
      </xsl:text>
</xsl:template>
</xsl:stylesheet>
```

RESULT:

```
1.a - 1st Street
1.b - 2nd Street
1.c - 3rd Street
2.a - First Street
2.b - Second Street
2.c - Third Street
```

set a numerical set of spaces, which will always be filled with `0` regardless of the relative size of the actual sequential count at any given node. For instance, the format model `001` will number sequentially as `001, 002, 003, ... 010, 011, 012`, etc., until `999` is reached.

9.7.6 The `lang` Attribute of `<xsl:number>`

The `lang` attribute is used to specify the language that is being used for numbering when the numbering is an alphabetic sequence. It accepts a two-character language value, such as "en" for English, from the ISO 639 specification, or a subcode, such as "en-US," for specific countries defined by the ISO 3166 specification. The XML recommendation[3] suggests using lowercase prefixes, followed by uppercase suffixes, even though the value of the `lang` attribute is not case-sensitive.

Using this attribute enables specific nuances of alphabetic order with languages other than English to be explicitly accommodated in `<xsl:number>`. If there is no language specified, the default value for the `lang` attribute is based on the language that is specified by the system environment or regional settings.

The value of the `lang` attribute can be interpreted as an attribute value template, or AVT (discussed in Section 6.6.1) when used with { }, allowing `lang` to be derived from an expression.

9.7.7 The **`letter-value`** Attribute

The `letter-value` attribute makes it possible to specify alphabetical representations of numbers. For instance, in English, Roman numerals are actually letters that are used as a sequence for numbering. When the language specified is English, however, Roman sequencing is handled with the `format` attribute.

If the language specified is something other than English, the `traditional` value for the `letter-value` attribute can be used to specify a letter sequencing other than alphabetic. When normal alphabetic sequencing is required for the language specified, the `letter-value` attribute should be specified as `alphabetic`. Note that this feature is implementation- and language-dependent.

The value of the `letter-value` attribute can also be interpreted as an AVT (discussed in Section 6.6.1) when used with { }, allowing `letter-value` to be derived from an expression.

9.7.8 The **`grouping-separator`** Attribute

The `grouping-separator` attribute makes it possible to specify the punctuation between groups of numbers. For instance, 1000 could be formatted as 1,000 with a comma, and it could also be formatted with a period as 1.000, using `grouping-separator="."` and `grouping-size="3"`.

3. The XML recommendation can be found at http://www.w3.org/TR/REC-xml.

This attribute works closely with the `grouping-size` attribute, which serves to identify how many digits or characters a group is broken into and, accordingly, where the separating punctuation mark is to fall. The two are effectively interdependent, and if only one of either the `grouping-separator` or `grouping-size` attribute is used, then it is ignored.

The value of the `grouping-separator` attribute can also be interpreted as an AVT (discussed in Section 6.6.1) when used with { }, allowing `grouping-separator` to be derived from an expression.

9.7.9 The `grouping-size` Attribute

The `grouping-size` attribute identifies how groups of numbers are to be separated when they are displayed, using the value in the `grouping-separator` attribute as the separating character . For example, using a value of 3 for `grouping-size` results in a separation every third digit, starting from the right and working towards the left, as in the grouping in the number 1,000,000.

Using `<xsl:number grouping-separator="." grouping-size="2">`, we can change this number display to `1.00.00.00`. Note, that when used in this context, the `"."` in the XPath connotation of "current node" is obviated.

The value of the `grouping-size` attribute can be interpreted as an AVT (discussed in Section 6.6.1) when used with { }, allowing `grouping-size` to be derived from an expression.

9.7.10 The `<xsl:fallback>` Instruction Element

The `<xsl:fallback>` instruction element is used to provide an alternative process when an XSLT instruction fails. The content for the `<xsl:fallback>` instruction is a template, and it has no attributes, as shown in the following element model definition:

```
<!-- Category: instruction -->
<xsl:fallback>
  <!-- Content: template -->
</xsl:fallback>
```

Normally, the processor signals an error if an instruction element that is not supported is used. The `<xsl:fallback>` instruction element catches the error and uses the instructions in the template provided instead of failing the process. If the `<xsl:fallback>` element is empty, the result is to output nothing. Note that this element is similar to a "catch" in some programming languages, which catches the error before it is sent through the process and redirects it to some other process. Example 9–27 demonstrates how we might use the `<xsl:fallback>` element with a hypothetical namespace with a prefix of `go`.

Example 9–27 : Using the `xsl:fallback` element.

```
<go:jump>
     <!-- some instruction elements here -->
<xsl:fallback>
     <!-- some alternative instruction elements here -->
</xsl:fallback>
</go:jump>
```

In this example, the contents of the `<xsl:fallback>` will be instantiated if the `<go:jump>` extension element is not supported by the processor. Of course, the namespace for the extension element must be declared in the stylesheet for the processor to work. It is an error to use a prefixed extension function without declaring the namespace for that prefix, and `<xsl:fallback>` is not intended to catch legitimate errors.

It should also be noted that `<xsl:fallback>` is an instruction element and only works at the instruction level—that is, it is only effective as a part of a template rule or as a child of `<xsl:template>`. This means that any extension elements defined by some other namespace as top-level elements cannot be "caught" using the `<xsl:fallback>` element. Unsupported top-level elements are simply ignored by the processor.

Controlling Output Options

- `<xsl:output>`
- `<xsl:strip-space>`
- `<xsl:preserve-space>`
- `<xsl:message>`

10

In this chapter, we will work with elements that are, for the most part, concerned with how the output from the stylesheet is handled or processed, and what kind of output it will be. The first element, `<xsl:output>`, is not used to *create* output (contrary to its name), but controls the logical structure of the output, and what kinds of processing-specific components are to be included or excluded. The other two top-level elements discussed in this chapter are the complementary pair `<xsl:strip-space>` and `<xsl:preserve-space>`. Notably, `<xsl:strip-space>` and `<xsl:preserve-space>` do not affect output directly; they govern the handling of whitespace in the *input* tree, which of course can affect the whitespace in the output result tree.

As another output option, messages such as logs and errors can be generated from the actual processing of the stylesheet using the `<xsl:message>` element, which is discussed in the last section of this chapter.

10.1 The `<xsl:output>` Top-Level Element

The `<xsl:output>` top-level element establishes the type of structure the output will contain (XML, HTML, or text) and provides attributes to select several different output options. It must be a child of the `<xsl:stylesheet>` or `<xsl:transform>` document element, and can occur anywhere within the document element, unless the `<xsl:import>` element is present, in which case it must come after that element. Its ten attributes, shown in the following element model definition, are optional and will be discussed individually in the following sections. This top-level element is always an empty element.

```
<!-- Category: top-level-element -->

<xsl:output

  method = "xml" | "html" | "text" | qname-but-not-
ncname

  version = nmtoken

  encoding = string

  omit-xml-declaration = "yes" | "no"

  standalone = "yes" | "no"

  doctype-public = string

  doctype-system = string

  cdata-section-elements = qnames

  indent = "yes" | "no"

  media-type = string />
```

Multiple `<xsl:output>` elements are allowed within one stylesheet and can also be imported from other stylesheets. However, the processor concatenates the information from each one into a single `<xsl:output>` element with all the effective values. If conflicts arise, the same conflict resolution for templates (discussed in Chapter 7) applies, except for the values of `cdata-section-elements` attributes, which are concatenated into one list.

In its primary capacity, `<xsl:output>` affects the form of the logical structure of the XSLT stylesheet's output. We use the phrase *logical structure* to underscore that formatting of output—"pretty-printing"—is not specifically the purview of XSLT, apart from any HTML LREs. The function of formatting is under the scope of the XSL formatting objects specification.[1] The formatting affected by `<xsl:output>` is at a more general level. The `<xsl:output>` element affects the *type* of output, HTML, text, or XML, not the human-readable or printable results. Whitespace and indenting of elements are affected, but things like running headers and footers are not. Character encoding, inclusion of DOCTYPE declarations, and similar kinds of output structural elements are specified using `<xsl:output>` and its attributes, as discussed in the following sections.

10.1.1 Attributes for `<xsl:output>`

The best way to enumerate the functions performed by `<xsl:output>` is through its attributes, which are the mechanisms by which it affects its results. We will introduce each of them in turn, according to the order in which they are found in the element model definition (shown above) from the W3C specification for XSLT, Section 16. These attributes are also discussed individually according to how they operate with each of the values of the `<xsl:output>` element's `method` attribute.

10.1.1.1 The `method` Attribute

The most frequently used attribute for `<xsl:output>` is the `method` attribute, which describes the overall file type, or logical structure, of the output XML document instance. If you are familiar with the *Save As* function in a word processor, which allows the choice of different file types, such as text-only or rich text format, you will see a similar functionality in the role played by the `method` attribute.

This attribute has three predefined values of `xml`, `html`, and `text`, and one user-defined value. The output from using a method equal to `xml` will always be a well-formed document. If the output method is `html`, the logical structure of the output document will be HTML, valid according to the version of HTML selected (and, correspondingly, *not*

1. See http://www.w3.org/TR/xsl/ for more information on XSL Formatting Objects.

equivalent to XHTML). Finally, in the case of `text`, the output is similar to a file whose content is only a text string or plain text file. We will attend to each output type in turn after generally introducing the balance of the `<xsl:output>` attributes.

There is also a fourth kind of output, shown in the element model definition above as *qname-but-not-ncname,* which can be defined by extensions supported by specific XSLT implementations of various processing software. Extensions are discussed in Chapters 12 and 13, which address processor-specific implementations. However, the following brief summary will provide an overview.

A QName is accepted as a fourth possible value for `method,` if there is a supported extension output type for that method. The QName must be prefixed by the namespace prefix for the extension output type. A namespace declaration must also be in effect for the prefix at the point in the XSLT stylesheet at which the output method is used.

10.1.1.2 The `version` Attribute

The `version` attribute for `<xsl:output>` is used to stipulate the version of the respective output type—applicable to `xml`, `html`, and conceivably, extension output types—as declared with the `method` attribute. For XML output, the current value would be 1.0 to match the current version of the XML specification. For HTML output, the default is assumed to be 4.0, unless it is necessary to choose HTML 2.0 for some specific purpose—perhaps to display the HTML LREs that are output in an older version of Netscape, for instance.

10.1.1.3 The `encoding` Attribute

The `encoding` attribute is used in combination with the `xml`, `html`, and `text` values for the `method` attribute, and specifies which encoding the output result tree will have for a particular character set. The result will be different for the different kinds of output specified under `method`. With an `xml` output, for instance, the stipulation of UTF-16 will create an `encoding` attribute with a value of `UTF-16` in the XML declaration of the resulting output XML file. With either `text` or `html` output, the processor will generate UTF-16 valid text. XSLT processors are not required to support all values of encoding, but they are required to respect both UTF-8 and UTF-16.

10.1.1.4 The `omit-xml-declaration` Attribute

The `omit-xml-declaration` attribute is only used when the `method` output is set to `xml`. It governs whether or not there must be an `XML` declaration at the beginning of the output XML document instance. The default, if left undeclared, is no, meaning that there *will* be an XML declaration. The only other possible value is yes, which omits the declaration from the output result tree.

10.1.1.5 The `standalone` Attribute

The `standalone` attribute establishes the value of the `standalone` attribute generated in the XML declaration of the output document. Its possible values are yes and no. It is only used when the `method` attribute has a value of `xml`, and is ignored otherwise since it is not applicable to the other output types. If the value of the `standalone` attribute is set to `yes`, the resulting XML document (including its DTD or any external parameter entities, if specified) is understood to be free from external declarations. External declarations, defined by the XML specification, are:

a. Attributes with default values, if elements to which these attributes apply appear in the document without specifications of values for these attributes

b. Entities (other than `amp`, `lt`, `gt`, `apos`, `quot`), if references to those entities appear in the document

c. Attributes with values subject to normalization, where the attribute appears in the document with a value which will change as a result of normalization

d. Element types with element content, if whitespace occurs directly within any instance of those types

References to external entities in a standalone document *are* valid as long as the entities are declared within the document. The following use of `<xsl:output>` shows the declaration of the `standalone` attribute:

```
<xsl:output method="xml" standalone="yes">
```

This use of the `<xsl:output>` element results in the following XML declaration in the output document:

```
<?xml version="1.0" standalone="yes"?>
```

10.1.1.6 The `doctype-public` Attribute

The `doctype-public` attribute is used to add a public identifier in the document type declaration of the output document. The value of the attribute is a string, which becomes the value of the public identifier in the output document. Note that the XSLT processor does not validate the string to ensure a proper identifier. The string is sent directly to the output document as it appears in the stylesheet. The `doctype-public` attribute is used with either the `html` or `xml` output method.

10.1.1.7 The `doctype-system` Attribute

The `doctype-system` attribute enables the declaration of a system identifier for the document type declaration in the output document. The value of the attribute is a string, in the form of a URL or relative path, which becomes the value of the system identifier in the output document. Note that the XSLT processor does not validate the string to ensure a proper identifier. The string is sent directly to the output document as it appears in the stylesheet. The `doctype-system` attribute is used with either the `html` or `xml` output method.

10.1.1.8 The `cdata-section-elements` Attribute

The `cdata-section-elements` attribute is used to list the element-type names in the output XML document whose text node children will be output as CDATA[2] sections. CDATA sections are used to escape portions

---

2. A CDATA section is a special kind of marked section that can include markup characters like & and <, without having to literally escape them using `&` and `<`.

of the output result tree that will possibly contain special characters that should not be escaped with character entity references.

As an example, some XML documents may contain a `<sample>` element that will be used to contain programming-specific code. Therefore, a `cdata-section-elements` attribute value of "`sample`" would stipulate that all text children of the `<sample>` element are to be output as CDATA sections. In other words, the text inside any `<sample>` element will appear in the output with the CDATA section delimiters in the form "`<![CDATA[original text]]>`", where "`original text`" is the original content of the text node. The CDATA section delimiters are `<![CDATA[` for the opening delimiter and `]]>` for the closing delimiter. These delimiters are special characters and are considered markup.

The sequence of two closing square brackets followed by a greater-than symbol (`]]>`), when found inside a CDATA section in the output, will cause an error. It is not valid for a CDATA section to contain another CDATA section. Note that the > symbol can appear in the CDATA section as the appropriate character entity reference `>` and still be considered part of the markup. If this sequence of characters is found in an LRE in the stylesheet or in an input element that will be treated as a CDATA section in the output, the processor will generate two individual CDATA sections, one containing the two `]]` and another containing the >.

If any special characters are found in the `<sample>` element's text node, the special characters are output as the correct character instead of the entity reference. So, if the text contains characters like & or <, or even XML character references like `&` or `<`, the real character will appear in the output instead of the character reference.

The `cdata-section-elements` attribute value can contain more than one element-type name if the names are separated by whitespace. It is used when the `method` attribute value is `xml`, and it is not used with any other type of output. Note that XT does not currently support this functionality.

10.1.1.9 The `indent` Attribute

The `indent` attribute can be used when either `xml` or `html` output is specified with the `method` attribute. When set to the value of `yes`, the hierarchical structure of the output result tree is indented, and in most cases, each element is on a separate line. This functionality provides a very user-friendly formatting of the output XML, since most processors by default ignore whitespace in the input and deliver "bunched up" XML. The XSLT processor has the discretionary option to implement this feature, and how it does so is also discretionary. The default value of the `indent` attribute, if left undeclared, is `no`.

Using the `indent` attribute with mixed content models will deliver unpredictable indentation. In other words, if the hierarchy of input elements contains text strings as siblings to other elements, the output from using `indent` set to `yes` can occasionally be unpredictable.

10.1.1.10 The `media-type` Attribute

The `media-type` attribute can be used with any value set with the `method` attribute, though uses with extension methods are not governed by XSLT. Values for this attribute are based on an external transport protocol called MIME.[3] For example, in an XML output document, the MIME type would be `text/xml`, and for HTML, `text/html`. If the XML being output is to be used as an application or data transport mechanism, the MIME type will be `application/xml`. If the output file type is text, the MIME type is `text/plain`. Because `xml` is the default for the `method` attribute, when there is no `method` specified, the default value of the `media-type` attribute is `text/xml`. The value of the `media-type` attribute can be used for clarifying how a given environment should handle the output file according to how—or if—it reads these kinds of MIME type declarations.

The two MIME media types applicable to XSLT and XML documents are `text/xml` and `application/xml`. These two media types are outlined in the W3C specification RFC2376. Additional media types may be registered in the future, and if one for XSLT specifically is registered, the new type should be supported by XSLT processors. An example of using the media-type attribute is as follows:

```
<xsl:output method="text" encoding="UTF-8" media-type="text/plain"/>
```

3. MIME is a type of external transport protocol like HTTP that provides information to the processor about the data being processed.

10.1.2 Working with the xml Output File Method

All of the `<xsl:output>` attributes are applicable to the `xml` output method, but may not be for other output types. For example, the `standalone` and `omit-xml-declaration` attributes are purely for XML output, while the others may apply to HTML or text, and possibly to extension output methods selectively, based on their function. The `xml` output method is the default output type unless, as described in Section 10.1.3 below, several output conditions are met that will cause the processor to generate HTML instead.

10.1.2.1 Using the `omit-xml-declaration` Attribute with XML Output

The `omit-xml-declaration` attribute controls the output of the XML declaration. If the `omit-xml-declaration` attribute is not specified, the XML declaration, `<?xml version="1.0"?>` will be included, as long as the output method is `xml`. The behavior of many of the other `<xsl:output>` attributes, such as `version`, `encoding`, and `standalone`, is somewhat predicated on whether there is an XML declaration. Using `<xsl:output method="xml" omit-xml-declaration="yes" />` will suppress the XML declaration in the output result tree.

10.1.2.2 The `version` Attribute with XML Output

Working with XML means this attribute has certain values already prescribed. Because the current version of the XML specification is 1.0, the only currently valid version number for `<xsl:output>` when the `method` attribute value is `xml` is 1.0. When the version of the W3C XML specification changes, the version for the XML specification in the output document can be changed using the `version` attribute of `<xsl:output>`.

Note that the current version of XT does not implement this function. The version for the XSL specification generated using XT is 1.0, regardless of the `<xsl:output>` `version` attribute.

10.1.2.3 The encoding Attribute with XML Output

If an encoding other than the default UTF-8 is desired in the XML declaration of the output document, the encoding attribute on <xsl:output> can be used to generate it. XSLT processors check the value of the encoding attribute and should signal an error if the value is not valid or is not a supported encoding type.

Encoding types are registered with the Internet Assigned Numbers Authority (IANA),[4] as defined in the W3C specification (RFC2278).[5] XML processors are not required to support anything other than UTF-8 and UTF-16, but according to the XML specification, the following character sets may be used:

> *In an encoding declaration, the values* "UTF-8"*,* "UTF-16"*,* "ISO-10646-UCS-2"*, and* "ISO-10646-UCS-4" *should be used for the various encodings and transformations of Unicode / ISO/IEC 10646; the values* "ISO-8859-1"*,* "ISO-8859-2"*,*... "ISO-8859-9" *should be used for parts of ISO 8859; and the values* "ISO-2022-JP"*,* "Shift_JIS"*, and* "EUC-JP" *should be used for the various encoded forms of JIS X-0208-1997.* (XML specification, Section 4.3.3)

The following <xsl:output> element shows the use of the encoding attribute:

```
<xsl:output method="xml" encoding="EUC-JP" />
```

This will output the following XML declaration in the output file:

```
<?xml version="1.0" encoding="EUC-JP"?>
```

The value of the encoding attribute is case-insensitive and must contain only printable ASCII characters. Additional user-defined character encoding sets are allowed, but if the specified encoding is not a charset registered with the IANA, it must start with X-.

4. See http://www.w3.org/TR/xslt#IANA.
5. See http://www.w3.org/TR/xslt#RFC2278.

10.1.2.4 The doctype-public and doctype-system Attributes with XML Output

The doctype-public and doctype-system attributes cause a DOCTYPE declaration to be output immediately following the XML declaration in the output result tree. The doctype-public attribute, which passes as its value a string that is a public identifier, will create a public document type declaration with the key word PUBLIC. The doctype-system attribute passes its value as a string in the form of a URI, which is a system identifier—either a URL or a system path—which may or may not resolve to an actual "place" on the file system or Internet. For example, using <xsl:output method="xml" doctype-system="http://www.my_store.com/my.dtd" /> generates a DOCTYPE declaration in the output result tree as follows:

```
<!DOCTYPE topelement SYSTEM "http://www.my_store.com/my.dtd">
```

When used together, the two attributes are combined into one DOCTYPE declaration with both PUBLIC and SYSTEM identifiers as follows:

```
<xsl:output method="xml"
      doctype-public="-//MY STORE//DTD MyDTD//EN"
      doctype-system="http://www.my_store.com/my.dtd" />
```

This use of <xsl:output> will produce the following DOCTYPE declaration *unless* there is an omit-xml-declaration attribute declared with a value of yes:

```
<!DOCTYPE topelement PUBLIC "-//MYSTORE//DTD MyDTD//EN"
"http://www.my_store.com/my.dtd">
```

The key word DOCTYPE is followed by the name of the top-level element of the XML document. The name for the document element, given in these examples as "topelement," is determined by the XSLT processor according to the element-type name of the first element node in the output document. The name is followed by the key word PUBLIC and the public declaration, if a public declaration exists. If the public declaration does not exist, the name is followed by the key word SYSTEM and the system declaration. If both declarations exist, the SYSTEM key word is dropped.

It is possible to use two different <xsl:output> elements to declare the system and public identifiers separately, but they are still combined into one DOCTYPE declaration in the output. Note that the XSLT processor does not validate the string content of the doctype-system or doctype-public attributes to ensure a proper identifier. The string is sent directly to the output document as it appears in the stylesheet.

10.1.2.5 The standalone Attribute with XML Output

When the standalone attribute is declared with <xsl:output>, the presence or absence of the standalone attribute in the XML declaration in the resulting XML document is determined.

The default value of this attribute is no; should the standalone attribute *not* be declared in the <xsl:output> element, the XML declaration will still be created in the result (assuming the omit-xml-declaration attribute has not been declared in <xsl:output> with a value of yes), but there will be no standalone attribute declared. When the standalone attribute is declared with a value of yes, the resulting XML document instance will have a standalone="yes" attribute node added to the XML declaration. See Section 10.1.1.5 for more information on the standalone attribute in the XML declaration. The following use of <xsl:output> shows the declaration of the standalone attribute:

```
<xsl:output method="xml" standalone="yes">
```

This use of the <xsl:output> element results in the following XML declaration:

```
<?xml version="1.0" standalone="yes"?>
```

10.1.2.6 The indent Attribute with XML Output

When the indent attribute value is yes, the processor has the option of indenting the XML output tree to reflect the hierarchy of the elements. The implementation of the indent attribute leaves some discretion to the XSLT processor, so there is no guarantee either of indentation or of consistency of results from one processor to another. In most cases, if the indent attribute is set to yes, the output structure will have line breaks and/or indents for each element.

The default value of the indent attribute is no. In other words, when this attribute is not declared, the output result tree reflects no hierarchically generated whitespace.

The XSLT specification indicates, “It is usually not safe to use indent="yes" with the document types that include element types with mixed content.” In other words, if the hierarchy of input elements contains text strings as siblings to other elements, the output from using indent set to yes can occasionally be unpredictable. Otherwise, the following declaration will make a conventional indented hierarchical representation:

```
<xsl:output method="xml" indent="yes" />
```

This would result in an output tree that, ideally, would look similar to the following:

```
<element>
      <sub-element>
            <sub-sub-element>Some text</sub-sub-element>
      </sub-element>
</element>
```

Note that XT does not provide any indentation, but does add line breaks for each element.

10.1.2.7 The cdata-section-elements Attribute with XML Output

CDATA sections in XML are used to escape character strings. Elements that are to be formatted as CDATA in the output result tree are identified by their element-type name, given as the value of the cdata-section-elements attribute. If there is more than one element to be output as CDATA, they should be itemized in the value of the attribute as a whitespace-separated list—in other words, listed with a space between each element-type name, with no commas or other separating tokens.

The creation of a CDATA section for an LRE called "sample" would involve the following use of <xsl:output>:

```
<xsl:output method="xml" cdata-section-elements="sample" />
```

This would apply to the following <sample> LRE from the stylesheet:

```
<sample>Some stuff goes in here</sample>
```

The LRE would be sent to the output result tree written as follows:

```
<sample><![CDATA[Some stuff goes in here]]></sample>
```

The cdata-section-elements causes the basic CDATA section delimiter syntax of <![CDATA[, followed by]]>, to be wrapped around the text of any element in the output result tree specified in cdata-section-elements.

Special character entities escaped with their defined character entity references in the input are resolved to their respective characters; for example, `<` is resolved upon output in a CDATA section as <.

For example, assume the stylesheet has the following content for the `<sample>` LRE:

```
<sample>&lt;example></sample>
```

The content of the LRE would be sent to the output, surrounded by the CDATA marked section delimiters, with the character entity reference `<` resolved to the appropriate character, <, as follows:

```
<sample><![CDATA[<example>]]></sample>
```

Further, if the LRE in the stylesheet has the CDATA section already marked, the output would be exactly the same. For example, the result of the following LRE is equivalent to the previous example:

```
<sample><![CDATA[<element>]]></sample>
```

There is a special character sequence that is specific to CDATA sections and is considered markup by the processor. The sequence of two closing square brackets followed by a greater-than symbol (`]]>`), when found inside an element specified as CDATA, will cause the processor to generate individual CDATA sections, one containing the two `]]` and another containing the >. It is not valid for a CDATA section to contain another CDATA section. Note that the > can appear in the LRE as the appropriate character entity reference of `>` and still be considered part of the disallowed markup. For example, suppose our `<sample>` LRE contained these specific characters as follows:

```
<sample>]]&gt;</sample>
```

The processor would generate the following element in the output result tree:

```
<sample><![CDATA[]]]]><!CDATA[>]]></sample>
```

While this may look like a plethora of square brackets, note that the first CDATA section contains the two from the original LRE, followed by the closing of that CDATA section. The second CDATA section contains the string—in this case, a resolved, predefined entity for the greater-than symbol, >—that followed the `]]` in the original LRE.

10.1.2.8 The `media-type` Attribute with XML Output

When using the `xml` output method, the default for this attribute is the `text/xml` value, but other values could be substituted, as warranted by the circumstances. For example, if the XML being output is to be used as an application or a data transport mechanism, the media type should be `application/xml`. Because `xml` is the default for the `method` attribute, when there is no `method` specified, the default value of the `media-type` attribute is `text/xml`.

The two MIME media types applicable to XSLT and XML documents are `text/xml` and `application/xml`. These two media types are outlined in the W3C specification RFC2376.

Note that if the `media-type` attribute is set to `text/xml`, the `encoding` attribute should not be specified because the `charset` parameter on the MIME type determines the character encoding method. If the `encoding` attribute is specified, it will be ignored, as stated in Appendix F of the XML recommendation. The relevant section is shown here:

> *[The] XML entity [may be] accompanied by encoding information, as in some file systems and some network protocols. When multiple sources of information are available, their relative priority and the preferred method of handling conflict should be specified as part of the higher level protocol used to deliver XML. Rules for the relative priority of the internal label and the MIME-type label in an external header, for example, should be part of the RFC document defining the text/xml and application/xml MIME types. In the interests of interoperability, however, the following rules are recommended:*
>
> - *If an XML entity is delivered with a MIME type of text/xml, then the* `charset` *parameter on the MIME type determines the character encoding method; all other heuristics and sources of information are solely for error recovery.*
> - *If an XML entity is delivered with a MIME type of application/xml, then the byte-order mark and encoding-declaration PI are used (if present) to determine the character encoding. All other heuristics and sources of information are solely for error recovery.*

These rules apply only in the absence of protocol-level documentation; in particular, when the MIME types text/xml and application/xml are defined, the recommendations of the relevant RFC will supersede these rules.

10.1.3 Working with the `html` Output File Method

Most of the attributes for the `<xsl:output>` element using the `xml` output method also apply to the `html` output method. However, there are three attributes that are not valid or do not apply to HTML because they are XML–specific: `omit-xml-declaration`, `standalone`, and `cdata-section-elements`. The remaining six attributes are discussed in the following sections. First, however, there are specific implementations of the `html` output method that should be discussed.

> **NOTE** There is no specific output type for XHTML,* though it is possible that extension elements for it will be added in the near future. XHTML output uses the same `<xsl:output>` attributes as the `xml` output method.
>
> *See the W3C specification for XHTML for more details: http://www.w3.org/MarkUp/.

10.1.3.1 Defaulting to the `html` Output File Method

There are circumstances under which the XSLT processor will default to the `html` output method, even when it is not explicitly declared. This is not to say that when the requirements for this are met, an explicit declaration of `xml` will itself be overridden. The following list is quoted from the W3C specification for XSLT, Section 16, with the quoted material in *italics*. The output method will default to `html` if all three of the following requirements are met:

1. *The root node of the result tree has an element child,*

2. *The expanded-name of the first element child of the root node (i.e., the document element) of the result tree has local part* `html` *(in any combination of upper- and lowercase) and a null namespace URI, and*
3. *Any text nodes preceding the first element child of the root node of the result tree contain only whitespace characters.*

These three requirements, when taken together as a whole, basically state that if the first element in the output document is the `<html>` element, the output method will default to `html` and the XML declaration will be omitted.

The first requirement states that the first node in the output document after the root must be an element and not a PI or comment. The second requirement states that the first element in the output document must be of the element-type name "html" and not case-specific. A "null namespace URI" only reflects the fact that the namespace for HTML is not an XML namespace and does not have a prefix, and is therefore considered an LRE.

> **NOTE** As discussed in Chapter 12, namespaces contain two parts: a prefix and a local part. If the namespace is expanded and the prefix is null, then the URI reference for the prefix is also understood to be null, and the element is considered an LRE by the processor. The exceptions to this rule are elements in the XSL namespace name, which do not need to be prefixed, and extension elements, if they are in a portion of the stylesheet that is defaulted with the extension namespace.

The third requirement states that if the first node in the document is text, it must only contain whitespace. In other words, the first object found in the output document cannot be text unless it is whitespace.

10.1.3.2 Using the `html` Output File Method

When `html` is the output method, whether explicitly declared with the `method` attribute in the `<xsl:output>` element or implicitly defaulted to based on the specific rules outlined in Section 10.1.3.1, the XSLT processor will follow certain guidelines for the output as specified by the XSLT specification:

1. Non-HTML element tags will be generated in the output just as they are with XML; a starting tag and an ending tag are required.
2. Any LRE elements that are not recognized as HTML elements will be treated as if they are XML tags.
3. HTML elements are recognized as HTML elements and sent to the output as required by the version of HTML specified with the version attribute of `<xsl:output>`.
4. Empty HTML tags will not have an end tag, and will not have a closing / inside the empty element tag as is done with XML. The empty elements recognized for HTML version 4.0 are: `area`, `base`, `basefont`, `br`, `col`, `frame`, `hr`, `img`, `input`, `isindex`, `link`, `meta`, and `param`. These elements will appear in the output in their HTML form as `<img>`, `<br>`, etc.
5. HTML is case-insensitive, so the XSLT processor will recognize them in any combination of case.
6. Like the `xml` output method, the default handling of special characters for the `html` method is to escape them, as long as the character has a defined entity reference for HTML. Characters like < and & will normally be sent to the output in their entity reference form of `<` and `&`. However, the escaping of special characters in the `script` and `style` elements will be turned off.
7. The `script` and `style` elements are analogous to the CDATA sections in XML, and special characters found in these elements should appear as their resolved characters in the output. If CDATA sections are found in these elements, they will also be resolved. For example, the `script` element may contain a programming-specific process sequence as follows:

   ```
   <script>if (a &lt; b) process()</script>
   or
   <script><![CDATA[if (a < b) process()]]></script>
   ```

   Both of these inputs would resolve to the following output in `html` output mode:

   ```
   <script>if (a < b) process()</script>
   ```

8. The special character < will not be escaped if it is found in an attribute because it is a valid character in HTML attributes.

9. The special character & in an attribute will not be escaped if it is immediately followed by a { character. For example, an element start-tag may be written in the stylesheet as follows:

```
<BODY bgcolor='&amp;{{randomrbg}};'>
```

This will be sent to the HTML output as:

```
<BODY bgcolor='&{randomrbg};'>
```

10. The HTML 4.0 Recommendation, Section B.2.1, outlines the specific method for escaping non-ASCII characters in URI attribute values when using the `html` output method
11. PIs, which in XML are terminated with `?>`, are terminated without the closing ? when in `html` output mode. PIs will be in the form `<?PI>` in HTML.
12. A holdover from SGML, Boolean value attributes in HTML can be minimized. This means that the attribute can appear in the element tag without a value, because the only possible value of the attribute is the same as the name of the attribute. Simply specifying the attribute sets its value. The `html` output method handles Boolean attributes in this way, sending them to the output in minimized form. For example, an element start-tag with a Boolean attribute may be written in the stylesheet as follows:

```
<OPTION selected="selected">
```

The HTML output of this element will be as follows:

```
<OPTION selected>
```

10.1.3.3 The `version` Attribute with HTML Output

Unlike the `xml` output method, the `version` attribute for the `html` output method does not generate a version number in the output document. It is used to control which version of HTML the processor will conform to when generating the output.

XSLT processors currently default to HTML version 4.0 to match the latest version of HTML. Unless otherwise stipulated, the absence of the `version` attribute in the `<xsl:output>` declaration will implicitly default the resulting HTML document instance to version 4.0.

In some cases, perhaps for the backward-compatibility of some systems, it may be necessary to use an older version of HTML for the output. In these cases, the version attribute will be used to signal the correct version to the processor, and the processor should generate the correct output.

10.1.3.4 The indent Attribute with HTML Output

When used with the html output method, the indent attribute works, depending on the XSLT processor's discretionary implementation, the same as it does with the xml output method. The use of whitespace to indicate the relative hierarchy of the descent of various elements nested one within another can vary from processor to processor, but the role of <xsl:output> is the same for both the xml and html output types. However, the processor will never interpret this attribute in such a way that it alters the default display handling of the HTML by the different browsers.

Note that XT does not support indentation with the html output method.

10.1.3.5 The encoding Attribute with HTML Output

When the html output method is used and the output document contains a <head> element, XSLT processors may generate a <meta> element to declare character set and media type values. The encoding attribute is used to generate the correct value for the charset attribute in the <meta> element. For example, <xsl:output method="html" encoding="UTF-16" /> would produce the following <meta> element in the HTML output:

```
<META http-equiv="Content-Type" content="text/html" charset="UTF-16">
```

This output assumes that the media-type attribute has not set a MIME output type other than the default of text/html.

Characters that are not supported by the selected encoding type should be escaped using the correct character entity reference, if defined for HTML, or a decimal numeric character reference. It is an error if the unresolvable character appears in a `script` or `style` element, or in a comment.

Note that Saxon generates the `<meta>` element for default as well as explicitly specified values of the `encoding` attribute, while XT only generates it if the encoding element is specified.

10.1.3.6 The `media-type` Attribute with HTML Output

As discussed in the previous section, when using the `html` output method, the XSLT processor should generate a `<meta>` element in the output document if the `<head>` element exists. The `media-type` attribute, when declared using `<xsl:output>`, is used to reset the default media type value of `text/html` to some other value, if need be, in the `content` attribute of the `<meta>` element.

Note that XT does not support the `media-type` attribute for the `html` output method.

10.1.3.7 The `doctype-system` and `doctype-public` Attributes with HTML Output

These attributes operate in the same way for the `html` output method as they do for `xml` output method (see Section 10.1.2.4). However, the determination of the document element name—which is done automatically by the processor for XML output based on the first element in the output document —is always going to be either `HTML` or `html`. The XSLT processor does not validate the string value of the `doctype-system` and `doctype-public` attributes to ensure a proper identifier. However, the correct system identifier to reference the W3C specification is http://www.w3.org/TR/html4/strict.dtd (the version number will be different if the chosen version is something other than 4.0). The correct public identifier for the latest HTML version is `-//W3C//DTD HTML 4.01//EN`. As with the `xml` output method for these attributes, if both are declared, the public identifier will come first.

These declarations are less commonly used in HTML than in XML, so this pair of attributes is not likely to be seen as frequently, but their use is recommended to support valid HTML documents. Nonetheless, apart from the automatic identification of the `html` document element, these attributes work almost identically with either `html` or `xml` output method.

10.1.4 Working with the `text` Output File Method

The `text` output method, as succinctly described by the W3C specification for XSLT, "outputs the result tree by outputting the string-value of every text node in the result tree in document order without any escaping" (Section 16.3).

This means that each node in the output result tree is examined, all entities are resolved, and the resulting text is sent to the output. If the input contains special characters that are not part of the markup, they are passed on to the output as the resolved characters.

There are only two relevant attributes for the `<xsl:output>` element using the `text` output method: `encoding` and `media-type`. The remaining attributes, `version`, `omit-xml-declaration`, `standalone`, `doctype-public`, `doctype-system`, `cdata-section-elements`, and `indent`, are not valid and are ignored by the XSLT processor when the method attribute is set to `text`.

10.1.4.1 The `media-type` Attribute with Text Output

The `media-type` attribute can be used with the text output method to define a media type other than the default for text, which is `text/plain`. If the output method is explicitly selected as `text`, a `media-type` attribute is not required, unless a value other than `text/plain` is required. An example of using the `media-type` attribute with a value other than `text/plain` is as follows:

```
<xsl:output method="text" media-type="model/vrml"/>
```

10.1.4.2 The `encoding` Attribute with Text Output

The `encoding` attribute is used to specify which character set the output result tree will have. When used with the `text` output method, the processor should generate valid encoded text.

The encoding of text is the process of converting the sequence of characters from the input tree, according to the value given for `encoding`, to generate the resulting sequence of bytes in the output. The default for this attribute is system-dependent.

XSLT processors are not required to support all values of encoding, but they are required to respect both UTF-8 and UTF-16. It is an error if a character that cannot be represented in the `encoding` value selected is used.

10.2 The `<xsl:strip-space>` and `<xsl:preserve-space>` Top-Level Elements

These elements form a complementary pair of XSLT top-level elements whose purpose is to govern the handling of whitespace in the input tree and, by implication, in the output result tree. Both elements have one required attribute, the `elements` attribute, whose value (*`tokens`*) is a whitespace-separated list of element-type names, as shown in the element model definitions for each element below:

```
<!-- Category: top-level-element -->
<xsl:strip-space
  elements = tokens />
```

```
<!-- Category: top-level-element -->
<xsl:preserve-space
  elements = tokens />
```

The <xsl:preserve-space> top-level element retains whitespace text nodes from the input elements listed in its elements attribute. The <xsl:strip-space> element has the opposite effect of <xsl:preserve-space>. Whitespace text nodes are stripped from the input prior to processing.

The value of the elements attribute contains a list of the elements that will be acted on to preserve the whitespace text nodes they contain, if used with <xsl:preserve-space>, or to strip them, if used with <xsl:strip-space>. All elements in the input document are defaulted to preserve space unless they are explicitly added to the <xsl:strip-space> elements attribute.

If there are conflicts in the matching of elements identified by their element-type name for either of the pair of these top-level elements in a given XSLT stylesheet, the standard rules of precedence discussed in Chapter 7 for <xsl:import> and <xsl:include>, and template rules in general, are used. Any <xsl:preserve-space> or <xsl:strip-space> elements with lower precedence due to being imported are ignored. The default priorities for the names (an element-type name or attribute name receives higher priority) determine precedence.

It should be noted that the <xsl:strip-space> and <xsl:preserve-space> elements do not operate on the text nodes of the specified elements unless those text nodes contain only whitespace. A text node with text other than whitespace will be sent to the output intact. Any excessive whitespace between words in a text node will appear as it did in the input.

For example, if a <block> in our Markup City contained extra whitespace, such as:

```
<block>1st Street                    </block>
<block>2nd          Street</block>
<block>             3rd Street</block>
```

Specifying "block" as the value for the elements attribute of <xsl:strip-space> *would not* remove the extra spaces. If, however, there were extra line breaks between <block> elements, specifiying "thoroughfare" as the parent of <block> elements would remove the extra line breaks between the <block>s, as shown in Example 10–1

Notice that the whitespace between text in a node is not stripped, but the extra line breaks, which are considered to be whitespace nodes, are stripped.

Example 10–1 : Removing line breaks from Markup City.

INPUT:

```
<?xml version="1.0"?>
      <thoroughfare>
                  <sidestreet>Bob Wallace Avenue</sidestreet>
                  <block>1st Street            </block>



                  <block>2nd       Street</block>


                  <block>          3rd Street</block>
                  <sidestreet>Woodridge Street</sidestreet>
      </thoroughfare>
```

STYLESHEET:

```
<?xml version="1.0"?>
<xsl:stylesheet xmlns:xsl="http://www.w3.org/1999/XSL/Transform"
                version="1.0">
<xsl:strip-space elements="thoroughfare"/>
<xsl:template match="*">
<xsl:copy-of select="."/>
</xsl:template>
</xsl:stylesheet>
```

OUTPUT:

```
<?xml version="1.0" encoding="utf-8"?>
<thoroughfare><sidestreet>Bob Wallace Avenue</sidestreet><block>1st
Street            </block><block>2nd      Street</block><block>
3rd Street</block><sidestreet>Woodridge
Street</sidestreet></thoroughfare>
```

10.3 Generating Error Messages and Logs

Error messages and log files are particularly important to programmers who need to debug or track changes in the processes of their code. XSLT provides a method, using `<xsl:message>`, to generate logs or messages, whether they are stored as files or sent to the screen as message windows, based on processor-specific implementations.

10.3.1 The <xsl:message> Instruction Element

The <xsl:message> instruction element is a way for the XSLT processor to communicate "outside" of itself and outside of the XSLT stylesheet being processed. It has one optional attribute, terminate, with a possible value of yes or no, as shown in the following element model definition. The content of the <xsl:message> element is a template, which means that other instruction elements can be used to build the structure of the final message.

```
<!-- Category: instruction -->
<xsl:message
```

```
terminate = "yes" | "no">
<!-- Content: template -->
</xsl:message>
```

If the terminate attribute is specified with a value of yes, the processor will send the message and terminate the processing of the stylesheet at that point. The default is no, meaning that the processor will continue to operate after the message has been output.

There is some discretion on the part of the XSLT processor as to the implementation of the output context and format for whatever message is to be given when <xsl:message> is triggered. It might appear in a message box on-screen, as a line at the command prompt, or it can be sent to a log file. The <xsl:message> element is triggered when the template rule containing it is instantiated; then the template contained within the <xsl:message> element determines the message displayed.

Using a modified fragment of our Markup City for Example 10–2, we can determine whether <block>s have names in text nodes or attribute nodes. The terminate attribute is set to yes to force the processor to terminate when the <xsl:message> element is activated by finding a <block> without a name attribute.

Example 10–2 : Using <xsl:message> to test for content.

INPUT:

```
<?xml version="1.0"?>
            <thoroughfare name="Whitesburg Drive">
                  <sidestreet>Bob Wallace Avenue</sidestreet>
                  <block name="1st Street"></block>
                  <block name="2nd Street"></block>
                  <block>3rd Street</block>
                  <sidestreet> Woodridge Street</sidestreet>
            </thoroughfare>
```

STYLESHEET:

```
<?xml version="1.0"?>
<xsl:stylesheet xmlns:xsl="http://www.w3.org/1999/XSL/Transform"
                version="1.0">
<xsl:template match="//block">
      <xsl:choose>
            <xsl:when test="@name">
                  <xsl:value-of select="@name" />
            </xsl:when>
            <xsl:otherwise>
                  <xsl:message terminate="yes">
                        <xsl:text>Unfortunately, </xsl:text>
                        <xsl:value-of select="." />
                        <xsl:text> is a street name that is a text
node, not an attribute, so processing will terminate now.</xsl:text>
                 </xsl:message>
           </xsl:otherwise>
     </xsl:choose>
</xsl:template>
</xsl:stylesheet>
```

MESSAGE GENERATED:

```
Unfortunately, 3rd Street is a street name that is a text
node, not an attribute, so processing will terminate now.
```

Using the <xsl:choose> structure, the match attribute of <xsl:when> tests for the presence of a name attribute in each <block>. If there is a name attribute, then its value is selected with

<xsl:value-of> and sent to the output result tree. The <xsl:otherwise> element matches any <block> found without a name attribute—3rd Street in this example—and the processor activates the <xsl:message>. The value of the text node is inserted into the text message using <xsl:value-of>. Because the terminate attribute on <xsl:message> is set to yes, the process terminates. Depending on the implementation of the processor, the valid content in the output result tree before the <xsl:message> element is activated may or may not be sent to the output.

XSLT Functions and Related XSLT Elements

- current(),document(), element-available(), format-number(), function-available(), generate-id(), key(), system-property(), unparsed-entity-uri()
- <xsl:key>
- <xsl:decimal-format>

11

The versatility of XSLT is greatly enhanced by the range of XPath functions (described in Chapter 5), which provide the ability to perform many sophisticated tasks. XSLT provides its own library of functions, specific to XSLT implementations, in addition to the core XPath library of functions. These XSLT functions are used within expressions and are declared by the XSLT specification in the same manner as XPath functions, using a function prototype, as shown in the following structure:

`Function:` *`return type`* **`name`** *`(arguments)`*

This chapter will discuss the nine XSLT functions, which are summarized in Table 11–1, as well as the two XSLT elements `<xsl:key>` and `<xsl:decimal-format>` and their relationships to the `key()` and `format-number()` functions, respectively. The reference number in the last column provides a quick lookup for the section of this chapter specifically applicable to a given function.

Table 11–1 XSLT functions

Function Name	*XSLT Function Group*	*Returns*	*Arguments*	*Argument Type*	*Ref.*
`current()`	Node-set	Node-set	None	None	11.1.2
`document()`	Node-set	Node-set	Object Node-set	Required Optional	11.1.1.1
`element-available()`	Boolean	Boolean	String	Required	11.3.1
`format-number()`	String	String	Number String String	Required Required Optional	11.2.3
`function-available()`	Boolean	Boolean	String	Required	11.3.2
`generate-id()`	String	String	Node-set	Optional	11.2.2
`key()`	Node-set	Node-set	String Object	Required Required	11.1.3
`system-property()`	String	Object	String	Required	11.2.1
`unparsed-entity-uri()`	String	String	String	Required	11.2.4

11.1 XSLT Function Groups

XSLT function groups follow the same conventions as XPath core function groups. There are four XPath function groups aligned with the four objects they produce: node-set, string, Boolean, and number. However, there are no XSLT functions in the number function group, so there is technically no XSLT number function group.

The XSLT functions that return node-sets are: `document()`, which works with material from external documents; `key()`, which provides an index-like addressing capability; and `current()`, which provides a way to explicitly address the current node in a given context. These three functions are in the node-set XSLT function group.

The XSLT functions that return strings are: `system-property()`, which is used to access information about the XSLT processor that is processing the stylesheet; `format-number()`, which is used to set specific parameters for the formatting of a number; `generate-id()`, which is used to create IDs for nodes, and `unparsed-entity-uri()`, which is used to return the value of entities. These four functions are in the string XSLT function group.

The XST functions that return a Boolean value are: `element-available()`, which checks to see if a particular element is supported by the processor being used; and `function-available()`, which checks to see if a particular function is supported in the processor being used. These two functions are in the Boolean XSLT function group.

11.1.1 Node-set XSLT Functions

The XSLT node-set function group augments the basic set of XPath node-set functions with the addition of a `document()` function for importing XML data from more than one source instance, a `current()` function for making explicit the current node regardless of the context node and the `key()` function, which, together with the `<xsl:key>` element, provide an index-like functionality for "looking up," or referencing, elements.

11.1.1.1 The `document()` XSLT Function

The `document()` XSLT function enables input for the XSLT stylesheet to come from more than one XML document instance source. By using `document()`, you can add the contents of an external XML document to the basic input source tree. The `document()` XSLT function is defined using the following function prototype:

`Function:` *`node-set`* **`document`** *`(object, node-set?)`*

Function Name	*Function Group*	*Function Return Type*	*Arguments*	*Argument Type*
`document()`	Node-set	Node-set	Object	Required
			Node-set	Optional

The `document()` function returns a node-set containing the root node of the document that is retrieved by the processor. The node-set returned by the `document()` function can be additionally qualified using a fragment identifier. Fragment identifiers select particular nodes in or descendants of the node-set. Fragment identifiers and their use are discussed in Section 11.1.1.3.

The first required argument of the `document()` function can be any object type, but if it is *not* a node-set, its value is converted to a string, which is interpreted as a URI. When the first argument *is* a node-set, each node in the node-set is evaluated and converted to a string. The strings resuting from each node in the node-set are then treated as if from individual calls by the `document()` function, resulting in a URI for each node.

The second argument is an optional node-set, and is used to identify an alternative base URI for the resolution of a relative URI in the first argument into an absolute URI.

11.1.1.2 Absolute, Relative, and Base URIs

The URI defined by the node-set in the second argument for the `document()` function can be either absolute or relative.

Absolute URIs can be in the form of an explicit URL, such as http://www.my_node-set.org/seminar.xml, or an explicit location path on a file system, such as c:\mydocs\seminar.xml.

Relative URIs are in the form of a URI or filename that is not explicitly pathed, such as *seminar.xml.* Relative URIs have a base URI, which is the default path or URL that will convert the relative path to an absolute path. Base URIs default to the base location in which the XSLT process is occurring.

A base URI is an absolute URI that can be used to convert a relative URI into an absolute URI. Concatenating a base URI and a relative URI will result in an absolute URI.

11.1.1.3 Fragment Identifiers

A fragment identifier in XSLT is used to select a subset of the nodes in the document that is returned by the `document()` function. This allows the selection of a child element in the document rather than the document element as the value returned by the `document()` function. If the resolved URI does not contain a node-set qualifier, the root node of the document is used as the node-set result. For example, adding `"//test"` to the end of the `document()` function as shown below changes the node-set returned by the `document()` function to the `<test>` element instead of the `<seminar>` element (assuming `seminar.xml` contains a `<seminar>` element that has a descendant called `<test>`).

```
document('seminar.xml')//test
```

> **NOTE** Fragment identifiers are defined in RFC2396* Uniform Resource Identifiers (URI): Generic Syntax, Section 4.1. The normal syntax for a fragment identifier is to add the path of the identifier at the end of the URI, separated from the URI by a hash (#). The RFC (Request For Comments) allows implementations to interpret and format the fragment identifiers according to media type. The implementation of fragment identifiers by XSLT processors is media type-specific, according to the media type of the resulting object retrieved by the URI. In relation to the `document()` function, fragment identifiers do not use the # symbol because the function returns a node-set. Selecting nodes in a node-set is accomplished using location paths, defined in the XPath specification. This means that a fragment identifier in XSLT must use an XPath pattern to select a subset of nodes.
>
> *See http://www.w3.org/TR/xpath#RFC2396.

11.1.1.4 The `document()` Function with a Non-Node-set First Argument

The first required argument of the `document()` function can be any object type, but if it is *not* a node-set, its value is converted to a string, which is interpreted as a URI. XSLT processors are not constrained to support any particular kind of URI, though most will resolve URLs. If the first argument to `document()` results in a URI of a type not supported by the XSLT processor, the processor can either report the error or just return an empty node-set.

The W3C specification implicitly requires that the document identified by a URI in the first argument to `document()` be a well-formed XML document. The document could take the form, for instance, of an XML-compliant HTML page one that was well-formed, at least or an XHTML page. However, if the document pointed to is not well-formed XML, the XSLT processor will either return an error or an empty node-set.

Suppose Markup City is to be augmented along the `<boulevard>` by the National Parks Service, and there is an online plan for a new park off of Old Chimney Road. With government funding being such a fickle process, the information on what the National Parks Service is planning will change regularly, so we might just want to get all the text information about the plan in its most up-to-date form from the government's Web site (`http://www.national_parks_service.gov`) each time we meet to discuss the new park. The information for the new `<park>` is located in a file called `monte_sano.xml` on their site. Example 11–1 shows the input file, the main stylesheet, the `monte_sano.xml` file and the stylesheet used to import it, as well as the result of the processing of the stylesheet.

In this example, we use an LRE to add a `<park>` element, and `<park>` is populated with the text contents of the `monte_sano.xml` file, retrieved by the `document()` function using the `<xsl:value-of>` instruction. Notice that the filename is in single quotes to specify that the first argument of the `document()` function is a string. The `<block>` LRE and `<xsl:apply-templates>` assure us that `Old Chimney Road` is still output as a named block.

Example 11–1 : Using the XSLT `document()` function.

INPUT 1:

```
<?xml version="1.0"?>
<boulevard>
            <block>Panorama Street</block>
            <block>Highland Plaza</block>
            <block>Hutchens Avenue</block>
            <block>Wildwood Drive</block>
            <block>Old Chimney Road</block>
            <block>Carrol Circle</block>
</boulevard>
```

STYLESHEET:

```
<?xml version="1.0"?>
<xsl:stylesheet xmlns:xsl="http://www.w3.org/1999/XSL/Transform"
               version="1.0">

<xsl:output indent="yes"/>
<xsl:strip-space elements="*"/>

<xsl:template match="block">
<block>
<xsl:apply-templates/>
</block>
</xsl:template>
<xsl:template match="boulevard/block[contains(., 'Old
Chimney')]">
<park>
<xsl:value-of select="document('http://
www.national_parks_service.gov/monte_sano.xml')" />
</park>
<block>
<xsl:apply-templates/>
</block>
</xsl:template>
</xsl:stylesheet>
```

Example 11–1 : Using the XSLT `document()` function (continued).

INPUT 2: monte_sano.xml:

```
<?xml version="1.0"?>
<park><name>Century Park</name>
</park>
```

RESULT:

```
<?xml version="1.0" encoding="utf-8"?>
<block>Panorama Street</block>
<block>Highland Plaza</block>
<block>Hutchens Avenue</block>
<block>Wildwood Drive</block>
<park>Century Park</park>
<block>Old Chimney Road</block>
<block>Carrol Circle</block>
```

> **NOTE** Use `<xsl:value-of select="document('monte_sano.xml')" />` (without the Web site reference) to access the contents of a file on the file system in the same directory as the stylesheet.

Working with `<xsl:value-of>` does not allow us to do much more processing with the elements in the file returned from the string URI. We could, however, access elements and attributes of the `monte_sano.xml` file by using the XSLT `<xsl:apply-templates>` instruction element, as shown below.

```
<xsl:apply-templates select=
"document('http://www.national_parks_service.gov/monte_sano.xml')" />
```

Now, since the contents of the `monte_sano.xml` file are available as child nodes, we can add template rules for the elements in the external file to restructure the new park according to the file's XML contents, as shown in Example 11–2.

In this example, each element in the second input document, called with the `document()` function, is addressed with a template rule. The template rule with a match on "`park`" uses an LRE to generate the `<park>` tags. Then it uses `<xsl:apply-templates>` to continue processing

Example 11–2 : Adding a park with `document()`.

INPUT 1:

```
<?xml version="1.0"?>
<boulevard>
            <block>Panorama Street</block>
            <block>Highland Plaza</block>
            <block>Hutchens Avenue</block>
            <block>Wildwood Drive</block>
            <block>Old Chimney Road</block>
            <block>Carrol Circle</block>
</boulevard>
```

INPUT 2: monte_sano.xml:

```
<?xml version="1.0"?>
<park><name>Century Park</name>
<facilities>
<pavilion quantity="10"/>
<restrooms quantity="20"/>
<playgrounds quantity="5"/>
<ballfield quantity="8"/>
</facilities>
<grounds>
<landscape/>
<sprinklers layout="3700"/>
<topography designation="6313"/>
<lighting/>
</grounds>
</park>
```

STYLESHEET:

```
<?xml version="1.0"?>
<xsl:stylesheet xmlns:xsl="http://www.w3.org/1999/XSL/Transform"
              version="1.0">

<xsl:output indent="yes"/>
<xsl:strip-space elements="*"/>
<xsl:template match="boulevard/block[contains(., 'Old
Chimney')]">
<xsl:apply-templates select="document('http://
```

Example 11–2 : Adding a park with `document()` (continued).

```
www.national_parks_service.gov/monte_sano.xml')" />
<block>
<xsl:apply-templates />
</block>
</xsl:template>

<xsl:template match="block">
<xsl:copy>
<xsl:apply-templates/>
</xsl:copy>
</xsl:template>

<xsl:template match="park">
<park>
<xsl:apply-templates/>
</park>
</xsl:template>


<xsl:template match="park//*[@*]">
<xsl:copy>
<xsl:value-of select="@*"/>
<xsl:apply-templates/>
</xsl:copy>
</xsl:template>

<xsl:template match="park/name">
<xsl:copy>
<xsl:value-of select="."/>
</xsl:copy>
</xsl:template>

</xsl:stylesheet>
```

RESULTS:

```
<?xml version="1.0" encoding="utf-8"?>
<block>Panorama Street</block>
<block>Highland Plaza</block>
<block>Hutchens Avenue</block>
<block>Wildwood Drive</block>
<park>
<name>Century Park</name>
```

Example 11–2 : Adding a park with `document()` (continued).

```
<pavilion>10</pavilion>
<restrooms>20</restrooms>
<playgrounds>5</playgrounds>
<ballfield>8</ballfield>
<sprinklers>3700</sprinklers>
<topography>6313</topography>
</park>
<block>Old Chimney Road</block>
<block>Carrol Circle</block>
```

the contents of the `<park>`. The template rule that matches on "`park//*[@*]`" is matching each element that is a decendant of `<park>`, but only if it has an attribute specified. The attribute may have any name, designated with the `@*` symbol. Elements without attributes are not matched, so they are handled by the built-in template rules (discussed in Chapter 3). The `<name>` element is matched and copied to the output using the `<xsl:copy>`, and the text is sent through to the output result tree because of the built-in template rule for text nodes.

11.1.1.5 Using `document()` to Reference the XSLT Stylesheet

The content of the XSLT stylesheet itself can be referenced using a pair of whitespace-separated quotes, `document(' ')`. This will return the root node of the XSLT *stylesheet* that contains the `document()` function call.

This use of the first argument to `document()` is analogous to the notation for "self" with "`.`" when referring to nodes. In other words, this space says, "Look in this stylesheet being processed right now." This is not affected by the fact that the `document()` function might be called from an included or imported set of template rules with the use of `<xsl:import>` and `<xsl:include>`. In that case, the local stylesheet is still the one in which the imported or included template rule is instantiated, not the one from which it was imported or included.

11.1.1.6 The document() Function with a Node-set First Argument

The first argument of the document() function can contain an expression, which can be used to generate the URI. For example, you could select an attribute node from the input document, which might contain the URI for the document to import. The document() function would then resolve the content of each node in the node-set to a string, resulting in a URI for each node. If there is more than one node in the node-set, each node is processed into a URI and each URI is resolved into a document that is used as input to the process. This way, more than one document can be included with one document() function.

Perhaps MarkupCity.xml contains another section called <city_plans>, with a section of <online> references to a government Web site containing comprehensive, up-to-date (at least by government standards) copies of the city plans as follows:

```
<city_plans><online href="monte_sano.xml"/></city_plans>
```

We would use an expression in the document() function to select the attribute node "href" and get its contents as follows:

```
document(//city_plans/online/@href)
```

Note that we do not use single quotes to designate the argument as a string. An argument without quotes as shown here is processed as an expression. This use of the document() function will access the document pointed to by the URI in the href attribute of any <online> element found, if it is a child of <city_plans>. For example, the XML input document might contain several <online> element children of the <city_plans> element, as shown below.

```
<city_plans>
<online href="http://www.local.gov/plans/parks.xml" />
      <online href="http://www.local.gov/plans/roads.xml" />
      <online href="http://www.local.gov/plans/recycle.xml" />
</city_plans>
```

Each of these href attributes would be resolved, and all three external documents would be returned from their URIs.

11.1.1.7 Using `document()` with Two Node-set Arguments

The second argument to the `document()` function, when used, provides the context for the URI in the first argument. This basically means that, if the URI in the first argument is a relative URI, the second argument can be used to resolve the relative URI into an absolute URI. A relative URI is resolved into an absolute URI by adding the base URI during processing. The processor uses several criteria to determine the base URI as follows:

1. If there is only one argument to the `document()` function and the URI resulting from that argument is a relative URI, the base URI comes from the element in the *stylesheet* that contains the `document()` function.
   a. If the element in the stylesheet comes from an included or imported stylesheet in another location, that location is used as the base URI for the relative URI.
   b. The default base URI is the location of the stylesheet.
2. If there are two arguments to the `document()` function, the base URI of the node-set in the second argument is used as the base URI for the relative URI in the first argument.
3. If the first argument is an absolute URI, the second argument is ignored.

Basically, when the second argument is added, the effect is generally only noticed when a relative URI is used. The second argument can then qualify the location, which will be the base URI for the first argument. Think of the second argument as a way of saying, "Look over there, instead." A simple example would be to use a relative path to the `monte_sano.xml` file as shown here:

```
document('monte_sano.xml')
```

Without the second argument, the processor would look in the same directory as the stylesheet that contains the element calling the `document()` function. Adding a second argument, we could redirect the processor to look in another directory, based on the location of that node-set.

This is especially helpful for elements that may be located in a different directory and reference using entities.

```
document('monte_sano.xml', city_plan)
```

By adding the `city_plan` second argument, the processor would look for an element in the input file called `city_plan` and use the absolute location of that element for the base URI of the `monte_sano.xml` file.

11.1.2 The `current()` XSLT Function

The `current()` XSLT function is used to get the current node that is being processed, regardless of where the function is being called. It takes no arguments, and its function return type is a node-set, as shown in the following function prototype:

Function: *node-set* **current()**

Function Name	*Function Group*	*Function Return Type*	*Arguments*	*Argument Type*
`current()`	Node-set	Node-set	None	None

When a template match is found by the XSLT processor and the given template rule is instantiated, each node in the node-set returned by that match is both the current node and the context for that template rule. However, expressions in the instruction elements within the template can change the context node when they are instantiated. Using the `current()` function in an instruction element expression returns the original node that was matched by the template rule.

The following examples, derived from the XSLT W3C specification, serve to clarify the distinction between the current node and the context node. The following two expressions for `<xsl:apply-templates>` are equivalent for an expression that is not contained in another expression:

```
<xsl:apply-templates select="current()" />
<xsl:apply-templates select="." />
```

However, when a predicate is used, the context node changes from subexpression to subexpression. The `current()` function, then, reaches *outside* the square brackets, as it were, to reference the original current node of the template that contains the expression. Again, the specification provides a good example:

```
<xsl:apply-templates select="//glossary/item[@name=./@ref]" />
```

This is looking for the `name` and `ref` attributes to have the same value that is, `name` and `ref` attributes of the item element. For that matter, then, you could also phrase this as the following:

```
<xsl:apply-templates select="//glossary/item[./@name=./ @ref]" />
```

which means the same thing. Accordingly, then, the redundancy here is underscored by:

```
<xsl:apply-templates select="//glossary/item[@name=@ref]" />
```

In all three cases, we are looking for `item` elements that are children of `glossary` elements, which have `name` and `ref` attributes whose *values are equal.* Now, notice the contrast when we use `current()`:

```
<xsl:apply-templates select="//glossary/item[@name=current()/@ref]" />
```

Here, `current()` is reaching *outside* the brackets. The node referenced by `current()` is the original context node of the template. As contradictory as it may sound, even though the current node and context nodes are often two different things, the `current()` function references the template's context node when used in a predicate. This is because at the level where the template is matched, the context node and the current node are the same node. By invoking `current()`, we are asking for any `ref` attributes of the original node that were matched with the match attribute of `<xsl:template>`. At the point in the predicate where the expression occurs, the context node is the `item` element in a `glossary` element.

11.1.3 The `key()` XSLT Function and the `<xsl:key>` Top-Level Element

The `key()` XSLT function is used to retrieve the value of a key that was previously defined using the `<xsl:key>` top-level element. Since keys need to be defined before they can be used, we will discuss the `<xsl:key>` element first.

11.1.3.1 The <xsl:key> Top-level Element

The <xsl:key> top-level element is used to associate a key with a node from the input XML document. Each key associated with a node also has a value defined with <xsl:key>. Getting and using the values of the keys defined with <xsl:key> involves the key() function, which is described in Section 11.1.3.2. The <xsl:key> element is an empty element that uses three required attributes, as shown in the following element model definition:

```
<!-- Category: top-level-element -->
<xsl:key
  name = qname
  match = pattern
  use = expression />
```

The <xsl:key> element uses the name attribute to create the name of a key. The match attribute's pattern is used to define the node to which the key will apply. The use attribute is an expression that defines the information to be used to apply a value to the key. These attributes are discussed in the following sections.

The <xsl:key> name Attribute

The required name attribute denotes the name by which the key will be referenced. This name is also used as the string required for the first argument to key(). The name must meet the criteria for a QName (see Chapter 12).

The <xsl:key> match Attribute

The match attribute uses a pattern expression to identify the node or set of nodes that will be associated with the key that is being defined. Once the node is matched, a value for the key for that node is assigned according to the specification supplied in the use attribute. Note that variable references (discussed in Chapter 8) are not allowed in the match attribute for <xsl:key>.

The `<xsl:key>` `use` *Attribute*

Once a node has been matched, the particular information that is to be used as the value for the key associated with that node is identified with the `use` attribute. The value for a key is often the value of an attribute in the element chosen by the pattern expression given for the `match` attribute. Since the value of the `use` attribute is a pattern expression, it can reference any node type in the input document. Note that variable references (discussed in Chapter 8) are not allowed in the `use` attribute for `<xsl:key>`.

Creating Keys with `<xsl:key>`

The `<xsl:key>` element is a top-level element, which means that keys must be defined at the stylesheet level, and cannot be defined in templates. The value of the keyed nodes can be extracted in a template using the `key()` function. The node-set matched using the match attribute of `<xsl:key>` is "indexed" prior to processing the input document with template rules. This means that the value of the key does not change after the creation of the key, and is not dependent on the context of a template rule.

Creating keys involves using all three attributes for the `<xsl:key>` element. The `name` attribute defines the name of the key, the `match` attribute is used to select the node set to associate with the key, and the `use` attribute selects the value to assign to the key.

For example, to use the value of an attribute node as the value of the key, reference the attribute in the `use` attribute of the `<xsl:key>` element:

```
<xsl:key name="key_name" match="*" use="@href" />
```

In this case, we're assigning a key named "key_name" to each node and assigning a value to the key using the value of the `href` attribute on that element.

In this example, every element node of the input source tree (designated by the *) will be assigned a key. If the node being matched has an `href` attribute, the value given for that `href` will be the key value that is assigned to that node. If the node being matched does not have an `href` attribute, the value of the key will be null and the key will not be accessible.

Using a version of Markup City that contains houses, we could create keys for the addresses, selecting only those houses that are off of Whitesburg Drive, taking advantage of `<xsl:key>`'s attributes to make that limitation, as shown in Example 11–3.

Example 11–3 : Setting up a set of keys with `<xsl:key>`.

INPUT:

```
<?xml version="1.0"?>
<main>
      <parkway>
            <thoroughfare>Governor Drive</thoroughfare>
<thoroughfare name="Whitesburg Drive">
                        <sidestreet name="Bob Wallace Avenue">
                        <block name="1st Street">
                              <house address="1200" />
                              <house address="1201" />
                              <house address="1202" />
                              <house address="1203" />
                        </block>
<block>2nd Street</block>
                        <block name="3rd Street">
                              <house address="1100" />
                              <house address="1101" />
                              <house address="1102" />
                              <house address="1103" />
                              <house address="1104" />
                              <house address="1105" />
                        </block>
                  </sidestreet>
                  <sidestreet name="Woodridge Street">
                        <house address="5624" />
                        <house address="5625" />
                        <house address="5626" />
</sidestreet>
</thoroughfare>
<thoroughfare name="Bankhead">
                  <sidestreet>Tollgate Road</sidestreet>
                        <block>First Street</block>
                        <block>Second Street</block>
                        <block>Third Street</block>
                  <sidestreet>Oak Drive</sidestreet>
            </thoroughfare>
      </parkway>
      <boulevard>
            <block>Panorama Street</block>
            <block name="Highland Plaza">
```

Example 11–3 : Setting up a set of keys with <xsl:key>(continued).

```
                    <house address="3410" />
                    <house address="3411" />
                    <house address="3412" />
                    <house address="3413" />
                    <house address="3414" />
                    <house address="3415" />
</block>
              <block>Hutchens Avenue</block>
              <block>Wildwood Drive</block>
              <block>Old Chimney Road</block>
              <block>Carrol Circle</block>
          </boulevard>
</main>
```

KEY RULE:

```
<xsl:key name="Whitesburg_houses"
      match="//*[@name='Whitesburg Drive']//house"
      use="@address" />
```

We've narrowed down the possible houses to be "keyed" by selecting only those that are descended from an element whose name attribute has the value Whitesburg Drive. It is not necessary to know whether Whitesburg Drive is a <parkway>, <thoroughfare>, or <boulevard>. For that matter, @name would be replaced if we did not know what the attribute name was by a generic search for any attribute with the value Whitesburg Drive, using the @* abbreviation in match="//*[@*='Whitesburg Drive']//house".

In any node that matches, the address attribute value would be used as the key, designated by the use="@address".

The resulting keyed object are stored in the processors memory, and can be represented as a table, as shown in Table 11–2.

The keys created here can be described in terms of the three parts mentioned above. There is the key's name, Whitesburg_houses, represented as the title of the table. Then there is the node itself, which in this case is an element identified in the match. Each node is associated with its

Table 11–2 Whitesburg_houses

Node	*Key*
<house address="1200" />	1200
<house address="1201" />	1201
<house address="1202" />	1202
<house address="1203" />	1203

key, which is chosen in the <xsl:key> element's use attribute, in this case as the address attribute of the house node.

Regardless of the kind of object designated by use, its value is converted to a string. If it is a node-set, it is converted to a string that is equivalent to the string value of one or more nodes designated by use.

The <xsl:key> element can be used several times with the same match value. This will add several different keys to each node in the node-set returned by the match, providing several different use values are given for each key on the same matched node. In addition, several keys can all share the same name, but have different match and use values, so that a particular category of information can be accessed several ways.

The nodes that have keys created in our example can be retrieved with the arguments given for the key() function,which is discussed in the next section.

11.1.3.2 The key() XSLT Function

The key() function and <xsl:key> element are interdependent. The key() XSLT function belongs to the node-set function group, returning a node-set from the evaluation of two required arguments, as shown in the following function prototype. The first argument must be a string, which evaluates to the name of the key as defined in the <xsl:key> element. The second argument can be any of the four types of objects node-set, string, Boolean, or number but evaluates to a string, and is used as the test for the value of the key.

Function: *node-set* **key**(*string, object*)

Function Name	*Function Group*	*Function Return Type*	*Arguments*	*Argument Type*
`key()`	Node-set	Node-set	String	Required
			Object	Required

The return value of the `key()` function is a node-set, and contains the nodes that have a key value equal to the value of the string of the second argument of the `key()` function. In other words, the value of the second argument is used to retrieve a list of nodes with the same key value.

For example, using the keys for houses set up in the previous section in Example 11–3, we can retrieve the houses that have keys, and ignore the ones that don't, using `<xsl:copy-of>` to get a copy of the keyed nodes, as follows:

```
<xsl:template match="house">
      <xsl:copy-of select="key('Whitesburg_houses', @address)"/>
</xsl:template>
```

The result of this template rule would copy only the houses that have a key named 'Whitesburg_houses' with the value equal to the same value as the current `<house>` element's address attribute.

> **NOTE** If you are a programmer, note the similarity of keys to arrays. Arrays have a name (the name of the array), a value (the value of an item in the array), and a return (the content of the array with that particular name and value). In this case, the return is the node that has the key. The only distinction is that an array can be thought to *contain* an item, whereas with keys, the item (node) has a key *attached to* it (there is no containership going on).

Think of keys as a way of adding "virtual" attributes to elements without changing the markup. The key name would be the same as an attribute name, and the key value would be the same as an attribute value. This explains why different nodes in a document can have the same key name and the same key value. For example, a key for the number of stories on a house would necessarily be the same for most houses, one, two, or maybe three.

```
<house stories="2">
<house stories="1">
<house stories="2">
```

Assume you've made a key with the name `stories` using `<xsl:key name="stories" match="house" use="@stories"/>`. Using `key('stories', '2')` will return all the `<house>` elements with a key of two stories, or the first and the third houses.

Unlike attributes, though, it *is* possible for one node to have more than one key of the same name, but with a different key value. This is useful if you want have several values on a node, but use the same key name. Let's say, for instance, you are keeping a list of all the houses that have a certain characteristic, such as bay windows. An element could not have two attributes called window. They would each need to be a different attribute name, as shown below.

```
<house window1="bay" window2="recessed">First House</house>
<house window1="gable" window2="bay">Second House</house>
<house window1="recessed" window2="gable">Third House</house>
```

Defining a key for each window type, however, you only need one name for the key, but you can use multiple values for the `use` attribute, as follows:

```
<xsl:key name="window"
     match="house"
     use="@window1 | @window2" />
```

The name of the node from which you are drawing your key value does not have to match the name of the key itself. If you have a key named `window`, then the value could be `bay`, `recessed`, `casement`, or `gable`. Your stylesheet could then say, "Give me all the houses that have `bay` windows." You wouldn't need to have separate key names for each type of window. This is particularly useful if you have several hundred kinds of windows! Example 11–4 shows a stylesheet using keys to make a report of two kinds of windows.

Using `<xsl:copy-of select="key('window', 'bay')"/>` would return any houses with bay windows, and `<xsl:copy-of select="key('window', 'recessed')"/>` would return any houses with recessed windows. Notice that `First House` is duplicated in

Example 11–4 : Using `key()` to pull nodes with multiple values for the same key.

INPUT:

```
<?xml version="1.0"?>
<block>
<house window1="bay" window2="recessed">First House</house>
<house window1="gable" window2="bay">Second House</house>
<house window1="recessed" window2="gable">Third House</house>
</block>
```

STYLESHEET:

```
<?xml version="1.0"?>
<xsl:stylesheet xmlns:xsl="http://www.w3.org/1999/XSL/Transform"
           version="1.0">

<xsl:output indent="yes"/>

<xsl:key name="window"
      match="house"
      use="@window1 | @window2" />
<xsl:template match="text()"/>
<xsl:template match="/">
<xsl:text>
Houses with Bay Windows
</xsl:text>
<xsl:copy-of select="key('window', 'bay')"/>
<xsl:text>

Houses with Recessed Windows
</xsl:text>
<xsl:copy-of select="key('window', 'recessed')"/>
</xsl:template>
</xsl:stylesheet>
```

RESULT:

```
Houses with Bay Windows
<house window1="bay" window2="recessed">First House</house>
<house window1="gable" window2="bay">Second House</house>
Houses with Recessed Windows
<house window1="bay" window2="recessed">First House</house>
<house window1="recessed" window2="gable">Third House</house>
```

the report, because it has both bay windows and recessed windows. There might be quite a few kinds of windows on a given group of houses, but only the ones specified would be selected.

11.2 String XSLT Functions

The XSLT string function group includes four functions: `system-property()`, `generate-id()`, `format-number()`, and `unparsed-entity-uri()`.

The `system-property()` function is not a string function in the purest sense, as it does not necessarily return a string as its function return type, but rather takes a string as a required argument. This function performs a sort of internal diagnostic check for system properties, and its resulting object is controlled by the namespace defining the system property.

The second function, `generate-id()`, enables the creation of unique identifiers for nodes in the input XML document instance. It can be used, for instance, to create an ID attribute for later use with the `id()` function.

The third string function, `format-number()`, works to adjust and control the formatting of numbers in the output. When the third argument to the `format-number()` function is used, it must be used in conjunction with the `<xsl:decimal-format>` top-level element.

Finally, the `unparsed-entity-uri()` function is used to extract PUBLIC or SYSTEM URI values from entities declared in a DTD.

11.2.1 The `system-property()` XSLT Function

The `system-property()` XSLT function is used to access the value of the system property named in its one required string argument, shown in the following function prototype. The function returns an object following the evaluation, which is the value of the system property being tested.

Function: *object* **system-property** (*string*)

Function Name	*Function Group*	*Function Return Type*	*Arguments*	*Argument Type*
`system-property()`	String	Object	String	Required

System properties can be defined by a namespace, and the value of each system property is controlled by the namespace that defines it. The string argument essentially passes the name of the system property as a query to the XSLT processor to determine its value. If the system value being tested has a prefix for a namespace, that namespace controls the values of the system properties. If no system property exists, the function returns an empty string.

The W3C specification for XSLT requires that any conforming XSLT processor be able to furnish values for the three specific system properties in the XSLT namespace as follows:

1. **`xsl:version`** — Generates the version of XSLT supported by the processor (which, for the time being, remains 1.0).
2. **`xsl:vendor`** — Gives the name of the vendor of the XSLT processor.
3. **`xsl:vendor-url`** — Provides a string with a URL that identifies the vendor of the XSLT processor's homepage, if that is the resolution of the URL that the vendor defines.

Using `<xsl:value-of>` in Example 11–5 to get the value of each of these three system properties results in the following for XT and Saxon, respectively.

Example 11–5 : Using `<xsl:value-of>` to extract XSL system properties.

XSLT Instructions:

```
<xsl:value-of select="system-property('xsl:version')"/>
<xsl:value-of select="system-property('xsl:vendor')"/>
<xsl:value-of select="system-property('xsl:vendor-url')"/>
```

Result Using XT:

```
1
James Clark
http://www.jclark.com/
```

Result Using Saxon:

```
1
SAXON 5.5.1 from Michael Kay of ICL
http://users.iclway.co.uk/mhkay/saxon/index.html
```

11.2.2 The `generate-id()` XSLT Function

The `generate-id()` function is used to generate a unique identifier for the first node in a node-set, specified by the node-set argument. It returns a string as its function return type, as shown in the following function prototype. If the optional argument is not provided, the context node is used. If an argument is provided, but contains an empty node-set, the result is an empty string.

Function: *string* **generate-id** (*node-set?*)

Function Name	*Function Group*	*Function Return Type*	*Arguments*	*Argument Type*
`generate-id()`	String	String	Node-set	Optional

The XSLT processor generates the string returned by the `generate-id()` function. The resulting string can be anything that the XSLT processing software was designed to generate; but, true to the requirements for an ID, it must begin with an alphabetic character.

The processor will always generate the same ID for the same node in document order, and the IDs will conform to the requirement that they be different for different nodes. However, it is possible that the same ID might not be generated for the same node each time the document is processed.

When the node-set argument is given, the ID is generated for the first node of the argument node-set in document order. If the result of evaluating the node-set in the argument is an empty node, the string will also be empty. When the node-set argument is not present, the ID is generated for the context node of the template rule in which the `generate-id()` function is called.

In Example 11–6, we will begin with the basic city with the new `<house>`s, which as yet have not been assigned addresses (notice that in this example, we have put the street names into attributes).

Notice, of course, that these are not the most natural-looking addresses when you run this stylesheet using XT, and they seem to be skipping some values. The values generated by the processor are incrementing by node. This is because XT generates IDs by counting nodes, but it counts all the nodes, including the element nodes, attribute nodes, and comment nodes, in the node tree of the entire input document. If there was text inside the `<house>` elements, the XT processor would also count that, and increment the number for each text node. In our example, the `<xsl:strip-space>` element is used to remove any additional text nodes that contain whitespace, because they would also increment the node count if not removed. The `<xsl:template match="text()"/>` removes any text, like `Oak Drive`, from elements that are not being matched, and `<xsl:output indent="yes"/>` adds nice formatting to the output. The template rule matching on `"block"` puts the `<block>` element in the output, as well as the name attribute for each `<block>`, and the template rule matching on `"house"` uses the `generate-id()` function to generate address attributes for each `<house>` element in the output.

Example 11–6 : Using the `generate-id()` function.

INPUT:

```
<?xml version="1.0"?>
<parkway>
            <!-- some thoroughfare's removed for brevity -->
      <thoroughfare name="Bankhead">
            <sidestreet name="Tollgate Road">
                  <block name="First Street">
                        <house></house>
                        <house></house>
                        <house></house>
                        <house></house>
                        <house></house>
                        <house></house>
                  </block>
                  <block name="Second Street">
                        <house></house>
                        <house></house>
                        <house></house>
                        <house></house>
                        <house></house>
                        <house></house>
                  </block>
                  <block name="Third Street">
                        <house></house>
                        <house></house>
                        <house></house>
                        <house></house>
                        <house></house>
                        <house></house>
                  </block>
            </sidestreet>
            <sidestreet>Oak Drive</sidestreet>
      </thoroughfare>
</parkway>
```

STYLESHEET:

```
<?xml version="1.0"?>
<xsl:stylesheet xmlns:xsl="http://www.w3.org/1999/XSL/Transform"
               version="1.0">
<xsl:template match="text()"/>
```

Example 11–6 : Using the `generate-id()` function (continued).

```
<xsl:output indent="yes"/>
<xsl:strip-space
      elements="block house parkway thoroughfare sidestreet"/>
<xsl:template match="block">
      <block name="{@name}">
      <xsl:apply-templates />
      </block>
</xsl:template>
<xsl:template match="house">
      <house>
            <xsl:attribute name="address">
            <xsl:value-of select='generate-id()' />
            </xsl:attribute>
      </house>
</xsl:template>
</xsl:stylesheet>
```

RESULT:

```
<?xml version="1.0" encoding="utf-8"?>
<block name="First Street">
<house address="N9"/>
<house address="N10"/>
<house address="N11"/>
<house address="N12"/>
<house address="N13"/>
<house address="N14"/>
</block>
<block name="Second Street">
<house address="N17"/>
<house address="N18"/>
<house address="N19"/>
<house address="N20"/>
<house address="N21"/>
<house address="N22"/>
</block>
<block name="Third Street">
<house address="N25"/>
<house address="N26"/>
<house address="N27"/>
<house address="N28"/>
<house address="N29"/>
<house address="N30"/>
</block>
```

11.2.3 The `format-number()` XSLT Function

The `format-number()` function is used to process a raw number and represent it as a formatted number (string) in the output. The function accepts three arguments and returns a string as its function return type, as shown in the following function prototype. The first two arguments are, respectively, a number and a string. Both arguments are required. The third argument is optional and is also a string.

Function: *string* **format-number** (*number, string, string?*)

Function Name	*Function Group*	*Function Return Type*	*Arguments*	*Argument Type*
`format-number()`	String	String	Number String String	Required Required Optional

The number supplied as the first argument to the `format-number()` function is converted to a string according to the format pattern indicated in the second argument. In other words, the second argument furnishes the model for the format conversion of the number in the first argument. The second argument is a string model that will bze used to format the number provided by the first argument. It is composed of a specific pattern, using characters derived by reference from the JDK 1.1 specification for numbers. The possible symbols are listed in Table 11–3.

Table 11–3 Formatting symbols for `format-number()`

Symbol	*Meaning*
0	A digit.
#	A digit, where using a zero is displayed as absent.

Table 11–3 Formatting symbols for `format-number()` (continued)

Symbol	*Meaning*
.	A period. Placeholder for decimal separator.
,	A comma. Placeholder for grouping separator.
;	A semi-colon. Separates formats.
-	A dash. Default negative prefix.
%	A percent symbol. Multiply by 100 and show as percentage.
?	A question mark. Multiply by 1000 and show as per mille.
$	Currency symbol. The currency symbol (#x00A4) is not supported by XSLT implementations of the `java.text.DecimalFormat` class. Use the real currency symbols for the appropriate country when required.
X	A letter or number. Any other characters can be used in the prefix or suffix.
'	A single quote. Used to quote special characters in a prefix or suffix.

For example, let's take any number, say 3.14159265358979323. If you wanted to represent this number as a number without any decimal characters, you would use the following:

```
<xsl:value-of select="format-number('3.14159265358979323', '#')"/>
```

This XSLT example would return any digit or digits before the decimal marker (the period "`.`"). It would first, of course, round the numbers according to the rules of the `round()` function (see Chapter 5). In this case, since rounding doesn't change the number before the decimal marker, the value returned is *3*. Since we are using the # symbol, any leading 0 digits (if any) will be dropped (e.g., if you had `003.14159265358979323` as your value).

Adding the decimal point and two digit markers to the second argument would return the "normal" value of pi, or *3.14*:

```
<xsl:value-of
     select="format-number('3.14159265358979323', '#.##')"/>
```

Let's say you wanted to format a number to be in the form of U.S. currency. The currency symbol is placed in front of the digit marker as appropriate:

```
<xsl:value-of
     select="format-number('3.14159265', '$#.##')"/>
```

This would return $3.14.

Of course, the full power of the `format-number()` function is not realized unless you have really large numbers. For example,

```
<xsl:value-of select=
     "format-number('141592653589793.23', ' US $#,###.##')"/>
```

Put the result in your bank account: US $141,592,653,589,793.22. You would lose a penny in the deal because of rounding, but that's not much when you have this kind of bank balance (the authors recommend donation of said pennies *en masse* to a central fund for lucidity in technical writing).

The third argument of the `format-number()` function is used to specify a different decimal format than the default. The default decimal format comes from the DecimalFormat[1] class of Java. The `format-number()` function works closely with the definitions for formatting decimal numbers from the Java Development Kit (JDK 1.1 and later), found in the java.text.DecimalFormat class. This argument requires the use of the `<xsl:decimal-format>` element, as discussed in the following section.

11.2.4 The `<xsl:decimal-format>` Top-Level Element

The `<xsl:decimal-format>` top-level element defines parameters for the display of decimal numbers. Issues such as the European style of

1. `DecimalFormat` is a concrete subclass of `NumberFormat` for formatting decimal numbers. It allows for a variety of parameters and localization to Western, Arabic, or Indic numbers. You can find more information about the Java DecimalFormatclass at http://java.sun.com/products/jdk/1.1/docs/api/java.text.DecimalFormat.html.

commas for decimal notation as opposed to the U.S. period style (e.g., with the `decimal-separator` attribute) are addressed by the attributes of `<xsl:decimal-format>`. This element must be present if there is a third argument given for `format-number()`. It has 11 attributes, as shown in the following element model definition, and is an empty element:

```
<!-- Category: top-level-element -->
<xsl:decimal-format
  name = qname
  decimal-separator = char
  grouping-separator = char
  infinity = string
  minus-sign = char
  NaN = string
  percent = char
  per-mille = char
  zero-digit = char
  digit = char
  pattern-separator = char />
```

The `<xsl:decimal-format>` element has a `name` attribute that is used to assign a unique name to the decimal format being created. If the third attribute of `format-number()` is used, its value must match one of the named decimal formats. The name allows several different versions of the `<xsl:decimal-format>` element to be used by the `format-number()` function. This is useful for localization of the output, or when presenting the same content in several different languages, for example.

The `<xsl:decimal-format>` element basically allows you to override the default characters used for the symbols in the pattern of the second argument to `format-number()`, shown previously in Table 11–3.

Quoting from the XSLT specification, with comments as necessary, the attributes for `<xsl:decimal-format>` are as follows. None of these attributes are required, including the `name` attribute.

1. **name** — *Specifies the name of the named decimal-format being declared.*

   The name is used as the third option for the `format-number()` function to call a specific named decimal format. When a name attribute is not used on the `<xsl:deci-`

mal-format> element, the decimal format defined by that element is used as the default decimal format.

2. **decimal-separator** — *Specifies the character used for the decimal sign; the default value is the period character (`.`).*

   This determines the actual character used to separate the real number from the decimal part of the number. This would be used, for instance, to make the European notation form of a number using a comma instead of a period. Its representation in the format pattern is the same as its output value that is, it looks the same in the output as it does in the pattern.

3. **grouping-separator** — *Specifies the character used as a grouping (e.g., thousands) separator; the default value is the comma character (`,`).*

   This determines the actual character used to separate groups of numbers. This is normally a comma, but might also be a period in some other countries or languages. Its representation in the format pattern is the same as its output value.

4. **percent** — *Specifies the character used as a percent sign; the default value is the percent character (`%`).*

   This determines the actual output character used to represent a percent symbol. Its representation in the format pattern is the same as its output value.

5. **per-mille** — *Specifies the character used as a per-mille sign; the default value is the Unicode per-mille character.*

   This determines the actual output character used to represent a per-mille symbol. Its representation in the format pattern is the same as its output value.

6. **zero-digit** — *Specifies the character used as the digit zero; the default value is the digit zero (`0`).*

   This determines the actual output character used to represent the digit zero. In some cases, for example, an X might be used to block out the zeros: $123.XX.

7. **digit** — *Specifies the character used for a digit in the format pattern; the default value is the number sign character (#).*

   This character is only used in the format pattern to represent digits. It is replaced by actual numbers in the output.

8. **pattern-separator** — *Specifies the character used to separate positive and negative subpatterns in a pattern; the default value is the semi-colon character (;).*

   When more than one format pattern applies to a given number, the patterns can be separated using this symbol. The processor will select the correct pattern from the values provided to format the output correctly.

9. **infinity** — *Specifies the string used to represent infinity; the default value is the string `Infinity`.*

   This specifies the particular character that represents infinity, which may appear in the result of formatting the number.

10. **NaN** — *Specifies the string used to represent the NaN value; the default value is the string `NaN`.*

    This specifies the particular characters or string that may appear in the result of formatting the number when the given value does not evaluate to a number.

11. **minus-sign** — *Specifies the character used as the default minus sign; the default value is the hyphen-minus character (-, #x2D).*[2]

    This specifies the particular character that may appear in the result of formatting the number if the number supplied is negative.

As an example, a decimal format named "dashed" can be created with the `<xsl:decimal-format>` top-level element as follows:

```
<xsl:decimal-format name="dashed" decimal-separator="," grouping-
separator="-" digit="X"/>
```

Using our previous example, we add the third argument to `format-number()` for the name of the decimal format we created, and change the pattern to fit the new format:

```
<xsl:value-of select="format-number('141592653589793.23', 'X-
XXX.XX', 'dashed')"/>
```

This would generate the output `141-592-653-589-793,22`.

Note that the `<xsl:decimal-format>` element and the third argument to the `format-number()` function are not implemented by XT.

2. #x2D is your plain, old, everyday, bread-n-butter minus sign.

11.2.5 The `unparsed-entity-uri()` XSLT Function

The `unparsed-entity-uri()` XSLT function is used to access the PUBLIC or SYSTEM value of an entity's URI. It has a function return type of string and requires one argument of type string, as shown in the following function prototype:

Function: *string* **unparsed-entity-uri** (*string*)

Function Name	*Function Group*	*Function Return Type*	*Arguments*	*Argument Type*
`unparsed-entity-uri()`	String	String	String	Required

The string returned by the function is the URI of the unparsed entity, which resolves to either the public identifier or the system identifier. Normally, the public identifier will be returned, depending on the preference of the XSLT processor being used, unless there is no public identifier declared. The declaration of the entity must be in the DTD, and the entity must be called using an entity reference in the document being processed, otherwise the function will return an empty string. If the URI returned by the function is a relative URI, it will be converted to an absolute URI using the base URI of the document that contains the entity declaration.

11.3 The Boolean XSLT Function Group

The Boolean XSLT function group addresses a circumstance that might well have crossed your mind. Specifically, if XSLT is extensible and different XSLT processors have their own specific extension elements and functions, what happens when an extension from one processor is called in an XSLT stylesheet being run on another processor that doesn't support that extension? Further, if this can and sometimes does generate an error that terminates the processing of the given XSLT stylesheet, is it possible to prepare in advance for this eventuality?

Many things in XSLT are contingent on which processor you are using, and the Boolean functions for XSLT are quite essential if your stylesheets are to be used in multiple environments, which might employ different XSLT processors. For instance, an XSLT stylesheet for a client who is likely to use Saxon might also have to be used in some places where only XT is running.

This is exactly the eventuality addressed by the two Boolean core functions for XSLT, which test if a given extension function or element is supported by the processor being used.

The `element-available()` and `function-available()` functions provide a contingency plan, if you will, for what happens in the event that a function or instruction element is not available in the chosen XSLT processing software. If a well-formed, conforming XSLT stylesheet includes instruction elements or functions that are supported by the chosen XSLT processor, all is well. If the processor doesn't support them, however, and the XSLT stylesheet uses those elements or functions (whether it hinges in part or in total on those elements or functions), the processor will stop and signal an error.

> **NOTE** It is not an error to include unsupported elements or functions in a template if that template is not instantiated. The processor will not test a function unless it is actually used in an expression that is instantiated.

11.3.1 The `element-available()` XSLT Function

The `element-available()` XSLT function is used to test whether the XSLT processor being used supports the instruction element or extension instruction element identified in the argument. It returns a Boolean as its function return type, and requires a single argument in the form of a string, as shown in the following function prototype:

Function: *boolean* ***element-available*** (*string*)

Function Name	*Function Group*	*Function Return Type*	*Arguments*	*Argument Type*
element-available()	Boolean	Boolean	String	Required

The string supplied for the argument of the element-available() function must be the name of the element being tested. If the name of the element has a namespace prefix that is the XSLT namespace (xsl), then the test is for an XSLT instruction element being supported. If the namespace is null, the element-available() element will return false. Any other namespaced name is a test for an extension element.

The most common use for this function is in combination with the <xsl:choose> instruction element. Sections of the stylesheet that are associated with an extension element that may not be supported by a processor can be contained within an <xsl:choose>, using <xsl:when> and <xsl:otherwise>. With the use of the element-available() function as the value of the test attribute for <xsl:when>, the processor will know when to handle it and when to ignore it. The <xsl:otherwise> gives an alternative action in case the result of the <xsl:when> test is not true.

In Example 11–7, we use the <xsl:document> element, which is defined in XSLT 1.1 WD, and may not be supported by some processors.

This stylesheet fragment keeps the <xsl:document> element from processing if the extension element is not supported by the processor. This example is presented as a full stylesheet in Example 13–6 of Chapter 13.

Example 11–8 shows a stylesheet to test each XSLT instruction element. Note that this stylesheet will return an error if using XT because the element-available() function is not implemented by XT.

Example 11–7 : Using the `element-available()` function.

```
<xsl:when test="element-available('xsl:document')">
      <xsl:document href="{@name | text()}.html">
            <html>
                  <head>
                  <title>
                        <xsl:value-of select="@name | text()"/>
                  </title>

                  </head>
                  <body>
                  <h2>
                        <xsl:value-of select="@name | text()"/>
                        </h2>
                        <xsl:apply-templates/>
                  </body>
            </html>
      </xsl:document>
</xsl:when>
```

Example 11–8 : Using the `element-available()` to test each XSLT instruction.

```
<?xml version="1.0"?>
<xsl:stylesheet xmlns:xsl="http://www.w3.org/1999/XSL/Transform"
      xmlns:go="my-extensions"
                version="1.0">
<xsl:output method="text"/>
<xsl:template match="/">
<xsl:text>
Supports  &lt;xsl:apply-imports> = </xsl:text>
<xsl:value-of select="element-available('xsl:apply-
imports')"/>
<xsl:text>
Supports  &lt;xsl:apply-templates> = </xsl:text>
<xsl:value-of select="element-available('xsl:apply-
templates')"/>
<xsl:text>
Supports  &lt;xsl:attribute> = </xsl:text>
<xsl:value-of select="element-available('xsl:attribute')"/>
<xsl:text>
Supports  &lt;xsl:call-template> = </xsl:text>
<xsl:value-of select="element-available('xsl:call-
template')"/>
<xsl:text>
```

Example 11–8 : Using the `element-available()` to test each XSLT instruction (continued).

```
Supports  &lt;xsl:choose> = </xsl:text>
<xsl:value-of select="element-available('xsl:choose')"/>
<xsl:text>
Supports  &lt;xsl:comment> = </xsl:text>
<xsl:value-of select="element-available('xsl:comment')"/>
<xsl:text>
Supports  &lt;xsl:copy> = </xsl:text>
<xsl:value-of select="element-available('xsl:copy')"/>
<xsl:text>
Supports  &lt;xsl:copy-of> = </xsl:text>
<xsl:value-of select="element-available('xsl:copy-of')"/>
<xsl:text>
Supports  &lt;xsl:element> = </xsl:text>
<xsl:value-of select= "element-available('xsl:element')"/>
<xsl:text>
Supports  &lt;xsl:fallback> = </xsl:text>
<xsl:value-of select= "element-available('xsl:fallback')"/>
<xsl:text>
Supports  &lt;xsl:for-each> = </xsl:text>
<xsl:value-of select="element-available('xsl:for-each')"/>
<xsl:text>
Supports  &lt;xsl:if> = </xsl:text>
<xsl:value-of select="element-available('xsl:if')"/>
<xsl:text>
Supports  &lt;xsl:message> = </xsl:text>
<xsl:value-of select="element-available('xsl:message')"/>
<xsl:text>
Supports  &lt;xsl:number> = </xsl:text>
<xsl:value-of select="element-available('xsl:number')"/>
<xsl:text>
Supports  &lt;xsl:processing-instruction> = </xsl:text>
<xsl:value-of select="element-available('xsl:processing-
instruction')"/>
<xsl:text>
Supports  &lt;xsl:text> = </xsl:text>
<xsl:value-of select="element-available('xsl:text')"/>
<xsl:text>
Supports  &lt;xsl:value-of> = </xsl:text>
<xsl:value-of select="element-available('xsl:value-of')"/>
<xsl:text>
Supports  &lt;xsl:variable> = </xsl:text>
<xsl:value-of select="element-available('xsl:variable')"/>
</xsl:template>
</xsl:stylesheet>
```

Example 11–8 : Using the `element-available()` to test each XSLT instruction (continued).

RESULT using Saxon:

```
Supports  <xsl:apply-imports> = true
Supports  <xsl:apply-templates> = true
Supports  <xsl:attribute> = true
Supports  <xsl:call-template> = true
Supports  <xsl:choose> = true
Supports  <xsl:comment> = true
Supports  <xsl:copy> = true
Supports  <xsl:copy-of> = true
Supports  <xsl:element> = true
Supports  <xsl:fallback> = true
Supports  <xsl:for-each> = true
Supports  <xsl:if> = true
Supports  <xsl:message> = true
Supports  <xsl:number> = true
Supports  <xsl:processing-instruction> = true
Supports  <xsl:text> = true
Supports  <xsl:value-of> = true
Supports  <xsl:variable> = true
```

11.3.2 The `function-available()` XSLT Function

The `function-available()` XSLT function checks for the support of a given function by the XSLT processor being used, whether it is an extension function or an XPath or XSLT function. It has a single required argument in the form of a string, as shown in the following function prototype. The value of the string should be a QName that expands to the name of the function whose support is being tested. The object returned is Boolean true if the function is supported, and false if it is not.

Function: *boolean* **function-available** (*string*)

Function Name	*Function Group*	*Function Return Type*	*Arguments*	*Argument Type*
`function-available()`	Boolean	Boolean	String	Required

The `function-available()` XSLT function can be used to test if the version of the XSLT processor being used supports XSLT or XPath functions, as well as whether an extension function is supported. If a function is used that is not supported, the processor will generate an error when the template or instruction calling that function is instantiated. If a function that is not supported is not called, it will not result in an error.

Although it is not an error to have an expression as the value of an argument, it must be a string value. Some implementations may not support expressions as arguments and will return a false value. For example, using `function-available(string(concat('doc', 'ument')))` is technically the same as using `function-available('document')`, yet it may result in a value of `false` even if the `document()` function is supported.

Example 11–9 shows a test for each XSLT function using the `function-available()` XSLT function. Of course, if the processor doesn't support the `function-available()` function, this stylesheet will not work. However, processors are required to support this function according to the XSLT specification.

Example 11–9 : Using `function-available` to test XSLT function support.

```
<?xml version="1.0"?>
<xsl:stylesheet xmlns:xsl="http://www.w3.org/1999/XSL/Transform"
                version="1.0">
<xsl:output method="text"/>
<xsl:template match="/">
<xsl:text>
Supports document() = </xsl:text>
<xsl:value-of select="function-available('document')"/>
<xsl:text>
Supports current() = </xsl:text>
<xsl:value-of select="function-available('current')"/>
<xsl:text>
Supports key() = </xsl:text>
<xsl:value-of select="function-available('key')"/>
<xsl:text>
Supports system-property() = </xsl:text>
<xsl:value-of select="function-available('system-property')"/>
<xsl:text>
Supports generate-id() = </xsl:text>
<xsl:value-of select="function-available('generate-id')"/>
<xsl:text>
Supports format-number() = </xsl:text>
<xsl:value-of select="function-available('format-number')"/>
<xsl:text>
Supports unparsed-entity-uri() = </xsl:text>
```

Example 11–9 : Using `function-available` to test XSLT function support (continued).

```
<xsl:value-of select="function-available('unparsed-entity-
uri')"/>
<xsl:text>
Supports element-available() = </xsl:text>
<xsl:value-of select="function-available('element-
available')"/>
<xsl:text>
Supports function-available() = </xsl:text>
<xsl:value-of select="function-available('function-
available')"/>
</xsl:template>
</xsl:stylesheet>
```

Result Using Saxon:

```
Supports document() = true
Supports current() = true
Supports key() = true
Supports system-property() = true
Supports generate-id() = true
Supports format-number() = true
Supports unparsed-entity-uri() = true
Supports element-available() = true
Supports function-available() = true
```

Result Using XT:

```
Supports document() = true
Supports current() = false
Supports key() = false
Supports system-property() = true
Supports generate-id() = true
Supports format-number() = true
Supports unparsed-entity-uri() = true
Supports element-available() = false
Supports function-available() = true
```

XSLT Processors, Extensions, and Java

- Extensions
- Conformance
- Namespaces
- Java
- Sun Microsystems® XSLTC
- Oracle® XML suite
- Microsoft® MSXML

12

As a form of XML, XSLT is by nature extensible. Extensions are additions to the standard library of elements and functions described in the previous chapters, created and supported by various XSLT processor implementations. With extensions, the potential ways XSLT can be used are limitless.

The W3C specification for XSLT, however, does not provide a way to define or control extensions, and extensions are not required to be implemented by processors.[1] What this means is that an XSLT stylesheet solution that works with one processor might well not work with others. For this reason, the XSLT `element-available()` and `function-available()` functions, and the `<xsl:fallback>` instruction element, can be used to test for support of extention elements and functions, and to provide for contingencies.

You may find that one processor or another suits your needs because of the platform on which it runs, its speed, the extensions it offers, or a combination of these. In this chapter, we will discuss three commerical products: Sun Microsystems® XSLTC, the Oracle® XML suite, and the Microsoft® MSXML, as well as Java and its installation procedures. Freeware XSLT

1. The W3C XSL committee is currently in the process of defining specifications for how extensions will be implemented. XSLT v1.1 will include extension functions and XSLT v2.0 will include extension elements.

processors Xalan, Saxon, and XT are discussed in Chapter 13. Information on these and other available tools can be obtained through the following URIs, among others:

```
http://xml.coverpages.org
http://oasis-open.org
http://www.xml.org
```

12.1 XSLT Processors

The fact that the processors we've chosen to discuss are largely Java-based is due only to the ubiquity of the platform and wide base of common familiarity with and knowledge of its interface. There are certainly implementations in Perl, Python, C++, and so on, accessible through the links above.

If there is any describable "methodology" for the processors we've chosen for detailed discussion here, it is nothing more other than the general amount of popular use, discussion traffic on the Internet, and the likely duration of continued development. Accordingly, we will discuss Xalan, Saxon, and XT in some detail in the following chapter. We have emphasized these shareware processors largely because of our own views on the open source movement.

The range of commercial processors is increasing almost monthly. For this reason, we have chosen to focus on freeware programs. However, we will discuss Sun Microsystems' XSLTC, Oracle's XML suite, and Microsoft's MSXML briefly in this chapter.

The remaining processors emphasized in this book are discussed in Chapter 13. We offer some detail on how to install these processors, as we have learned that many aspects of Java `CLASSPATH`s and other details necessary to set up an XSLT processor, which may be obvious to programmers, are not always as clear to a markup expert. The majority of each processor's discussion, however, is devoted to explaining the extensions each has.

We make no effort to evaluate the processors, though we do report features of the W3C specification not implemented if any and any observable aspects noted by developers, such as memory footprint and speed. This is presented only to save the legwork of gathering this information and summarizing it, rather than to formally endorse or advocate the respective assessments. Before we introduce the processors and their extensions, however, we'll first give a general overview of the concept of extensions and their use according to the W3C specification for XSLT, as well as the mechanics of using them regardless of which software they are supported by in an XSLT stylesheet.

12.2 Extension Elements and Functions

In its simplest sense, an extension element is any element not prescribed in the W3C specification for XSLT. Of course, LREs are also not prescribed; however, LREs are not software-dependent and do not have to be namespaced. Extension elements are first visually distinguished by their namespace prefix. The same is true of extension functions insofar as extension functions are always namespaced. In fact, XSLT elements and functions are namespaced also, but their namespaces are derived by implicit inheritance from the *default namespace* defined in the document element. As we will see, it is possible to define extension attributes and functions, as well as extension top-level elements.

The W3C specification only describes the use of extension instruction elements and extension functions, expressly contrasting them with LREs. Specifically, if an extension element occurs within a template, it is considered an instruction element rather than an LRE, as long as that namespace has been defined and is available to the context of the extension element. An interesting consequence is that the W3C specification for XSLT does *not* address the use of extension top-level elements.

Nonetheless, processors such as Saxon have added extension top-level elements, so there *will* be discussion of them here in this chapter. Remember, the uses of and behavior for these extensions is processor-specific and not, as of XSLT 1.0, prescribed by the W3C specification.

12.3 Namespaces

Namespaces identify the particular markup vocabulary from which element-type names and attribute names are derived. They are important because, for example, when using links, the idea of embedding linked content from other documents raises the problem of possible duplicate element-type names and attribute names with different meanings. For instance, if the element-type name "body" was used in two different ways, such as by an auto parts manual and by a physician's desktop reference, how should this be handled?

It is essential that element-type names and attribute names be distinguishable in the way that, for example, the particular meaning of *element* in *chemical element* is distinguishable from its meaning in *markup element*. Another way to think of the issue is in terms of surnames. For example, lots of folks are named John, and an inconvenience (especially for those named John) can arise from the somewhat unsavory uses of john but a surname (like Gardner or Jacobjingleheimerschmidt) disambiguates "a john" from "John Smith," "John Doe," or "the john." Namespaces allow a unique identification of a name by providing a way for them to be differentiated.

12.3.1 Theory of a Namespace

A namespace is, well, a space for a name. Element-type names or an attribute names are qualified with a prefix, a sort of short name or alias for the namespace. Each namespace is declared prior to using its prefix, either in the same element in which it is used or in an ancestor element. The declaration of the namespace contains a URI that (hopefully) points to something that regulates that namespace.

> **NOTE** The prefix is necessary because URI constructs are not allowed in element and attribute names and would render a document invalid if used as such.

Any XSLT element-type name is *qualified* with a namespace, and as such, it is called a QName. A QName is an element-type name preceded by a prefix, with a separating colon. In essence, if an element-type name has a colon (`:`), you can be sure it is a QName and, accordingly, indicates an element with a namespace. Element-type names without colons are not QNames, then, and can be referred to as no-colon names, or NCNames.

When declaring a namespace, you must specify what the prefix of the namespace will be, and the name of the namespace, which is usually a URI (Uniform Resource Identifier) giving at least in human terms information that identifies the namespace according to its lineage or pedigree. The URI could also point to a DTD or Schema for the declared namespace.

> **NOTE** We are deliberately avoiding what is and has been a huge topic of debate about the declaration of a namespace. There are some who feel the URI must always resolve to a particular DTD or schema, others feel it never should, and a range of passionate opinions fall between. The Namespace Specification allows for a particular namespace URI to resolve to a "place"–such as a Web resource as well as for it not to resolve to a place. Quoting from the Namespace Specification: "The namespace name, to serve its intended purpose, should have the characteristics of uniqueness and persistence. It is not a goal that it be directly usable for retrieval of a schema (if any exists)."

A namespace declaration is similar to a DOCTYPE declaration, only it is found in a different part of the XML document instance. It is not a child of the root; it is an attribute on an element. The examples in this chapter concern the declarations of XSLT namespaces, but those that might be found in XML documents will be similar. It is not the purpose of this chapter to provide a comprehensive guide to writing namespaces, but rather, to enable you to effectively recognize and use them with XSLT. Namespaces become very important for distinguishing extensions to XSLT that different XSLT processors implement, and as such are discussed further in Chapter 12.

12.3.2 Anatomy of a Namespace

A namespace must be declared before it can be used. Declaring a namespace such as `xmlns:xsl="http://www.w3.org/1999/XSL/Transform"` defines a prefix and the value of the namespace name, which is usually a URI pointing to the namespace owner. The prefix (`xsl`, in this example) follows the XML namespace declaration, `xmlns`. The XML namespace declaration is the reserved attribute name, `xmlns` (which happens to be the prefix for the `xmlns` namespace), followed by the `:` separator. Immediately following the separator is the prefix being defined, followed by an equal sign, which separates it from the address or URI of the namespace.

The address or URI of the namespace is only used to identify the namespace; whether it resolves to a location or a schema is irrelevant. It is only intended to be a unique value that can be used to differentiate elements from two separate sources that may happen to have the same name.

Figure 12–1 illustrates an example of a namespace declaration. Notice that there is what appears to be a Web address (or URI) for the name of the namespace. In fact, this particular namespace name is a specific Web address; if you type it into a browser, you'll get a Web page on the W3C Web site. This namespace URI is not actually controlling the content of the document in relation to any specification, but it serves as a placeholder for the future of such an engine. The Namespaces recommendation does not preclude that the URI be a specific address.

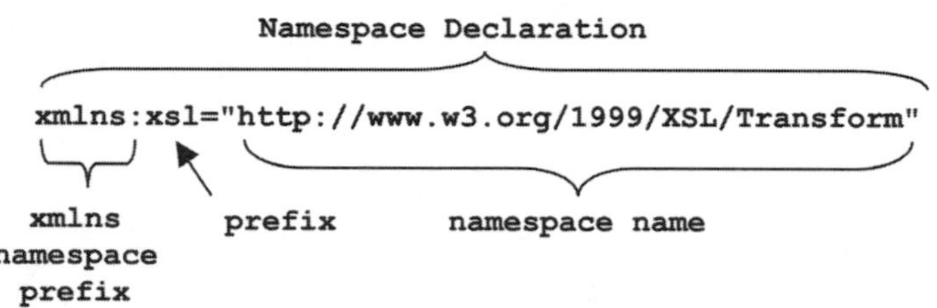

Figure 12–1 Anatomy of a namespace declaration.

A namespace declaration, unless it is `xml` or `xmlns`, must be declared in the element it is used in or in an ancestor of that element. The `xmlns` namespace declaration attribute is therefore allowed in any XML element. To actually *use* a namespace in an element tag, the prefix (`xsl`, in this example) should appear before the element-type name, with a colon (`:`) between them:

```
<xsl:template match="body">
```

12.3.3 Default Namespace

In any XSLT stylesheet there is a default namespace that does not need to be declared. The XML namespace, for example, is implicitly declared (see Section 12.3.7) and can be used anywhere in the stylesheet (as seen using the `xml:space` attribute). The default namespace for an XSLT stylesheet can be changed by declaring a new namespace and removing its prefix from the declaration.

In Example 12–1, the XHTML[2] namespace is declared and made the default namespace of the document by removing the prefix.

Example 12–1 : An LRE stylesheet declaring the XHTML namespace as the default namespace.

```
<html xsl:version="1.0"
        xmlns:xsl="http://www.w3.org/1999/XSL/Transform"
        xmlns="http://www.w3.org/TR/XHTML">
    <head>
        <title>My document title.</title>
    </head>
    <body>
        <p>My document content.</p>
    </body>
</html>
```

12.3.4 Qualified Names (QNames) and No-Colon Names (NCNames)

Namespaces contain two rather esoteric parts: QNames and NCNames. An NCName is a no-colon name, or a name without a colon, while a QName is a name with a colon. Strangely enough, each part of a qualified name (the parts around the colon) is an NCName. So if `iowa:season` is a QName, `iowa` and `season` individually are both NCNames. However, they each have their own signification.

A QName has two parts: an optional prefix and a local part. The prefix is associated with a namespace, which is expanded into a URI using the namespace declared for that prefix. The local part is the name of the object in the document instance. The prefix and the local part are separated by a colon. With or without a prefix, both element-type names and attribute names are QNames.

The *name* of an XSLT object is the combination of the expanded prefix (if used) and the local part of the QName, and is referred to as the expanded name. If a QName does not have a prefix, the local part is consid-

2. For more on XHTML, see http://www.w3.org/TR/xhtml1/. However, be aware that there is now only one XHTML, but the example in the W3C specification for XSLT reflects a prior phase, since rescinded, in which XHTML had three possible namespaces.

ered the name of the XSLT object. The default namespace defined in the stylesheet is *not* used as a prefix for QNames that do not have prefixes.This discussion on names and prefixes may be quite confusing, but suffice it to say that the names of most objects in XSLT are governed by the XML naming rules for names:

1. A name must start with either a letter or an underscore character (_).[3]
2. The remaining characters in a name must be one of the following:
   - Letter
   - Digit
   - Period (.)
   - Dash (-)
   - Underscore (_)
   - Combining characters
   - Extenders

Combining characters and extenders are special characters derived from the Unicode character database (listed in Appendix B of the XML specification).

In addition to element-type names and attribute names, internal XSLT objects must be named using QNames. Internal XSLT objects are defined by the XSLT specification as one of six types: specifically, a named template, a mode, an attribute set, a key, a decimal-format, and a variable or parameter.

3. XML names also allows a colon (:), but this is reserved for use with namespaces.

12.3.5 The XSL Namespace

The document element (<xsl:stylesheet> or <xsl:transform>) of an XSLT stylesheet contains a namespace declaration that defines the document as an XSLT stylesheet. This namespace always uses the same format. Once the namespace has been declared, XSLT elements are recognized by the processor using the "xsl" prefix in the element-type name. Notice from the examples used previously that each instruction and top-level XSLT element contains the "xsl" prefix followed by a colon, as in <xsl:template>. If these elements did not have the prefix, the processor would assume them to be LREs and this would either invalidate the stylesheet, or send the LREs to the output.

The declaration of the XSL namespace for any XSLT stylesheet occurs as an attribute in the document element. The prefix for the XSLT namespace is `xsl`, reflecting the relationship of XSLT to XSL (XSLT is part of XSL). The declaration is made as follows:

```
<xsl:stylesheet
        xmlns:xsl="http://www.w3.org/1999/XSL/Transform"
        version="1.0">
```

Notice in this case that the namespace is actually being declared in an attribute on an element that is already using the prefix. Although it may appear that the prefix is being used before it is declared, this is a perfectly valid way to declare and use a namespace.

The namespace declaration is preceded by the reserved namespace declaration attribute name `xmlns`. XSLT processors recognize the `xmlns` attribute as the beginning of a declaration for a namespace. The following attribute model definition shows the appropriate structure of the `xmlns` attribute.

```
ATTRIBUTE: xmlns:xsl CDATA #FIXED
VALUE = "http://www.w3.org/1999/XSL/Transform"
```

The prefix `xmlns` is used only for namespace bindings and is not itself bound to any namespace name. (W3C REC-xml-names-19990114, Namespaces in XML, Section 4)

Following the `xmlns` namespace declaration, the prefix that will be used for the given namespace is given, followed by an equals sign and the value of the attribute, which is a URI.

> **NOTE** The prefix is not `xslt`, but `xsl`. `XSLT` is a subset of XSL. The larger, complete styling specification includes another set of functions for formatting only. All QNames from either XSLT or XSL are part of XSL, so they have the same namespace.

12.3.6 Using Other Namespaces

XSLT, as an "extensible" language, can be extended to include elements other than those in the base set specified by the W3C. For instance, James Clark's XT has several functions that were added beyond the basic set specified in version 1.0 of the XSLT specification. Because these additional functions are commonly used, we might want to declare a namespace for XT extensions in the document element as follows:

```
<xsl:stylesheet
      xmlns:xsl="http://www.w3.org/1999/XSL/Transform"
      version="1.0"
      xmlns:xt="http://www.jclark.com/xt">
```

Thereafter, any extension elements used in the stylesheet would have the `xt` namespace prefix, while the normal XSLT elements would still have the `xsl` namespace prefix. Because the XT namespace is declared on the document element, all elements in the document can use the declared namespace if required.

12.3.7 The Default XML Namespace

XSLT stylesheets, being part of XML, have a default XML namespace that does not need to be declared.

There are two XML-specific attributes that use the XML namespace and can be used in XSLT: `xml:lang` and `xml:space`. The `xml:space` attribute is discussed in detail in Section 2.5.1.6 in connection with the document element. The `xml:lang` is not treated specially by XSLT since there is an XSLT-specific attribute (`lang`) that covers the same functionality. The XSLT `lang` attribute is discussed in Chapter 9.

12.3.8 Declaring the Extension Namespace and Its Applicability

As elsewhere in this book, the easiest way to explain how an extension element namespace applies is to look at the logical structure of the XSLT stylesheet as an XML document instance. When an extension element namespace is declared in the document element, that namespace declaration applies to the entire stylesheet. It does not, however, apply to imported or included stylesheets. Thus, if you wanted it to apply James Clark's XT to an entire XSLT stylesheet, you could declare the namespace for it, as shown below.

```
<xsl:stylesheet xmlns:xsl="http://www.w3.org/1999/XSL/Transform"
                version="1.0"
                xmlns:xt=http://www.jclark.com/xt>
```

If you were using only one particular extension element in the context of only one template rule, you might declare the namespace only on that element, as shown below using the Saxon namespace.

```
<xsl:template match="something" saxon:trace="yes"
     xmlns:saxon="http://icl.com/saxon">
```

If your XSLT stylesheet uses `<xsl:fallback>` with `element-available()` and `function-available()` to provide contingencies for unsupported elements or functions, you might more likely use the `extension-element-prefixes` attribute in the document element to provide a list of the possible namespaces, so that all possible processors are covered. This makes an XSLT stylesheet truly portable.

It is important to remember that conforming XSLT processors are not required to signal an error if an unsupported extension is encountered. Therefore, as you are fine-tuning or debugging a stylesheet, be sure and check that any extensions you are using are supported before assuming it's a deficiency in your stylesheet composition skills! At the same time, because some XSLT processors do not support the entire W3C specification, but may also have their own extension functions and/or elements, it can be confusing to trace the source of incorrect output. Comparing your chosen components to those supported by your particular processor is the first step in resolving an issue.

12.3.9 Processor Extensions, Java Additions, and Future W3C XSLT Specifications

In spite of the title of this section, we are not forecasting the future of XSLT. However, there is a crossover between the wish list for future XSLT specifications both publicly discussed and formally specified in the XSLT specification and the actual extensions provided by most mainstream XSLT processors.

The specification lists some 22 targeted goals as possible future additions to the current XSLT W3C specification. Among them are items such as IDREF functionality, which could serve, for instance, as a complement to the `id()` function. Other items are DTD and/or schema support, entity reference support, conditional expressions, case-insensitive comparisons, increased access to RTFs, and more.

However, the extensibility of XSLT has made it possible that "the future is now" on some wish list items, depending on what processor you choose. One of the most frequently requested and widely implemented extensions to XSLT is the ability for a single XSLT stylesheet to create several different output files. For instance, Xalan implements this as `<xalan:write>`, Saxon as `<saxon:output>`, and XT as `<xt:document>` extension instruction elements. This raises the issue of portability because the same functionality is available from each XSLT processor, but in different syntax. Thus, a portable XSLT stylesheet would need to use `<xsl:fallback>` to support the various processors on which it might be run to insure comparable results. These types of shared extensions, as well as the unique offerings with specific XSLT implementations, are discussed individually with the respective processors in which they are implemented.

Another item on the wish list is a common Java binding mechanism for external functions written in Java. Currently, four of the processors we discuss have very similar approaches to this: Xalan (with a few variations), Saxon, XT, and Oracle. The details of each are best explained in the product documentation that accompanies them. Additional information can be obtained through the respective Web sites for each XSLT processor.

12.3.10 Conforming XSLT Processors and the OASIS XSLT Conformance Committee

Throughout this book, we frequently use the phrase "conforming XSLT processor," or "processor that conforms to the W3C specification for

XSLT." Just what does *conforming* mean, and who decides whether the processor conforms?

Until very recently, there has not been a specific way to assign a label of "conforming" to any XSLT processor that had any industry acceptance. However, one of the ongoing efforts of the Organization for the Advancement of Structured Information Standards, OASIS, has been the chartering of conformance committees and establishment of conformance testing parameters.

These conformance committees are not evaluative bodies in the sense that the committee members pass judgment on one software implementation or another. Quite the contrary, the committees are charged with the task of detailed research into the full implications of what a W3C specification means, both in its prescribed and proscribed behavioral descriptions for any software implementation. From this research is derived a set of conformance tests and prescriptions for how they are to be implemented, and their results evaluated. Industry implementations may then access these tests and apply them to their own software, or to the software they are evaluating, to determine levels of conformance and desirability. It is not a "speed test" or memory footprint test as much as a finely tuned filter for finding precise levels of granularity in subtle nuances of how every implication of the specification is or is not met by a given software implementation.

Currently, G. Ken Holman of Crane Softwrights Ltd., a leading developer who uses XSLT and the author of a comprehensive, regularly updated resource on XSLT, is the chair of the XSLT/XPath Conformance Technical Committee. Representatives from the National Institute for Standards in Technology (NIST) a branch of the U.S. government in addition to established experts in markup technology such as Mulberry Technologies, which, among other things, is home to the XSL-list email list (http://www.mulberrytech.com/) and representatives from industry, such as IBM and Sun Microsystems, fill the seats on the committee. These are collaborative efforts of voluntary service that serve the wider needs of the XML community. For instance, a rich set of thousands of detailed XSLT tests was contributed through David Marston, the IBM/Lotus representative, while many tests are being received from other sources such as Sun and Microsoft, among others.

The test suite, which will be available at http://www.oasis-open.org/, allows users and corporations to access an independent, nonprofit-generated set of tests for evaluating XSLT software under consideration for use in whatever XML deployment they are designing. Similarly, programmers of XSLT processors have a ready benchmark by which to progressively evaluate the robustness of their implementations. OASIS will ultimately address the gamut of XML-related technologies and provide a valuable resource to the information industry. You are encouraged to utilize the committee's work in evaluating software. It is a useful learning exercise as well to run these tests, as they cover the specification in greater detail than does any single publication on XSLT or XPath.

12.4 Java

Each implementation of XSLT that we've chosen to emphasize is described according to three basic characteristics. First, the installation is explained in sufficient detail that users unfamiliar with, for example, Java CLASSPATHs, will still be able to take advantage of the software that requires them. Second, the various special extensions added by each package are presented. Finally, any caveats or unimplemented features are noted, not as an evaluation, but as a summary of frequently discussed aspects of the software that are useful in planning how to work with XSLT stylesheets and how to utilize XSLT processing software.

In Section 12.3.1, we offer an opportunity to learn to install the JDK (Java Development Kit) that is required for most XML processing software, especially for XSLT. It is too often the case that packages come with the somewhat unhelpful line "Install JDK 1.1.6 or later" and little else. This means chasing around the Internet to find the JDK, figuring out which version to use, making sense of `PATH`s vs. `CLASSPATH`s, and often never even getting Java, let alone an XSLT processor or XSLT stylesheet, running. This book was designed to *not* take for granted that everyone already knows everything about Java. For those who do know the JDK, skip Section 12.3.1; for those who don't, we hope it helps, as we wrote it out of our own frustration with too much Java-related technology being taken for granted and too little help available.

12.4.1 Getting Java Going on Your Solaris/UNIX, Macintosh, or Windows Machine

The processors emphasized here all work predominantly with the JDK. Most assume or prefer JDK 1.1.6 or later, and some work best with JDK 1.2. In general, you are almost always safest with JDK 1.1.8 or later, but in many cases, XSLT processors are designed with increased convenience or simplicity if you have JDK 1.2 (also called, somewhat confusingly, Java 2). For example, Java 2 does not require the additional installation of Swing, which further simplifies the use of the GUI for Xalan, designed by Eric Lawson.

In essence, you are going to learn how to install a Java Virtual Machine, sometimes called a Java VM, or JVM. The JVM and JDK are not necessarily the same thing, and the nuances are important if you are programming in Java. They are not pivotal for XSLT. All you really need is a general idea what the JDK does on your system so that you can get the most out of your XSLT processor. In short, think of the JDK as being like your operating system.

If you work on Solaris, the JDK is an environment, so to speak, in which Java applications can run. The same thing applies to a Macintosh or Windows machine; the JDK is a "layer" on top of the basic operating system. The JDK runs like an application *on top of* the Mac OS (operating system) or Windows 95, 98, or NT basic OS. Then, a Java application in this case, the XSLT processor runs on top of that. If it sounds complex, don't worry; the beauty of Java is that you are largely insulated from this and your machine is insulated from crashes when you run a Java application.

It may prove worthwhile to add a little memory to your machine, because these layers do take up space, especially if the XML document instances you are transforming with your XSLT stylesheets are large. At a *minimum,* 64MB of RAM is needed for Windows, and realistically, not less than 128MB are required. At a *minimum,* the same is required for Macintosh, but realistically, unless you have a lot of time on your hands to wait while it runs, you need 128MB or more. Mac OS 7.6 or later is a bare minimum, but you should really have 8.1 or later. You can always use virtual memory, but this is going to be as slow as your hard drive already is because, of course, that's what virtual memory uses.

For Solaris and UNIX, you are usually on a shared network, so this is less of a problem, but you are going to want to carve out a little extra memory (we'll show you how) when you run the XSLT processor. If you have a Sun

Ultra, for instance, don't even *try* to work with less than 64MB of RAM, and again, realistically, you will be need 128MB (just using swap doesn't help because, again, virtual memory is as slow as your hard drive).

Another advantage is that one Java application runs on Java for Mac, or Java for Windows, or Java for UNIX, largely transparently. That's why you will read about Java parsers or XSLT processors more than Windows or Macintosh processors; the Java XSLT processor can run on either, for the most part.

So, to get the benefits of Java and to start using XSLT processors, you will need to get the JDK that is appropriate for your machine. Once you have that "Java operating system" ready, you can run all the Java XML processing software you want. That's a great advantage of Java too; once the JVM is installed, you've instantly made a whole new world of software available to yourself much or most of which is also free!

12.4.1.1 Accessing a Java Virtual Machine

If you are on a Solaris or UNIX system, chances are there is already a JVM installed (if not, there are instructions in Section 12.3.1.2). Contact your system administrator to find out where it is on the system so you know in what directory to look for the settings described below for each XSLT processor. Usually, it will be the location of the Java classes, so you can set a Java CLASSPATH to point to them.

You can also find the JVM yourself with a little persistence. Using a command-line window (terminal, in Solaris), type `java`. If a set of instructions for running Java comes up, you are all set. If not, you will need to do a couple more things.

1. Try to find the JVM by changing into your root directory. Type `cd /` at the command line.
2. Test to see if there is a Java version running by typing `Java -version`.
3. Type `find . -name 'java' -print`.
4. Set your environment to point to the path by typing:

   ```
   setenv CLASSPATH=/java/classes/classes.zip
   ```

   Note that this assumes you are using csh, not ksh or Bourne shell. The path shown here may change depending on where java is on your system.

5. If you know where your XSLT processor files are, you can do all this in one step by separating each with a colon (`:`) as below for an installation of XT where the XT files are all in your `usr/bin` directory.

   a. For pre-JDK 1.2:

```
setenv CLASSPATH=/usr/bin/xt/sax.jar:/usr/bin/xt/xt:/java/classes/classes.zip
```

   b. For JDK1.2+:

```
setenv CLASSPATH=/usr/bin/xt/sax.jar:/usr/bin/xt/xt:.
```

6. You can also make this permanent if you're comfortable editing your `.cshrc` file; just add the following line to it (exactly as above, but with `set` rather than `setenv`, and remember that `/java/classes/classes.zip` is only for pre-JDK 1.2; otherwise only a "`.`" period is needed).

   a. For pre-JDK 1.2:

```
set CLASSPATH=/usr/bin/xt/sax.jar:/usr/bin/xt/xt:/java/classes/classes.zip
```

   b. For JDK1.2+:

```
set CLASSPATH=/usr/bin/xt/sax.jar:/usr/bin/xt/xt:.
```

If you work with Internet Explorer 5.0 or later (actually 4.0 or later, but we recommend 5.0), there is a JVM built in, which can be used with either Instant Saxon or the Windows version of XT. In these two cases, the Saxon or XT processor comes preconfigured to access the JVM that is part of IE. You can download IE 5.0 at http://www.microsoft.com. The instructions for using Instant Saxon or XT Windows version are quite simple once you have IE 5.0, which is free and automatically installs all you need if you follow the default settings in the installation wizard.

12.4.1.2 Setting Up a JVM on Solaris/UNIX (Linux, too)

Most of these installations are very similar, so we will generalize here. When you choose the specific package you need, detailed instructions will lead you through the particulars.

The most important thing here is to be sure you get the right version of the JVM when you download. It requires a few additional steps to work in UNIX or Solaris, but it's still quite easy and should not take more than an hour with a reliable, fast Ethernet Internet connection. If you skipped Section 12.3.1.1, reading it could save a *lot* of time if—and it is highly likely that this is the case—the JVM is already on your system.

If not, go to the Sun site at http://www.java.sun.com and download the JDK file (1.1.8 or later). Get the SPARC or Intel Solaris version as needed. For instance, with Java 2, you might download the Solaris SPARC file `1.2.2_05_jdk_sparc.tar.Z`. Root privileges are not necessary to install or run Java.

1. Choose a directory in which to install, such as the common `/usr/local/bin` or `/usr/bin` or `/local/bin` (sometimes Solaris installs work most transparently when you use `/opt`), and copy the files into it if they are not already there.
2. Use `uncompress 1.2.2_05_jdk_sparc.tar.Z` to unzip, then use `tar xvf 1.2.2_05_jdk_sparc.tar` to unarchive, or untar, the file.
3. Untarring the file creates all necessary directories and subdirectories.
4. Set your environment permanently by changing your `.cshrc` file; for instance, if you are installing into `/usr/bin`, add the following line to your `.cshrc`.
   a. For pre-JDK 1.2:

   ```
   set CLASSPATH=/usr/bin/java/classes/classes.zip
   ```

   b. For JDK1.2+:

   ```
   set CLASSPATH=.
   ```

On Windows, remember to use the semi-colon (;) and reverse slash (\).

5. If you do not want to make this permanent, you can simply set this each time with:

    a. For pre-JDK 1.2:

```
setenv CLASSPATH=/usr/bin/java/classes/classes.zip
```

    b. For JDK1.2+:

```
setenv CLASSPATH=.
```

You are now ready to run the XSLT processor on your Solaris, UNIX, or Linux system by augmenting this CLASSPATH with the location of the XSLT files you have chosen to use. Test the installation by typing `java` at the prompt, or `java -version` to see if it's the version you thought you installed.

12.4.1.3 Installing the JDK on Windows

When you choose to run Java on Windows, you will download either one large `.zip` file or several small files from http://java.sun.com. Whichever you choose, follow the instructions for dealing with the multiple or single files as appropriate (it is recommended that, to avoid errors, waiting the additional time for downloading the single file is worth it). Put the downloaded file into a folder on your PC, such as `c:\utilities` or `c:\java`, and unzip it with WinZip (likely on your machine; otherwise, do a simple search on the Web and download it). You can double-click on the `.zip` file with WinZip on your system and it will open up. Then, double-click the resulting executable file and follow the auto-prompts through the installation process with the install wizard.

Once you've gone through the install, you need to add a few lines to your `autoexec.bat` file, which you will find by using Notepad and looking for it on the root `c:\directory` (remember to choose "All" in the Files of Type pulldown in the Open File window). The change to PATH identifies the actual program location. CLASSPATH identifies the class file locations. If you installed the JDK to `c:\jdk1.2.2`, program files like `javac` are in `c:\jdk1.2.2\bin`, and the class files are in c:\jdk1.2.2\lib\classes.zip. Add the following lines (assuming you have installed the JDK into c:\java, though the wizard will often choose something like c:\jdk1.2.2) to your autoexec.bat file:

```
PATH ......;C:\jdk1.2.2\bin;.......
SET CLASSPATH=.
```

The "......" denote whatever directories are already in your PATH; be sure to separate each one with a semicolon, though no semicolon is added at the end of the line, and do not use spaces or hard returns. If you are using Windows NT, you can specify the path by going to Start, Control Panel, System, Environment. Test to see if you have been successful by typing java at a c:\ prompt in a DOS window (go to Start, Run, and type cmd), or to see if you have the right version running in case there was another previously installed or conflicting version type c:\java -version.

12.4.1.4 Installing Java on a Macintosh

Setting up Java on a Macintosh is extremely simple. You need only to run the install and all the paths for running Java will be correct. The only paths you will need to add are those for whatever XSLT software you choose.

First, get the Mac MRJ 2.2.2. Next, you need to get the Java for Mac that has JBindery. It comes with the MRJ SDK. You can find the MRJ 2.2 SDK for free at http://developer.apple.com/java/text/download.html#sdk (it takes a few minutes from home, less on Ethernet). Macintosh Runtime for Java Software Development Kit 2.1 is fine if you have it. Now install it by double-clicking the icon, following all the automatic presets. When it's done, you will see the MRJ SDK 2.1 directory on your hard drive, inside that is a folder called Tools, and one called Application Builders. It is inside the Application Builders where you will find the JBindery folder (if not, remove MRJ, reinstall with the Custom option, and select *all* components).

12.5 Commercial XSLT Processors

As noted, we are only describing three commercial XSLT processors due to limits of space and the simple pragmatics of how widespread and commonly used they are. These three processors are Sun Microsystem's XSLTC, Oracle's XML suite, and Microsoft's MSXML.

12.5.1 Sun Microsystems' XSLTC

Sun Microsystems' XSLTC (XSLT Compiler) is a unique addition to the XSLT processor realm in that it produces translets per stylesheet, which greatly reduce the amount of memory consumed by the DOM, in most cases, and often substantially increase speed. It is also possible to protect your stylesheet composition with the Sun translets, as they are compiled byte-code rather than human-readable XML document instances. This approach brings the promise of sophisticated transformations with a small enough memory footprint to work with wireless devices. This very new technology is significantly different from a conventional XSLT processor.

The latest tests at Sun show that XSLTC is typically 30% faster, if not more, than XT. The following table (provided by Sun) of some contributed XSL stylesheets shows a sample of processing speeds.

	XSLTC	**XT**	**Saxon**	**Xalan**
test1	2.3	2.76	3.96	6.16
test2	2.1	2.98	4.4	5.98
test3	2.98	4	4.26	14.1
test4	4.18	4.72	6.3	12.48
test5	3.74	5.78	5.82	10.1
test6	4.7	7.5	6.6	11.84
test7	2.08	4.5	3.98	7.22

12.5.2 Oracle® XML Developer's Kit (XDK)

Oracle provides a suite of XML tools in its XML Developer's Kit (XDK), which is available for Java, C, C++, and PL/SQL. This suite includes an XML parser and an XSLT processor, as well as other useful XML tools. XSLT support is provided with version 2 of the XML parser, which can be downloaded from the Oracle Technology Network Web site at http://technet.oracle.com/tech/xml. The Oracle XDK is free, and it is fully supported for Oracle customers who have an existing support plan. Anyone using the

Oracle XDK can also take advantage of free technical assistance provided through the XML Discussion Forum on Oracle Technet. The XDK can also be redistributed under the terms of the Oracle license.

The Oracle XML Parser is available in a standalone command-line version, or Libraries for Java, C, C++, and PL/SQL. It supports DOM2, SAX2, XML Namespaces 1.0, and XML Schema, and also runs on Oracle 8*i* and Oracle Application Server.

The XSLT processor supports the W3C XSLT Recommendation 1.0 and the W3C XPath Recommendation 1.0.

12.5.3 Installing the Oracle XSL Processor

The XSLT processor is included with the XML parser download. The Oracle XML parsers can be downloaded from the Oracle Technology Network Web site at http://technet.oracle.com/tech/xml. Select the appropriate XDK language version, and then click on the "Software" icon.

> **NOTE** You must be a registered Oracle Technology Network member to have access to download software. Membership is free, but you may have to fill out a registration form prior to downloading software.

Software version choices are listed in Table 12–1

Table 12–1 Software for XSLT and Oracle

Software	*Platform*
Java v2	UNIX, Windows NT
C	Linux, Sun Solaris, Windows NT
C++ v2	Linux v2.0.2, Sun Solaris v2.0.4, HP Unix, Windows NT v2.0.3
PL/SQL	UNIX, Windows NT

The appropriate programming environment for each version should be installed and configured prior to installing the parser. For example, if you download the Java version, Java JDK-1.1.x or higher should be installed on your system. Also, since the files are zipped, either GNU gzip on UNIX or the WinZip executable on Windows should be available to unzip the files.

Once the appropriate software is installed and the zipped parser file has been downloaded, unzip the file into a directory of your choice and configure your system to add the directory and parser to your PATH and CLASSPATH environment variables.

The Oracle XSL processor has a command line utility as well as libraries. The download includes sample files. The command to run the XSL processor on the sample files is:

```
java oracle.xml.parser.v2.oraxsl <sample xsl file> <sample xml file>
```

12.5.4 Microsoft® MSXML

The October 2000 Microsoft XML Parser (MSXML) 3.0 final release provides a complete implementation of XSLT/XPath and complete conformance to the specifications from the W3C and the OASIS Test Suite.[4]

Complete implementation of XSLT/XPath is of course the key. Previous versions of the Microsoft Parser did not support certain elements and functions of the XSLT and XPath specifications. The specific changes in this release include support for the `<xsl:decimal-format>` element, the `unparsed-entity-uri()` and `format-number()` functions, and the namespace axis.

Microsoft's original implementation of MSXML (for Internet Explorer® 5) contained functionality that was not implemented in the final XSLT or XPath specifications. However, those ideas contributed to the development of a new W3C Proposal, XML Query Language (XQL),[5] and also led to the creation of a new W3C working group, the XML Query group.

MSXML 3.0 continues to support the previous XSL language WD-XSL,[6] which integrated the XQL extensions. Since this language is obsolete, Microsoft encourages people to move to compliant XSLT as soon as practical.

---

4. There are a few minor bugs in this release, which Microsoft is addressing with Web releases.
5. See http://www.w3.org/TandS/QL/QL98/pp/xql.html.
6. See http://www.w3.org/TR/WD-xsl.

The Microsoft web site provides complete documentation for XSLT, XML, and SAX2, including MSXML extensions. The documentation is included in the installation for the 3.0 Version of the XML SDK and can be downloaded from:

```
http://msdn.microsoft.com/xml/default.asp
XML Downloads ➔ XML ➔ MSXML SDK 3.0 Release
```

The files are installed in the \Program Files\Microsoft XML Parser SDK folder on your system. The documentation is in the Docs directory, and can be accessed by clicking on the xmlsdk30.chm file.

12.5.4.1 MSXML Extension Elements and Functions

The Microsoft XSLT Processor extends the XSLT and XPath specifications with one extension element, `<msxsl:script>`, and one extension function, `node-set()`.

The `<msxsl:script>` Extension Element

The `<msxsl:script>` extension element is a top-level element (a child of `<xsl:stylesheet>` or `<xsl:transform>`) and contains script blocks that define global variables and functions for script extensions. It has two attributes: `language`, which is used to specify the scripting language of the script block it contains; and `implements-prefix`, a required attribute used to associate a namespace prefix with the script block, as shown in the following element model definition. The `<msxsl:script>` element does not allow child elements.

```
<!-- Category: extension top-level element -->
<msxsl:script
  language = "language-name"
  implements-prefix = "prefix of user's namespace">
</msxsl:script>
```

Calling the script function using the `<xsl:value-of>` instruction element executes the script block and converts the result into a text string. The `select` attribute of the `<xsl:value-of>` element passes in the parameters required by the function. The script blocks defined by `<msxsl:script>` are globally available to all XSLT elements.

The optional `language` attribute specifies the active scripting language for the function defined in the script block. It accepts the same values that are allowed on the `<script>` element in HTML. The processor uses the default language Microsoft JScript® if no other language is specified, or if the attribute is not specified.

The required `implements-prefix` attribute is used to associate a namespace prefix with the script block. The namespace must be declared prior to the use of the `<msxsl:script>` element. The value of the attribute is the prefix declared by the namespace.

Example 12–2 comes directly from the Microsoft SDK[7] documentation, and shows an example of the declaration of the `user` namespace, as well as the declaration and calling of a script block.

Example 12–2 : Using the `<msxsl:script>` function.

```
<xsl:stylesheet xmlns:xsl="http://www.w3.org/1999/XSL/Transform"
                xmlns:msxsl="urn:schemas-microsoft-com:xslt"
                xmlns:user="http://mycompany.com/mynamespace"
                version="1.0">
      <msxsl:script language="JScript" implements-prefix="user">
        function xml(nodelist) {
          return nodelist.nextNode().xml;
        }
      </msxsl:script>

      <xsl:template match="/">
        <xsl:value-of select="user:xml(.)"/>
      </xsl:template>
</xsl:stylesheet>
```

12.5.4.2 The `node-set()` Extension Function

The MSXML `node-set()` function enables the conversion of a tree into a node set. The result is a single node that contains the root node of the tree. The function return type of this function is a node-set. Its one required argument is a string, as shown in the function prototype below. The string

7. Much of the information for this section comes directly from the Microsoft SDK 3.0 documentation. All copyrights for Microsoft and the MSXML, as stated in the copyright page of the SDK, apply.

is processed in a manner defined by the msxsl namespace to convert the string into a node-set. The function must be called using the msxsl namespace prefix, unless the msxsl prefix is declared to be the default namespace of the stylesheet.

Function: *node-set* **msxml:node-set** (*string*)

Function Name	*Function Group*	*Function Return Type*	*Arguments*	*Argument Type*
node-set()	Node-set	Node-set	String	Required

One of the features that was removed from the original MSXML implementation, in order to support conformance, was the ability to use variable references in pattern expressions. Because you cannot use variable references in a pattern, it is not possible to have arbitrary patterns that return a node-set. For example, the use of the $var variable in <xsl:for-each select="$var/el"> is not allowed, but the node-set() function gets around this limitation, as shown below:

```
<xsl:for-each select="msxsl:node-set($var)/el)">
```

The result of the evaluation of the select expression is a node-set consisting of <el> nodes which are descended from whatever element is defined in the var variable. The content of the <xsl:for-each> element will then apply to each node in the node-set.

12.5.5 Installing the Latest Microsoft XML Parser

Download the current version of MSXML from the Microsoft Web site at:

```
http://msdn.microsoft.com/xml/default.asp
XML Downloads ➔ XML ➔ MSXML Parser 3.0 Release
```

The Download screen will appear n the window on the right hand side. Click on the "Download" icon, accept the end-user license agreement, and select "save to disk." This will install a file called "msxml3.exe" on your system. Double click on this file to install the software. Note: You must have the Microsoft Windows Installer version 1.1 loaded on your machine prior to running this installation. It can be downloaded from the same window that was used to download the MSXML parser, but may already be included in your system if you have the latest version of Microsoft Office or Windows NT. The installer will run and install the program, but will not tell you where or how to use it.

Installing the 3.0 version will not overwrite any previous versions of MSXML on your system unless it is installed specifically using the "replace" mode. This means that your programs will continue to use the older version of the parser until you replace it with the new version using the xmlinst.exe installer tool, which can be downloaded from:

```
http://msdn.microsoft.com/xml/default.asp
XML Downloads ➔ XML ➔ Xmlinst.exe Installer Tool.
```

The Microsoft web site recommends installing Internet Explorer 4.01 Service Pack 1 or later in order for this beta release to function properly. The latest version of Internet Explorer can be downloaded from:

```
http://www.microsoft.com/windows/ie/default.htm
```

Xalan, Saxon, and XT

- Xalan-C++ and Xalan-J
- Saxon
- XT
- Multiple output documents

13

In this chapter, we will discuss three freeware XSLT processors: Xalan, Saxon, and XT. Each section contains an overview of the product, an installation guide, and details about any extensions that are implemented by the processor.

13.1 Xalan

Xalan, an XSLT processor originally developed by Scott Boag at Lotus (now part of IBM), was donated to the Apache XML Project as part of their open source endeavor. A team of engineers at Lotus drives the development of both Xalan-C++ (using C++) and Xalan-J (using Java). Both versions implement XSLT 1.0 and XPath 1.0.

Like every XSLT processor, both Xalan-C++ and Xalan-J require an XML parser to validate the input XML document instance, and use the Apache parser, Xerces. They can work with other parsers, but you would have to write an interface to do so.

The Apache Web site includes both the C++ and Java versions, as well as a complete set of test files, the API, and documentation, which can be found at:

http://xml.apache.org/xalan-c/
http://xml.apache.org/xalan-j/

13.1.1 Xalan-C++

If you are working with very large documents, or need to work in a multithreaded application environment, Xalan-C++ provides functionality and speed that surpasses Xalan-J. The installation includes a command-line processor as well as a simplified C++ and C API for performing standard transformations. The documentation includes lots of samples to get started with, along with full source code and a complete description of each C++ class. This provides the ability to build your own applications to include Xalan-C++ with relative ease.

The latest version of Xalan-C++ can be found on the Apache Web site at http://xml.apache.org/xalan-c. Zipped files are available for Windows 32, Red Hat Linux 6.1, AIX 4.3, HP-UX 11, and Solaris 2.6 (UNIX versions are tarred with gnu tar). Each download comes with documentation, sample applications, and the complete Xalan-C++ source tree.

In addition to the command-line version of Xalan-C++ for transformations, which is available immediately upon installation, the download provides the C++ classes required to implement and build user-defined applications.

When you download Xalan-C++, the latest version of Xerces-C++ is also included. Xerces-C++ is an XML parser that validates XML according to version 1.0 of the XML specification.[1] The shared library provides the capability to generate, manipulate, and parse XML documents, and provides high performance, modularity, and scalability.

13.1.1.1 Installing Xalan-C++

Unzip the file that you downloaded from the Apache Web site into the directory of your choice. This will create two directories, one for xml-xalan and one for xml-xerces.

You must modify your system and library paths to point to the executable directory as follows:

1. See http://www.w3.org/TR/REC-xml.

Windows:

```
PATH=xml-xalan\c\Build\Win32\VC6\Release
```

Red Hat Linux:

```
PATH=xml-xalan/c/bin
LD_LIBRARY_PATH=xml-xalan/c/lib
```

or copy `libxalan-c1_1.so` to `/usr/lib`

AIX:

```
PATH=xml-xalan/c/bin
LIBPATH=xml-xalan/c/lib
```

or copy `libxalan-c1_1.a` to `/usr/lib`

HP-UX 11:

```
PATH=xml-xalan/c/bin
SHLIB_PATH=xml-xalan/c/lib
```

or copy `libxalan-c1_1.a` to `/usr/lib`

Solaris:

```
PATH=xml-xalan/c/bin
LD_LIBRARY_PATH=xml-xalan/c/lib
```

or copy `libxalan-c1_1.so` to `/usr/lib`

13.1.1.2 Using Xalan-C++ Command-line

Once you've installed the executable file and modified your Path statement, the Xalan-C++ command-line version is ready to go.

Using a command-line DOS or terminal window, type `testXSLT`. This will give you a message with the arguments available for Xalan-C++ on the command-line. The command-line version requires at least two arguments, with their corresponding flags: `-in` for the input filename, and `-xsl` for the XSLT stylesheet. All the other arguments, including the output filename, are optional:

```
testXSLT -in XMLFileName -xsl XSLFileName [-out OutFileName] [args]
```

Where:

`testXSLT` is the command to run Xalan-C++
`XMLFileName` is the input XML file name
`XSLFileName` is the name of your XSLT stylesheet
`[OutFileName]` is the optional output file name
`[args]` are additional optional arguments

The installation directory structure includes a *samples* directory with several basic sample applications, under *install-directory\xml-xalan\c\samples* on Windows or *install-directory/xml-xalan/c/samples* on UNIX. The samples are precompiled, each with their own executable with the same name as the directory. For example, using the command-line in the *install-directory/xml-xalan/c/samples/SimpleTransform* directory, type `SimpleTransform` to run the test. This will take the `foo.xml` file and process it according to the `foo.xsl` stylesheet, producing a `foo.out` output file. You can also use the command-line executable directly by typing:

```
testXSLT -in foo.xml -xsl foo.xsl -out foo.out
```

Xalan-C++ includes other command-line arguments (not case-sensitive), listed in Table 13–1 below:

Table 13–1 Command-line options for Xalan-C++

Argument	*Action/Effect*
`-IN` *inputXMLFileName*	InputXMLURL.
`-XSL` *stylesheetFileName*	XSLTransformationURL.
`-OUT` *outputFileName*	OutputFileName.
`-ESCAPE` chars	Which characters to escape—default is <>&"'\r\n.
`-EER`	Expand entity references—default is not to expand.
`-V`	Version info.
`-QC`	Quiet Pattern Conflicts Warnings.
`-Q`	Quiet Mode.
`-INDENT` *number*	Number of spaces to indent each level in output tree—default is 0.

Table 13–1 Command-line options for Xalan-C++ (continued)

Argument	*Action/Effect*
`-VALIDATE`	Validate the XSL and XML input—default is not to validate. If a DTD is specified in the input XML document, this will validate the XML using that DTD.
`-TT`	Trace the templates as they are being called.
`-TEXT`	Use simple Text formatter.
`-TG`	Trace each result tree generation event.
`-TS`	Trace each selection event.
`-TTC`	Trace the template children as they are being processed.
`-XML`	Use XML formatter and add XML header.
`-NH`	Don't write XML header. Requires that the -XML flag be set.
`-HTML`	Use HTML formatter to generate HTML 4.0.
`-NOINDENT`	Turns off HTML indenting. Requires that the -HTML flag be set.
`-STRIPCDATA`	Strip CDATA sections of their brackets, but do not escape. Requires that either the -XML or -HTML flag be set.
`-ESCAPECDATA`	Strip CDATA sections of their brackets, and escape. Requires that either the -XML or -HTML flag be set.

Table 13–1 Command-line options for Xalan-C++ (continued)

Argument	*Action/Effect*
`-PARAM` *name expression*	Set a stylesheet parameter. String value expressions should be enclosed in single quotes (').

If you don't want to use the optional arguments, there is a compiled executable that is set up to run a basic transformation with just the input filename, XSLT stylesheet name, and the optional output filename. All the defaults are used, and the flags (`-in`, etc.) are not required:

```
XalanTransform XMLFileName XSLFileName [OutFileName]
```

Where:

`XalanTransform` is the command to run Xalan-C++
`XMLFileName` is the input XML file name
`XSLFileName` is the name of your XSLT stylesheet
`OutFileName` is the optional output file name

13.1.1.3 Extending Xalan-C++

Xalan-C++ provides the ability to create your own extension functions. See the Xalan-C++ documentation, provided with the download or on the Apache Web site at http://xml.apache.org/xalan-c/extensions.html for information on creating extension functions.

Xalan-C++ does not support creating extension elements at this time. Currently, support for extension elements is planned for version 1.4.

13.1.1.4 Limitations of Xalan-C++

There are several known limitations to the current version on Xalan-C++, including:

- Does not support 20 or more digits of numerical precision after the decimal.

- The namespace axis does not return the default "xml" namespace.
- Does not support `case-order` and `lang` attributes in `<xsl:sort>`.
- Does not support extension elements

The Xalan development mailing list (xalan-dev@xml.apache.org) is a good place for users to report bugs and other issues. Any bugs that are reported should be specified as Xalan-C++ issues on the subject line.

13.1.1.5 Internationalization with Xalan-C++

Xalan-C++ provides support for internationalization with the addition of the International Components for Unicode™ (ICU)[2] from IBM's Developerworks.

The ICU provides support for number formatting using the XPath `format-number()` function, Unicode-style collation using the `<xsl:sort>` XSLT element, and character encoding using UTF-16.

> **NOTE** Xalan-C++ ignores the format pattern and optional decimal-format name arguments for `format-number()` unless you install the ICU.

To get the ICU:

1. Download and unzip the latest ICU source files from the IBM developerWorks open source page: `http://oss.software.ibm.com/developerworks/opensource/icu/project/download/index.html`
2. Do an ICU build according to the build instructions in the *readme.html* that is included with the download. When installing on Windows, the ICU should be on the same drive and at the same level as your installation of Xalan-C++.
3. Set the ICU_DATA environment variable as shown in the *readme.html*.

2. See http://oss.software.ibm.com/developerworks/opensource/icu/project/index.html.

13.1.2 Xalan-J

Xalan-J takes a unique approach to the conventional representation of the input XML document instance. It can represent the XML document instance's nodes as an array, in a representation called the Document Table Model. This allows Xalan-J to outperform some other XSLT processors under certain conditions, such as with large documents. To learn more, consult the Xalan-J documentation. In these files are details about the features listed below; we have only summarized them here to aid in your selection of an appropriate XSLT processor, and we've included the various connectivity options with Java and applets, or wrappers.

If you choose to add functions and are familiar with Java or JavaScript, for example, Xalan-J uses the Bean Scripting Framework (BSF) for adding functionality. Java and JavaScript have both been tested according to the documentation. This is the reason for adding the `bsf.jar` and `bsfengines.jar` files with the command-line installation (described in Section 13.1.2). Otherwise, you do not need to add these to your CLASSPATH to use Xalan-J programmatically, or through the command line.

We will present two ways to work with Xalan-J. The first is the conventional command-line method, and the second involves an excellent and extremely convenient GUI interface developed by Eric Lawson of ISOGEN/DataChannel. In fact, one of the features of Xalan-J is that it can be run either by command-line or by its Java API. Additionally, it can be run within an applet or servlet, similar to the interface provided by Lawson, included on the CD.

13.1.3 Using Xalan-J with Eric Lawson's GUI

Using Xalan-J with the GUI by Eric Lawson is simple and convenient. Assuming that you have Java installed as described in Chapter 12, you only need the `XSLTConv.zip` file included on the CD (*XSLTConv.zip* in the */software/Xalan/Lawson_GUI* directory). The following instructions are derived from the *readme* file. The instructions below will work with either Windows or UNIX. Macintosh is slightly different, as a command-line is not so readily available in the Mac OS.

The application is basically a graphical front end for the Xalan-J XSLT processor, which takes advantage of Xalan's predilection for being easily run from within an applet. This application frees users from having to actually install Xalan, because it contains all the necessary classes required to perform XSLT Transformations. This also frees users from having to use Xalan-J through the command-line, which can be very repetitive typing-wise, and liberates users from having to deal with some of the underlying complexity of XSLT processors once Java is on the system.

Java version 1.1.6 or greater with Swing 1.01 or greater should be installed, or any Java 2 installation (1.2 or greater we recommend Java 1.2). Simply copy the `xsltconv.jar` file into a directory of your choice. Then, type the following onto the command-line of a UNIX terminal window or an MS-DOS window (via Start, run, cmd):

```
java -jar xsltconv.jar
```

Make sure you run this from the directory where you copied the XSLT-Converter files. Once the XSLT Transform window comes up, using it is very simple. Either type in the location of your files, along with filenames for the files you want processed by Xalan. Alternately, you can just click the Browse button next to each field XML Source File, XSLT Stylesheet, and Output File and, just as you would use any graphical interface File/Open command, point and click to select the files to be used.

One thing to remember is that the Output File field is not likely to be browsable to a file because, presumably, until it's output, it doesn't exist! Alternately, you can click Browse, open up the File Chooser, and then select the directory you wish the output file to be placed in. Then, type the name of the desired file into the File Chooser (as this file may not exist yet), and click Select File. To actually invoke your XSLT stylesheet and convert the files, simply click the Transform button and the XSLT processor will perform the transformation.

13.1.4 Installing the Basic Command-line Interface for Xalan-J

Using the command-line interface for Xalan-J affords access to a number of extensions and "switches" you can invoke when you run it. Xalan-J requires that you also have the Xerces parser, so you will need to download both it and Xalan-J from http://xml.apache.org/dist/xalan-j/ and http://xml.apache.org/dist/xerces-j/. If you plan to run XSLT extensions, you need `bsf.jar` and `bsfengines.jar`, both of which are included in the Xalan-Java distribution. Remember, we suggest that you use JDK 1.2+ so that your settings are simpler. To run the extensions, include `bsf.jar` and `bsfengines.jar` in the CLASSPATH.

Unzip the files into the directory you wish to use for running Xalan-J and make the following changes to your system.

1. At the very least, you must include `xalan.jar` and `xerces.jar` on the system CLASSPATH. Thus, where you had a basic " . ", you would modify it as follows:

```
set CLASSPATH=/usr/bin/xalan/xerces.jar:/usr/bin/xalan/xalan.jar:.
```

   For your `.cshrc` on Solaris/UNIX or `autoexec.bat` file on Windows, remember to use a semicolon (`;`) and the reverse slash (\). For temporary on Solaris/UNIX:

```
setenv CLASSPATH=/usr/bin/xalan/xerces.jar:/usr/bin/xalan/xalan.jar:.
```

2. To run the sample applications, include `xalansamples.jar`. Thus, where you had a basic `.:/usr/bin`, you would modify it as follows:

```
set
CLASSPATH=/usr/bin/xalan/xerces.jar:/usr/bin/xalan/xalan.jar:.:/usr/bin/xalan/xala
nsamples.jar
```

   For your `.cshrc` on Solaris/UNIX, use a colon separator, or use a semicolon for the `autoexec.bat` file on Windows, and remember to use the reverse slash (\).

```
setenv
CLASSPATH=/usr/bin/xalan/xerces.jar:/usr/bin/xalan/xalan.jar:.:/usr/bin/xalan/xala
nsamples.jar
```

   and so on, with the `:` separator on Solaris/UNIX. To use the extensions, add them as follows:

```
set CLASSPATH=/usr/bin/xalan/xerces.jar:/usr/bin/xalan/xalan.jar:.:
/usr/bin/xalan/xalansamples.jar:/usr/bin/xalan/bsf.jar:
/usr/bin/xalan/bsfengines.jar
```

   For your `.cshrc` on Solaris/UNIX, use a colon separator, or use a semicolon for `autoexec.bat` on Windows, and remember to use the reverse slash (\).

```
setenv CLASSPATH=/usr/bin/xalan/xerces.jar:/usr/bin/xalan/xalan.jar:.:
/usr/bin/xalan/xalansamples.jar:/usr/bin/xalan/brf.jar:
/usr/bin/xalan/bsfengines.jar
```

13.1.5 Using Xalan-J with the Command-line Interface and Extensions

Once you have Xalan-J installed for command-line usage, you have several options when invoking it, which can affect the kinds of output and processing that take place. Be sure your CLASSPATH is set as above and that you have Java correctly installed. The basic invocation is as follows:

```
java org.apache.xalan.xslt.Process -in source.xml -xsl stylesheet.xsl
-out output.xml
```

Notice that `-in`, `-xsl`, and `-out` precede the XML document instance, the XSLT stylesheet, and result file, respectively. The initial invocation of `java` simply invokes the JVM, and the `org.apache.xalan.xslt.Process` implements the actual XSLT processing class. If you are using the Microsoft virtual machine, use `jview` instead of `java`.

There are several additional aspects of running Xalan-J from the command line, such as having the ability to set a parameter value from "outside" the XSLT stylesheet. Thus, within the XSLT stylesheet, you might have a declared parameter that would be invoked somewhat differently each time you ran the XSLT stylesheet through Xalan.

```
<xsl:param name="birthday" value="******" />
```

Here, you could input the date, if your stylesheet was in some way dependent on the time at which it was run.

```
java org.apache.xalan.xslt.Process -PARAM birthday '09-13-63' -in
source.xml -xsl process_date.xsl -out result.xml
```

Notice how `-PARAM` takes two arguments: the declared `name` value of `<xsl:param>` and the actual value set at the moment the XSLT stylesheet is processed that particular time.

There is a range of these command-line switches beginning with "`-`" that you can use with Xalan-J. The command-line utility can take the flags and arguments listed in Table 13–2 (these flags, or switches, are case-insensitive, and note that all of them begin with the Xalan-perfunctory "`-`").

Table 13–2 Xalan-J arguments and flags to be invoked at runtime

Argument	*Action/Effect*
`-IN` *filename*	Input filename.
`-XSL` *filename*	XSL transformation URL.
`-OUT` *filename*	Output filename.
`-LXCIN` *filename*	Compiled stylesheet filename in.
`-LXCOUT` *filename*	Compiled stylesheet filename out.
`-PARSER` *classname*	Fully qualified class name of parser liaison.
`-V`	Displays version information.
`-QC`	Quiet pattern conflicts warning.
`-Q`	Quiet mode.
`-LF`	Use linefeeds only on output; default is CR/LF.
`-CR`	Use carriage returns only on output; default is CR/LF.
`-INDENT` *number*	Number of spaces to indent each level in output tree; default is 0.
`-TT`	Trace the templates as they are being called.
`-TG`	Trace each result tree generation event.
`-TS`	Trace each selection event.
`-TTC`	Trace the template children as they are being processed.

Table 13–2 Xalan-J arguments and flags to be invoked at runtime (continued)

Argument	*Action/Effect*
`-VALIDATE`	Validate the XML and XSL input; validation is off by default.
`-EDUMP` *filename*	Do stackdump on error, output to optional filename.
`-XML`	Use XML formatter and add XML header.
`-TEXT`	Use simple text formatter.
`-HTML`	Use HTML formatter.
`-PARAM` *name expression*	Set a stylesheet parameter.

13.1.6 Xalan-J Extensions

Xalan-J has three built-in extension elements that together provide the functionality to send the output to several different files from a single input XML document instance. These elements are `<redirect:open>`, `<redirect:write>`, `<redirect:close>` and, together, are called the Xalan-J Redirect Extension. In addition, Xalan-J implements two extension elements, `<lxslt:script>` and `<lxslt:component>`, that allow user-defined extensions to be processed. The Xalan-J namespace must be declared on or before the Xalan-J extension elements as follows:

```
xmlns:lxslt="http://xml.apache.org/xslt"
```

Because the Xalan-J product was originally an implementation of the LotusXSL product, that namespace can also be used as follows:

```
xmlns:lxslt="http://xsl.lotus.com/"
```

13.1.6.1 Xalan-J Redirect Extension

The Redirect extension includes three elements that redirect portions of your XSLT stylesheet output to multiple files: `<redirect:open>`,

<redirect:write>, and <redirect:close>. If you use the <redirect:write> element alone, the extension opens a file, writes to it, and closes the file immediately. If you want direct control over the opening and closing of files while your XSLT stylesheet is being processed by Xalan, use the <redirect:open> and <redirect:close> elements.

When the redirect extension elements are used, the redirect namespace should be declared, in addition to the Xalan-J namespace, using the following declaration:

```
xmlns:redirect="org.apache.xalan.xslt.extensions.Redirect"
```

Note that the redirect prefix should also be added the the extension-element-prefixes attribute on the document element. The following element model defiinitions show the structure of each of these elements:

```
<!-- Category: extension-element -->
<redirect:write
select = expression
  file = string >
 <!-- content: (template) -->
</redirect:write>
<!-- Category: extension-element -->
<redirect:open
  select = expression
  file = string
/>
<!-- Category: extension-element -->
<redirect:close
  select = expression
  file = string
/>
```

Each of these elements includes an optional file attribute and/or an optional select attribute to designate the output file. If you use file, this attribute requires a string. It can be used to directly specify the output filename, in a sense "hardwiring" it. The select attribute takes an XPath expression, so you can use it to dynamically generate the output filename with the evaluation of the contents of the expression. Using both attributes causes the Redirect implementation to first evaluate the value of the select attribute. This is a sort of contingency processing model, as

Xalan-J "falls back" to the string value of the `file` attribute if the `select` attribute expression does not return a valid filename.

The `<redirect:open>` and `<redirect:close>` elements must be used together. Both elements are empty, but the `<redirect:close>` element acts as a closing tag for the `<redirect:open>` element. The file that is opened with `<redirect:open>` must be closed with an `<redirect:close>` element with the same `file` or `select` attribute value.

Example 13–1, from the Xalan-J documentation,[3] shows the use of the Redirect extentions.

13.1.6.2 Xalan-J User-Defined Extensions

The Xalan-J namespace provides support for the `<lxslt:component>` extension element and its `<lxslt:script>` sub-element. Together these elements allow users to define their own extensions that will be implemented by the Xalan-J processor.

13.1.6.3 The Xalan-J `<lxslt:component>` Extension Element

The `<lxslt:component>` element is used to define the prefix for a user-defined namespace, as well as the names of any extension functions or elements that are being created. It has three attributes, prefix, functions, and elements. The following element model definition shows the structure of the `<lxslt:component>` element:

```
<!-- Category: extension-element -->
<lxslt:component
  prefix= prefix
  functions="func-1 func-2 ...func-n"
  elements="elem-1 elem-2 ...elem-n"
  namespace-uri = string >
  <!-- content: (lxslt:script) -->
</lxslt:component>
```

This element contains the `<lxslt:script>` element used to define the extension function or element. The `prefix` attribute is used to specify the

3. This is from the Xalan-Java Class Redirect.htm file in the Xalan-J documentation.

Example 13–1 : Using Redirect with Xalan.

```
<?xml version="1.0"?>
<xsl:stylesheet xmlns:xsl="http://www.w3.org/XSL/Transform/1.0"
     version="1.0"
     xmlns:lxslt="http://xml.apache.org/xslt"
     xmlns:redirect="org.apache.xalan.xslt.extensions.Redirect"
     extension-element-prefixes="redirect">

   <xsl:template match="/">
     <out>
       default output.
     </out>
     <redirect:open file="doc3.out"/>
     <redirect:write file="doc3.out">
       <out>
         <redirect:write file="doc1.out">
           <out>
             doc1 output.
             <redirect:write file="doc3.out">
               Some text to doc3
             </redirect:write>
           </out>
         </redirect:write>
         <redirect:write file="doc2.out">
           <out>
             doc2 output.
             <redirect:write file="doc3.out">
               Some more text to doc3
               <redirect:write select="doc/foo">
                 text for doc4
               </redirect:write>
             </redirect:write>
           </out>
         </redirect:write>
       </out>
     </redirect:write>
     <redirect:close file="doc3.out"/>
   </xsl:template>
</xsl:stylesheet>
```

namespace prefix for the user-defined functions. The functions attribute is used to specify the names of the extension functions being defined, and the elements attribute is used to specify the names of the extension elements being defined. Both functions and elements attributes are required. The values for the functions and elements attributes are a list of names separated by whitespace. The namespace-uri attribute is used to specify a URI for the namespace prefix specified in the prefix attribute.

The Xalan-J documentation provides the following implicit DTD fragment for <lxslt:component>.

```
<!ELEMENT lxslt:component (lxslt:script)>
<!ATTLIST lxslt:component
  prefix CDATA #IMPLIED
  namespace-uri CDATA #IMPLIED
  elements NMTOKENS #REQUIRED
  functions NMTOKENS #REQUIRED>
```

13.1.6.4 The Xalan-J <lxslt:script> Extension Element

For each <lxslt:component> element you must include an <lxslt:script> element to define the extension element or function. The <lxslt:script> element is similar to the <xsl:script> element specified in the XSLT 1.1 WD.[4] It has two attributes: lang and script. The following element model definition shows the structure of the <lxslt:script> element:

```
<!-- Category: top-level-extension-element -->
<lxslt:script
  lang = string

  src = string >
<!-- content: (#PCDATA) -->

/>
```

4. See http://www.w3.org/TR/xslt11.

The `lang` attribute is used to specify the name of the scripting language that the function uses, and the `src` attribute is used to specify the fully qualified class name. For example, if the extension is implemented in Java, the `lang` would be `javaclass`, the `src` would be the class name, and the `<lxslt:script>` element would be empty, as follows:

```
<lxslt:script lang="javaclass" src="classname"/>
```

If the extension is implemented in JavaScript, the `lang` would be `javaScript`, and the `<lxslt:script>` element would contain the JavaScript code. Example 13–2 from the Xalan-J documentation shows an example of a JavaScript implementation.

Example 13–2 : Using `<lxslt:script>` to define an extension using JavaScript.

```
<lxslt:component prefix="counter"
                 elements="init incr" functions="read">
  <lxslt:script lang="javascript">
    var counters = new Array();

    function init (xslproc, elem) {
      name = elem.getAttribute ("name");
      value = parseInt(elem.getAttribute ("value"));
      counters[name] = value;
      return null;
    }

    function read (name) {
      // Return a string.
      return "" + (counters[name]);
    }

    function incr (xslproc, elem)
    {
      name = elem.getAttribute ("name");
      counters[name]++;
      return null;
    }
  </lxslt:script>
</lxslt:component>
```

The new extension elements and function can then be used in a template as shown in Example 13–3.

Example 13–3 : Using Xalan-J with User-defined Extensions.

```
<xsl:template match="/">
    <HTML>
      <H1>Names in alphatebical order</H1>
      <counter:init name="index" value="1"/>
      <xsl:for-each select="doc/name">
        <xsl:sort select="@last"/>
        <xsl:sort select="@first"/>
        <p>
        <xsl:text>[</xsl:text>
        <xsl:value-of select="counter:read('index')"/>
        <xsl:text>]. </xsl:text>
        <xsl:value-of select="@last"/>
        <xsl:text>, </xsl:text>
        <xsl:value-of select="@first"/>
        </p>
        <counter:incr name="index"/>
      </xsl:for-each>
    </HTML>
  </xsl:template>
```

13.2 Saxon

Michael Kay has contributed what might be considered one of the most robust and versatile XSLT processors with his Saxon product. It has one of the largest sets of built-in extension top-level elements, instruction elements, and functions. It also runs on Java and is regularly updated at the source Web site, http://users.iclway.co.uk/mhkay/saxon.

Saxon includes a servlet that allows it to be invoked directly from a URL entered into a browser. You might think of Saxon as the "programmer's XSLT processor," due to its extended documentation for adding extensions, event handlers, and so forth (see the *api-guide.html* file in the Saxon user documentation).

The Saxon XSLT processor is available in two forms, a "complete" Saxon API for Java, and a simple command-line version of the processor, called Instant Saxon.

The complete Saxon API contains a Java library, which supports a similar processing model to XSL, but allows full programming capability, which you need if you want to perform complex processing of the data or to access external services such as a relational database. It includes a typical set of `.jar` files that are added to the CLASSPATH environment, and also contains utilities such as a DTD generator and other goodies, including documentation.

The simple version, Instant Saxon, runs straight from a Windows command-line. The Microsoft JVM must be installed on the system prior to using Instant Saxon. However, if you use Internet Explorer 4 or later, the JVM will already be on your system. The Instant Saxon installation does not emphasize the extras or the documentation, so it may be worth downloading both versions just to get these. The Instant Saxon installation comes bundled with the AElfred XML parser from Microstar.[5]

13.2.1 Installing Full Saxon on Solaris/UNIX or Windows Java

If you are installing the full Saxon product, you will need the JDK 1.2 (1.1.6+ will do, but is not recommended). Kay notes that the current version is compiled with Java 2 and will run with 1.1, but will not compile under 1.1. If you do not use the default Aelfred parser included with Saxon, you will also need a SAX1 or SAX2 parser, such as XP.

The core program for working with objects is a JAR file, `saxon.jar`, which you must include on your CLASSPATH.We will continue to work with the model introduced above, which assumes you will put this in a `/usr/bin` directory, likely called `/usr/bin/saxon`.

You can find additional user documentation, covering both the XSLT and Java interfaces, included in the Saxon package as JAVADOC specifications. These package summaries give an overview in the form of a user guide. In addition, there is an introductory overview, included with the documentation provided with Saxon.

Saxon comes with a bundled XML parser, a modified copy of the AElfred parser, adapted to notify comments to the application. Saxon has been tested successfully in the past with Lark, MSXML, SUN Project X, Oracle XML, Xerces, xml4j, and XP. Use of a SAX2-compliant parser is preferred,

5. See www.microstar.com.

as SAX1 does not allow XML comments to be passed to the application. However, Saxon works with either. All the relevant classes must be installed on your Java CLASSPATH. The following examples assume that you will use the default `xp.jar` XML processor and that you have put it in your directory with Saxon.

At the very least, you must include `saxon.jar` and `xp.jar` on the system CLASSPATH. Thus, where you had a basic " . ", you would modify it as follows:

```
set CLASSPATH=/usr/bin/saxon/xp.jar:/usr/bin/saxon/saxon.jar:.
```

Use the above for your `.cshrc` on Solaris/UNIX; or for an `autoexec.bat` file on Windows, do the same syntax, but remember to use the semicolon (`;`) and reverse slash (\).

```
setenv CLASSPATH=/usr/bin/saxon/xp.jar:/usr/bin/saxon/saxon.jar:.
```

To run full Saxon, unless you've attached some applet wrapper or invoked it from a URL in a browser (in which case, you should review the Saxon documentation *index.html* file), open a command line window and run it with the following syntax:

```
saxon [options] source.xml stylesheet.xsl [params . . .]
```

13.2.2 Installing Instant Saxon on Windows

All you need to install Instant Saxon is the download zip file located at http://users.iclway.co.uk/mhkay/saxon. You do not need to add any extra parsers or to modify PATH or CLASSPATH environment variables, provided you have IE 4+ (IE 5 recommended) on your Windows 95, 98, or NT/2000 machine. Unzip the file in the directory where you plan to use Saxon and you are ready to go.

To run Instant Saxon on Windows, use a command-line or DOS window (select Start, Run, and type cmd) and run it with the following syntax:

```
saxon [options] input.xml stylesheet.xsl [params . . .]
```

Options and parameters for Instant Saxon are described in the following sections. The `input.xml` and `stylesheet.xsl` represent filenames for the input XML document and the XSL stylesheet being used, respectively.

13.2.3 Saxon Options

Saxon has a number of command-line options that are used when invoking Saxon with an XSLT stylesheet (see Table 13–3). The options must precede the `input.xml` and the `stylesheet.xsl` filenames on the command-line:

```
saxon [options] input.xml stylesheet.xsl [params . . .]
```

Table 13–3 Command-line options for Saxon

Argument	*Action/Effect*
`-a`	Used with XML documents that directly contain a stylesheet. This means that the filename for the stylesheet on the command line is not required. See Chapter 2, Section 2.7 for more information on including XSLT stylesheets in an XML document.
`-ds | -dt`	Selects which internal tree model is to be used. -dt (which is the default) selects the "tinytree" model, and -ds selects the traditional tree model.
`-l`	Saxon implements a line numbering function `saxon:line-number()`, to access the line number for each line in the input document. This option enables (turns on) the line numbering for the source document.
-m classname	Used with the `<xsl:message>` element to control the output of messages as a new document. Must be used with the com.icl.saxon.output.Emitter class.

Table 13–3 Command-line options for Saxon (continued)

Argument	*Action/Effect*
`-r` classname	Used with the `document()` function in the `<xsl:include>` and `<xsl:import>` elements to resolve URIs into a source document. Also used with the -u option to process the URIs of the input file and stylesheet file provided on the command-line.
`-o` filename	Used to provide a filename for the output from the processor. This option checks the extension of the filename provided to determine the output file type if one is not explicitly specified with the method attribute of `<xsl:output>`.
`-t`	Displays the version and timing information.
`-T`	Displays stylesheet tracing information. Also enables (turns on) the line numbering for the source document.
`-TL` classname	Signals the processor to use a TraceListener. The name of a user-defined class, which must implement com.icl.saxon.trace.TraceListener, is specified with the classname.
`-u`	Provides the ability to use URLs for the input and stylesheet filenames on the command line. If the filenames start with "http:" or "file:" they are assumed to be URLs, and this option is not required.

Table 13–3 Command-line options for Saxon (continued)

Argument	*Action/Effect*
`-w0, w1, or w2`	Saxon implements 3 levels of recovery when an error occurs. The level can be specified on the command-line as: w0 - recover silently, w1 - recover after writing out a warning message w2 - signal the error and do not attempt recovery The default is `w1`.
`-x` classname	The SAX parser used to process the XML files can be specified using this option. The classname specifies a Java class that implements the org.xml.sax.Parser or org.xml.sax.XML-Reader interface.
`-y` classname	The SAX parser used to process the XSLT files can be specified using this option. The classname specifies a Java class that implements the org.xml.sax.Parser or org.xml.sax.XMLReader interface.
`-?`	Displays the help for Saxon's command-line syntax.

13.2.4 Saxon Command-line Parameters

Saxon provides the ability to submit parameter values through the command-line at run-time to update global parameters defined in the stylesheet with the `<xsl:param>` top-level element. The parameters must follow the filenames for the input XML document and the XSLT stylesheet on the command-line as follows:

```
saxon [options] input.xml stylesheet.xsl [params . . .]
```

A parameter value is passed to the stylesheet in the form *name=value*, where *name* is the name of the parameter defined in the stylesheet with `<xsl:param>`, and *value* is the new value for the parameter. If the parameter is not declared in the stylesheet, the parameter from the command-line is ignored. Parameter values that contain spaces should be surrounded with double quotes on the command-line.

13.2.5 Saxon Extensions

Saxon includes what is one of the largest collections of built-in extensions. They include extension top-level elements, extension functions, extension attributes, and extension instruction elements. The following material is excerpted and annotated from the material included from the current download of Saxon (this is from the *extensions.html* file in the Saxon documentation). The most up-to-date documentation is available at http://users.iclway.co.uk/mhkay/saxon/. Kay provides the following preface to users of the Saxon extensions:

> These extension functions and elements have been provided because there are things that are difficult to achieve, or inefficient, using standard XSLT facilities alone. As always, it is best to stick to standard if you possibly can: and most things are possible, even if it's not obvious at first sight.

13.2.5.1 Saxon Attribute Extensions

Saxon implements the following extension attributes: trace, allow-avt, disable-output-escaping,[6] method,[7] indent-spaces, character-representation, omit-meta-tag, and next-in-chain.

---

6. The `disable-output-escaping` attribute has been implemented in the XSLT specification and is no longer a Saxon extension.
7. The method attribute is from the XSLT1.0 specification, but Saxon adds support for QName values.

The use of the Saxon extension attributes requires that the Saxon namespace be declared either in the document element, an element that uses the extension, or an ancestor of the element that uses the extension. The Saxon namespace is declared using the following format:

```
xmlns:saxon="http://icl.com/saxon"
```

The `saxon:trace` *Extension Attribute*

This attribute can be used on either the document element or an `<xsl:template>` element, and turns on echoing of the instantiation for each template rule. The reporting is sent to the standard error output, whether the command-line or a GUI window, as implemented by the application.

If you use this attribute on the document element, all the top-level elements are listed along with their import precedence. All contained template rules are then traced as well. The default value for `saxon:trace` is no, as shown in the following attribute model definition:

```
EXTENSION ATTRIBUTE:  saxon:trace (yes|no) "no"
VALUE = (yes|no) "no"
```

Use this attribute on either the `<xsl:stylesheet>` or `<xsl:transform>` document elements, or a template rule as follows:

```
<xsl:template match="block" saxon:trace="yes">
```

The `saxon:allow-avt` *Extension Attribute*

This extension attribute is used with the `<xsl:call-template>` instruction element. This attribute lets the value given for the `name` attribute of `<xsl:call-template>` to be interpreted as an attribute value template, when the value is surrounded by curly-braces { } (see Chapter 6, Section 6.6.1). Since attribute value templates are not normally allowed as the value for the `name` in `<xsl:call-template>`, adding the extension attribute will prevent a processor error. The default value for `saxon:allow-avt` is no, as shown in the following attribute model definition:

```
EXTENSION ATTRIBUTE:  saxon:allow-avt (yes|no) "no"
VALUE = (yes|no) "no"
```

Use the `saxon:allow-avt` attribute as follows to permit AVT's in the value for `name`:

```
        <xsl:call-template name="{$some_variable}"
    saxon:allow-avt="yes" >
```

The `saxon:disable-output-escaping` *Extension Attribute*

The `disable-output-escaping` attribute has been implemented in the XSLT specification and is no longer a Saxon extension. Its use can be found in Chapter 3 in conjunction with the `<xsl:value-of>` element, and Chapter 6 in conjunction with the `<xsl:text>` element.

The `method` *Attribute with Saxon*

The `method` attribute of `<xsl:output>` and `<xsl:document>` is not an extension attribute, but its value can contain a QName that is governed by a processor. The prefix of the QName must be a valid namespace prefix. We use `saxon` as the prefix in the following examples, however it can be any valid prefix. Saxon implements the method attribute with the values shown in Table 13–4.

Table 13–4 Values of QNames Implemented by the Saxon processor[a]

QName	*Action*
Saxon:fop	Directs output to Apache's FOP processor (which must be installed separately from www.apache.org), which implements the developing W3C formatting objects, or FO, portion of XSLT.
Saxon:xhtml	Outputs the result tree in XHTML format. This follows the same rules as method="xml," except that it follows the guidelines for making the XML acceptable to legacy HTML browsers. Specifically (a) empty elements such as are output as , and (b) empty elements such as <p/> are output as <p></p>. The indent attribute defaults to "yes," and indenting follows the HTML rather than XML rules. Other attributes may be specified as for XML output, e.g. cdata-section-elements and omit-xml-declaration.

Table 13–4 Values of QNames implemented by the Saxon processor[a] (continued)

QName	*Action*
Saxon:classname	The fully qualified class name of a class that implements either the SAX org.xml.sax.DocumentHandler interface, or the SAX2 org.xml.sax.ContentHandler interface, or that is a subclass of the com.icl.saxon.output.Emitter class. If such a value is specified, output is directed to the user-supplied class.

a. The information for this table comes directly from the Saxon 6.2.2 documentation.

Use the `method` attribute as follows:

```
<xsl:output method="saxon:fop"/>
```

The `saxon:indent-spaces` Extension Attribute

The `saxon:indent-spaces` controls the amount of indentation that is generated when the file output method is XML or HTML, and indent is set to yes on either `<xsl:output>` or `<xsl:document>` elements. The value of the attribute must be an integer.

The value for `saxon:indent-spaces` is a number, as shown in the following attribute model definition:

```
EXTENSION ATTRIBUTE:  saxon:indent-spaces NMTOKEN #IMPLIED
VALUE = Number
```

Use the `saxon:indent-spaces` attribute as follows:

```
<xsl:output saxon:indent-spaces="10"/>
```

The `saxon:character-representation` Extension Attribute

This attribute is used with `<xsl:output>` or `<xsl:document>`, and controls how non-ASCII characters are represented in the output. It works with the two method values, `xml` and `html`.

When used with the `xml` method, its value can be either `decimal` or `hex`.

When used with the `html` method, the value has two strings, separated by a semicolon. The first string controls how non-ASCII characters within the character encoding is represented, the values being `native`, `entity`, `decimal`, or `hex`. The second string controls how characters outside the encoding will be represented, the values being `entity`, `decimal`, or `hex`.

The value for `saxon:character-representation` is a string, as shown in the following attribute model definition:

```
EXTENSION ATTRIBUTE:  saxon:character-representation CDATA #IMPLIED
VALUE = String
```

Use the `saxon:character-representation` attribute as follows:

```
<xsl:output method="xml" saxon:character-representation="hex"/>
```

The `saxon:omit-meta-tag` *Extension Attribute*

This attribute is used with `<xsl:output>` and the `html` method. The normal action of the `html` output method is to generate a <META> tag immediately after the <HEAD> tag, containing details of the media type and character encoding. Setting this attribute to "yes" causes this output to be suppressed.

The values for `saxon:omit-meta-tag` are yes or no, as shown in the following attribute model definition:

```
EXTENSION ATTRIBUTE:  saxon:omit-meta-tag (yes|no) "no"
VALUE = (yes|no) "no"
```

Use the `saxon:omit-meta-tag` attribute as follows:

```
<xsl:output method="html" saxon:omit-meta-tag="yes"/>
```

The `saxon:next-in-chain` *Attribute*

The saxon:next-in-chain attribute is used with either <xsl:output> or <xsl:document> to direct the output to another stylesheet. The output is then used as the input for the new stylesheet. The value of the attribute is the URL of the new stylesheet. The output stream must always be pure XML, and attributes that control the format of the output (e.g., method, cdata-section-elements, etc.) will be ignored. The output of the second stylesheet will be directed to the destination that would have been used for the first stylesheet if no saxon:next-in-chain attribute were present. When used with <xsl:output>, the original transformation result destination is used. When used with <xsl:document>, the file specified by the href attribute is used. The value for saxon:next-in-chain is a URL, as shown in the following attribute model definition:

```
EXTENSION ATTRIBUTE:  saxon:next-in-chain CDATA
#IMPLIED
VALUE = URL
```

Use the saxon:next-in-chain attribute as follows:

```
<xsl:output saxon:next-in-chain="http://mystyles/newstyle.xsl"/>
```

13.2.5.2 Saxon Extension Elements

Saxon adds four top-level extension elements: <saxon:handler>, <saxon:preview>, <saxon:function>, and <saxon:script>, as well as eight instruction extension elements: <saxon:assign>, <saxon:doctype>, <saxon:entity-ref>, <saxon:group>, <saxon:item>, <saxon:output>, <saxon:return>, and <saxon:while>.

To use Saxon extension elements, their namespace must be declared and the extension-element-prefixes attribute on the document element must include the saxon value.

All these extensions are available to either full Saxon or Instant Saxon. However, to use the external Java calls as with <saxon:output> you may need the accompanying documentation, which comes with full Saxon.

The `<saxon:handler>` *Top-Level Extension Element*

The `<saxon:handler>` top-level extension element is similar to `<xsl:template>`, and has the same uses for the `match`, `mode`, `name`, and `priority` attributes, as shown in the following element model definition:

```
<!-- Category: top-level-extension-element -->
<saxon:handler

 handler = classname
  match = pattern
  name = qname
  priority = number
  mode = qname>
/>
```

This element is sorted for precedence of instantiation in equal standing with any other `<xsl:template>` element. Its function is to call a user-written JavaNodeHandler with the mandatory `handler` attribute. The JavaNodeHandler and the `<saxon:handler>` element are explained in detail in the Saxon documentation (begin with the *extensions.html* file in the Saxon documentation).

The `<saxon:preview>` *Top-Level Extension Element*

This top-level extension element is designed to facilitate more efficient handling of large documents. In the traditional XSLT stylesheet processing model, each template rule is evaluated for a match to determine if it will be instantiated in turn. This means that the entire input XML document instance is parsed for a match for every single template rule—very time- and system-resource consuming.

With `<saxon:preview>`, the relevant parts of the input source, those which find the template match, are processed as soon as they are parsed, then removed from the virtual document tree, saving on memory resources. In effect, it is possible to break the transformation of the document source into a series of separate smaller transformations. The elements listed in the mandatory `elements` attribute are "disregarded" by the Saxon processor after they have been treated according to whatever mode has been stipulated in the mandatory `mode` attribute. The results are written to the output result tree, but those elements in the input XML document instance are ignored in subsequent evaluation of other templates in the XSLT stylesheet. The following element model definition shows the structure of `<saxon:preview>`.

```
<!-- Category: top-level-extension-element -->
<saxon:preview
  mode = qname
  elements = qnames >
  <!-- Content: (xsl:param*, template) -->
</saxon:preview>
```

The `<saxon:preview>` element can be used to simply weed out undesired input elements by using it as a template that does nothing—in other words, give it no children instruction elements, only the list of elements to be ignored for that mode.

The `<saxon:function>` Top-Level Extension Element

The top-level `<saxon:function>` extension element is used to declare an extension function. It contains a template, preceded by zero or more `<xsl:param>` elements. It has a required `name` attribute whose value is a QName, evaluating to a URI, as shown in the following element model definition:

```
<!-- Category: top-level-extension-element -->
<saxon:function
  name = qname >
  <!-- Content: (xsl:param*, template?,
saxon:return*, xsl:fallback?) -->
</saxon:function>
```

The function definition contains zero or more `<saxon:return>` instructions to define the return value. The Saxon documentation provides additional information for defining functions using the <saxon:function> element.

An example of using <saxon:function> from the Saxon Documentation is as follows:

```
<saxon:function name="my:initial">
    <xsl:param name="size"/>
    <saxon:return select="substring(.,1,$size)"/>
</saxon:function>
<xsl:template match="text()">
    <xsl:value-of select="my:initial(3)"/>
</xsl:template>
```

The <saxon:script> *Top-Level Extension Element*

The <saxon:script> element is a top-level element that is equal to <xsl:script>, defined in XSLT 1.1 WD. The reason Saxon provides this element is so it can be used in stylesheets that are shared and used with different processors. Any processor other than Saxon will ignore this element.

For example, to use an extension function like xx:intersection(), you can define the Saxon implementation as follows:

```
<saxon:script implements-prefix="xx" language="java"
     src="java:com.icl.saxon.functions.Extensions">
```

The following element model definition shows the structure of the <saxon:script> element:

```
<!-- Category: top-level-extension-element -->
<saxon:script
  implements-prefix = ncname
  language = "ecmascript" | "javascript" | "java" |
qname-but-not-ncname
  src = uri-reference
  archive = uri-references >
  <!-- Content: #PCDATA -->
</saxon:script>
```

The `<saxon:assign>` *Extension Element*

This function provides a very useful feature that allows XSLT variables and parameters to be dynamically updated in the context of a template rule. Currently, XSLT variables and parameters, as codified in the W3C specification, cannot be updated other than in the case of a parameter with the use of `<xsl:with-param>`, which has limited uses. For example, you might have a declared variable of `birthday` that has been assigned to a variable as follows:

```
<xsl:variable name="birthday" select="{@date}" />
```

You can then update it to make an employee password a combination of start date, Social Security number, and birthdate.

```
<xsl:template match="password">
      <xsl:attribute>
            <xsl:value-of select="@ssn" />
            <saxon:assign name="birthday"
            expr="concat($birthday, @start-date" />
      </xsl:attribute>
</xsl:template>
```

This extension instruction element can also contain a template, as shown in the element model definition below:

```
<!-- Category: instruction-extension-element -->
<saxon:assign
  name = qname
  select = node-set-expression >
  <!-- Content: (template) -->
</saxon:assign>
```

The variable being updated must have been defined using the extension attribute `saxon:assignable="yes"`. The value of the variable is determined either using the `select` attribute or by instantiating the template it contains.

The `<saxon:doctype>` *Extension Element*

The `<saxon:doctype>` instruction element is used to insert a document type declaration into the current output file. It has no attributes, and its content is a template, as shown in the element model definition below.

The template is instantiated to create an XML document that represents the DTD to be generated.

> **NOTE** If this element is present the `doctype-system` and `doctype-public` attributes of `<xsl:output>` are ignored.

```
<!-- Category: instruction-extension-element -->
<saxon:doctype>
  <!-- Content: (template) -->
</saxon:doctype>
```

The Saxon documentation provides detailed information on the output format and usage of the `<saxon:doctype>` element. An example of using `<saxon:doctype>` from the Saxon documentation is as follows:

```
<xsl:template match="/">
  <saxon:doctype xsl:extension-element-prefixes="saxon">
  <dtd:doctype name="booklist"
       xmlns:dtd="http://icl.com/saxon/dtd" xsl:exclude-result-
prefixes="dtd">
    <dtd:element name="booklist" content="(book)*"/>
    <dtd:element name="book" content="EMPTY"/>
    <dtd:attlist element="book">
      <dtd:attribute name="isbn" type="ID" value="#REQUIRED"/>
      <dtd:attribute name="title" type="CDATA" value="#IMPLIED"/>
    </dtd:attlist>
    <dtd:entity name="blurb">'A <i>cool</i> book with &gt;
200 pictures!'</dtd:entity>
    <dtd:entity name="cover" system="cover.gif" notation="GIF"
    <dtd:notation name="GIF" system="http://gif.org/"/>
  </dtd:doctype>
  </saxon:doctype>
  <xsl:apply-templates/>
</xsl:template>
```

The `<saxon:entity-ref>` *Extension Element*

This instruction element allows HTML entities such as ` ` to be generated in HTML output when the `<xsl:output>` top-level element has a `method` attribute of `html`. Use the element as follows:

```
<saxon:entity-ref name="nbsp" />
```

This empty element has one required attribute, `name`, as shown in the element model definition below:

```
<!-- Category: instruction-extension-element -->
<saxon:entity-ref
 name = qname
/>
```

The <saxon:group> *Extension Element*

The grouping mechanism provided by <saxon:group> allows iteration over nodes selected in an expression returning a node-set. The required `select` attribute is used to define the nodes which will be used for the iteration, as shown in the following element model definition:

```
<!-- Category: instruction-extension-element -->
<saxon:group
  select = node-set-expression
  group-by = string >
  <!-- Content: (xsl:sort*, template?, saxon:item, template?) -->
</saxon:group>
```

This instruction element is similar in function to <xsl:for-each>. It also requires a `group-by` attribute to determine how the grouping is to be done whose value is a string expression that is applied to each item selected under the `select` attribute. This element can have <xsl:sort> children and must have a <saxon:item> children (see the section immediately below). The other instructions contained in <saxon:group> are performed once for each item in the group selected by the `select` attribute of the parent <saxon:group>.

The <saxon:item> *Extension Element*

This element is the required child of the <saxon:group> element, and stipulates the items within a group. XSLT instructions outside of <saxon:item> are executed once for each group that qualifies in the `group-by` attribute of the <saxon:group>. The XSLT instructions that are *children* of <saxon:item> are executed once per item. This element has no attributes, and contains a template, as shown in the element model definition below:

```
<!-- Category: extension-element -->
<saxon:item>
  <!-- Content: (template) -->
</saxon:item>
```

The <saxon:output> Extension Element

This element allows redirection of output to different files of all result tree nodes produced within the <saxon:output> tags. After its contents have been executed and placed in the respective files, the output destination reverts back to the previous output destination stipulated when the XSLT stylesheet was invoked. This element is equal to the <xsl:document> element that is specified in XML 1.1 WD, which is implemented by many processors. Note that in previous versions of Saxon, <saxon:output> had additional functionality that has been removed. The <saxon:output> element is shown in the following element model definition:

```
<!-- Category: instruction-element -->
<saxon:output
  href = { uri-reference }
  method = { "xml" | "html" | "text" | qname-but-not-ncname }
  version = { nmtoken }
  encoding = { string }
  omit-xml-declaration = { "yes" | "no" }
  standalone = { "yes" | "no" }
  doctype-public = { string }
  doctype-system = { string }
  cdata-section-elements = { qnames }
  indent = { "yes" | "no" }
  media-type = { string } >
  <!-- Content: (template) -->
</saxon:output>
```

The <saxon:return> Extension Element

The <saxon:return> element is used to exit from a function, and provides a return value. It is only used within a <saxon:function> element, and it must not have any following sibling instructions other than <xsl:fallback>. However, there can be more than one

<xsl:return> instruction in a function, for example, one in each branch of an <xsl:choose>.

The <saxon:return> element has one optional select attribute, whose value is an expression. The expression is evaluated and its value is sent as the return value of the function. If the select attribute is not used, the template in the <saxon:return> element is instantiated and the result is returned as a result tree fragment. The following element model definition shows the structure of the <saxon:return> element.

```
<!-- Category: extension-element -->
<saxon:return
  select = expression >
  <!-- Content: (template) -->
</saxon:return>
```

The <saxon:while> Extension Element

This element adds an iteration feature that processes as long as some given condition is true. The condition is a Boolean expression in the mandatory test attribute. To prevent endless looping, the <saxon:assign> element is required as a child to <saxon:while> and sets a variable that is updated at some point in the loop in order to terminate it.

```
<!-- Category: instruction-extension-element -->
<saxon:while
test = expression >
  <!-- Content: (template?, saxon:assign, template?) -->
</saxon:while>
```

An example of using <saxon:while>, from the Saxon documentation, is as follows:

```
<xsl:variable name="i" expr="0"/>
<saxon:while test="$i &lt; 10">
    The value of i is <xsl:value-of select="$i"/>
    <saxon:assign name="i" expr="$i+1"/>
</saxon:while>
```

13.2.5.3 Saxon Extension Functions

Saxon implements twenty-seven extension functions, ranging in application from basic existence to conditional functions. These functions include: saxon:after(), saxon:before(), saxon:difference(), saxon:distinct(), saxon:evaluate(), saxon:eval(), saxon:exists(), saxon:expression(), saxon:forAll(), saxon:getUserData(), saxon:hasSameNodes(), saxon:highest(), saxon:if(), saxon:ifNull(), saxon:intersection(), saxon:leading(), saxon:lineNumber(), saxon:lowest(), saxon:max(), saxon:min(), saxon:nodeSet(), saxon:path(), saxon:range(), saxon:setUserData(), saxon:sum(), saxon:systemId(), and saxon:tokenize().

To invoke a Saxon function, the Saxon namespace must be declared at or above the element calling the function. A typical use of a Saxon extension function is shown below:

```
<xsl:template match="something">
      <xsl:apply-templates
            select="saxon:distinct($some_nodeset)" >
</xsl:template>
```

More details about these functions and updates for newly added functions are available at http://users.iclway.co.uk/mhkay/saxon.

The documentation notes that these extension functions have a very simple source code for the most part which can be used as templates, or models, by users for writing their own extensions.

The after() *Extension Function*

Function: *node-set* **after** *(node-set-1, node-set-2)*

The after() function returns a node-set with all the nodes in node-set-2 that follow (in document order) at least one node of node-set-1. Its function return type is node-set, and it contains two node-set arguments.

The before() *Extension Function*

Function: *node-set* **before** *(node-set-1, node-set-2)*

The before() function returns a node-set with all the nodes in node-set-2 that precede (in document order) at least one node of node-set-1. Its function return type is node-set, and it contains two required node-set arguments.

The `difference()` *Extension Function*

Function: *node-set* **difference** *(node-set-1, node-set-2)*

The `difference()` function compares the two arguments and returns a node-set of those nodes in node-set-1 that are *not* in node-set-2. Its function return type is node-set, and it contains two required node-set arguments.

The `distinct()` *Extension Function*

Function: *node-set* **distinct** *(node-set-1, stored-expression)*

This function returns a node-set based on evaluating all the nodes in the set given in the first argument that a duplicate string value as the stored-expression in the second argument. Its function return type is node-set, and it contains two arguments, the first a required node-set and the second an optional string.

If the second argument is not used, the string that is used as a comparison is the string value of the current node. Every node following will be compared, removing any duplicates.

An example from the Saxon documentation is as follows:

```
<xsl:for-each select="saxon:distinct(surname,
saxon:expression('substring(.,1,1)')">
```

This function will process the first surname starting with each letter of the alphabet in turn.

The `eval()` *Extension Function*

Function: *string* **eval** *(stored-expression)*

The `eval()` function evaluates the expression stored as its argument and returns the string value of that expression. See the `saxon:expression()` function for information about generating stored-expressions. The function return type is string, and it contains one string argument, which is an expression. The following example comes from the Saxon documentation:

```
saxon:eval(saxon:expression(concat(2, $op, 2)))
```

The `evaluate()` *Extension Function*

Function: *string* **evaluate** *(string)*

This function evaluates the expression that is passed in as a string argument and returns its value as a string. This allows the calculation of a variable, for instance, at runtime, based on the evaluation of this expression. One use might be to dynamically determine a sort key for `<xsl:sort>` based on different contingencies for various input XML document instances. The function saxon:evaluate(string) is shorthand for saxon:eval(saxon:expression(string)).

The `exists()` *Extension Function*

Function: *boolean* **exists** *(node-set-1, stored-expression)*

The `exists()` function is used to test whether the value of the stored-expression in the second argument is true for any node in the node-set supplied in the first argument. The function return type is boolean, and it has two required arguments, a node-set and a string (expression).

The `expression()` *Extension Function*

Function: *string* **expression** *(string)*

This function is used to create a stored expression that can be used in other Saxon extension functions. It contains one required argument, a string which must be an expression. Its function return type is string.

The `forAll()` *Extension Function*

Function: *boolean* **forAll** *(node-set-1, stored-expression)*

This function tests each node in the node-set provided in the first argument against the expression in the second argument. If each node in the node-set evaluates to true, the function returns true. Otherwise it returns false. It has two required arguments, a node-set and a string (expression). Its function return type is Boolean.

An example of using this function, from the Saxon documentation, is as follows:

```
saxon:forAll(sale, saxon:expression('@price * @qty &gt; 1000'))
```

This will return true if for every child `<sale>` element of the context node, the product of price and qty exceeds 1000.

The `getUserData()` *Extension Function*

`Function:` *`string`* **`getUserData`** *`(string)`*

This function returns a string value of the predefined user data associated with the context node. The user data is predefined using the `saxon:setUserData()` function. It has one required argument, a string, and its function return type is a string.

The `hasSameNodes()` *Extension Function*

`Function:` *`boolean`* **`hasSameNodes`** *`(node-set-1, node-set-2)`*

The `has-same-nodes()` function returns a Boolean true if node-set-1 and node-set-2 have exactly the same nodes (not merely an intersection). This is different from the XSLT = operator, which only compares the string values of nodes. The function has two required arguments, both node-sets, and its function return type is Boolean.

The `highest()` *Extension Function*

`Function:` *`node-set`* **`highest`** *`(node-set1, stored-expression)`*

This function returns a node-set of the one node that has the highest numerical value, evaluated as if using the `number()` function. If the second argument is used, the expression is evaluated and the node that is returned is the one that has the highest value according to that expression. NaN values are ignored. The function has one required attribute, a node-set, and one optional argument, a string (expression). Its function return type is node-set.

An example of using this function, from the Saxon documentation, is as follows:

```
saxon:highest(sale, saxon:expression('@price * @qty'))
```

This will evaluate price times quantity for each child `<sale>` element, and return the node for which this has the highest value.

The `if()` *Extension Function*

`Function:` *`object`* **`if`** *`(condition, value1, value2)`*

This function allows conditionals as part of an XPath expression. The first argument must be a Boolean function, such as `contains()`, or a similar test. If it is true, then it returns the value of the first argument; if it is false, it returns the value of the second argument. The function has three arguments, the first is a Boolean, the second and third are of type object (they can be of any type, node-set, string, number, or Boolean). Its function return type is object, the same type as the value of the argument being returned.

The `ifNull()` *Extension Function*

Function: *boolean* **ifNull** *(java-object)*

This function returns true if the java-object provided as the required argument is null. Its function return type is Boolean, and its one required argument is of type string (java-object).

The `intersection()` *Extension Function*

Function: *node-set* **intersection** *(node-set-1, node-set-2)*

This function will return a node-set containing only those nodes common to both node-set-1 and node-set-2, and discards all others. The function has two required arguments, both node-sets, and its function return type is node-set.

An added convenience is that the arguments can be a union of tests with the | operator to test one of several node-sets. This is very handy to use, for instance, with keys, as it can determine what both arguments have in common.

The `leading()` *Extension Function*

Function: *node-set* **leading** *(node-set-1, stored-expression)*

This function evaluates the expression in the second argument and returns each node in the node-set of the first argument that evaluates to true, up to, but not including, the first node that returns a false value. The function has two required arguments, a node-set and a string (expression), and its function return type is node-set.

An example of using this function, from the Saxon documentation, is as follows:

```
saxon:leading(following-sibling::*, saxon:expression('self::para'))
```

This will return the `<para>` elements following the current node, stopping at the first element that is not a `<para>`.

The `lineNumber()` *Extension Function*

Function: *number* **lineNumber**()

This function is used to determine the line number, in document order, of the input XML document at the point where it is used. It can be used with

<xsl:message>, for instance, to diagnose where a match is or is not happening for a given template rule. The function has no arguments, and its function return type is a number.

Make sure line numbering is turned on by adding the -l option on the command-line.

The `lowest()` *Extension Function*

`Function:` *`node-set`* **`lowest`** *`(node-set-1, stored-expression)`*

This function returns a node-set of the one node that has the lowest numerical value, evaluated as if using the `number()` function. If the second argument is used, the expression is evaluated and the node that is returned is the one that has the lowest value according to that expression. NaN values are ignored. The function has one required attribute, a node-set, and one optional argument, a string (expression). Its function return type is node-set.

An example of using this function, from the Saxon documentation, is as follows:

```
saxon:lowest(sale, saxon:expression('@price * @qty'))
```

This will evaluate price times quantity for each child <sale> element, and return the node for which this has the lowest value.

The `max()` *Extension Function*

`Function:` *`number`* **`max`** *`(node-set-1, stored-expression)`*

This function returns a number which is the highest possible value of the evaluation of the expression in the second argument for each node in the node-set of the first argument. The `number()` function is used implicitly to evaluate the string value of each node prior to testing, and if there is no second argument, the highest value of that evaluation is returned. This function has one required argument, a node-set, and one optional argument, a string (expression). Its function return type is number.

An example of using this function, from the Saxon documentation, is as follows:

```
saxon:max(sale, saxon:expression('@price * @qty'))
```

This will evaluate price times quantity for each child <sale> element, and return the maximum amount.

The `min()` *Extension Function*

Function: *number* **min** *(node-set-1, stored-expression)*

This function returns a number which is the lowest possible value of the evaluation of the expression in the second argument for each node in the node-set of the first argument. The `number()` function is used implicitly to evaluate the string value of each node prior to testing, and if there is no second argument, the lowest value of that evaluation is returned. This function has one required argument, a node-set, and one optional argument, a string (expression). Its function return type is number.

An example of using this function, from the Saxon documentation, is as follows:

```
saxon:min(sale, saxon:expression('@price * @qty'))
```

This will evaluate price times quantity for each child `<sale>` element, and return the minimum amount.

The `nodeSet()` *Extension Function (obsolete)*

Function: *node-set* **nodeSet** *($fragment)*

This function is now obsolete: a result-tree-fragment is now converted implicitly to a node-set if it is used in a context where a node-set is required.

The `path()` *Extension Function*

Function: *string* **path**()

The `path()` function returns the string value of the path (XPath pattern expression) of the context node. It has no arguments, and its function return type is string.

The `range()` *Extension Function*

Function: *node-set* **range** *(number-1, number-2)*

The `range()` function allows two arguments to be converted to numbers according to the XSLT `number()` function, and then further rounds them to nearest integers. A new node-set is then made which contains one node for each integer in the range, starting with the first number and all the integers between and including the last number. The values of the numbers are converted to strings and stored as the values of the nodes in the new node-set. Its two required arguments are both numbers, and its function return type is node-set.

For example, range(2, 5) creates a node-set with four nodes with string values 2, 3, 4, and 5.

The main intended usage, as stated in the Saxon documentation, is `<xsl:for-each select="range($from, $to)">` which simulates a conventional for-loop in other programming languages.

The `setUserData()` *Extension Function*

`Function:` *`string`* **`setUserData`** *`(string, value)`*

This function associates property information with the context node that can then be accessed with the `getUserData()` extension function (within the same stylesheet). It has two arguments, both strings, although the second string contains an expression. The string value of the first argument is used as the name for the property. The value of the property is assigned using the second argument, which is an expression. The function return type for `setUserData()` is an empty string, because the values are retrieved using the `getUserData()` function.

The `sum()` *Extension Function*

`Function:` *`number`* **`sum`** *`(node-set-1, stored-expression)`*

This function evaluates the expression in the second argument and applies it to each node in the node-set of the first argument. Each value is then added up to provide a total sum of the numbers of the nodes. If the result of any node is NaN, the total will be NaN.

An example of using this function, from the Saxon documentation, is as follows:

```
saxon:sum(sale, saxon:expression('@price * @qty'))
```

This will evaluate price times quantity for each child `<sale>` element, and return the total amount.

The `systemId()` *Extension Function*

`Function:` *`string`* **`systemId`**`()`

This function returns the system identifier or URI of the XML entity that contains the context node. Its function return type is a string, and it has no arguments.

The `tokenize()` *Extension Function*

`Function:` *`node-set`* **`tokenize`** *`(string-1, string-2?)`*

This function builds a new node-set containing a node for each token in the first argument. The first argument is converted to a string, as with the XSLT `string()` function (see Chapter 5). This string is treated then as a whitespace-separated list of tokens. The second argument can set a delimiter other than whitespace, such as a comma. It can be used to break out, word by word, the contents of a sentence, for example. This function contains one required argument and one optional argument, both of type string, and its function return type is node-set.

13.3 XT

James Clark has been a driving force in specification design and authorship for markup technology. He was instrumental in the codification of the W3C specification for XSLT as its editor and was also principle author of the W3C specification for XPath. His processor, XT, is universally acknowledged as far and away the leanest, meanest, and fastest. It was no small shock to the markup community when he announced that he is no longer building revisions and upgrades. There is a list at the end of this section of the limitations in XT, as documented on James Clark's Web site. There is good news, however; a group called 4XT is taking on the task of developing XT further, and their Web site, http://www.4xt.org, documents their efforts.

Clark's XML parser, XP, is also highly regarded and is the default in countless implementations for this reason. In addition, XP allows comments to be passed to the application.

XT is designed as a filter for SAX, the Simple API for XML. It is a parallel technology to the DOM and has some distinct advantages over DOM, apart from the wide industry base of preference for SAX. XT takes the stream of SAX events from the XML processor e.g., XP as input, and outputs them to the result tree as an additional stream of SAX events.

It is well worthwhile to begin with XT simply due to its speed, and then move to another processor if and when additional functionality is required. Note that while XT conforms meticulously to the W3C specification for XSLT and XPath, as you might expect from a processor born of the editor for both specs, it does not implement all of the spec, most notably and regrettably omitting support for `key()`. In addition, `<xsl:fallback>`, `<xsl:namespace-alias>` element, the `extension-element-prefixes` attribute, and the `element-available()` function are not implemented. The optional third argument to `format-number()` and the `<xsl:decimal-format>` element are not supported. XT does not allow access to the namespace axis and you cannot add the `xsl:exclude-result-prefixes` attribute to literal result elements (it is allowed on the document element, however).

XT has a simple executable for Windows that runs in the same way as Instant Saxon. If you use it with a JVM other than the Internet Explorer engine, you will need to modify CLASSPATHS. When you download XT from Clark's site, the XP processor comes with it, so we will describe the installation of both together.

13.3.1 Installing XT for Windows

Download the `xt.exe` file from James Clark's site at http://www.jclark.com. You do not need to add any extra parsers or to modify PATH or CLASSPATH, provided you have IE 4+ (IE 5 recommended) on your Windows 95, 98, or NT/2000 machine. Unzip the file in a directory where you plan to use XT and you are ready to go.

To run Instant XT on Windows, select Start, Applications, MSDOS, and in the window, run it with the following syntax:

```
xt source.xml stylesheet.xsl output.xml [name=param]
```

The `name` is a name value for inserting a parameter's value at runtime, with the syntax of `param=value`, with `name` as the parameter's name declared in `<xsl:param>`, and `value` as whatever value you assign at runtime. In place of the parameter, you can stipulate the name of your output file.

13.3.2 Installing XT and XP on UNIX

If you are running XT, you will need the JDK 1.2 (1.1.6+ will do, but is not recommended) installation, described in Chapter 12. You will also need XP, which is included with the download of the XT processor from James Clark's site. The core program for working with the objects is a JAR file, `xt.jar`, which you must include on your CLASSPATH. We will continue to work with the model introduced in Chapter 12, which assumes you will put this in a `/usr/bin` directory, likely called `/usr/bin/XT`.

If you have followed the instructions above, you will have JDK 1.2.2, which will work fine. The following examples assume that you will use the default `xp.jar` XML processor and that you have put it in your directory with Saxon.

At the very least, you must include `xt.jar` and `xp.jar` on the system CLASSPATH. Thus, where you had a basic "`.`" you would modify it as follows:

1. If you know where your XSLT processor files are, you can do all this in one step by separating each with a colon (`:`) for an installation of XT, where the XT files are all in your `usr/bin` directory (see details in Chapter 12):
   a. For pre-JDK 1.2:

```
setenv CLASSPATH=/usr/bin/xt/sax.jar:/usr/bin/xt/xt:/java/classes/classes.zip
```

   b. For JDK 1.2+:

```
setenv CLASSPATH=/usr/bin/xt/sax.jar:/usr/bin/xt/xt:.
```

2. You can also make this permanent if you're comfortable editing your `.cshrc` file; just add the following line to it (exactly as above, but with `set` rather than `setenv`, and remember that `/java/classes/classes.zip` is only for pre-JDK 1.2; otherwise only a "`.`" period is needed):
   a. For pre-JDK 1.2:

```
set CLASSPATH=/usr/bin/xt/sax.jar:/usr/bin/xt/xt:/java/classes/classes.zip
```

   b. For JDK 1.2+:

```
set CLASSPATH=/usr/bin/xt/sax.jar:/usr/bin/xt/xt:.
```

13.3.3 Installing XT and XP on Macintosh

First, you need to download the Java for Mac that has JBindery. It comes with the MRJ SDK. You can find the MRJ 2.1 SDK (Macintosh Runtime for Java Software Development Kit) for free at http://developer.apple.com/java/text/download.html#sdk (it takes a few minutes from home, less on Ethernet). Now install it by double-clicking the icon and following all the automatic presets. When it's done, you will see the MRJ SDK 2.1 directory on your hard drive, with a JBindery folder (if not, trash MRJ, reinstall with custom, and select *all* components).

Now you need the files for XT, from James Clark's site. Be sure to choose the Java versions, not the Windows. You will need XT and XP. Get them from http://www.jclark.com/xml/xt.html, or get direct anonymous FTP from ftp://ftp.jclark.com/pub/xml/xp.zip and ftp://ftp.jclark.com/pub/xml/xt.zip. Unzip these and put all the XT files in one folder called "xt" inside the JBindery folder which is nested several folders inside of the MRJ folder (inside MRJ is a folder called Tools, and one called Application Builders. It is inside the Application Builders where you will find the JBindery folder) on your hard drive. Do the same with XP (except put its files in the JBindery folder in their own folder called "xp").

If you want to make your own applets after you have more experience with XSLT, and change the input and output filenames, just run JBindery itself and change the filenames in the Command window, as shown in Figure 13–1.

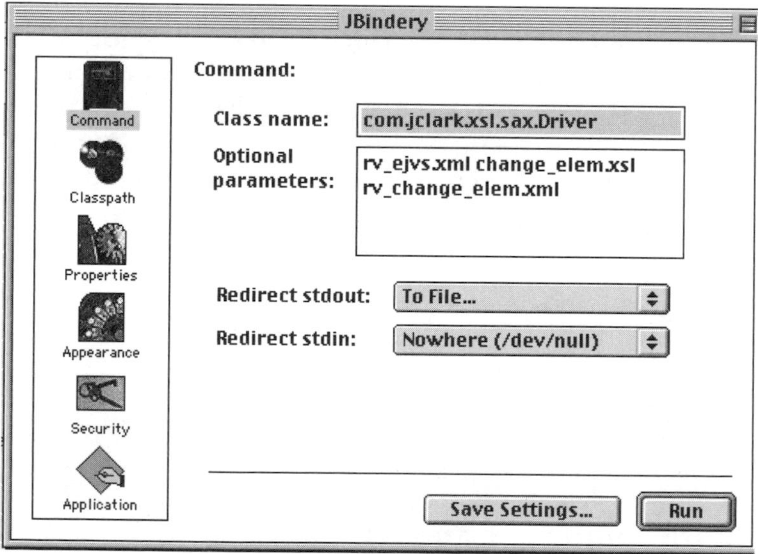

Figure 13–1 Screenshot of the JBindery Command window.

Then Save as Application in the JBindery folder with whatever name you wish, which means you can then run these applets by double-clicking the application (that is, as long as you are not changing the input, stylesheet, and output filenames).

You may also encounder Not Found/Directory Path errors. That comes from a trickier screen. If you look at the JBindery window, the lefthand icon list has a Properties icon, and this could be a source of troubles. You need to add the following two lines to the bottom left and bottom right windows (it'll spill over the viewable space of the window, so type carefully), respectively:

1. On the left window, add:
   `jclark.xsl.sax.parser`
2. On the right window, add:
   `com.jclark.xml.sax.Driver`

If done correctly, it should look like the window in Figure 13–2. The top large window fills in of its own accord as you use JBindery.

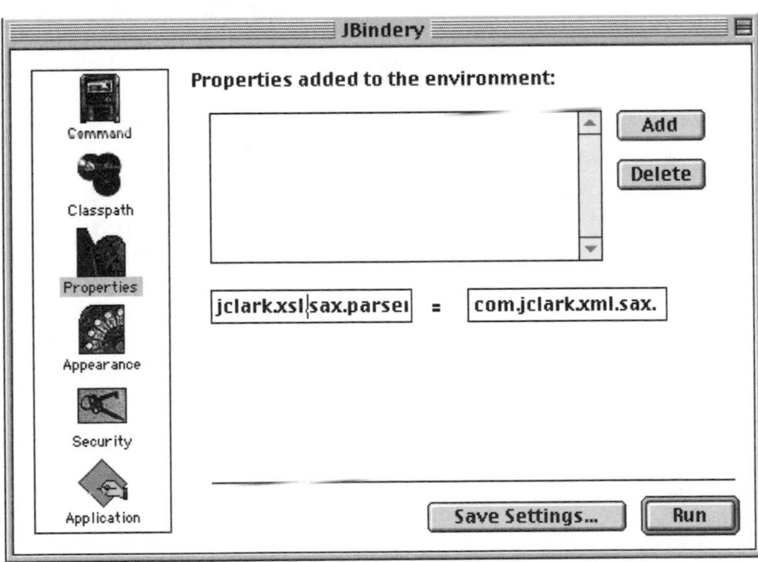

Figure 13–2 The JBindery Properties window for XT.

You should also have the appropriate .jar files in your CLASSPATH window. Assuming you've unzipped stuff all to the JBindery directory, your window should look like Figure 13–3.

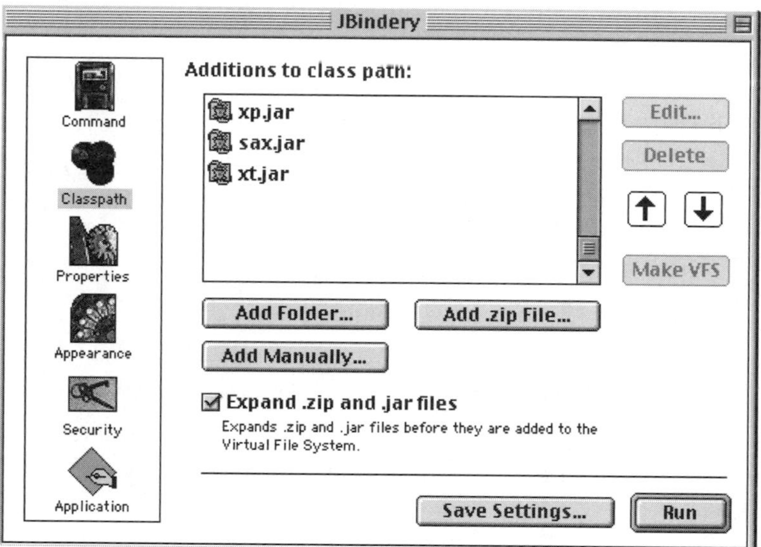

Figure 13–3 The JBindery CLASSPATH window.

If it does not, use the Add .zip File button to select the appropriate .jar files, as shown through the Finder interface it provides.

It's important to remember that you will primarily use the JBindery folder while you're learning. Over time, as you gain confidence, you will likely want to work with different directories and the JBindary folder will likely get very crowded!

13.3.4 XT Extensions

XT implements one extension element: `<xt:document>`, and one extension attribute: `xt:nxml`. It also includes three extension functions: `node-set()`, `intersection()`, and `difference()`.

The XT namespace must be declared if any extensions are to be used. The following example shows the proper way to declare the XT namespace:

```
xmlns:xt="http://www.jclark.com/xt"
```

13.3.4.1 The xt:nxml Extension Attribute

The xt:nxml value for the method attribute on <xsl:output> enables certain specific non-XML characters to be output which simply using <xsl:output> with method set to text would not allow.

Using xt:nxml as the output method stipulates a number of subelements to mark characters for a sort of "escaping" so the processor and parser do not signal an error. These subelement are shown in Table 13–5.

Table 13–5 Subelements escaped by xt:nxml

QName	*Action*
<nxml></nxml>	Contains the <char>, <data>, <escape>, and <control> elements.
<char></char>	Allows a non-XML character to be output, such as ASCII control characters outside the default accepted set.
<data></data>	Allows special characters to be, or to remain, escaped throughout processing.
<escape></escape>	Allows a special character and how it should be escaped to be defined by the user, for example, without using &.
<control></control>	Allows characters to be output directly with no escaping; it sort of forces a straight-through processing without additional treatment, not unlike CDATA sections.

James Clark's XT documentation shows the following example of using the xt:nxml method:

```
<xsl:stylesheet
  xmlns:xsl="http://www.w3.org/1999/XSL/Transform">
<xsl:output method="xt:nxml" xmlns:xt="http://www.jclark.com/xt"/>
<xsl:template match="/">
<nxml>
<escape char="\">\\</escape>
```

```
<data>&amp;&lt;&gt;\</data>
<control>&amp;&lt;&gt;\</control>
</nxml>
</xsl:template>
</xsl:stylesheet>
```

This will generate the following output:

```
&<>\\&<>\
```

13.3.4.2 The <xt:document> Extension Element

The <xt:document> element is used to produce multiple output files from a single XML document instance. It has a mandatory href attribute whose value must be the relative URL for an output file. Its value can be interpreted as an attribute value template. In addition, all the same attributes that are allowed on the <xsl:document> element can be used with <xt:document>.The content of the <xt:document> element is a template, as shown in the following element model definition.

```
<!-- Category: instruction-element -->
<xt:document
  href = { uri-reference }
  method = "xml" | "html" | "text" | qname-but-not-ncname
  version = nmtoken
  encoding = string
  omit-xml-declaration = "yes" | "no"
  standalone = "yes" | "no"
  doctype-public = string
  doctype-system = string
  cdata-section-elements = qnames
  indent = "yes" | "no"
  media-type = string >
  <!-- Content: template -->
</xt:document>
```

See Section 13.4 for an example of an XSLT stylesheet designed for multiple-document output from either Saxon, Xalan, or XT.

13.3.4.3 The `node-set()` Extension Function

`Function:` *`node-set`* **`node-set`** *`($fragment)`*

This function takes a result tree fragment and converts it to a node-set. This function provides the ability to choose parts of the result tree while it is still in process and treat those parts with additional template rules. The function return type of this function is node-set, and its one required attribute is a node-set.

13.3.4.4 The `intersection()` Extension Function

`Function:` *`node-set`* **`intersection`** *`(node-set-1, node-set-2)`*

This function returns a node-set containing the nodes common to two node-sets. Nodes from the first argument that are also found in the node-set in the second are returned as a new node-set. This function has two required arguments, both of type node-set, and its function return type is also a node-set.

13.3.4.5 The `difference()` Extension Function

`Function:` *`node-set`* **`difference`** *`(node-set-1, node-set-2)`*

This function returns a node-set containing the difference between two node-sets. Nodes from the first argument that are not found in the node-set in the second are returned as a new node-set. This function has two required arguments, both of type node-set, and its function return type is also a node-set.

13.3.5 XT Limitations

James Clark list the limitations and known bugs for the XT processor as follows. The following features of the XSLT PR are not yet implemented:

- the element extension mechanism (the `extension-element-prefixes` and `xsl:extension-element-prefixes` attributes, the `<xsl:fallback>` element, and the `element-available()` function)

- keys (the `<xsl:key>` element, and the `key()` function)
- the `<xsl:decimal-format>` element and the optional third argument on the `format-number()` function
- the `namespace` axis
- forwards-compatible processing
- the `xsl:exclude-result-prefixes` attribute on literal result elements (the `exclude-result-prefixes` attribute on `<xsl:stylesheet>` *is* implemented)
- The `xml` output method ignores the `encoding` and `cdata-section-elements` attributes on `<xsl:output>`.

The following are some known bugs:

- Many errors that the XSLT specification requires to be reported are silently ignored.
- Comments and processing instructions occurring in the DTD are not excluded from the data model.
- The `node()` node-test does not work in match patterns (it does work in expressions).
- The `document()` function does not pay attention to the HTTP `content-type` header.
- The `<xsl:import>` element does not conform to the requirement that when `xsl:include` is used to include a stylesheet, any `<xsl:import>` elements in the included document are moved up in the including document to after any existing `<xsl:import>` elements in the including document.
- The HTML output method may get confused if you embed namespace-qualified XML elements with the HTML.

Improvement is needed in the following areas:

- The implementation of the `<xsl:number>` element is slow.
- Error reporting is often not as helpful as it might be.
- No error recovery is attempted after an error is reported.
- The `document()` function does not support fragment identifiers in URIs for any media types.

13.4 Generating Multiple Output Files Using Saxon, Xalan, or XT

Example 13–4, drawn from the earlier Markup City examples, shows how `<xt:document>`, `<saxon:output>`, and Xalan's Redirect extensions can be used in one XSLT stylesheet. We use `<xsl:fallback>` to make sure the stylesheet can run on systems using any of these processors with almost identical output. Note that even though XT does not support `<xsl:fallback>` and `element-available()`, it will find its own recognized extensions in this stylesheet and process them, thus still giving consistent output.

Example 13–4 : XML for stylesheets using multiple processors.

```
<?xml version="1.0"?>
<parkway>
            <thoroughfare>Governor Drive</thoroughfare>
            <thoroughfare name="Whitesburg Drive">
                  <sidestreet name="Bob Wallace Avenue">
                        <block>1st Street</block>
                        <block>2nd Street</block>
                        <block>3rd Street</block>
                  </sidestreet>
                  <sidestreet>Woodridge Street</sidestreet>
            </thoroughfare>
            <thoroughfare name="Bankhead">
                  <sidestreet name="Tollgate Road">
                        <block>First Street</block>
                        <block>Second Street</block>
                        <block>Third Street</block>
                  </sidestreet>
                  <sidestreet>Oak Drive</sidestreet>
            </thoroughfare>
</parkway>
```

In our example, we might want to chop up the `<thoroughfare>` elements in Markup City into individual XML data instances for further detailed work. Think of it as separating the city into districts for specific councilpersons to represent. We might want to use Clark's `<xt:docu-`

ment> instruction element (or the <saxon:output> element) to do this. The territory to be divvied up consists of the offshoots of <parkway>.

Our goal is to get a single HTML page for each <thoroughfare>. In Example 13–5, we'll use <xt:document> and several LREs to do this (note that we've declared the XT namespace URI properly in the document element).

Example 13–5 : Using the <xt:document> extension element.

```
<?xml version="1.0"?>
<xsl:stylesheet xmlns:xsl="http://www.w3.org/1999/XSL/Transform"
      version="1.0"
      xmlns:xt="http://www.jclark.com/xt"
      extension-element-prefixes="xt">

<xsl:output omit-xml-declaration="yes"/>

<xsl:template match="text()"/>

<xsl:template match="thoroughfare">
      <xt:document href="{@name | text()}.html">
      <html>
      <head><title><xsl:value-of select="@name |
text()"/></title></head>
      <body>
      <h2><xsl:value-of select="@name | text()"/></h2>
      <xsl:apply-templates/>
      </body>
      </html>
</xt:document>
</xsl:template>
<xsl:template match="sidestreet">
      <dl>
            <dt>
                  <xsl:value-of select="@name | text()" />
            </dt>
            <dd>
                  <ul>
                        <xsl:apply-templates/>
                  </ul>
            </dd>
</dl>
```

Example 13–5 : Using the <xt:document> extension element (continued).

```
</xsl:template>

<xsl:template match="block">
      <li>
            <xsl:value-of select="@name | text()" />
      </li>
</xsl:template>

</xsl:stylesheet>
```

The attribute value template in the href attribute on <xt:document> provides access to the value of either the attribute or the text name of the <thoroughfare>.

The <xt:document> instruction element creates three new HTML files, one for each <thoroughfare>, containing the <sidestreet> and <block> children of each respective <thoroughfare>.

A contingency for this stylesheet would be very difficult if there were no processors that could handle the multiple outputs. In fact, it basically couldn't be done. We could make a contingency for whether a given processor that does multiple outputs is available though, for instance between XT or Saxon. In Example 13–6 we'll use a couple of more XSLT instruction elements, <xsl:when> and <xsl:otherwise>, children of <xsl:choose>.

We basically repeated the entire XT-dependent template, which used <xt:document>, within the context of an <xsl:choose> element. Each <xsl:when> element tests for the availability of an extension element, using the element-available() function. If the element is available, then the instructions under the <xsl:when> element are instantiated. If element-available() returns false for all the <xsl:when> elements, then the <xsl:otherwise> is instantiated. The <xsl:document> function shown here is defined in the XSLT 1.1 WD. Note that, since XT does not support the element-available() function, the stylesheet will fail using XT.

Example 13–6 : Using contingencies for extension elements.

```
<?xml version="1.0"?>
<xsl:stylesheet xmlns:xsl="http://www.w3.org/1999/XSL/Transform"
      version="1.0"
      xmlns:xt="http://www.jclark.com/xt"
      xmlns:saxon="http://icl.com/saxon"
      xmlns:lxslt="http://xml.apache.org/xslt"
      xmlns:redirect="org.apache.xalan.xslt.extensions.Redirect"
      extension-element-prefixes="xt saxon lxslt redirect">

<xsl:output omit-xml-declaration="yes"/>

<xsl:template match="text()"/>

<xsl:template match="thoroughfare">
<xsl:choose>
      <xsl:when test="element-available('xt:document')">
            <xt:document href="{@name | text()}.html">
                  <html>
                        <head><title><xsl:value-of select="@name |
text()"/></title></head>
                        <body>
                              <h2><xsl:value-of select="@name |
text()"/></h2>
                              <xsl:apply-templates/>
                        </body>
                  </html>
            </xt:document>
      </xsl:when>
      <xsl:when test="element-available('saxon:output')">
            <saxon:output file="{@name | text()}.html">
                  <!-- use Saxon pre 6.2.2 version and the "file"
                        attribute for saxon:output support -->
                  <html>
                        <head><title><xsl:value-of select="@name |
text()"/></title></head>
                        <body>
                              <h2><xsl:value-of select="@name |
text()"/></h2>
                              <xsl:apply-templates/>
                        </body>
                  </html>
            </saxon:output>
      </xsl:when>
      <xsl:when test="element-available('xsl:document')">
```

Example 13–6 : Using contingencies for extension elements (continued).

```
            <xsl:document href="{@name | text()}.html">
                  <html>
                        <head><title><xsl:value-of select="@name |
text()"/></title></head>
                        <body>
                              <h2><xsl:value-of select="@name |
text()"/></h2>
                              <xsl:apply-templates/>
                        </body>
                  </html>
            </xsl:document>
      </xsl:when>

      <xsl:when test="element-available('redirect:write')">
            <redirect:write select="{@name | text()}.html">
                  <html>
                        <head><title><xsl:value-of select="@name |
text()"/></title></head>
                        <body>
                              <h2><xsl:value-of select="@name |
text()"/></h2>
                              <xsl:apply-templates/>
                        </body>
                  </html>
            </redirect:write>
      </xsl:when>
      <xsl:otherwise>
            <h2><xsl:value-of select="@name | text()"/></h2>
      <xsl:apply-templates/>
      </xsl:otherwise>
</xsl:choose>
</xsl:template>

<xsl:template match="sidestreet">
      <dl>
            <dt>
                  <xsl:value-of select="@name | text()" />
            </dt>
            <dd>
                  <ul>
                        <xsl:apply-templates/>
                  </ul>
            </dd>
      </dl>
```

Example 13–6 : Using contingencies for extension elements (continued).

```
</xsl:template>
<xsl:template match="block">
      <li>
            <xsl:value-of select="@name | text()" />
      </li>
</xsl:template>

</xsl:stylesheet>
```

Appendix A
Case Studies

This appendix provides examples that use many of the XPath and XSLT functions as well as the XSLT elements presented in this book. They are drawn directly, or otherwise derived, from real-world applications of XSLT. They have been chosen for their high likelihood of applicable relevance to most readers' needs. Each example is included on the CD.

There are many more uses of XSLT than are represented here. Be sure to review the examples of the `<xsl:key>` top-level element and `key()` function in Jeni Tennison's contributed Appendix B, "Grouping Using the Muenchian Method," as well as the unique application of XSLT to the classic N-Queens problem in artificial intelligence, by Oren Ben-Kiki, in Appendix C.

In this appendix, we've included a sample of work with library records stored in the Machine Readable Record (MARC) format as part of a significant XML project currently underway at Emory University by the American Theological Library Association's Center for Electronic Resources in Theology and Religion. MARC records are an early standard for electronic card catalogues used for over 20 years by libraries around the world. In this example, MARC records converted to XML with an excellent shareware tool by Bob Pritchett at Logos Software (http://www.logos.com/marc/marc.asp) are mined for linking to individual images of each page of the journal article referenced by any given MARC record. Another example represents a common situation encountered with complex documents representing several types of markup DTDs and two different texts. It shows how to reformat the tags and separate the versions for selective publication.

The first set of examples represents a comprehensive range of ways to work with lists in XSLT and XPath to create HTML and plain text lists of varying formats and complexity.

A.1 Lists

Each of these list examples becomes successively more complex, beginning with a simple HTML output with LREs and building toward layered sublists using <xsl:number>. All examples except the last one work with the simple structure of the list shown in Example A–1.

A.1.1 Simple HTML Lists from XML with Literal Result Elements

The stylesheet in Example A–1 converts the input list to basic HTML output with ordered and unordered lists.

In this example, we directly match <list> elements, based on their type attribute (@) value of ordered or unordered, with a simple insertion of HTML ordered (<ol>) and unordered (<ul>) LREs. The <item> elements are then transformed into <li> elements. The use of <xsl:apply-templates> assures that the children of the matched elements are processed. The first <xsl:template> model establishes the basic <html> and <body> wrappers used to make browser-readable HTML, as shown in the sample output. Notice also that it is possible to create HTML output without using <xsl:output> and setting its `method` to `html`, as long as the output is well-formed, per XML rules.

A.1.2 ASCII/Text-only Lists from XML Input

Using the <xsl:output> element with the `method` attribute set to `text`, it is possible to take the same XML document instance as in Example A–1 and get simple text from it, also as a numbered list. We'll add `position()` and <xsl:value-of> to create the sequential number-

Example A–1 : Making HTML lists.

INPUT:

```
<?xml version="1.0"?>
<list type="ordered" prefix="number">
<item>item 1 in list level 1</item>
<item>item 2 in list level 1</item>
<item>item 3 in list level 1</item>
<item>item 4 in list level 1, with a sub-list:
<list type="unordered" prefix="bullet">
<item>item 1 in list level 2</item>
<item>item 2 in list level 2</item>
<item>item 3 in list level 2</item>
</list>
</item>
<item>item 5 in list level 1</item>
<item>item 6 in list level 1</item>
</list>
```

STYLESHEET:

```
<?xml version="1.0"?>
<xsl:stylesheet
      xmlns:xsl="http://www.w3.org/1999/XSL/Transform"
      version="1.0">
<!-- This stylesheet takes an XML list
     and converts it to HTML list format -->

<xsl:template match="/">
      <html>
      <body>
      <xsl:apply-templates/>
      </body>
      </html>
</xsl:template>

<xsl:template match="list[@type='ordered']">
      <ol>
             <xsl:apply-templates/>
      </ol>
</xsl:template>

<xsl:template match="list[@type='unordered']">
      <ul>
      <xsl:apply-templates/>
```

Example A–1 : Making HTML lists (continued).

```
      </ul>
</xsl:template>

<xsl:template match="item">
      <li>
           <xsl:apply-templates/>
      </li>
</xsl:template>

</xsl:stylesheet>
```

OUTPUT:

```
<html>
<body>
<ol>
<li>item 1 in list level 1</li>
<li>item 2 in list level 1</li>
<li>item 3 in list level 1</li>
<li>item 4 in list level 1, with a sub-list:
<ul>
<li>item 1 in list level 2</li>
<li>item 2 in list level 2</li>
<li>item 3 in list level 2</li>
</ul>
</li>
<li>item 5 in list level 1</li>
<li>item 6 in list level 1</li>
</ol>
</body>
</html>
```

ing in Example A–2, which was otherwise made possible in HTML by a browser rendering the list tags properly. Notice especially how `<xsl:text>` is used to format the text output similarly to how `<pre>` in HTML pre-formats HTML output.

Since we are not using LREs, and since we have text-only output, the `<list>` elements are not necessary for the output, other than to have the value of their `type` attributes determine whether `<item>`s selected for processing in either template will be ordered or unordered. We've used a predicate (`[]`) test for which attribute value is to be selected so that the

Example A–2 : XSLT for an XML list converted to an ASCII list.

STYLESHEET:

```
<?xml version="1.0"?>
<xsl:stylesheet
      xmlns:xsl="http://www.w3.org/1999/XSL/Transform"
      version="1.0">

<xsl:output method="text"/>
<xsl:strip-space elements="*"/>

<!-- This stylesheet takes an XML list
     and converts it to a text list format -->

<xsl:template match="list[@type='ordered']/item">
      <xsl:value-of select="position()"/><xsl:text>.
</xsl:text><xsl:apply-templates/>
<xsl:text>
</xsl:text>
</xsl:template>

<xsl:template match="list[@type='unordered']/item">
<xsl:text>
</xsl:text>
      <xsl:text>    -   </xsl:text><xsl:apply-templates/>
</xsl:template>

</xsl:stylesheet>
```

RESULT:

```
1.  item 1 in list level 1
2.  item 2 in list level 1
3.  item 3 in list level 1
4.  item 4 in list level 1, with a sub-list:
    -  item 1 in list level 2
    -  item 2 in list level 2
    -  item 3 in list level 2
5.  item 5 in list level 1
6.  item 6 in list level 1:apply-templates/>
```

corresponding <item> children of either <list> element can be processed. The technique of splitting into two different lines for the starting and ending tags of <xsl:text> shows how to get a hard return between each item.

Several things are different in this example. First, working with <xsl:output> set to method="text", we need no XML tags in the output. That being the case, it is necessary to find a way to generate numbers for the numbered, or ordered, portions of the list. We need to do some formatting, so for each of the items in the <list> with the ordered attribute type value, we use <xsl:value-of> and position() to calculate what number should be assigned to each item. Using <xsl:text>, we mandate that a period follows each <xsl:value-of> with position() to set up nicely formatted numbers, followed by two spaces. Then, the actual list content is simply processed as a child of each <item> (remember, text() nodes are possible children of elements, so when <xsl:apply-templates> processes the children of each <item>, it is the text contained in the tags that is processed). Notice that we have suppressed any blank space children using the <xsl:strip-space> element.

For the unordered list, we're relying heavily on <xsl:text> in a similar manner to enable a certain formatting with dashes and spaces. Otherwise, <xsl:apply-templates> assures the proper output of the actual text content the text() child nodes of each <item> child to the <list> element with the type attribute set to a value of unordered.

A.1.3 Additional Text-only Formatting from XML with <xsl:number>

Working with <xsl:number>, it becomes possible to perform additional formatting on the output list, which is only possible with the basic functionality introduced in the preceding examples. We can get the same output as in Example A–2, but do not need as many <xsl:text> elements to do so. The <xsl:output> method is still text, and the match on each <list> item is still a path expression with a predicate ([]) test on the attribute values to determine ordered or unordered. However, inside the templates, we are working specific formatting options for the numbers, as shown in Example A–3.

Example A–3 : XSLT for XML list converted to ASCII list using `<xsl:number>`.

```
<?xml version="1.0"?>
<xsl:stylesheet xmlns:xsl="http://www.w3.org/1999/XSL/Transform"
          version="1.0">

<xsl:output method="text"/>

<!-- This stylesheet takes an XML list
     and converts it to a text list format -->

<xsl:template match="list[@type='ordered']/item">
<xsl:number value="position()" format="1. "/>
<xsl:apply-templates/>
<xsl:text>
</xsl:text>
</xsl:template>

<xsl:template match="list[@type='unordered']/item">
<xsl:text>
</xsl:text>
     <xsl:text>    -  </xsl:text><xsl:apply-templates/>
</xsl:template>

</xsl:stylesheet>
```

Notice that we have left the unordered template the same, as there is no need to use `<xsl:number>`, of course, if it is unordered. The `format` value of `<xsl:number>` is just a standard 1 followed by a period and a space, a task that required the careful use of `<xsl:text>` in previous examples is simplified here. You could also specify something like "A. " for this and get capital alphabetical ordering (for more, see Chapter 9, Section 9.7). Splitting the `<xsl:text>` element into two lines, as shown above, provides the hard return between each item. A more deeply-nested list is shown in Example A–4.

Example A–4 : Using <xsl:number> with formatting.

INPUT:

```
<?xml version="1.0"?>
<xsl:stylesheet xmlns:xsl="http://www.w3.org/1999/XSL/Transform"
          version="1.0">

<xsl:output method="text"/>
<xsl:strip-space elements="*"/>

<!-- This stylesheet takes an XML list
     and converts it to a text list format -->
<xsl:template match="list[@type='ordered']/item">
<xsl:number value="position()" format="A. "/>
<xsl:apply-templates/>
<xsl:text>
</xsl:text>
</xsl:template>

<xsl:template match="list[@type='unordered']/item">
<xsl:text>
</xsl:text>
      <xsl:text>    -  </xsl:text><xsl:apply-templates/>
</xsl:template>
</xsl:stylesheet>
```

OUTPUT:

```
A. item 1 in list level 1
B. item 2 in list level 1
C. item 3 in list level 1
D. item 4 in list level 1, with a sub-list:

    -  item 1 in list level 2
    -  item 2 in list level 2
    -  item 3 in list level 2
E. item 5 in list level 1
F. item 6 in list level 1
```

A.1.4 Multi-level Text Outline

The XML list in Example A–5 has a more deeply layered structure, with sub, sub-sub, and further embedded sub-lists. Making a representative output of this structure in text form can be done very well with the same tools, but applied in more detail. We begin with a slightly more complex input XML source. The stylesheet will generate a list formatted to look like an outline.

In this example, we're doing a more complex formatting of the output to look like a traditional outline in a text document. Using the format attribute of `<xsl:number>` makes this possible. In addition, we are also using `<xsl:text>` to create or "force" indentation of the sub-levels of the outline.

If you look closely at the XSLT stylesheet, you will notice that apart from a successively longer path in the `<xsl:template>` `match` attribute, each template repeats a fairly regular structure. The `<xsl:text>` element is used to increase the indent level, then `<xsl:number>` draws its value from `position()` and a `format` value that changes its style each time, as required by the successive step down the outline form.

A.2 MARC Records: The ATLAS Project from ATLA-CERTR at Emory University

MARC records for electronic card catalogues in libraries have been in use for some two to three decades. They have become most prevalent in the last 15 years, as the increased power and affordability of digital equipment has become more available to libraries—one of the most invaluable and almost utterly under funded knowledge stores of humankind.

The MARC style is very simple, but remarkably powerful for data representation and categorization. This is accomplished with a carefully counted syntax in which the entire beginning of each record is a series of eight-digit sequences identifying each part of the record (title, author, etc.), how many characters each contains, and where in the sequence of characters each ends.

MARC is not XML. There are no < > tags in MARC. It is therefore necessary to convert MARC to XML. Again, because the string-tagging system in MARC is so very orderly, it is not difficult to convert MARC records to XML. Each part of a library lookup record is identified in MARC by its starting position in the numerical sequence of characters forming the record

Example A–5 : Outline formatting for a deeply nested list.

INPUT:

```
<?xml version="1.0"?>
<list>
<item>item 1 in list level 1</item>
<item>item 2 in list level 1</item>
<item>item 3 in list level 1</item>
<item>item 4 in list level 1, with a sub-list:
<list>
<item>item 1 in list level 2</item>
<item>item 2 in list level 2</item>
<item>item 3 in list level 2, with a sub-list:
<list>
<item>item 1 in list level 3</item>
<item>item 2 in list level 3</item>
<item>item 3 in list level 3, with a sub-list:
<list>
<item>item 1 in list level 4</item>
<item>item 2 in list level 4</item>
<item>item 3 in list level 4, with a sub-list:
<list>
<item>item 1 in list level 5</item>
<item>item 2 in list level 5</item>
<item>item 3 in list level 5, with a sub-list:
<list>
<item>item 1 in list level 6</item>
<item>item 2 in list level 6</item>
<item>item 3 in list level 6</item>
</list>
</item>
<item>item 4 in list level 5</item>
<item>item 5 in list level 5</item>
</list>
</item>
<item>item 4 in list level 4</item>
<item>item 5 in list level 4</item>
</list>
</item>
<item>item 4 in list level 3</item>
<item>item 5 in list level 3</item>
</list>
</item>
<item>item 4 in list level 2</item>
```

Example A-5 : Outline formatting for a deeply nested list (continued).

```
<item>item 5 in list level 2</item>
</list>
</item>
<item>item 5 in list level 1</item>
<item>item 6 in list level 1</item>

</list>
```

STYLESHEET:

```
<?xml version="1.0"?>
<xsl:stylesheet xmlns:xsl="http://www.w3.org/1999/XSL/Transform"
           version="1.0">

<xsl:output method="text"/>
<xsl:strip-space elements="*"/>

<!-- This stylesheet takes an XML list
     and converts it to a text list outline format
     regardless of list type, using list levels -->

<xsl:template match="list//list">
<xsl:apply-templates/>
<xsl:text>
</xsl:text>
</xsl:template>

<!-- 1st list level -->
<xsl:template match="list/item">
<xsl:number value="position()" format="I. "/>
<xsl:apply-templates/>
<xsl:text>
</xsl:text>
</xsl:template>

<!-- 2nd list level -->
<xsl:template match="list/item/list/item">
<xsl:text>
      </xsl:text><xsl:number value="position()" format="A. "/>
<xsl:apply-templates/>
</xsl:template>
```

Example A–5 : Outline formatting for a deeply nested list (continued).

```
<!-- 3rd list level -->
<xsl:template match="list/item/list/item/list/item">
<xsl:text>
            </xsl:text>
<xsl:number value="position()" format="1. "/>
<xsl:apply-templates/>
</xsl:template>

<!-- 4th list level -->
<xsl:template match="list/item/list/item/list/item/list/item">
<xsl:text>
                  </xsl:text>
<xsl:number value="position()" format="a. "/>
<xsl:apply-templates/>
</xsl:template>

<!-- 5th list level -->
<xsl:template match="list/item/list/item/list/item/list/item/
list/item">
<xsl:text>
                              </xsl:text>
<xsl:number value="position()" format="i. "/>
<xsl:apply-templates/>
</xsl:template>
</xsl:stylesheet>
```

OUTPUT:

```
I. item 1 in list level 1
II. item 2 in list level 1
III. item 3 in list level 1
IV. item 4 in list level 1, with a sub-list:

      A. item 1 in list level 2
      B. item 2 in list level 2
      C. item 3 in list level 2, with a sub-list:

            1. item 1 in list level 3
            2. item 2 in list level 3
            3. item 3 in list level 3, with a sub-list:

                  a. item 1 in list level 4
                  b. item 2 in list level 4
                  c. item 3 in list level 4, with a sub-list:
```

Example A–5 : Outline formatting for a deeply nested list (continued).

```
                        i. item 1 in list level 5
                        ii. item 2 in list level 5
                        iii. item 3 in list level 5
                        iv. item 4 in list level 5
                        v. item 5 in list level 5

                  d. item 4 in list level 4
                  e. item 5 in list level 4
             4. item 4 in list level 3
             5. item 5 in list level 3

      D. item 4 in list level 2
      E. item 5 in list level 2

V. item 5 in list level 1
VI. item 6 in list level 1
```

(a start tag in XML correlates to this), and the length in number of characters of that piece of information (an end tag in XML indicates this point of closure for the information). There is also a three-digit string that identifies what kind of information is represented (title, etc.), like an XML element name.

Fortunately, while it is possible to wrap a MARC record in XML tags and use a complex set of XPath functions and expressions (e.g., `count()`, `substring-after()`, and so on), there is already software that does this. We highly recommend a freeware program called marcxml.exe (alas, Windows only) from Bob Pritchett at Logos, Inc. (*http://www.logos.com/marc/marc.asp*).

The following archive and access procedure was developed at Emory University by the American Theological Library Association's Center for Electronic Resources in Theology and Religion (ATLA-CERTR). ATLA-CERTR has undertaken a project in which over 50 years of issues from 50 journals in philosophy, ethics, religion, and so forth are being scanned as images for archival integrity and are also being keyed in with the Text Encoding Initiative (TEI) DTD in XML, a service provided by Pacific Data Conversion Corporation. The initial point of access is through MARC records from the comprehensive catalogue of resources maintained by ATLA (a 50 x 50 journal/year subset of the one-of-a-kind resource for theology, ethics, religion, philosophy and biblical studies carefully maintained by the Chicago-based nonprofit organization). To accomplish this task and to maintain a completely standards-based XML solution, the MARC records required translation into XML, as well as further processing.

The Logos software simply takes a command line in an MS-DOS window with the name of the program, the input MARC, and the output XML filename you choose. It runs very quickly, even on extremely large MARC files, and produces well-formed XML. An output MARC record in XML is shown as the input in Example A–6.

The three-digit numbers in the `tag` attribute values are MARC identifiers for the kind of information, like `773` for the kind of journal, and the `<subfield>`s identify citations and so forth. One of the first projects at ATLA-CERTR was to test an Oracle database back-end with the MARC records and links to the images of the journal articles. In the case of the record in Example A–6, the pages of this article were 7 through 19 (see `<data-field tag="773" ind1="0">` at the end of `<record>` and `<subfield>` with `code` equal to `g`). This set of numbers was not individually marked, and sometimes the format varied, so it was not easy to recognize the page numbers. Plus, of course, in a large database, there could be many page 7s, 8s, 9s, and so forth. Therefore, a unique identifier was needed to make each page from this record distinct from duplicate numbers in different records.

In addition, to make the pages browsable in a traditional Internet browser, we needed to have forward and backward links and to have each page formatted with information from the author and title fields as well. It so happens that the specification for MARC records sets aside in the control field a unique identifier field for each record (one of the very first strings of numbers in each record), such as the number `"001"` in the following line taken from Example A–6:

```
<control-field tag="001">ario19990010001002</control-field>
```

First, however, we needed to select the subset of records that represented our initial set of test-scanned images of article pages a few journals of various types.

Using the stylesheet shown in Example A–6, we fed over 500MB of data into an XSLT processor to extract the less than 100K of total records for our initial test. The first template selected the root element, `<marc>`, which was the standard output from the Logos marcxml.exe conversion program. With `<xsl:copy>`, we copied that basic element and processed only

Example A–6 : Processing an XML version of a MARC record.

INPUT:

```
<?xml version="1.0"?>
<record type="naa">
      <control-field tag="001">ario19990010001002</control-field>
      <control-field tag="003">ATLA</control-field>
      <control-field tag="005">19990802145817.0</control-field>
      <control-field tag="008">990802s1998    xx           000  0eng
d</control-field>
      <data-field tag="040">
            <subfield code="a">ATLA</subfield>
            <subfield code="c">ATLA</subfield>
      </data-field>
      <data-field tag="100" ind1="1">
            <subfield code="a">Malone, Patricia.</subfield>
      </data-field>
      <data-field tag="245" ind1="1" ind2="0">
            <subfield code="a">Religious Education and Prejudice among
Students Taking the Course Studies of Religion :</subfield>
            <subfield code="b">[bibliog, tables]</subfield>
      </data-field>
      <data-field tag="650" ind2="4">
            <subfield code="a">Religions</subfield>
            <subfield code="x">Study.</subfield>
      </data-field>
      <data-field tag="650" ind2="4">
            <subfield code="a">Prejudices.</subfield>
      </data-field>
      <data-field tag="650" ind2="4">
            <subfield code="a">Toleration, Religious.</subfield>
      </data-field>
      <data-field tag="650" ind2="4">
            <subfield code="a">Students</subfield>
            <subfield code="x">Religious life.</subfield>
      </data-field>
      <data-field tag="651" ind2="4">
            <subfield code="a">Australia</subfield>
            <subfield code="x">Education.</subfield>
      </data-field>
      <data-field tag="773" ind1="0">
            <subfield code="a">British Journal of Religious
Education</subfield>
```

Example A–6 : Outline formatting for a deeply nested list (continued).

```
            <subfield code="g">21 (Aut 1998), p. 7-19</subfield>
            <subfield code="x">0141-6200</subfield>
      </data-field>
</record>
```

STYLESHEET:

```
<?xml version="1.0"?>
<xsl:stylesheet xmlns:xsl="http://www.w3.org/1999/XSL/Transform"
                version="1.0">

<xsl:output type="xml" indent="yes"/>

<!-- Semeia, vols 73-76, issues 1 -->
<!-- JBL, Vol 114, 115 issues 1-4 0021-9231-->
<!-- Biblical Archaeologist, Vol 60, issues 1-4 0006-0895-->
<!-- JAAR, Vol 65, issue 1 0095-571X-->
<xsl:template match="marc">
<xsl:copy>
<xsl:apply-templates mode="copy"
 select="record[data-field/subfield='0002-7189']"/>
<xsl:apply-templates mode="copy"
 select="record[data-field/subfield='0021-9231']"/>
<xsl:apply-templates mode="copy"
 select="record[data-field/subfield='0006-0895']"/>
<xsl:apply-templates mode="copy"
 select="record[data-field/subfield='0095-571X']"/>
</xsl:copy>
</xsl:template>

<xsl:template mode="copy" match="*">
<xsl:copy>
<xsl:copy-of select="@*"/>
<xsl:apply-templates mode="copy"/>
</xsl:copy>
</xsl:template>

</xsl:stylesheet>
```

those `<record>` children whose ISSN[1] numbers contained in the `<subfield>` child of a `<data-field>` element, as tested in the predicate (`[]`) matched our chosen #'s. Then, to be sure we got all the attributes as well-remember, `<xsl:copy>` does not copy attributes—we used `<xsl:copy-of>` and a `match` on all attributes with `@*`. We used the `copy` mode. With this simple stylesheet, we got the subset we needed for this particular test. However, the original challenge still remained: to get individual pages for each page in the article that corresponded to the citation in the MARC record. In addition, those HTML pages had to be made unique among references to duplicate page numbers in other journals.

For example, a "start" page was required, as well as a header for each page, so that the image of the page would be called in a browser page, which would also display basic reference information in human-readable form, including the title, journal, citation, and author.

The XSLT stylesheet in Example A–7, developed primarily by G. Ken Holman of CraneSoftwrights, Ltd., is presented in parts, along with commentary. Assume a starting MARC XML file similar to the sample record in Example A–6. It uses the XT `xt:document` extension element (you could also use `saxon:output`) for producing multiple output files from a single MARC XML input file.

There are several major tasks accomplished by this stylesheet. The first template has to set up the basic breakout of page ranges and the "homepage" for all the articles in the chosen subset (for instance, in our first demo, this was per-journal issue within a per-journal directory structure). This first step is performed with the `xt:document` element to create the homepage (index.htm) and individual article pages for each journal.[2] There are a number of qualifications to be considered, as MARC records do not require any specific order or sorting and the structure of the text() nodes can be different. After a basic match for the template on the root or document element (with /), and once the name of the output document is declared to be the index.htm file, the contents of that index.htm file must be created by the child elements.

1. Journals and books have unique numerical identifiers called ISSN and ISBN numbers, respectively.
2. The sample XML file on the CD only contains several MARC records, as the ATLA database is quite large and only a few records are required to make this example illustrative.

Example A–7 : Processing MARC XML files into HTML pages.

```
<?xml version="1.0" ?>
<xsl:stylesheet xmlns:xsl="http://www.w3.org/1999/XSL/Transform"
version="1.0" xmlns:xt="http://www.jclark.com/xt">
  <xsl:output method="html" />
<xsl:template match="/">

<xt:document href="index.htm">
<!--
make index page
  -->
<!--
each entry creates a set of files
  -->
<xsl:for-each select="//record/*[@tag='773']">
  <xsl:variable name="cite_elem" select="*[@code='g']" />
  <xsl:variable name="citation" select="normalize-space($cite_elem)" />
  <xsl:variable name="numseqs"
select="substring-after($citation,'p. ')" />
  <xsl:variable name="start"
select="number(substring-before($numseqs,'-'))" />
  <xsl:variable name="end" select="number(substring-after($numseqs,'-
'))" />
  <xsl:param name="basename" select="concat(../control-field[@tag=001], '-
')" />
<!--
check number validity before linking
  -->
<xsl:if test="string($start) != 'NaN' and string($end) != 'NaN'">
<p>
<a href="{$basename}{$start}.htm">
  <xsl:value-of select="*[@tag='245']" />
  </a>
  </p>
  </xsl:if>
  </xsl:for-each>
  </xt:document>
<!--
make each set of pages
  -->
<xsl:for-each select="//record/*[@tag='773']">
```

Example A–7 : Processing MARC XML files into HTML pages (continued).

```
<xsl:variable name="cite_elem" select="*[@code='g']" />
  <xsl:variable name="citation" select="normalize-space($cite_elem)" />
  <xsl:variable name="numseqs"
select="substring-after($citation,'p. ')" />
  <xsl:variable name="start"
elect="number(substring-before($numseqs,'-'))" />
  <xsl:variable name="end" select="number(substring-after($numseqs,'-
'))" />

<xsl:choose>
<xsl:when test="string($start) = 'NaN' or $start &lt; 0">
  <xsl:message>start value unacceptable</xsl:message>
  </xsl:when>
<xsl:when test="string($end) = 'NaN' or $end &lt; 0">
  <xsl:message>end value unacceptable</xsl:message>
  </xsl:when>
<xsl:when test="$start &gt; $end">
  <xsl:message>start value unacceptable</xsl:message>
  </xsl:when>
<xsl:otherwise>
<xsl:call-template name="makepages">
  <xsl:with-param name="basename" select="concat(../control-
field[@tag=001], '-')" />
<!--
 with-param name="prev"     use default
  -->
  <xsl:with-param name="start" select="$start" />
  <xsl:with-param name="end" select="$end" />
  </xsl:call-template>
  </xsl:otherwise>
  </xsl:choose>

  </xsl:for-each>
  </xsl:template>
<xsl:template name="makepages">
<!--
make a set of pages from start to end
  -->
<xsl:param name="basename" />
  <xsl:param name="prev" />
```

Example A–7 : Processing MARC XML files into HTML pages (continued).

```
<!--
number of previous page
  -->
  <xsl:param name="start" select="-1" />
<!--
number of this page
  -->
  <xsl:param name="end" select="-1" />
<!--
number of last page
  -->
<!--
produce this document from set
  -->
<xt:document href="{$basename}{$start}.htm">
<p>
  <xsl:value-of select="*[@tag='773']" />
  </p>
<!--
item information
  -->
<xsl:choose>
<!--
previous link
  -->
<xsl:when test="not($prev)">
<p>
  <a href="index.htm">Index page</a>
  </p>
  </xsl:when>
<xsl:otherwise>
<p>
<a href="{$basename}{$prev}.htm">
  Page
  <xsl:value-of select="$prev" />
  </a>
  </p>
  </xsl:otherwise>
  </xsl:choose>
<xsl:choose>
<!--
next link
  -->
```

Example A–7 : Processing MARC XML files into HTML pages (continued).

```
<xsl:when test="$start &lt; $end">
<p>
<a href="{$basename}{$start + 1}.htm">
  Page
  <xsl:value-of select="$start + 1" />
  </a>
  </p>
  </xsl:when>
<xsl:otherwise>
<p>
  <a href="index.htm">Index page</a>
  </p>
  </xsl:otherwise>
  </xsl:choose>

<p>
  Page
  <xsl:value-of select="$start" />
  </p>
<!--
item information
  -->
  <img src="{$basename}{$start}.gif" alt="Page {$start} Image" />
<!--
image
  -->
  </xt:document>
<!--
produce next document from set
  -->
<xsl:if test="$start &lt; $end">
<!--
only if available
  -->
<xsl:call-template name="makepages">
 <xsl:with-param name="basename" select="$basename" />
  <xsl:with-param name="prev" select="$start" />
  <xsl:with-param name="start" select="$start + 1" />
  <xsl:with-param name="end" select="$end" />
  </xsl:call-template>
  </xsl:if>
 </xsl:template>

</xsl:stylesheet>
```

We begin with what we know. First, we know that the citation data is contained in the <data-field> with the 773 attribute tag. We select each one with <xsl:for-each> and a selection on this journal's <data-field>. We can safely choose any element (*) with an attribute tag value of 773 as follows:

```
<xsl:for-each select="//record/*[@tag='773']">
```

Next, we create a series of variables that build on one another for narrowing down and removing ambiguity from the particular string of page numbers that interests us. Since string functions have specific input node types for their arguments, we'll work with variables to avoid errors. First, a variable called cite_elem is made with <xsl:variable> to identify the particular element whose text() node we're going to use. In this case, it is the <subfield> child of the <data-field> element with tag 773, which has a code value of g. In MARC parlance, the g indicates the citation details for an article. So, we select the element child (*) with a predicate test ([]) for the attribute code to be g for any element (*) that is the child of the currently selected node using

```
<xsl:variable name="cite_elem" select="*[@code='g']" />
```

Next, we need to make sure there are no extra spaces in the section with the page numbers, so we use normalize-space() to normalize the space in the text() node referenced by the cite_elem variable; we call this the citation variable: normalize-space($cite_elem). Note that when you call a variable for an argument in a function, you do not have to put it in quotes, but you must precede it with the $ token.

```
<xsl:variable name="citation" select="normalize-space($cite_elem)"
/>
```

Now that the citation variable has been identified and "cleaned up," we can begin to extract the page numbering sequences we'll use. Creating a variable called numseqs, we can identify the page numbers by choosing the substring-after() the p (now that we've normalized spaces). This gives us a numseqs variable value, which is the string of representative page numberings (such as 7–19).

```
<xsl:variable name="numseqs" select="substring-after($citation,'p. ')"
/>
```

Next, we'll pare this down even further, using the dash (-) to get the starting number for a variable called start and the ending number for a variable called end. We'll use substring-before() for the number preceding the dash and `substring-after()` for the number that follows it.

```
<xsl:variable name="start" select="number(substring-before($numseqs,'-'))" />
<xsl:variable name="end" select="number(substring-after($numseqs,'-'))"
/>
```

We can now work with the `start` and `end` numbers and be confident that the normalized space and substring functions are giving us the specific digits we want. Using `<xsl:message>`, we make sure that, in case this is a record with typos or we've gotten an improper page number representation, there is some alert to this effect. We'll use the NaN (not a number) token to test whether the `$start` and `$end` variables are "not NaN" in other words, the double-negative will affirm a positive. If they are not a non-number, then they are a number. We'll use the `<xsl:if>` test to determine this, and if they pass the test, LREs will create the basic HTML tags we need for making the reference links to the start page of the articles. We will then create a parameter to get the unique field name from the control field for the base name of the file, which will be used in the link from the index page (a dash is added with the `concat()` function).

```
<xsl:param name="basename" select="concat(../control-field[@tag=001],
'-')" />
```

Assuming the NaN test is passed, then the LRE for the hypertext link is to the file whose name is created with the basename and the start number appended with `.htm`.

```
<a href="{$basename}{$start}.htm">
```

The two AVTs with { } get the basename and the starting page number. The actual text that is the link, for user-friendliness, is the title of the article, retrieved by `<xsl:value-of>`, selecting the contents of the element (`*`) whose attribute `tag` is `245` the `MARC` indicator for a title.

```
<xsl:value-of select="*[@tag='245']" />
```

The content of the `xt:document` element creates an index page, whose contents are links, which use the titles of the articles from each MARC record to link to the first page image of each respective article.

We will now move on to the creation of the individual per-page HTML files to hold each scanned article page's image. We will work with another `<xsl:for-each>` to establish an iterative approach. Everything begins with the same set of variables as before (remember, they must be redeclared) to establish exactly what range of page numbers is to be used for making the pages.

```
<xsl:for-each select="//record/*[@tag='773']">
<xsl:variable name="cite_elem" select="*[@tag='773']/*[@code='g']" />
  <xsl:variable name="citation" select="normalize-space($cite_elem)" />
  <xsl:variable name="numseqs"
select="substring-after($citation,'p. ')" />
  <xsl:variable name="start"
select="number(substring-before($numseqs,'-'))" />
  <xsl:variable name="end" select="number(substring-after($numseqs,'-
'))" />
```

We then use another `<xsl:choose>` and a set of `<xsl:when>` elements to make sure the page number variables are valid. If they are, the `<xsl:otherwise>` element is selected and we create the individual HTML files for each page number with a call to a named template.

```
<xsl:call-template name="makepages">
```

We add an `<xsl:with-param>` element to pass the values of the page numbers and basename to the named template.

```
  <xsl:with-param name="basename"
      select="concat(../control-field[@tag=001], '-')" />
  <xsl:with-param name="start" select="$start" />
  <xsl:with-param name="end" select="$end" />
```

These pages have to have “next” and “previous” HTML links for "turning the virtual pages" of the journal article. Now that the model is set with `$basename` for naming and making the individual output files in HTML with `xt:document`, it is time to use the template that is actually called for doing so.

```
<xsl:template name="makepages">
```

Remember that when `name` is used with `<xsl:template>`, a `match` attribute is not required.

The initial pair of `$prev` and `$basename` parameters are declared, but no values are given because values for each MARC record will be invoked on-the-fly with `<xsl:with-param>`, which can recalculate a parameter when used, for instance, in `<xsl:call-template>`.

```
<xsl:param name="basename" />
<xsl:param name="prev" />
```

To begin building the pages, we need to increment the `$start` and `$end` values sequentially to one less than their starting value, so that by checking for a value greater than the former or latter, we'll know or the processor will know we've made "enough" pages.

```
  <xsl:param name="start" select="-1" />
<!--
number of this page
  -->
  <xsl:param name="end" select="-1" />
```

Next, we make the actual pages, again with `xt:document`. Each successive current node in `<xsl:for-each>` which called the `makepages` template is processed.

```
<xt:document href="{$basename}{$start}.htm">
<p>
  <xsl:value-of select="*[@tag='773']" />
  </p>
```

The `xt:document` function is concatenating the `$basename` defined in the template with `<xsl:with-param>`, into which this template is called as `makepages`. This is added to the `$start` variable and an `.htm` extension to make the first page of the article. Then we use some `<p>` LREs to make the citation information (from the `773` `<data-field>`) appear as a human-readable reference on each HTML page created.

Next, with `<xsl:when>` inside an `<xsl:choose>` element, we test to see if there is a `$prev` value:

```
<xsl:when test="not($prev)">
<p>
  <a href="index.htm">Index page</a>
  </p>
  </xsl:when>
```

If there is not, we just make a link to the homepage (index.htm) since we are on the first page of the article and the only place to go back to is the index page of articles. If there is a `$prev` value, we skip to the `<xsl:otherwise>` element to make a link to the previous page.

```
<xsl:otherwise>
<p>
<a href="{$basename}{$prev}.htm">
  Page
  <xsl:value-of select="$prev" />
  </a>
  </p>
  </xsl:otherwise>
```

The actual text, which is the blue-colored browser link, is the page number (the word Page is added with actual text), and we use `<xsl:value-of>` to select that actual page number value.

We then make the next page link for readers to continue reading additional pages (e.g., from page 8 to page 9), using a new `<xsl:choose>` element.

```
<xsl:choose>
<!--
next link
  -->
<xsl:when test="$start &lt; $end">
<p>
<a href="{$basename}{$start + 1}.htm">
  Page
  <xsl:value-of select="$start + 1" />
  </a>
  </p>
  </xsl:when>
```

We use `<xsl:when>` to be sure that our `$start` variable is less than `$end` (in other words, that we haven't finished remember, `makepages` is called into an `<xsl:for-each>` loop in the previous template of the stylesheet, so we have to have termination conditions). If it is less, then we make a link with LREs by concatenating the `$basename` MARC record identifier to distinguish this string of pages from another from a different issue or volume, along with the `$start` variable incremented by 1 to an `.htm` suffix for the HTML link reference. The actual human-readable blue link text is, again, the word "Page" followed by the page number of that next page being linked to, retrieved with `<xsl:value-of>`, selecting the `@start +1` page number.

We've not finished making pages yet, just parts of their content, as we've not yet even put in the image files! is to account for what to do when `$start` is *not* less than `$end`. In other words, what do we do when we are actually *on* the last (`$end`) page in the `<xsl:for-each>` iteration for each article represented by a MARC record? We already set up a link like that for `$prev` if we're on the first page: When we're on the first page, we can only go "back" to the main index of articles for that journal.

```
<xsl:otherwise>
<p>
  <a href="index.htm">Index page</a>
  </p>
```

```
        </xsl:otherwise>
```

In the final parts of this `xt:document` instruction, the actual image of the scanned article page itself has to be inserted. We just take the `$start` variable and place it before the `.gif` suffix, along with the `$basename` identifier. For the additional pages beyond `$start`, as you will see, we simply increment +1—remember, again, this is used in an `<xsl:for-each>`, where it is called as a template for each MARC record and each page represented by the article cited in that record. We prefix the scanned image with the word "Page" and the current page number using a <p> LRE.

```
      <p>
        Page
        <xsl:value-of select="$start" />
        </p>
      <!--
      item information
        -->
        <img src="{$basename}{$start}.gif" alt="Page
      {$start} Image" />
      <!--
      image
        -->
        </xt:document>
```

The actual scanned article page image is displayed, using the HTML `<img>` element, for reader convenience in reading the citation (e.g., journal name, data, page numbers). The images are stored in directories named and structured by journal ISSN and issue, in practice.

We use the `<xsl:call-template>` element recursively inside the `<xsl:if>` element to make the rest of these pages. We test with `<xsl:if>` to see if there are remaining pages if `$start`, as iterated by +1, is less than `$end` and if so, `makepages` continues to be called. This portion of the template is recursive, as we are calling the template in which this template occurs. However, the `<xsl:if>` test gives us our stop criteria.

```
<xsl:if test="$start &lt; $end">
  <xsl:call-template name="makepages">
     <xsl:with-param name="basename" select="$basename" />
     <xsl:with-param name="prev" select="$start" />
     <xsl:with-param name="start" select="$start + 1" />
     <xsl:with-param name="end" select="$end" />
  </xsl:call-template>
</xsl:if>
```

A.3 The Harvard-Kyoto Classics Project with Vedic Literature

The academic work done with XML is varied in many ways and is still in its exploratory stages. An international collaboration between Dr. Michael Witzel of Harvard University and colleagues at Kyoto University, Japan, led by H. Nakani and M. Tokunaga, is working to reconstruct an entire catalogue of the classics of Asian, East Asian, and South Asian sacred literature under the title "Towards a Reconstitution of Classical Studies." It will be done in XML with unprecedented complexity, richness of links, and other aspects of XML technology.

A multitude of ancient texts have been entered into computer formats over the past decades, beginning with the valiant and noble efforts of Lehman and Ananthanarayanan in 1971, with the *Rig Veda* and *Shatapatha Brahmana,* two ancient texts of India dating as far back as pre-1800 B.C.E. Formats were a problem, and even when markup was used, differing DTDs and tag names were employed, some in SGML/TEI (Text Encoding Initiative) tags, some in plain text, and some in HTML. In addition, there are multiple versions of the texts particularly of important texts like the *Rig Veda* (RV). In this applied example, we will see how the use of XML and XSLT is still readily possible, even when the actual content is not known, but the logical structure of the tags is.

In Example A–8a, we see one such example where the version by Lubotsky, designed to remove changes in spelling due to sound combinations of words, is combined with a version maintained in the TITUS project at Frankfurt University by Jost Gippert (*http://titus.uni-frankfurt.de/texte/texte.htm*). These versions have been woven with TEI `<div>` tags, nonconforming IDs (remember, IDs need to begin with a nonnumeric, therefore alphabetic, character), and HTML tags.

In this project, we wanted to separate the "L" (Lubotsky) version from the "T" (TITUS) version, for some high-precision searching in pure XML, with no HTML tags, but with proper IDs (which could be validated if needed) and tag names that reflected the actual common naming among scholars (like *paada* for each little part of a verse, also called a *mantra*). Notice that if you open the resulting file in a browser, it looks like

Example A–8a : XML input from the *Rig Veda*.

```
<?xml version="1.0"?>

<html>
<body bgcolor="#ffffff">

<div class="Rgveda">

<hr size="8" />
<br />
<font size="5"><b>Mandala I</b></font>
<br />
<hr width="200" />
<br />

<div1 class="maNDala" id="1">
<dl>
<div2 class="hymn" id="1.1">

<div3 class="verse" id="1.1.1">
<a name="1.1.1"></a>
<dt>
1.1.1
</dt>

<dd>
<ol class="mantra" type="a">
      <li class="T">
agni;m ILe puro;hitaM yajJa;sya deva;m Rtvi;jam /
<ul>
<li class="L">
agni;m ILe puro;hitam
</li>
<li class="L">
yajJa;sya deva;m Rtvi;jam /
</li>
</ul>
</li>
</ol>
<ol type="a" start="3" class="mantra">
<li class="T">
ho;tAraM ratnadhA;tamam //
<ul>
<li class="L">
ho;tAram ratnadhA;tamam //
```

Example A–8a : XML input from the *Rig Veda* (continued).

```
</li>
</ul>
</li>
</ol>
</dd>
</div3>

<div3 class="verse" id="1.1.2">
<a name="1.1.2"></a>
<dt>
1.1.2
</dt>

<dd>
<ol class="mantra" type="a">
      <li class="T">
agni;H pU;rvebhir R;Sibhir I;Dyo nU;tanair uta; /
<ul>
<li class="L">
agni;H pU;rvebhiH R;SibhiH
</li>
<li class="L">
I;DyaH nU;tanaiH uta; /
</li>
</ul>
</li>
</ol>
<ol type="a" start="3" class="mantra">
<li class="T">
sa; devA;M; e;ha; vakSati //
<ul>
<li class="L">
sa; devA;n A; iha; vakSati //
</li>
</ul>
</li>
</ol>
</dd>
</div3>
</div2>
</dl>
</div1>
</div>
</body>
</html>
```

Figure A–1, with definition lists (`<dl>`) used to format the verse numbers and so forth.

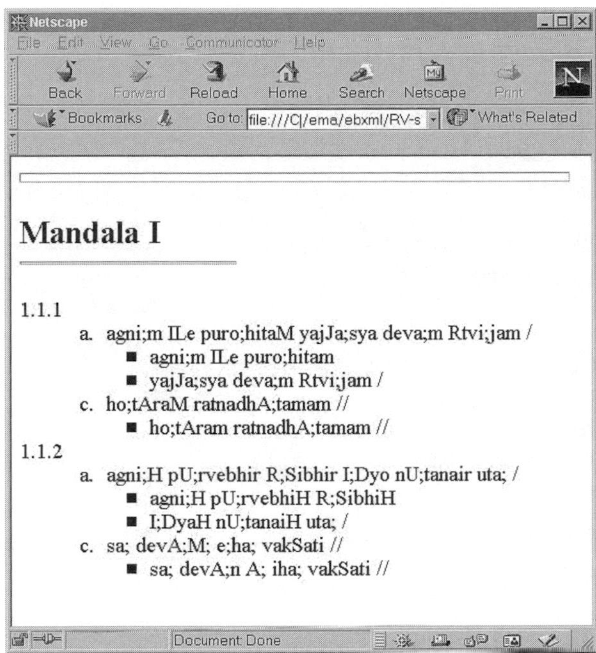

Figure A–1 Browser view of the hybrid XML-HTML *Rig Veda.*

This HTML formatting is not necessary for the raw processing in XML where we wanted tags for specific rhythms of meter, deities addressed in the hymn, author, and so forth were to be added and individual word strings searched. This did not require the HTML format, the extra `<dl>`, `<dt>`, and `<dd>` tags, or the "T" version. So, a simple series of XPath matches would give us the "L" versions in the output by selecting them and using `xsl:apply-templates`. In addition, we can easily remove the "T," or "TITUS" versions, because they are located only in ordered lists `<ol>`. The "L" versions are in unordered lists (`<ul>`). Thus when we do an `<xsl:template>` match on an `<ol>` (which is the T version we want to get rid of for our research use), and *not* use `xsl:apply-templates` in other words, give an empty body to the template they are simply removed from the output. We are still preserving the TEI `<div>` tag structure, however. The first template matches on the root and processes all children with <xsl:apply-templates>, as shown in Example A–8b.

Example A–8b : Stylesheet to create HTML.

```
<?xml version="1.0"?>
<xsl:transform xmlns:xsl="http://www.w3.org/1999/XSL/Transform">
<xsl:output method="xml" indent="yes" xml-declaration="yes"/>
<xsl:strip-space elements="*"/>
<!-- 1 -->
  <xsl:template match="/">
    <xsl:apply-templates />
  </xsl:template>
<!-- 2 -->
  <xsl:template match="li">
    <xsl:copy>
      <xsl:apply-templates select="@*"/>
      <xsl:apply-templates select="text()"/>
    </xsl:copy>
  </xsl:template>
<!-- 3 -->
  <xsl:template match="div3">
    <xsl:copy>
      <xsl:apply-templates select="@*"/>
      <xsl:apply-templates select="dt"/>
      <xsl:apply-templates select="dd"/>
    </xsl:copy>
  </xsl:template>
  <!-- 4 -->
  <xsl:template match="dd">
    <xsl:copy>
      <xsl:apply-templates select=".//ul"/>
    </xsl:copy>
  </xsl:template>
  <!-- 5 -->
  <xsl:template match="dl">
    <xsl:copy>
      <xsl:apply-templates select=".//div2"/>
    </xsl:copy>
  </xsl:template>
```

Example A–8b : Stylesheet to create HTML (continued).

```
<!-- 6 -->
  <xsl:template match="div">
    <xsl:copy>
      <xsl:apply-templates select="@*"/>
      <xsl:apply-templates select=".//div1"/>
    </xsl:copy>
  </xsl:template>
  <!-- 7 -->
<xsl:template match="*|@*|text()">
    <xsl:copy>
      <xsl:apply-templates select="*|@*|text()"/>
    </xsl:copy>
  </xsl:template>
</xsl:transform>
```

The second template matches on `<li>`, or list items, and copies them with `<xsl:copy>`. The use of `<xsl:apply-templates>` preserves the attributes and actual text nodes.

The `<div3>` element is matched in the third template and copied, and its definition list children, `<dt>` and `<dd>`, are processed along with the attributes.

Those `<dd>` elements are matched and copied in the fourth template, along with any `<ul>` node branches thus preserving the "L" versions, which are contained in the `<ul>` tags, and processing them to the output result tree.

With the fifth template matching on `<dl>`, the main definition list is matched and preserved with `<xsl:copy>`, and all its `<div2>` node branch children are preserved with `<xsl:apply-templates>`. This maintains the basic TEI tag format (thoughit is not a valid TEI document in this use).

The `<div>` and `<div1>` tags are then processed to the output tree in the sixth template, along with their attributes (we'll use these for IDs later).

Finally, text and attributes are output using the seventh template.

The result is a Lubotsky-only version of the sample file that looks like Example A–8c. This is well-formed XML, which will also display in a browser.

Next, we want to remove all the HTML tags—the `<html>`, `<body>`, `<dl>`, and so forth. Further, we want to change the abstract TEI `<div>` tags to the terms scholars use for the levels of division in the *Rig Veda*

Example A–8c : Resulting HTML file after "cleaning" input tags.

```
<?xml version="1.0" encoding="utf-8"?>
<html>
<body bgcolor="#ffffff">
<div class="Rgveda">
<div1 class="maNDala" id="1">
<dl>
<div2 class="hymn" id="1.1">
<div3 class="verse" id="1.1.1">
<dt>
1.1.1
</dt>
<dd>
<ul>
<li class="L">
agni;m ILe puro;hitam
</li>
<li class="L">
yajJa;sya deva;m Rtvi;jam /
</li>
</ul>
<ul>
<li class="L">
ho;tAram ratnadhA;tamam //
</li>
</ul>
</dd>
</div3>
<div3 class="verse" id="1.1.2">
<dt>
1.1.2
</dt>
<dd>
<ul>
<li class="L">
agni;H pU;rvebhiH R;SibhiH
</li>
<li class="L">
I;DyaH nU;tanaiH uta; /
</li>
</ul>
<ul>
<li class="L">
sa; devA;n A; iha; vakSati //
```

Example A–8c : Resulting HTML file after "cleaning" input tags (continued).

```
</li>
</ul>
</dd>
</div3>
</div2>
</dl>
</div1>
</div>
</body>
</html>
```

book/div1, hymn/div2, and verse/div3 and label the individual unordered list segments (`<ul>`) as the more common term *paada,* meaning foot. In Sanskrit and Vedic, a foot of divine meter is considered a footstep of the gods in a sense, so the term applies. If the word seems familiar, the Western podiatrist, who treats feet, derives from the same root word.

We also need to recreate the `id` attributes with an alphabetic prefix of `rv` at each level, using `<xsl:attribute>` and `<xsl:text>` to add `rv` to the `<xsl:value-of>` of the existing `id` attributes. In each case, LREs for book/div1, hymn/div2, and verse/div3 are inserted to remove the more abstract TEI element-type names for scholars unfamiliar with the otherwise versatile academic DTD. The `<xsl:apply-templates>` element processes the children of each matched element to the result tree. See Example A–9a.

Now, we want to remove the `dt` elements that remain. We do this with an empty `<xsl:template>` that matches on them and puts nothing in their place. Following that, the `<paada>` LRE replaces the remaining HTML `<ul>` tags for the individual verse portions.

The result output is shown in Example A–9b, now nearly ready for detailed research, with only the basic tags, so more complex XSLT stylesheets can be added (you can see other such stylesheets in a prior publication by one of the authors at *http://www1.shore.net/~india/ejvs, http://www.asiatica.org/publications/ijts/default.asp,* and *http://nautilus.shore.net/~india/ejvs/ejvs0601/ejvs0601.html*). This new stripped down version is a much smaller and correspondingly speedier file to use. In case you're wondering at this point, *agni* is the Vedic word for fire, and this hymn is a famous praise of fire in the rituals. The first line says, "Agni I call upon, the priest." The fire was considered a priest because, as the smoke rose to the

Example A–9a : XHTML-to-XML conversion and calculation of `id` attributes with XSLT.

```
<xsl:stylesheet xmlns:xsl="http://www.w3.org/1999/XSL/Transform"
                version="1.0"
                >

<xsl:output type="xml" indent="yes"/>

<xsl:template match="div1">
<book>
      <xsl:attribute name="id">
            <xsl:text>rv</xsl:text><xsl:value-of select="@id" />
      </xsl:attribute>
<xsl:apply-templates />
</book>
</xsl:template>

<xsl:template match="div2">
<hymn>
      <xsl:attribute name="id">
            <xsl:text>rv</xsl:text><xsl:value-of select="@id" />
      </xsl:attribute>
<xsl:apply-templates />
</hymn>
</xsl:template>
<xsl:template match="div3">
<verse>
      <xsl:attribute name="id">
            <xsl:text>rv</xsl:text><xsl:value-of select="@id" />
      </xsl:attribute>
<xsl:apply-templates select="*" />
</verse>
</xsl:template>
<xsl:template match="dt" />
<xsl:template match="ul">
<paada>
            <xsl:apply-templates />
</paada>
</xsl:template>

</xsl:stylesheet>
```

Example A–9b : Resulting XML file.

```
<?xml version="1.0"?>
<book id="rv1">

<hymn id="rv1.1">
<verse id="rv1.1.1">
<paada>

agni;m ILe puro;hitam


yajJa;sya deva;m Rtvi;jam /

</paada>
<paada>

ho;tAram ratnadhA;tamam //


</paada>
</verse>
<verse id="rv1.1.2">
<paada>

agni;H pU;rvebhiH R;SibhiH


I;DyaH nU;tanaiH uta; /

</paada>
<paada>

sa; devA;n A; iha; vakSati //

</paada>
</verse>
</hymn>

</book>
```

sky, it "carried" the message of the ritual to the deities (see http://vedavid.org/diss/ for more).

Now, the only other thing that makes this a more usable text is to mark the individual <paada> elements with more detail. In Vedic parlance, each few syllables forming a mantra is sub-sequenced with a, b, c, d, and so on. These verses have a through d sections (some go up to g and h), and every other one is marked for example, a and c. To aid in identification for our new workhorse text of the *Rig Veda,* we're going to add `id` attributes to the <paada>s and format them with <xsl:number>. Example A–10a presents the stylesheet, with comments. As usual, the first template match on the root assures processing of the entire input XML document instance.

Example A–10a : Using XSLT to enhance data identification in XML: basic source copying.

```
<xsl:stylesheet xmlns:xsl="http://www.w3.org/1999/XSL/Transform"
                version="1.0"
                >

<xsl:output type="xml" indent="yes" />

<xsl:template match="/">
            <xsl:apply-templates />
</xsl:template>
<xsl:template match="paada">
<xsl:copy>
<xsl:attribute name="id">
      <xsl:value-of select="../@id" />
      <xsl:copy>

      <xsl:number format="a" value="position() -2"
            letter-value="alphabetic" />

      </xsl:copy>
</xsl:attribute>
            <xsl:apply-templates />
</xsl:copy>
</xsl:template>
<xsl:template match="*|@*|text()">
    <xsl:copy>
      <xsl:apply-templates select="*|@*|text()"/>
    </xsl:copy>
  </xsl:template>

</xsl:stylesheet>
```

We begin by matching on <paada>. It is copied with <xsl:copy>. Then, the <xsl:attribute> instruction adds an attribute named id. To get the proper verse id as the base of the id for each <paada>, we select its value (we could also use AVTs ({ }) here, see Chapter 6, Section 6.6.1). The simple path that gets the <xsl:value-of> of the parent (..) attribute id furnishes this base. Next, we want to calculate sub-identifiers a, c, e, and so on for each <paada>, based on its position. The <xsl:number> instruction element allows us to format it as a letter. Further, the value is set by the current position, minus two spaces (there is text and then an attribute node, and we only want to count the node that is the paada itself: the first is a, third is c, and so on). The children are processed to the output XML document instance with <xsl:apply-templates>.

The last template assures output of any unmatched elements, attributes, and text nodes.

The resulting output XML document instance, ready for detailed book, hymn, verse, and now *paada* identification, is shown in Example A–10b.

Just to take this one step further, let's use XSLT to search this new text we've created. We can create a simple template to do this. With all the standard <xsl:output> and by removing the whitespace with <xsl:strip-space>, we can match on the path to a <paada> (you could imagine replacing "verse" with an author, for instance, to get all <paada>s by that author) to start the template. Then, a simple <xsl:if> test with the contains() function searches for a <paada> containing Ile. When that is found, <xsl:copy-of> copies its ancestor, for instance, so we get the entire verse context for our match, as shown in Example A–11a.

Example A–11b is the output result of the search. It is important to remember, however, that XSLT is not a proper query language, nor was it intended to be one. It works well for many query-like functions, but as has been said when all you have is a hammer, everything looks like a nail. At a certain point, querying with XSLT and XPath is going to run into intractable limits, including processor power. The reader might notice that, in effect, we're using XPath with XSLT here to "query" in a database sense. Future evolving standards from the W3C will weave a query langauge in XML, XQL, together with these standards. Until then, these kinds of content-based selections from a large resource are still quite efficient depending on how much detail is there in the tagging of your source.

Example A–10b : Resulting XML document instance.

```
<book id="rv1">

<hymn id="rv1.1">
<verse id="rv1.1.1">
<paada id="rv1.1.1a">

agni;m ILe puro;hitam


yajJa;sya deva;m Rtvi;jam /

</paada>
<paada id="rv1.1.1c">

ho;tAram ratnadhA;tamam //

</paada>
</verse>
<verse id="rv1.1.2">
<paada id="rv1.1.2a">

agni;H pU;rvebhiH R;SibhiH


I;DyaH nU;tanaiH uta; /

</paada>
<paada id="rv1.1.2c">

sa; devA;n A; iha; vakSati //

</paada>
</verse>
</hymn>

</book>
```

Example A–11a : A simple content-based search query with XSLT.

```
<xsl:stylesheet xmlns:xsl="http://www.w3.org/1999/XSL/Transform"
                version="1.0">
<xsl:output type="xml" indent="yes"/>
<xsl:strip-space elements="*" />

<xsl:template match="verse/paada">
   <xsl:if test="contains(., 'ILe')">
          <xsl:copy-of select='ancestor::verse'/>
     </xsl:if>
</xsl:template>
</xsl:stylesheet>
```

Example A–11b : Resulting XML document instance from XSLT search query.

```
<?xml version="1.0" encoding="utf-8"?>
<verse id="rv1.1.1">
<paada id="rv1.1.1a">

agni;m ILe puro;hitam


yajJa;sya deva;m Rtvi;jam /

</paada>
<paada id="rv1.1.1c">

ho;tAram ratnadhA;tamam //

</paada>
</verse>
```

Remember that, using XSLT, we can add more detailed categories, like who wrote a hymn, its meter, and other information. This makes it possible to further contextualize the search with XPath, such as requesting all <paada>s composed by Agastya, in the *jagati* meter, dedicated to Agni, containing the word *tanuu*. This and other plans are in the works from Harvard and Kyoto, including a use of Topic Maps and XLink.

Appendix B
Grouping Using the Muenchian Method

by Jeni Tennison

Grouping is a common problem in XSLT stylesheets. How do you take a list of elements and arrange them into groups? One of the most common situations in which it occurs is when you are getting XML output from a database. The database usually gives you results that are structured according to the records in the database. If it's an address book, for example, it might give you something like:

```
<records>
      <contact id="0001">
            <title>Mr</title>
            <forename>John</forename>
            <surname>Smith</surname>
      </contact>
      <contact id="0002">
            <title>Dr</title>
            <forename>Amy</forename>
            <surname>Jones</surname>
      </contact>
      -
</records>
```

The problem is how to turn this flat input into a number of lists, grouped by surname, to give something like:

```
Jones,<br />
      Amy (Dr)<br />
      Brian (Mr)<br />
Smith,<br />
      Fiona (Ms)<br />
      John (Mr)<br />
```

There are two steps in getting to a solution:

1. identifying what the surnames are
2. getting all the contacts that have the same surname

Identifying what the surnames are involves identifying one contact with each surname within the XML, which may as well be the first one that appears in it. One way to find these is to get those contacts that do not have a surname that is the same as a surname of any previous contact:

```
contact[not(surname = preceding-sibling::contact/surname)]
```

Once these contacts have been identified, it's easy to find out their surnames and to gather together all the contacts that have the same surname:

```
<xsl:apply-templates
     select="/records/contact[surname = current()/surname]" />
```

The trouble with this method is that it involves two XPaths that take a lot of processing for big XML sources (such as those from big databases). Searching through all the preceding siblings with the *preceding-siblings* axis takes a long time if you're near the end of the records. Similarly, getting all the contacts with a certain surname involves looking at every single contact each time. This makes it very inefficient.

The Muenchian Method is a method developed by Steve Muench for performing these functions in a more efficient way, using keys. Keys work by assigning a key value to a node and giving you easy access to that node through the key value. If there are lots of nodes that have the *same* key value, then *all* those nodes are retrieved when you use that key value. Effectively, this means that if you want to group a set of nodes according to a particular property of the node, then you can use keys to group them together.

Let's take our address book above. We want to group the contacts according to their surname, so we create a key that assigns each contact a key value that is the surname given in the record. The nodes that we want to group should be matched by the pattern in the `match` attribute. The key value that we want to use is the one that's given by the `use` attribute:

```
<xsl:key name="contacts-by-surname" match="contact" use="surname" />
```

Once this key is defined, if we know a surname, we can quickly access all the contacts that have that surname. For example,

```
Key('contacts-by-surname', 'Smith')
```

will give all the records that have the surname `'Smith'`. So it's easy to satisfy the second thing we needed to do (get all the contacts with the same surname):

```
<xsl:apply-templates select="key('contacts-by-surname', surname)" />
```

The first thing that we needed to do, though, was identify what the surnames were, which involved identifying the first contact within the XML that had a particular surname. We can use keys again here. We know that a contact will be part of a list of nodes that is given when we use the key on its surname: the question is whether it will be the first in that list (which is arranged in document order) or further down. We're only interested in the records that are first in the list.

Finding out whether a contact is first in the list returned by the key involves comparing the contact node with the node that is first in the list returned by the key. There are a couple of generic methods of testing whether two nodes are identical:

1. compare the unique identifiers generated for the two nodes (using `generate-id()`):

```
contact[generate-id() =
          generate-id(key('contacts-by-surname', surname)[1])]
```

2. see whether a node-set made up of the two nodes has one or two nodes in it—nodes can't be repeated in a node-set, so if there's only one node in it, then they must be the same node:

```
contact[count(. | key('contacts-by-surname', surname)[1]) = 1]
```

Once you've identified the groups, you can sort them in whatever order you like. Similarly, you can sort the nodes within the group however you want. Here is a template, then, that creates the output that we specified from the XML we were given from the database:

```
<xsl:key name="contacts-by-surname" match="contact" use="surname" />
<xsl:template match="records">
      <xsl:for-each select="contact[count(. | key('contacts-by-
surname', surname)[1]) = 1]">
```

```
            <xsl:sort select="surname" />
            <xsl:value-of select="surname" />,<br />
            <xsl:for-each select="key('contacts-by-surname', surname)">
                <xsl:sort select="forename" />
                <xsl:value-of select="forename" /> (<xsl:value-of
select="title" />)<br />
            </xsl:for-each>
      </xsl:for-each>
</xsl:template>
```

The Muenchian Method is usually the best method to use for grouping nodes together from the XML source to your output because it doesn't involve trawling through large numbers of nodes, and it's therefore more efficient. It's especially beneficial where you have a flat output from a database, for example, that you need to structure into some kind of hierarchy. It can be applied in any situation where you are grouping nodes according to a property of the node that is retrievable through an XPath.

The downside is that the Muenchian Method will only work with an XSLT processor that supports keys. This rules out James Clark's XT and pre-May 2000 versions of MSXML. In addition, using keys can be quite memory intensive, because all the nodes and their key values have to be kept in memory. Finally, it can be quite complicated to use keys where the nodes that you want to group are spread across different source documents.

Appendix C

Using XSLT for the Artificial Intelligence "N-Queens" Problem

by Oren Ben-Kiki

We are pleased to include a unique use of XSLT devised and summarized below by Oren Ben-Kiki. The N-Queens problem is discussed in many places dealing with artificial intelligence search algorithms. It is a problem which simply asks how to place the maximum number of queens on a chess board such that no queen can attack another (while I was writing a draft of this book, my niece Anna Marie was avidly occupied—using pawns—for some 27 minutes before finding a solution).

It was originally attributed to Max Bezzel in the German chess magazine Schach in 1848.[1] *It was called the 8-Queens problem and was eventually republished in 1850, catching the attention of mathematicians seeking to solve all possible arrangements (there are 92). It was generalized to "n-Queens" under the work of E. Netto in 1901, who summarized it as the n x n chessboard problem (i.e., 4 x 4, 8 x 8). The 4 x 4 version became something of a craze in the United States, under the name 15-puzzle in the 1870s. Mathematicians again*

1. A detailed discussion of N-Queens, from which the notes in the foreword are derived, is found with bibliographical references for further reading in Russell and Norvig's excellent AI text, *Artificial Intelligence: A Modern Approach* (Upper Saddle River, NJ: Prentice Hall, 1995, pp. 85ff.).

examined it in this iteration, with publications emerging in the American Journal of Mathematics. It began to be used on computers and revealed itself as a useful tool for comparing search algorithm performance in 1967. In 1986, it was shown that the n x n version's shortest possible solution belonged to a special class of problems—known as NP-complete (nondeterministic polynomial)—which are "most extreme" in difficulty.

Oren Ben-Kiki has worked with XSLT for some time and is currently Vice-President of R&D at Rich FX, Ltd. He devised this solution some time ago, in the early months of the XSLT specification. He annotated the solution below as a courtesy to the readers of this book. As an added point of interest, Oren has included a comparison set of statistics for a C++ solution at the end of his presentation below.

—John Robert Gardner

C.1 Architecture

C.1.1 Overall structure

Aside from headers, the stylesheet consists of two sets of templates.
The first set computes the set of solutions to the N-Queens problem. It is built around the following principle: each template invocation is responsible for emitting all the solutions to the problem, given that part of the solution is known. The second set is in charge of formatting each solution into an HTML table for display. It processes a solution row by row and column by column, emitting the relevant HTML table tags for displaying the resulting chessboard.

C.1.2 Solution representation

To make this architecture work, we need some way to represent a solution during the execution of the stylesheet. The first set of templates would build this representation and the second set would convert it to HTML. Since we are working in XML, the immediate solution that comes to mind is something like:

```
<solution>
      <queen row="0" column="0"/>
      ...
</solution>
```

Alas, this doesn't work. The reason is that once such a solution (or part of it) is created, XSLT does not allow us to do anything with it except emit it to the output document. This is because any XML generated by an XSLT fragment is considered to be a *result tree fragment*. In order to further process such fragments, we would need to apply templates to them. However, templates can only be applied to node-sets. Currently, XSLT does not allow us to convert a result tree fragment into a *node-set*. Allowing this operation opens up many interesting possibilities for writing stylesheets, and several XSLT processors support it as an extension. It is best to stick to standard XSLT whenever possible, so we will use strings to represent solutions instead. The scheme used in the stylesheet is based on the insight that there can be only one queen in each row (this insight is also used to efficiently search for all the valid solutions). Therefore, to represent a solution, all we need is the column number for each queen. To allow processing the solution string, we separate the column numbers by - characters. Thus, the following solution to the 4-Queens problem is represented as -1-3-0-2-:

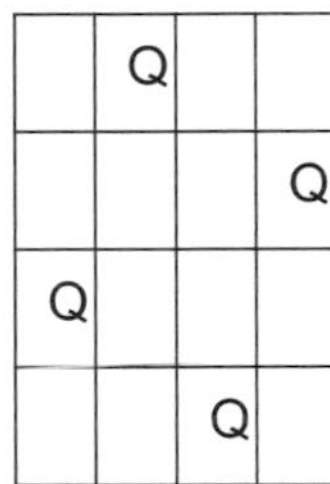

Another thing we need is to represent a part of a solution. The representation we have chosen makes it possible by using a prefix of the full solution string. For example, `-1-` represents placing the first queen as in the above solution, without saying anything about the rest of the queens.

A final subtle point is that the leading `-` in the representation is there for a reason (see Section C.2.2.2). However, in templates processing each column number in the solution, this becomes a nuisance. We therefore strip the leading "`-`" before invoking such templates.

C.1.3 Implementing Loops

The final part of the architecture is the concept of loops and how to implement them in XSLT. A loop is the application of the same processing steps to a list of different inputs. Typically in XSLT, these inputs are available in the input document, allowing two ways of achieving this. The easiest is to write the following:

```
<xsl:for-each select="... the list of inputs ...">
... repeated processing steps would otherwise be here, removed for brevity
</xsl:for-each>
```

Sometimes it is worthwhile to factor out the repeated processing to a separate template and use:

```
<xsl:apply-templates select="... the list of inputs ..."/>... repeated
processing steps would otherwise be here, removed for brevity ...
<xsl:template match="... the list of inputs ...">
... repeated processing steps would otherwise be here, removed for
brevity ...</xsl:template>
```

This is mostly useful when the same processing steps are invoked from multiple templates. In such cases, it may be impossible to write a match pattern that will identify the list of inputs and will not be triggered from undesired areas of the input document. To solve that, it is best to use a mode:

```
<xsl:apply-templates mode="bloop" select="... the list of inputs ..."/>
...
<xsl:template mode="bloop" match="*">
... repeated processing steps would otherwise be here, removed
for brevity ...</xsl:template>
```

Specifying a mode ensures that the template will only be invoked from the matching `<xsl:apply-template>` calls, and nowhere else.

At any rate, our problem here is that for us, the list of inputs can't exist in the input document. The input document is just one element, and we'll need to perform many repeated operations, such as printing all the rows of a solution, all the columns in each row, and so on.

It turns out that this is possible in XSLT, with some effort. The general technique is that for each loop, we need to write a template along the following lines:

```
<xsl:template name="RepeatedWorkForManyInputs">
<xsl:param name="ListOfTheRestOfTheInputs"/>
... other parameters repeated here ...
<xsl:if test="... there is at least one more input in the list ...">
<!-- ... do the work for the first input in the list ... -->
<xsl:call-template name="RepeatedWorkForManyInputs">
<xsl:with-param
```

```
        name="ListOfTheRestOfTheInputs">
<!-- ... the (possibly empty) list of the rest of the inputs ...-->
    </xsl:with-param>
<!--... other parameters ...-->
    </xsl:call-template>
    </xsl:if>
    </xsl:template>
```

> **NOTE** Computer scientists call this technique for implementing loops *tail recursion*. *Recursion* is defined as a function (or, in our case, a template) invoking itself. Tail recursion is the special case where the invocation appears as the very last thing in the body of the function.
>
> This technique was originally invented as part of researching a family of computer languages known as *functional languages*. It turned out that it is relatively easy to optimize systems such that the tail recursive form is as efficient as a direct loop implementation; in fact, in most such languages, both forms are implemented in exactly the same way, internally.
>
> People quickly found out, however, that having an explicit loop construct in the language is much easier to work with. Therefore every practical functional language has some sort of an explicit loop construct.
>
> XSLT is still a young language, and it is conceivable that a future version of it will contain better support for loops. In the meantime, we are forced to use tail recursion whenever we need to loop on lists that are not a part of the input document.

C.2 The Stylesheet

C.2.1 Headers

The stylesheet starts with standard "boilerplate" headers.

Declare it as an XML document:

```
<?xml version="1.0" encoding="ISO-8859-1"?>
```

A copyright notice:

```
<!--
Copyright (C) 2000 Oren Ben-Kiki
```

```
This stylesheet is public domain. However, if you
modify it or decide to use it as part of an XSLT
benchmark/testing suite, I'd appreciate it if you
let me know at oren@ben-kiki.org
-->
```

A descriptive comment:

```
<!--
This XSL stylesheet will convert an XML document
of the form:
<BoardSize>8</BoardSize>
Into an HTML document listing all 8x8 chess boards
containing 8 queens such that no one threatens
another.
It uses XSLT version 1.0, as per
http://www.w3.org/TR/1999/REC-xslt-19991116
-->
```

Now we get to the stylesheet itself. Since we would like to emit HTML output, we need to supply an `<xsl:output>` element. Providing a public doctype isn't strictly necessary, but it is good form. It helps browsers realize which brand of HTML you are using.

```
<xsl:stylesheet version="1.0"
                xmlns:xsl="http://www.w3.org/1999/XSL/Transform">
<xsl:output method="html"
            doctype-public="-//W3C//DTD HTML 4.0 Transitional//EN"/>
```

C.2.1.1 BoardSize

```
<xsl:template match="BoardSize">
```

This template will match the single element expected in the input document. It is a pretty standard template, emitting the overall HTML document structure and invoking the `PlacedQueens` template to actually generate all the solutions to the problem. The parameters to `PlacedQueens` are:

```
<html>
  <head>
    <title>
      <xsl:text>Solutions to the </xsl:text>
      <xsl:value-of select="."/>
      <xsl:text>-Queens problem</xsl:text>
    </title>
```

```
      </head>
      <body>
        <h1>
          <xsl:text>Solutions to the </xsl:text>
          <xsl:value-of select="."/>
          <xsl:text>-Queens problem</xsl:text>
        </h1>
        <xsl:call-template name="PlaceQueenInRow">
          <xsl:with-param name="BoardSize"
select="."/>
          <xsl:with-param name="Row" select="0"/>
          <xsl:with-param name="PlacedQueens"
select="'-'"/>
        </xsl:call-template>
      </body>
    </html>
</xsl:template>
```

C.2.2 Compute the Set of Solutions

C.2.2.1 PlaceQueensInRow

```
<xsl:template name="PlaceQueenInRow">
  <xsl:param name="BoardSize"/>
  <xsl:param name="PlacedQueens"/>
  <xsl:param name="Row"/>
```

This template will emit all the solutions to the problem, given that all the queens in the rows up to `Row` were already placed. This placement is given in `PlacedQueens`, and is represented as described in Section C.1.2.

Thus, the first invocation specified `Row="0"` and `PlacedQueens="-"`, indicating that no queens have yet been placed, and therefore requests emitting all the possible solutions to the problem. An invocation with `Row="1"` and `PlacedQueens="-1-"` would request to emit only the solutions where the queen in the first row is placed in the second column, and so on. Note that there may be zero, one, or several such solutions; the template's task is to print (as HTML) each and every valid solution, or nothing at all if there are none. This principle is used in all the rest of templates in this section.

```
  <xsl:choose>
    <xsl:when test="$Row = $BoardSize">
```

This template is called repeatedly as parts of solutions are generated, with increasing `Row` values. Eventually, all the queens will be placed. In this case, we are actually given a complete solution, not just part of one. All that remains to be done is to print it. Note that here we strip the leading - from the placement string to make it easier to process.

```
      <xsl:call-template name="PrintBoard">
        <xsl:with-param name="BoardSize" select="$BoardSize"/
          >
        <xsl:with-param name="PlacedQueens"
                        select="substring-
          after($PlacedQueens, '-')"/>
      </xsl:call-template>
    </xsl:when>
    <xsl:otherwise>
```

In the general case, however, we are given only a partial solution—for example, just the two first queens out of four. In this case, we need to explore all the possible columns where the third queen can be placed. `PlaceQueenInColumn` will do this for us.

```
      <xsl:call-template name="PlaceQueenInColumn">
        <xsl:with-param name="BoardSize" select="$BoardSize"/
          >
        <xsl:with-param name="PlacedQueens"
          select="$PlacedQueens"/>
        <xsl:with-param name="Row" select="$Row"/>
        <xsl:with-param name="Column" select="0"/>
      </xsl:call-template>
    </xsl:otherwise>
  </xsl:choose>
</xsl:template>
```

C.2.2.2 PlaceQueenInColumn

```
<xsl:template name="PlaceQueenInColumn">
  <xsl:param name="BoardSize"/>
  <xsl:param name="PlacedQueens"/>
  <xsl:param name="Row"/>
  <xsl:param name="Column"/>
```

This template will emit all the solutions to the problem, given that all the queens in the rows up to `Row` were already placed. This placement is given in `PlacedQueens`, and is represented as described in Section C.1.2. The queen to be placed at the specified `Row` must be placed at or after the given `Column`.

This is our first loop template. We need to go over each column, check whether it is valid to place a queen there, and if so, emit all the solutions with the queen placed in that column. Therefore, this template follows the form described in Section C.1.3. The complete list of inputs is the integers `0`, `1`, ..., `BoardSize - 1`. The `Column` parameter serves as the list of the rest of the inputs; the remaining integers are those no smaller then `Column`.

```
<xsl:if test="$Column &lt; $BoardSize">
```

Test whether there are more inputs to process—that is, verify we haven't finished checking all the columns. If we haven't, do the repeated processing steps. These apply to the next input—in our case, the specified column.

```
<xsl:if test="not(contains($PlacedQueens,
                           concat('-', $Column, '-')))">
```

The first step is to ensure that no previously placed queen was assigned the same column. We use a small trick here, using string operations to do that. Given our representation, we can check that no queen was placed in column 1 by looking for the substring `-1-` in the `PlacedQueens` string. This is why we need the leading `-`; if it weren't there, we'd miss on checking the column of the queen in the first row. Checking just for `1-` doesn't work when working with large problems (e.g., in the 12-Queens problem, it would match the placement `-11-`).

If no queen was placed in this column, we still need to check that there is no queen placed in the same diagonal. Here we can't use any string tricks, so we have to resort to using another loop, testing this column against each of the previously placed queens in turn. Again, we strip the leading `-` from the string to make it easier to process.

```
    <xsl:call-template name="TestQueenPosition">
      <xsl:with-param name="BoardSize" select="$BoardSize"/>
        <xsl:with-param name="PlacedQueens" select="$PlacedQueens"/>
      <xsl:with-param name="Row" select="$Row"/>
      <xsl:with-param name="Column" select="$Column"/>
      <xsl:with-param name="TestQueens"
                  select="substring-after($PlacedQueens, '-')"/>
      <xsl:with-param name="Offset" select="$Row"/>
    </xsl:call-template>
  </xsl:if>
```

Finally, there is the recursive invocation. We invoke the same template, but tell it to start working from the next column. Eventually, we will reach the end of the row and we will be done.

```
    <xsl:call-template name="PlaceQueenInColumn">
      <xsl:with-param name="BoardSize" select="$BoardSize"/>
      <xsl:with-param name="PlacedQueens" select="$PlacedQueens"/>
      <xsl:with-param name="Row" select="$Row"/>
      <xsl:with-param name="Column" select="$Column + 1"/>
    </xsl:call-template>
  </xsl:if>
</xsl:template>
```

C.2.2.3 TestQueenPosition

```
<xsl:template name="TestQueenPosition">
  <xsl:param name="BoardSize"/>
  <xsl:param name="PlacedQueens"/>
  <xsl:param name="Row"/>
  <xsl:param name="Column"/>
  <xsl:param name="TestQueens"/>
  <xsl:param name="Offset"/>
```

This template will emit all the solutions to the problem, given that all the queens in the rows up to `Row` were already placed. This placement is given in `PlacedQueens`, and is represented as described in Section C.1.2. The tentative placement of the queen in `Row` is in the specified `Column`. It needs to be verified that this placement is not on the same diagonal as any of the queens whose placement is listed in `TestQueens`, such that the offset in rows between the newly placed queen and the first queen in this list is given in `Offset`. `TestQueens` is in the same format as `PlacedQueens`, minus the leading `-`.

Again, this is a loop template. We need to check each of the `TestQueens` to see they are not on the same diagonal as the proposed placement. Only if none are, we may try to place additional queens in the remaining rows. Unlike the previous template, in this case the list of inputs is a real list, represented as a string.

```
  <xsl:choose>
    <xsl:when test="not($TestQueens)">
```

There are no more queens to test. This means that the newly placed queen was not on the same diagonal as any of the previous ones. We still need to place the rest of the queens, in the rows below the current one.

Invoking `PlacedQueenInRow` again will do this for us, by asking it to start one row down and adding this row's placement into `PlacedQueens`.

```
        <xsl:call-template name="PlaceQueenInRow">
          <xsl:with-param name="BoardSize" select="$BoardSize"/>
          <xsl:with-param name="PlacedQueens">
            <xsl:value-of select="$PlacedQueens"/>
            <xsl:value-of select="$Column"/>
            <xsl:text>-</xsl:text>
          </xsl:with-param>
          <xsl:with-param name="Row" select="$Row + 1"/>
        </xsl:call-template>
      </xsl:when>
      <xsl:otherwise>
```

Otherwise, there are more queens to test.

```
        <xsl:variable name="NextQueenColumn"
                      select="substring-before($TestQueens, '-')"/>
        <xsl:if test="not($Column = $NextQueenColumn + $Offset)
                      and not($Column = $NextQueenColumn - $Offset)">
```

The new queen is on the same diagonal as the next queen to test if the offset in rows is identical to the offset in columns. Using a variable here makes the code a bit more readable. If we pass this test, we move to the recursive invocation to test the rest of the queens (if any). Since we are dealing with a physical list here, we have to pass it the tail of the list as well as update the diagonal's offset.

```
          <xsl:call-template name="TestQueenPosition">
          <xsl:with-param name="BoardSize" select="$BoardSize"/>
            <xsl:with-param name="PlacedQueens" select="$PlacedQueens"/>
          <xsl:with-param name="Row" select="$Row"/>
          <xsl:with-param name="Column" select="$Column"/>
          <xsl:with-param name="TestQueens"
                          select="substring-after($TestQueens, '-')"/>
          <xsl:with-param name="Offset" select="$Offset - 1"/>
        </xsl:call-template>
      </xsl:if>
    </xsl:otherwise>
  </xsl:choose>
</xsl:template>
```

C.2.3 Print a Solution

C.2.3.1 PrintBoard

```
<xsl:template name="PrintBoard">
  <xsl:param name="BoardSize"/>
  <xsl:param name="PlacedQueens"/>
```

This template will print a single solution to the problem as an HTML table. Like the `BoardSize` template, it doesn't do much but generate the overall structure and invoke `PrintBoardRow` to actually do the work. `PlacedQueens` contains the solution to print, as described in Section C.1.2, minus the leading `-`.

```
  <hr/>
  <table border="1">
    <xsl:call-template name="PrintBoardRow">
      <xsl:with-param name="BoardSize" select="$BoardSize"/>
       <xsl:with-param name="PlacedQueens" select="$PlacedQueens"/>
      </xsl:call-template>
  </table>
</xsl:template>
```

C.2.3.2 PrintBoardRow

```
<xsl:template name="PrintBoardRow">
  <xsl:param name="BoardSize"/>
  <xsl:param name="PlacedQueens"/>
```

This template will print a row (actually, all the remaining rows) of a solution to the problem. This is a pretty simple loop template; the only complication is that it invokes a nested loop template to print the columns in each row. `PlacedQueens` contains the remaining part of the solution to print, as described in Section C.1.2, minus the leading `-`.

```
  <xsl:if test="$PlacedQueens">
```

Test that the remaining part of the solution to print is not empty.

```
    <tr>
      <xsl:call-template name="PrintBoardColumn">
        <xsl:with-param name="ColumnsLeft" select="$BoardSize"/>
        <xsl:with-param name="QueenColumn"
                        select="substring-before($PlacedQueens, '-')"/>
      </xsl:call-template>
    </tr>
```

The repeated processing steps are as follows: print all the columns in the next row (inside a `<tr>` element), using a nested loop template; followed by the recursive call, given the placement of the remaining rows to print.

```
    <xsl:call-template name="PrintBoardRow">
      <xsl:with-param name="BoardSize" select="$BoardSize"/>
      <xsl:with-param name="PlacedQueens"
                      select="substring-after($PlacedQueens, '-')"/>
    </xsl:call-template>
  </xsl:if>
</xsl:template>
```

C.2.3.3 PrintBoardColumn

```
<xsl:template name="PrintBoardColumn">
  <xsl:param name="ColumnsLeft"/>
  <xsl:param name="QueenColumn"/>
```

This template will print a column (actually, all the remaining columns) of a row of a solution to the problem. This is the simplest loop template in the stylesheet. The list to process is all the remaining columns, whose numbers are given in `ColumnsLeft`. A queen is placed in one of these columns; it is given in `QueenColumn`. This number is relative to the remaining columns; that is, when it is zero, the next column to print (the first in the list of remaining columns) is the one containing the queen. It is possible to rewrite this template to use an absolute queen column, but that would require us to pass an additional parameter (the `BoardSize`).

```
  <xsl:if test="not($ColumnsLeft = 0)">
```

Test that there are more columns to print.

```
    <td>
      <xsl:choose>
        <xsl:when test="$QueenColumn = 0">Q</xsl:when>
        <xsl:otherwise> </xsl:otherwise>
      </xsl:choose>
    </td>
```

The repeated processing step here is simply to print the column. If this is where the queen is placed, put a Q in it; otherwise, use a nonbreaking space (some browsers require this to force them to draw the border around the cell). Note that we can't use the symbolic name ` ` because the XSLT processor does not recognize it.

Next is the recursive call, starting at the next column and with an adjusted queen column number.

```
      <xsl:call-template name="PrintBoardColumn">
        <xsl:with-param name="ColumnsLeft" select="$ColumnsLeft - 1"/>
        <xsl:with-param name="QueenColumn" select="$QueenColumn - 1"/>
      </xsl:call-template>
    </xsl:if>
  </xsl:template>
</xsl:stylesheet>
```

C.3 Final notes

The above stylesheet was tested using James Clark's XT XSLT processor. I also wrote a C++ implementation. Running both on my computer yielded the results in Table C–1.

Table C–1 Comparing processing speed between between XSLT and C++ for solving N-Queens

Number of Queens	*Number of Solutions*	*Time to run in XSLT*	*Time to run in C++*
4	2	1.0 second	0.065 seconds
6	4	1.5 second	0.065 seconds
8	92	8.5 seconds	0.065 seconds
10	724	3.0 minutes	0.180 seconds

XT is a pretty fast XSLT processor. It is just not optimized for the kind of processing this stylesheet performs. Not only that, while the stylesheet does print all the solutions to the N-Queens problem, it does not print a serial number by each. It turns out that doing so is a non-trivial problem. To achieve this, the stylesheet would need to collect all the valid solutions into a single long string, and only then print them one by one, as opposed to printing each solution the moment it was found. That would probably make it even less efficient. There's no such problem in the C++ program.

This demonstrates that while it is possible to perform general-purpose computations in XSLT, it may be impossible to do so in an efficient manner. In general, the techniques demonstrated in this stylesheet (using loop templates and using strings to represent complex data) do not scale well for large processing tasks.

It is doubtful that this situation will change in the future. XSLT was not design for such tasks. Instead, it provides standard mechanisms for accessing external functionality from an XSLT stylesheet, using extension elements and extension functions.

It is therefore important to assess the practicality of writing a complex processing task in XSLT as opposed to providing it as an extension function. As long as XSLT is used for small amounts of data, such as a single HTML page, the need for portability may well favor implementing the task in straight XSLT. For large amounts of data, such as processing large archives, the loss of portability may well be worth the huge increase in efficiency.

Index

A

B

C

D

E

F

O

T

U

V

W

X

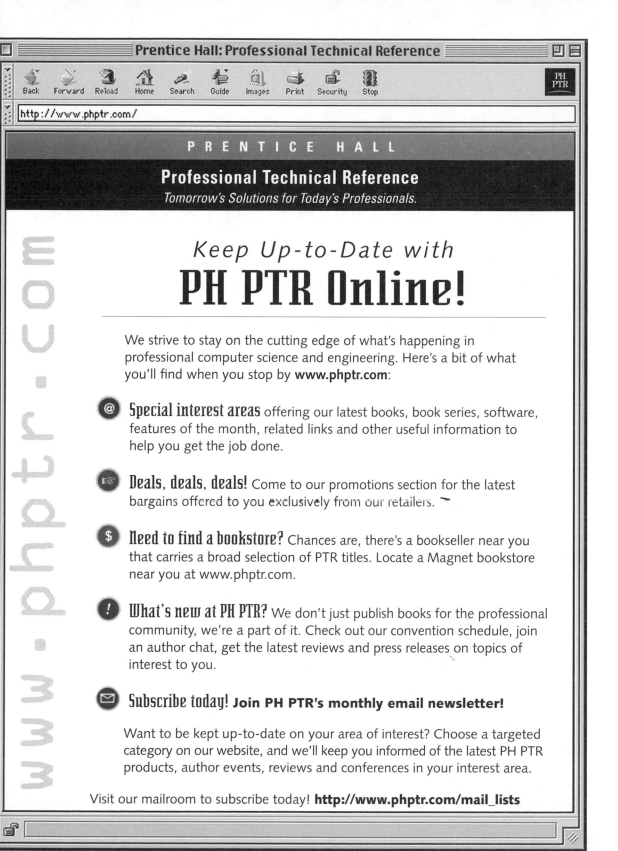

LICENSE AGREEMENT AND LIMITED WARRANTY

READ THE FOLLOWING TERMS AND CONDITIONS CAREFULLY BEFORE OPENING THIS CD PACKAGE. THIS LEGAL DOCUMENT IS AN AGREEMENT BETWEEN YOU AND PRENTICE-HALL, INC. (THE "COMPANY"). BY OPENING THIS SEALED CD PACKAGE, YOU ARE AGREEING TO BE BOUND BY THESE TERMS AND CONDITIONS. IF YOU DO NOT AGREE WITH THESE TERMS AND CONDITIONS, DO NOT OPEN THE CD PACKAGE. PROMPTLY RETURN THE UNOPENED CD PACKAGE AND ALL ACCOMPANYING ITEMS TO THE PLACE YOU OBTAINED THEM FOR A FULL REFUND OF ANY SUMS YOU HAVE PAID.

1. **GRANT OF LICENSE:** In consideration of your purchase of this book, and your agreement to abide by the terms and conditions of this Agreement, the Company grants to you a nonexclusive right to use and display the copy of the enclosed software program (hereinafter the "SOFTWARE") on a single computer (i.e., with a single CPU) at a single location so long as you comply with the terms of this Agreement. The Company reserves all rights not expressly granted to you under this Agreement.

2. **OWNERSHIP OF SOFTWARE:** You own only the magnetic or physical media (the enclosed CD) on which the SOFTWARE is recorded or fixed, but the Company and the software developers retain all the rights, title, and ownership to the SOFTWARE recorded on the original CD copy(ies) and all subsequent copies of the SOFTWARE, regardless of the form or media on which the original or other copies may exist. This license is not a sale of the original SOFTWARE or any copy to you.

3. **COPY RESTRICTIONS:** This SOFTWARE and the accompanying printed materials and user manual (the "Documentation") are the subject of copyright. The individual programs on the CD are copyrighted by the authors of each program. Some of the programs on the CD include separate licensing agreements. If you intend to use one of these programs, you must read and follow its accompanying license agreement. You may not copy the Documentation or the SOFTWARE, except that you may make a single copy of the SOFTWARE for backup or archival purposes only. You may be held legally responsible for any copying or copyright infringement which is caused or encouraged by your failure to abide by the terms of this restriction.

4. **USE RESTRICTIONS:** You may not network the SOFTWARE or otherwise use it on more than one computer or computer terminal at the same time. You may physically transfer the SOFTWARE from one computer to another provided that the SOFTWARE is used on only one computer at a time. You may not distribute copies of the SOFTWARE or Documentation to others. You may not reverse engineer, disassemble, decompile, modify, adapt, translate, or create derivative works based on the SOFTWARE or the Documentation without the prior written consent of the Company.

5. **TRANSFER RESTRICTIONS:** The enclosed SOFTWARE is licensed only to you and may not be transferred to any one else without the prior written consent of the Company. Any unauthorized transfer of the SOFTWARE shall result in the immediate termination of this Agreement.

6. **TERMINATION:** This license is effective until terminated. This license will terminate automatically without notice from the Company and become null and void if you fail to comply with any provisions or limitations of this license. Upon termination, you shall destroy the Documentation and all copies of the SOFTWARE. All provisions of this Agreement as to warranties, limitation of liability, remedies or damages, and our ownership rights shall survive termination.

7. **MISCELLANEOUS:** This Agreement shall be construed in accordance with the laws of the United States of America and the State of New York and shall benefit the Company, its affiliates, and assignees.

8. **LIMITED WARRANTY AND DISCLAIMER OF WARRANTY:** The Company warrants that the SOFTWARE, when properly used in accordance with the Documentation, will operate in substantial conformity with the description of the SOFTWARE set forth in the Documentation. The Company does not warrant that the SOFTWARE will meet your requirements or that the operation

of the SOFTWARE will be uninterrupted or error-free. The Company warrants that the media on which the SOFTWARE is delivered shall be free from defects in materials and workmanship under normal use for a period of thirty (30) days from the date of your purchase. Your only remedy and the Company's only obligation under these limited warranties is, at the Company's option, return of the warranted item for a refund of any amounts paid by you or replacement of the item. Any replacement of SOFTWARE or media under the warranties shall not extend the original warranty period. The limited warranty set forth above shall not apply to any SOFTWARE which the Company determines in good faith has been subject to misuse, neglect, improper installation, repair, alteration, or damage by you. EXCEPT FOR THE EXPRESSED WARRANTIES SET FORTH ABOVE, THE COMPANY DISCLAIMS ALL WARRANTIES, EXPRESS OR IMPLIED, INCLUDING WITHOUT LIMITATION, THE IMPLIED WARRANTIES OF MERCHANTABILITY AND FITNESS FOR A PARTICULAR PURPOSE. EXCEPT FOR THE EXPRESS WARRANTY SET FORTH ABOVE, THE COMPANY DOES NOT WARRANT, GUARANTEE, OR MAKE ANY REPRESENTATION REGARDING THE USE OR THE RESULTS OF THE USE OF THE SOFTWARE IN TERMS OF ITS CORRECTNESS, ACCURACY, RELIABILITY, CURRENTNESS, OR OTHERWISE.

IN NO EVENT, SHALL THE COMPANY OR ITS EMPLOYEES, AGENTS, SUPPLIERS, OR CONTRACTORS BE LIABLE FOR ANY INCIDENTAL, INDIRECT, SPECIAL, OR CONSEQUENTIAL DAMAGES ARISING OUT OF OR IN CONNECTION WITH THE LICENSE GRANTED UNDER THIS AGREEMENT, OR FOR LOSS OF USE, LOSS OF DATA, LOSS OF INCOME OR PROFIT, OR OTHER LOSSES, SUSTAINED AS A RESULT OF INJURY TO ANY PERSON, OR LOSS OF OR DAMAGE TO PROPERTY, OR CLAIMS OF THIRD PARTIES, EVEN IF THE COMPANY OR AN AUTHORIZED REPRESENTATIVE OF THE COMPANY HAS BEEN ADVISED OF THE POSSIBILITY OF SUCH DAMAGES. IN NO EVENT SHALL LIABILITY OF THE COMPANY FOR DAMAGES WITH RESPECT TO THE SOFTWARE EXCEED THE AMOUNTS ACTUALLY PAID BY YOU, IF ANY, FOR THE SOFTWARE.

SOME JURISDICTIONS DO NOT ALLOW THE LIMITATION OF IMPLIED WARRANTIES OR LIABILITY FOR INCIDENTAL, INDIRECT, SPECIAL, OR CONSEQUENTIAL DAMAGES, SO THE ABOVE LIMITATIONS MAY NOT ALWAYS APPLY. THE WARRANTIES IN THIS AGREEMENT GIVE YOU SPECIFIC LEGAL RIGHTS AND YOU MAY ALSO HAVE OTHER RIGHTS WHICH VARY IN ACCORDANCE WITH LOCAL LAW.

ACKNOWLEDGMENT

YOU ACKNOWLEDGE THAT YOU HAVE READ THIS AGREEMENT, UNDERSTAND IT, AND AGREE TO BE BOUND BY ITS TERMS AND CONDITIONS. YOU ALSO AGREE THAT THIS AGREEMENT IS THE COMPLETE AND EXCLUSIVE STATEMENT OF THE AGREEMENT BETWEEN YOU AND THE COMPANY AND SUPERSEDES ALL PROPOSALS OR PRIOR AGREEMENTS, ORAL, OR WRITTEN, AND ANY OTHER COMMUNICATIONS BETWEEN YOU AND THE COMPANY OR ANY REPRESENTATIVE OF THE COMPANY RELATING TO THE SUBJECT MATTER OF THIS AGREEMENT.

Should you have any questions concerning this Agreement or if you wish to contact the Company for any reason, please contact in writing at the address below.

Robin Short

Prentice Hall PTR

One Lake Street

Upper Saddle River, New Jersey 07458

About the CD-ROM

For best results, use a Web browser to open the file *index.htm* on the CD-ROM. This index provides links to all the examples and reference material included on the CD-ROM, as well as links to current versions of the software.

System Requirements

- Windows, MAC, Unix, or Linux operating system
- CD-ROM drive
- Any Internet Browser

Examples

A complete set of all the examples in the book can be found in the Examples directory, listed by chapter.

Software

Software programs for several XSLT processors are provided on the CD-ROM in accordance with the copyright notices for each vendor. They are:

- Eric Lawson's Xalan-J GUI
- Instant Saxon
- Saxon
- Xalan C++
- Xalan J
- XT

The manufacturer's installation instructions for the other individual XSLT processors can be found on the Web site for that particular software.

License Agreement

Use of the *XSLT and XPath* CD-ROM is subject to the terms of the License Agreement and Limited Warranty on the preceding pages.